Embodiment and Cognitive Science

This book explores how people's subjective, felt experiences of their bodies in action provide part of the fundamental grounding for human cognition and language. Cognition is what occurs when the body engages the physical and cultural world, and it must be studied in terms of the dynamical interactions between people and the environment. Human language and thought emerge from recurring patterns of embodied activity that constrain ongoing intelligent behavior. We must not assume cognition to be purely internal, symbolic, computational, and disembodied, but seek out the gross and detailed ways in which language and thought are inextricably shaped by embodied action. *Embodiment and Cognitive Science* describes the abundance of empirical evidence from many disciplines, including work on perception, concepts, imagery and reasoning, language and communication, cognitive development, and emotions and consciousness, that support the idea that the mind is embodied.

Raymond W. Gibbs, Jr. is Professor of Psychology at the University of California, Santa Cruz. He is the author of *The Poetics of Mind* and *Intentions in the Experience of Meaning*. He is coeditor (with G. Steen) of *Metaphor in Cognitive Linguistics* and editor of the interdisciplinary journal *Metaphor and Symbol*.

Embodiment and Cognitive Science

RAYMOND W. GIBBS, JR.
University of California, Santa Cruz

CAMBRIDGE
UNIVERSITY PRESS

CAMBRIDGE UNIVERSITY PRESS
Cambridge, New York, Melbourne, Madrid, Cape Town, Singapore, São Paulo

Cambridge University Press
32 Avenue of the Americas, New York, NY 10013-2473, USA

www.cambridge.org
Information on this title: www.cambridge.org/9780521811743

First published 2005

A catalog record for this publication is available from the British Library.

Library of Congress Cataloging in Publication data

Gibbs, Raymond W.
Embodiment and cognitive science / Raymond W. Gibbs, Jr.
p. cm.
Includes bibliographical references and index.
ISBN 0-521-81174-0 – ISBN 0-521-01049-7 (pbk.)
1. Mind and body. 2. Cognitive science. I. Title.
BF151.G53 2005
153 – dc22 2005000709

ISBN 978-0-521-81174-3 hardback
ISBN 978-0-521-01049-8 paperback

Transferred to digital printing 2008

Contents

Acknowledgments

I thank Greg Bryant, Christin Izett, Melissa Newman, and Nicole Wilson for their important comments on earlier versions of some of the chapters in this book. Ben Bergen and Alan Cienki and his students at Emory University also offered extremely helpful comments on parts of this book. Many conversations with Herb Colston and Guy Van Orden were critical in sharpening some of the ideas discussed here.

Many thanks to Phil Laughlin and the entire staff at Cambridge University Press for their wonderful support and expertise while this book was being written and produced for publication.

This book is dedicated to Christin Izett in appreciation of her love and support throughout the writing of this book.

1

Introduction

Embodiment in the field of cognitive science refers to understanding the role of an agent's own body in its everyday, situated cognition. For example, how do our bodies influence the ways we think and speak? Consider the following narrative written by a 23-year-old woman, Sandra, who was asked to describe a recent, important life event. Sandra began her narrative by noting that she was engaged to be married to an older man who worked in the computer industry in northern California. Quite recently, Sandra's fiancé asked her to sign a prenuptial agreement and this request evoked many feelings that Sandra struggled to deal with.

> I know that I shouldn't be so naive about this sort of thing, but when he presented me with a draft of the agreement, it was so formal and legal and felt so cold to me that I just broke down crying. I simply couldn't stand to see our future relationship be reduced to questions of money. It seemed like Barry didn't trust me, or that he lacked faith in our future. I had always thought that we were in this together, going forward as partners as we started dating, got serious, then engaged, and hopefully soon married. Now my parents want me to consult with a lawyer to insure I don't get screwed by the pre-nup.
>
> I'm trying hard to find the right balance between understanding Barry's needs to protect himself and my own needs for emotional security ... I'm trying to be flexible about the whole thing ... I love Barry and I know he loves me and I wish that the feeling of love would be enough to sustain us through anything. But the idea of getting divorced, even before we have been married, makes me ill. Everyone tells me that I'll get over this and that doing the pre-nup is probably the right thing to do. That may be so. The wedding is in August. Hopefully by that time, I'll be mellow about what we're going through right now.

This narrative is not particularly remarkable in terms of how Sandra described her recent experience. However, a closer look at what is said reveals how various embodied experiences help structure the narrative. For example, Sandra commented early on that "I couldn't stand to see our future relationship be reduced to questions of money," referring to the physical experience of standing, or failing to remain standing, to describe how she felt about her relationship becoming so centered on money issues. Later on, Sandra said, "I had always thought that we were in this together, going forward as partners as we started dating, got serious, then engaged, and hopefully soon married." At this moment, Sandra clearly talked of her relationship in terms of being physically together with her boyfriend as they started out on a journey, beginning when they first began dating, soon traveling to the point of getting serious, and then moving forward along a path toward the eventual destination of marriage.

Sandra also noted her struggle "to find the right balance between understanding Barry's needs to protect himself and my own needs for emotional security." This emotional experience is referred to metaphorically, as if Sandra were physically balancing two opposing weights while trying to remain upright. As she worked to come to terms with her fiancé's request for a prenuptial agreement, Sandra was "trying to be flexible about the whole thing," again showing that she is conceptualizing her emotional experience as if her body must adjust to remain flexible in order not to be injured when confronted with physical burdens. Finally, Sandra hoped for her wedding that "by that time, I'll be mellow about what we're going through right now," referring to the physical obstacle that she and her fiancé were struggling to overcome along the path of their relationship journey.

Sandra's narrative illustrates how the ways we think about our experiences may be shaped by embodiment. She specifically talked of her mental/emotional experiences in terms of recurring patterns of embodied action (e.g., standing, being flexible, movement along paths toward goals, remaining balanced). Sandra was likely not conscious of the embodied character of her words, and readers probably do not think of her emotional experiences as specific embodied actions. Yet Sandra's description of her emotional experiences in terms of embodied action is not a linguistic accident, but demonstrates how embodiment provides the foundation for how people interpret their lives and the world around them.

What must a body be like for it to support cognition, language, and consciousness? Did Sandra's embodied experience shape the way she thought about particular topics, or did she merely talk that way? One of the traditional beliefs in the cognitive sciences is that intelligent behavior, including the ability to perceive, think, and use language, need not arise from any specific bodily form. Thermostats, computers, robots, and brains in vats may all, under the right circumstances, exhibit sophisticated cognitive skills. Under this view, cognitive systems are best characterized in terms of their functional states (i.e., their logical and computational processes) without concern for how these states are physically realized (i.e., as human brains, silicon chips, or robots). The building materials that shape the contents of mental life simply do not matter. Minds may be realized in flesh, silicon, or even cream cheese (Putnam, 1975). To be in a specific mental state is simply to be in a physical device of whatever type satisfies a specific formal/functional description.

This traditional conception of mind and body has imposed serious limitations on the scholarly study of mental life in cognitive science. Although psychologists and others readily admit that much knowledge is derived from sensory perception, few scholars, until recently, have emphasized the importance of kinesthetic action in theoretical accounts of how people perceive, learn, think, experience emotions and consciousness, and use language. This book advances the idea that the traditional disembodied view of mind is mistaken, because human cognition is fundamentally shaped by embodied experience. My aim is to describe the way in which many aspects of cognition are grounded in embodiment, especially in terms of the phenomenological experience of our bodies in action. Embodiment may not provide the single foundation for all thought and language, but it is an essential part of the perceptual and cognitive processes by which we make sense of our experiences in the world.

Why has cognitive science been so neglectful of embodiment in constructing theories of perception, cognition, and language? The denial of the body in consideration of human thought has been part of the Western intellectual tradition since the time of the ancient Greeks. Perhaps the best voice for this earlier view was Plato, as shown in the following dialogue from the "Phaedo":

> All these considerations, said Socrates, must surely prompt serious philosophers to review the position in some such way as this... So long as we keep the body and our soul contaminated with this imperfection, there is no chance of our ever attaining satisfactorily to our object, which we assert to be the truth.... The body fills us with loves and desires and fears and all sorts of nonsense, with the result that we literally never get an opportunity to think at all about anything... That is why, on all these accounts, we have so little time for philosophy.... It seems, to judge from the argument, that the wisdom which we desire and upon which we profess to have set our hearts will be attainable only when we are dead... It seems that so long as we are alive, we shall continue closest to knowledge if we avoid as much as we can all contact and association with the body, except when they are absolutely necessary, and instead of allowing ourselves to become infected with its nature, purify ourselves from it until God himself gives us deliverance. (Hamilton & Cairns, 1961: 49)

Plato viewed the body as a source of distraction in intellectual life that must be eradicated in the practice of philosophy. Separation of the mind and body and the hierarchical ordering of mind over body haunt the history of Western philosophical accounts of knowledge from Plato, Aristotle, and Augustine through to Descartes and Kant. For example, in early Christian writings, bodily sensations and desires were rivaled in contests against a higher form of Truth, or closeness to God. As St. Augustine wrote in the fifth century, "More and more, O Lord, you will increase your gift in me, so that my soul may follow me to you, freed from the concupiscence which binds it, and rebel no more against itself" (Augustine, 1961: 234). Augustine fixed the body as a source of sin, weakness, and the measure against which the strength of his will toward God is knowable.

In the 17th century, Rene Descartes' struggle with a purely material body and a perfectly insubstantial mind led him to propose that the body is, in fact, an idea in the mind (Descartes, 1984, 1985). The body's materiality, along with other objects that are impressed upon body substances, is a literalization of this idea in our experience. When we pay attention to it, the body materializes, and we become aware of the body as an object. However, as our attention centers on other things, or on thought itself, the body disappears.

Mental phenomena, according to Descartes, have no place in the quantifiable world of physics, but have a completely autonomous status: "I am a substance the whole nature or essence of which is to think, and which for its existence does not need any place or depend on any material thing" (Descartes, Discourse, Part IV). Descartes distinguished, then, between physical substances ("res extensa"), which can be measured and divided, and thinking substances ("res cogitans"), which are unextended and indivisible. The human body, including the brain and nervous system, belongs to the first group, whereas the mind, including all thoughts, desires, and volitions, belongs to the second.

Cartesian dualism arose from Descartes' claim that he could doubt the existence of physical objects, including his own body, but not the existence of his thoughts or thinking. Although Descartes worried about possible interactions of mind and body, Cartesian dualism evolved into an epistemological tradition that separated the mind as rational, thinking, immaterial, and private from the body as an irrational, corrupt, and physical substance that merely provided public, physical exertion on the material world. This bifurcation of the person into mind and body has subsequently given rise to many other dualisms, including subjective as opposed to objective, knowledge as opposed to experience, reason as opposed to feeling, theory as opposed to practice, and verbal as opposed to nonverbal. Cartesianism has also led to the romantic view of the body as the last bastion of what is natural, unspoiled, preconceptual, and primitive in experience. Bodily movement is viewed as behavior, with little relevance to language, thought, or consciousness, and not as meaningful action.

The Western tradition since Descartes has generally assumed that the body is a solid object and the self, in particular the mind, is an ethereal subject mysteriously infused into the body object. Throughout history, the mind has been modeled as a series of different material objects (e.g., a hydraulic machine, a telephone switchboard, a hologram, a digital computer).

Cognitive science, as an interdisciplinary research enterprise, came into being in the 1950s with the rise of the MIND IS A COMPUTER metaphor, which resulted from technological advances in computing machinery. Alan Turing (1950) outlined a method for assessing the question "Can machines think?" Following in Descartes' footsteps, Turing emphasized the importance of drawing a "fairly sharp line" (p. 434) between a person's physical capacities and his/her intellectual abilities. Turing asked us to consider a scenario that included three people – a man (A), a woman (B), and an interrogator of unspecified sex (C). The interrogator was in a separate room from the man and the woman, and the interrogator's task was to determine which of the two was a man and which was a woman on the basis of their written answers to certain questions (e.g., "What is the length of your hair?"). It is A's task to confuse the interrogator and B's task to help. The test proper comes into play by swapping the man (A) with a machine. If the interrogator makes the same set of judgments, deductions, and guesses after the swap as before (i.e., the interrogator is unable to distinguish the machine's answers from the man's answers), then the machine has passed the "Turing test." The machine whose behavior is indistinguishable from the intellect of the man is the machine that thinks.

Cognitive science models of intelligent human activity have mostly continued to assume, like Turing, that cognition is autonomous, logical, and disembodied. In his history of cognitive science, Gardner (1985) claimed that the exclusion of the body was, in fact, a benign methodological decision: "Though mainstream cognitive scientists do not necessarily bear any animus against the affective realm, against the context that surrounds any actor or thought, or against historical or cultural analyses, in practice they attempt to factor out these elements to the maximum extent possible ... This may be a question of practicality: if one were to take into account these individualizing and phenomenalistic elements, cognitive science might well become impossible" (p. 41).

Some cognitive scientists question whether the exclusion of the phenomenological body, along with other aspects of experience such as emotion and consciousness, is merely a methodological issue, and not really constitutive of what cognitive scientists believe is essential about cognition. Of course, many scholars now try to avoid the strict separation of mind and body assumed by Cartesian dualism. The most popular strategy, especially in recent decades, has been to reduce mental events to brain processes and replace internal explanations with instrumental ones. In some cases, the reduction of mind to brain carries with it the reduction of body to brain. Neuroscientists, for instance, seldom acknowledge the role played by the body as a whole in the cognitive operation of the brain. The body is reduced to its representation in the somatosensory cortex and is considered important only to the extent that it provides the raw sensory input required for cognitive computations. In other cases, the body is first reduced to the mind, and then reduced to the brain. This is especially true in psychology, where the body is first treated as an intentional object (i.e., an image, a mental representation) and then reduced to neural computations.

Contemporary philosophers argue over whether a physical body is necessary for knowledge and cognition, often by considering the implications of different thought experiments in which the mind may be divorced from critical aspects of bodily experience. For instance, consider the following scenario:

> Imagine a brilliant neuroscientist named Mary, who has lived her entire life in a room that is rigorously controlled to display only various shades of black, white, and grey. She learns about the outside world by means of a black/white television monitor, and being brilliant, she manages to transcend these obstacles. She becomes the world's greatest neuroscientist, all from within this room. In particular, she comes to know everything there is to know about the physical structure and activity of the brain and its visual system, of its actual and possible states. (Churchland, 1985: 22)

Philosophers argue, based on examples like the above, over whether qualia (i.e., the phenomenal character of our experience), such as one's subjective sensations of color, must be mental states that are causally related to the neurophysiology of the brain (see Churchland, 1984; Jackson, 1982, 1986). These scenarios, however, dramatically fail to recognize the need for a real living body in knowing about the world. There is no acknowledgment of Mary as a living person, made of flesh, blood, and bone, who moves and has awareness of the felt qualities of her own actions. Mary's first-person experiences of her own body in relation to the environment provide knowledge that is "qualitatively incommensurate" with whatever may be happening in her own brain, or anyone else's (Sheets-Johnstone, 1999: 167). Mary learns about qualia because she subjectively experiences them through her own bodily actions. Knowledge of a set of abstract propositions, such as Mary's understanding of the neurophysiology of color vision, means nothing unless a person experiences in some embodied sense the physical world to which these propositions refer (Sheets-Johnstone, 1999).

Cognitive psychologists, like many philosophers, often fail to recognize the significance of embodied action in the study of human mental life. Most experimental investigations of perception and cognition occur in laboratory situations where a person passively observes stimuli and then responds in some specified manner to what has been presented. In some instances, the person is physically restricted in his or her movements (e.g., head rests are used in psychophysical experiments). In cases where the participant must move to respond to stimuli, such as having to push a button or speak aloud, psychologists work hard to eliminate the movement from their theoretical understanding of the processes involved in perception and cognition. Cognitive processes, especially, are viewed as strictly mental phenomena that have little to do with embodied experience. The body is the vessel for the mind and brain, but has negligible importance in characterizing the essence of mental life.

However, the situation is now changing. Consider just three examples of how psychologists now pay attention to embodied action when studying different cognitive phenomena. First, the classic empirical work on mental imagery investigates possible correspondences between mental imagery and visual perception. For example, participants in one classic study were presented with two-dimensional drawings of pairs of three dimensional objects. The participants' task was to determine whether the two represented objects were identical except for orientation (Shepard & Metzler, 1971). Some of the figures required rotation solely within the picture plane, whereas others required rotation in depth ("into" the page). The general result was that, whether for two- or three-dimensional rotations, participants seemed to rotate the objects mentally at a fixed rate of approximately 60 degrees/second. For many years, psychologists assumed that cognitive abilities, such as those observed in mental rotation studies, demonstrate the tight link between visual perception and mental imagery. Although numerous studies examine people's kinesthetic and motor imagery, scholars traditionally have not searched for explicit relations between kinesthetic activity and mental imagery.

However, recent work suggests that many aspects of visual and motor imagery share a common representational, and possibly neuropsychological, substrate. Various studies demonstrate that the ability to transform mental images is linked to motor processes, so that rotating one's hands in the direction opposite to the required mental rotation slows down the speed of mental rotation (Wexler, Kosslyn, & Berthoz, 1998). Researchers now claim that "visuomotor anticipation is the engine that drives mental rotation" (Wexler et al., 1998). Under this view, similar mechanisms drive both visual image transformation and the production of embodied movements. The ability to plan movements as simulated actions, and not as actual motor plans, may be the common element underlying embodied action and mental imagery performance (Johnson, 2000). These new developments in cognitive psychology illustrate how correcting for a previous neglect of embodied experience in experimental studies leads to a richer picture of the importance of embodiment in human cognition.

Psycholinguists have also slowly begun to seek out the embodied foundation of linguistic structure and meaning. Recall Sandra's earlier comment in response to her fiancé's request for a prenuptial agreement that "I couldn't stand to see our future relationship be reduced to questions of money." Why is it that Sandra used the word "stand" to refer to an abstract, mental experience of her adjusting to her fiancé's demand? Traditional studies on how people process ambiguous, or polysemous, words such as "stand" generally assume that each sense of a word is listed as part of its entry in the mental lexicon. For example, do people immediately access all the possible senses for the word "stand," with context determining which meaning is appropriate afterward? Or does context constrain lexical access so that only the correct meaning of "stand" is accessed during immediate utterance interpretation? These empirical questions have been studied extensively (Gorfein, 2001).

Psycholinguists rarely ask whether people have intuitions about why "stand," or any polysemous word, has the variety of meanings it does. Recent studies, however, demonstrate that people's intuitions about the meanings of "stand" are shaped by their embodied experiences of standing (Gibbs, Beitel, Harrington, & Sanders, 1994). Thus, people tacitly recognize that Sandra's use of "stand" has a metaphorical meaning that is related to their embodied experiences of struggling to remain physically upright when some physical force acts against them. People's understandings of linguistic meanings are not divorced from their embodied experiences, but rather are fundamentally constrained by them in predictable ways.

Following Piaget's early writings, developmental psychology has also started to meaningfully explore how embodied action may underlie children's acquisition of perceptual/conceptual knowledge. For example, infants' interest in things that move assists them in understanding some cause-effect relations in the physical world. Sophisticated studies indicated that infants 12 months old and younger are capable, in the right setting, of making causal attributions to the behavior of objects they see in the world (Gergely, Nadasdy, Csiba, & Biro, 1995; Spelke, Philip, & Woodward, 1995). The infant's developing sensitivity to causal relations may underlie the acquisition of a concept for agency (i.e., things move because of internal forces or human intentions).

These studies, however, despite their brilliance, situate the child as a passive observer who learns to reason about the physical world by visual inspection of real-world events. Several experiments now demonstrate the importance of the child's bodily exploration of the physical world in learning about objects and their behaviors (Adolph, 1997, 2000; Bertenthal, Campos, & Kermoian, 1994; Hertenstein, 2002; Needham, Barrett, & Peterman, 2002). This empirical work suggests that many basic concepts may arise from rudimentary bodily actions and young children's felt experiences of them. Causation and agency, for example, may be rooted in infants' phenomenological sense of their own bodies' interactions with objects and other people. Even before infants possess any ability to physically manipulate objects with their hands and feet, they directly experience cause and effect from the movement of their lips, tongues, and mouths during breastfeeding, or from chewing food, which transforms it to something that can be swallowed easily. An encouraging trend in developmental psychology is greater attention given to infants' phenomenological experience in relation to cognitive growth.

These brief examples illustrate how looking for embodied action in thought and language may provide a different picture of human cognition than has traditionally been assumed within cognitive science. Much recent work in cognitive science views embodiment as a matter of brain states and neural activity. We have indeed learned a great deal from these neuroscientific studies. However, as Roger Sperry noted over sixty-five years ago, "An objective psychologist, hoping to get at the physiological side of behavior, is apt to plunge immediately into neurology trying to correlate brain activity with modes of experience. The result in many cases only accentuates the gap between the total experience as studied by the psychologist and neuronal activity as analyzed by the neurologists. But the experience of the organism is integrated, organized, and has its meaning in terms of coordinated movement" (1939: 295).

The psychologist Scott Kelso more recently suggested, "It is important to keep in mind . . . that the brain did not evolve merely to register representations of the world; rather, it evolved for adaptive actions and behaviors. Musculoskeletal structures coevolved with appropriate brain structures so that the entire unit must function together in an adaptive fashion . . . it is the entire system of muscles, joints, and proprioceptive and kinesthetic functions and appropriate parts of the brain that evolve and function together in a unitary way" (1995: 268).

The brain is certainly part of an integrated dynamic system devoted to the moment-by-moment embodied dynamics of everyday life. Viewing the brain simply as an information-processing or computational device, as the center of cognition, ignores the centrality of animate form in human thought (Sheets-Johnstone, 1999).

This book describes the ways that perception, concepts, mental imagery, memory, reasoning, cognitive development, language, emotion, and consciousness have, to varying extents, groundings in embodiment. My strategy in exploring the significance of embodiment in the study of these topics adopts what may be called the "embodiment premise":

> People's subjective, felt experiences of their bodies in action provide part of the fundamental grounding for language and thought. Cognition is what occurs when the body engages the physical, cultural world and must be studied in terms of the dynamical interactions between people and the environment. Human language and thought emerge from recurring patterns of embodied activity that constrain ongoing intelligent behavior. We must not assume cognition to be purely internal, symbolic, computational, and disembodied, but seek out the gross and detailed ways that language and thought are inextricably shaped by embodied action.

The key feature of this premise is the idea that understanding the embodied nature of human cognition demands that researchers specifically look for possible mind-body and language-body connections. Understanding embodied experience is not simply a matter of physiology or kinesiology (i.e., the body as object), but demands recognition of how people dynamically move in the physical/cultural world (i.e., the body experienced from a first-person, phenomenological perspective). The mind (its images, thoughts, representations) is created from ideas that are closely related to brain representations of the body and to the body's continued activities in the real world.

Fortunately, there is an accumulating body of empirical evidence showing how embodied activities shape human cognition. In the spirit of cognitive science, this "empirical" evidence includes data collected from controlled laboratory studies, naturalistic field observations, neuropsychological case studies, linguistic research, artificial intelligence (and artificial life) modeling, and various phenomenological studies and reports. To be sure, many of the scholars whose studies are described here may not entirely agree with my interpretation of their work as support for "embodied" cognition. Some of these disagreements center around what is meant by the terms "embodied" and "embodiment." I argue that "embodiment" may refer to, at least, three levels of personhood (see Lakoff & Johnson, 1999): neural events, the cognitive unconscious, and phenomenological experience. Although amazing advances have been made in understanding neural processes, insignificant attention has been given to people's phenomenological experience in explaining many aspects of perception, cognition, and language. I address this problem in the pages that follow.

At the same time, special emphasis will be given in the following chapters to two important developments in cognitive science. The first is the approach to cognition known as dynamical systems theory. Dynamical approaches emphasize the temporal dimensions of cognition and the ways in which an individual's behavior emerges from interactions of brain, body, and environment. Simple and complex behavioral patterns are higher-order products of self-organization processes. Virtually all living organisms self-assemble, or are self-organizing systems, "as emergent consequences of nonlinear interaction among active components" (Kelso, 1995: 67). Self-organized patterns of behavior emerge as stable states from the interaction of many subsystems. Yet the emerging higher-order behavior is also capable of "enslaving" lower-level components in such a way that behavioral patterns can often be described by relatively few dimensions. Much of the emphasis, then, in dynamical systems theory is on the structure of spaces of possible behavioral trajectories and the internal and external forces (i.e., couplings between brain, body, and world) that shape these trajectories as they unfold. More specifically, dynamical systems theory is a set of mathematical tools that can be applied to characterize different states of the system as these evolve in time. In this way, a dynamical view aims to describe how the body's continuous interactions with the world provide for coordinated patterns of adaptive behavior, rather than focusing on how the external world become represented in the inner mind.

A dynamical approach rejects the idea that cognition is best understood in terms of representational content (either for neurons or for parts of the mind), or that cognitive systems can be decomposed into inner functional subsystems or modules. Linear decomposition of cognitive performance into functional subsystems (i.e., "boxology") is inadequate to understand the dynamical systems that cut across brain-body-world divisions. Most researchers working within a dynamical framework adopt the conservative strategy of seeing how far one can go in explaining various behavioral data without invoking representational explanations. Dynamical systems theory has had its most profound effect in cognitive science in the study of perception/action relations, or couplings, and in the development of situated, embodied agents, or robots, capable of minimally cognitive behavior. Although there is debate over whether dynamical approaches can "scale up" to explain higher-order aspects of cognition, including language use and consciousness, I am enthusiastic about this perspective because it directly acknowledges the interaction of an agent's physical body (including its brain and nervous system), its experience of its body, and the structure of the environment and social context to produce meaningful adaptive behavior.

As will become evident in what follows, a dynamical perspective is not given to all of the topics discussed in this book, mostly because such applications are still in their infancy, and because my purpose here is not to argue for a single metatheory that explains all cognition. Nonetheless, understanding cognition as an embodied activity demands recognition of the situated dynamics that serve to generate meaningful behavior in a complex world.

A second area of special emphasis in this book will be the important work in cognitive linguistics on the embodied nature of mind and language. Cognitive linguistics does not view language as arising from an autonomous part of the mind/brain, but seeks to discover the ways in which linguistic structures are related to and motivated by human conceptual knowledge, bodily experience, and the communicative functions of discourse (Croft & Cruse, 2004; Lakoff & Johnson, 1999). One of the many notable findings from cognitive linguistic research is that the body serves as a significant resource for people's understanding of many abstract concepts. Metaphor is especially important in mapping experiences of the body to help structure abstract ideas that are fundamental to how people speak and think. Although the research from cognitive linguistics is controversial, given its heavy emphasis on language, and the individual intuitions of linguists, I aim to give cognitive linguistic evidence its proper position in cognitive science as a leading empirical and theoretical force in establishing the importance of embodiment for human cognition.

Overall, there is currently enough empirical evidence to present a fuller, more embodied picture of human cognition than has typically been the case in the cognitive sciences. Most generally, experiences of the body are represented as ideas in the mind, and the body provides valuable resources for off-loading cognition such that mind is distributed across brain, body, and world interactions. This new view of the embodied mind has the following specific characteristics, which will be explored in more detail in the following chapters:

- Concepts of the self, and who we are as persons, are tightly linked to tactile-kinesthetic activity.
- Embodiment is more than physiological and/or brain activity, and is constituted by recurring patterns of kinesthetic, proprioceptive action that provide much of people's felt, subjective experience.
- Perception is not something that only occurs through specific sensory apparatus (e.g., eyeballs and the visual system) in conjunction with particular brain areas, but is a kinesthetic activity that includes all aspects of the body in action. Perception is tightly linked to subjunctive thought processes whereby objects are perceived by imagining how they may be physically manipulated.
- Many abstract concepts are partly embodied, because they arise from embodied experience and continue to remain rooted in systematic patterns of bodily action.
- Human minds evolved with neural resources that are primarily devoted to perceptual and motoric processing, and whose cognitive activity consists largely of on-line interaction with the environment.
- Cognitive processes are not located exclusively inside a person's skin as computations upon mental representations (e.g., propositions, productions, mental images, connectionist networks). Cognitive processes are partly constituted by physical and bodily movements and manipulations of objects in real-world environments. Cognitive mechanisms have evolved to operate in conjunction with environmental structures. Thus, cognitive processes are composed of both internal processes and bodily manipulation of external objects outside the skin.
- Language reflects important aspects of human conceptualization and thus is not independent from mind (i.e., as a separate module). Systematic patterns of linguistic structure and behavior are not arbitrary, or due to conventions or purely linguistic generalizations, but are motivated by recurring patterns of embodied experience (i.e., image schemas), which are often metaphorically extended.
- Memory, mental imagery, and problem solving do not arise from internal, computational, and disembodied processes but are closely linked to sensorimotor simulations.
- Children's developing perception and cognition begins with and is rooted in embodied action.

- Emotion, consciousness, and language evolved, and continue to exist in many ways, as extensions of animate motion.
- Bodies are not culture-free objects, because all aspects of embodied experience are shaped by cultural processes. Theories of human conceptual systems should be inherently cultural in that the cognition that occurs when the body meets the world is inextricably culturally based.

Some of these ideas are not entirely new, but descend from a variety of scholarly works, in many academic disciplines, that have explored the body in mind. These developments, described in the chapters that follow, have decisively influenced the ways cognitive scientists now think about, and empirically examine, cognitive behavior. My arguments in favor of the embodied mind, again, do not imply that embodied experience is the sole underlying factor driving human cognition. Many of the above characteristics of the embodied mind do not tell the whole story of why concepts, language, development, emotions, and consciousness take the particular forms they do in human life. However, I attempt to make a strong case for the importance of embodiment in providing a better blueprint for how cognitive scientists study and describe minds. The time is right for this kind of reappraisal of the body's role in human cognition. Our bodies, and our felt experiences of our bodies in action, finally take center stage in the empirical study of perception, cognition, and language and in cognitive science's theoretical accounts of human behavior.

2

Bodies and Persons

Each of us feels some intimate connection between who we are and our bodies. When someone punches my nose, I, Raymond W. Gibbs, Jr., and not someone else, experience pain. When I wonder if I feel happy, I consider this in terms of my own embodied being, and not someone else's. When I experience the pleasures of sex, the discomfort of feeling cold, or the fatigue from running five miles, I clearly know that my body is the sole source of these sensations.

Yet when I think about the existence of God, or try to solve a complex math problem, I have little awareness that my body has a place in my thoughts. Cognitive processes seemingly occur with little input from our bodies. The very act of perception focuses on perceptual objects/events out in the world in such a way that the body recedes into the background and feels almost unnecessary (Leder, 1990). This "corporeal disappearance" allows us, for better or worse, to objectify the body. We see the body as a material object, whereas the self and the mind are ethereal entities that somehow mysteriously invade or permeate the body. The traditional maxim of "mind over matter" captures the common belief that the immaterial mind rules supreme over the corporeal body.

What is the relationship between persons and their bodies? One may argue that oneself, one's person, is a pure thinking being, similar to that envisaged by Descartes. After all, there are many times when my true essence as a person seems utterly immaterial, as when my body becomes fatigued, ill, or disfigured, yet I still believe that my "self" is unchanged. The person I am, my self-conception, feels unrelated to my body, with my body only being the vehicle for my thoughts. But this kind of quick introspectionist analysis may be misleading, and due as much to one's cultural "folk beliefs" as it is to veridical phenomenological insight. Systematic examination of one's experience of the self and its relation to having a particular kind of body suggests that personhood may be deeply connected to bodies. A body is not just something that we own, it is something that we are.

I claim that the regularities in people's kinesthetic-tactile experience not only constitute the core of their self-conceptions as persons, but form the foundation for higher-order cognition.

This chapter begins to shape the outline for this claim, setting the stage for more detailed consideration of various perceptual, cognitive, and linguistic phenomena that follow in later chapters. I begin by considering traditional conceptions about personhood, the ways we notice our bodies, the difference between body schema and body image, the importance of movement in our experiences as "persons," disordered bodies, culture and embodiment, and the three levels of embodiment that make up the totality of who and what we are as persons. My specific aim here is to begin closing the mind-body gap, so persistent in the Western view of mind, by establishing a tight connection between our sense of ourselves as unique persons and our bodies. Recent attempts within cognitive science to talk of the "embodied mind" too often do so in the context of specific properties of the brain. But there is a great need to understand embodiment as a aspect of whole persons interacting with one another and the world around them.

The First-Person Perspective

The intimate connection between who we are as persons and our bodies has recently been explored by the philosopher Lynne Baker (2000). She argued that a "person" is constituted by a human body, but a "person" is not identical to his or her body. A human organism is a person by virtue of having a capacity to adopt a "first-person perspective." Under this view, persons are not distinguished from other things by virtue of having certain mental states, conscious or otherwise. Many mammals have mental states of belief and desire, and many mammals also have conscious states. Instead, the distinguishing mark of human persons is their capacity to have a complex mental property – a first-person perspective that allows me, for instance, to conceive of my body and mental states as my own, to have various intentional states such as believing, desiring, hoping, fearing, and so on, and to be self-conscious about the plans and goals I decide to pursue. From a first-person perspective, I can think about myself as myself (e.g., "I wonder whether I'll be happy in ten years"), which demonstrates that I have some concept of myself as myself (Baker, 2000: 92). Even if totally paralyzed, an individual has a first-person relation to his or her own body if the thought "I wonder if I'll ever be able to move my legs again" can be entertained (Baker, 2000: 94).

Two human persons may be distinguished from one another by the fact that they are constituted by different bodies, each of which supports different first-person intentional states. Thus, any replica of me has a first-person relation to his body, not mine. Moreover, a single body cannot constitute two persons at the same time. A single person may sometimes feel as if he or she is different persons at different times (e.g., The Three Faces of Eve), and a commissurotomy patient may be manipulated in an experimental situation into simultaneously trying to put on his pants with one hand and trying to take them off with the other. But these are examples of a disordered, single first-person perspective, and not of two different first-person perspectives within the same body (Baker, 2000: 108, but also see the discussion below of conjoined twins). Although a human body starts out as entirely organic, it can acquire nonorganic parts. An artificial leg that I think of as my own, and that I can move merely by intending to move it, becomes a part of my (still human) body. How much of the human body may be replaced and still remain a human body? Technology will surely have an increasing role in supplementing and extending the body. The philosopher Andy Clark (2003) claims that the melding of flesh and machine is a natural progression in our long-developing capacity to incorporate tools into our living environments to reduce the demands placed on brains and minds (see Chapter 5). But as long as we continue to be sustained by organic processes, to some significant extent, each of us should be considered to have a genuine human body.

These observations illustrate the central importance of how we define who we are as persons in terms of our first-person bodily perspective. Moreover, nothing can be your body if there is no you. At the very least, linking first-person bodily perspective with some concept of the self goes against arguments that we are mere bundles of respiring cells, or computer programs, or that our existence as human persons is a metaphysical illusion. Each of these ideas has been seriously debated within the history of philosophy. Some contemporary philosophers, for example, maintain that the phrases "human body" and "one's body" introduce much philosophical confusion and should be avoided in discussions of personal identity (Olson, 2003). Even if one's personhood may be more than the body, there is no self without a body.

Bodies and World

One traditional belief in Western cultures is that human bodies are separate from the external world. Many cognitive scientists embrace this idea by assuming that individuals learn to know the world by re-presenting it to their minds. Human bodies, through the five major senses, are conduits for this re-presentation of the world. Yet bodies are independent of the world as defined by the boundaries of skin (i.e., metaphysical or person-world dualism).

But many philosophers and cognitive scientists now reject person-world dualism and advocate that persons be understood, and scientifically studied, in terms of organism-environment mutuality and reciprocity. For example, Merleau-Ponty (1962) claimed that the body exists primordially, before there is thought or a reflected world, and the world exists for us only in and through the body. Phenomenology shows how the environment and people's perceptions of it are interrelated. As Merleau-Ponty wrote: "My body is the fabric into which all objects are woven, and it is, at least in relation to the perceived world, the general instrument of my 'comprehension'" (1962: 235). Contrary to Descartes, who saw self-knowledge as the foundation of one's knowledge of the world and others persons, Merleau-Ponty suggested that the full explanation of our knowledge of self arises from participatory interaction with our embodied existence. When we consider the concept of time, for instance, Merleau-Ponty argued that it is not helpful to think of time as a river that flows through our lives, independent of and precedent to our relation to it. We do not "observe" time as it goes by. Instead, time comes into being as a function of our embodied interaction with the world.

A more recent perspective on person-environment mutuality is the enactive view of personhood and cognition (Varela, Thompson, & Rosch, 1991). The enactive view has the explicit goal to "negotiate a middle path between the Scylla of cognition as recovery of a pregiven outer world (realism), and the Charybdis of cognition as the projection of a pregiven world (idealism)" (p. 172). Cognition is understood as enaction, or a history of structural couplings that "brings forth a world" either by taking part in an existing world, as happens during development and maturation, or by shaping a new one, as happens over the history of a species. Because enaction consists partially in coupling, the agent and the world are not really separate, because they are "mutually specifying." A person's world is determined by the agent's behavior and the sensorimotor capabilities that allow the individual to cope with a local situation. What people perceive depends upon what they are able to do, and what they do, in time, alters what they perceive. "Perception and action, sensorium and motorium are linked together as successfully emergent and mutually selecting pattern" (p. 163). When a person enacts or brings forth a world, the person and the world are coupled. This possibility does not imply that the body and mind are one and the same. But our bodies are closely defined, and experienced, in terms of the specific actions we engage in as we move about the world.

Our bodies and the world are different, although they can be seemingly absorbed into one another on many occasions. Philosopher Drew Leder describes this embodied coupling of self and the world in the following personal example (Leder, 1990: 165): "I am walking down a forest path. Yet, I am not attending to my world in a bodily or mindful way. I am caught up in my own worries – a paper that needs completion, a financial problem. My thoughts are running their private race, unrelated to the landscape. I am dimly aware of the sights and sound of nature, but it is a surface awareness. The landscape neither penetrates into me, nor I into it. We are two bodies.

"Yet, once again, it is possible to imagine an existential shift. Over time, through the rhythm of my walking, the calmness of the scene, my mind begins to quiet. Something catches my ear – the trilling of a bird. I glance up in time to see the bird hopping from branch to branch, its bright colors shining in the sunlight. I gradually become aware of other birds, other songs, and, as if awakening from a dream, realize that I stand in the midst of a wild chorus. I am beginning to absorb the world around me and become absorbed in it."

Does this experience sound familiar? As Leder comments, "The boundaries between the inner and outer thus become porous. As I close my eyes, I feel the sun and hear the bird songs both within-me and without-me. They are not sense data internal to consciousness, but neither are they 'out there' somewhere. They are part of a rich body-world chasm that eludes dualistic characterization" (Leder, 1990: 165–6). The world becomes alive for us from being incorporated into our bodies, while, at the same time, we experience ourselves being absorbed into the body of the world. This fusion of body and world makes it difficult, at times, to strictly distinguish between the two. Gregory Bateson's (1972) famous example of the blind person who experiences the tip of his walking stick as part of his bodily being illustrates this problem. The clothes we wear, our eyeglass, hearing aids, artificial hearts, and other prosthetic devices are not natural parts of our bodies at birth, but eventually becomes so to some individuals. Postmodern philosophers, and science fiction enthusiasts, explore the consequences of blurring the self/other dichotomy with advances in technological devices that extend the body and integrate nonorganic material with human flesh. These developments work to dissolve any clear boundary between bodies and world.

Bodies and Selves

The cultural anthropologist Clifford Geertz once suggested that the Western view of the self is: "A bounded, unique, more or less integrated motivational and cognitive universe, a dynamic center of awareness, emotion, judgment, and action organized into a distinctive whole and set contrastively both against other such wholes and against a social and natural background" (Geertz, 1979: 229). Many Westerners agree that this definition captures a great deal of the essence of how people conceive of themselves. But this definition does not explicitly acknowledge the body's role in the creation of a self-concept.

There has historically been a strong tendency to conceive of the self as indivisible, and separate from any bodily incarnation. Following in Descartes' footsteps, the 18th-century Scottish philosopher Thomas Reid famously wrote, "A part of a person is a manifest absurdity. When a man loses his estate, his health, his strength, he is still the same person, and has lost nothing of his personality. If he has a leg or an arm cut off, he is the same person he was before. The amputated member is no part of his person, otherwise it would have a right to his estate, and be liable for part of his engagements. It would be entitled to a share of his merit and demerit, which is manifestly absurd. A person is something individual . . . My thoughts, and actions, and feelings change every moment; they have no continued, but a successive existence; but the self or I, to which they belong is permanent, and has the same relation to all the succeeding thoughts and actions which I call mine" (from Flanagan, 2002: 173).

Reid's attempt to locate the self in the immaterial, an echo to the "I think therefore I am" maxim, does not necessarily hold up to phenomenological examination. Many people perceive their selves, the coherence of what we think of as the "self," as being founded on the perceived unity and boundedness of the body. As William James observed over 100 years ago, "The nucleus of the 'me' is always the bodily existence felt to be present at the time" (James, 1890; 194). Our identity through time consists in the identity of our bodies (Ayer, 1936).

Part of our felt sense of ourselves as persons comes from how sensory information is correlated in experience. I know who I am, and that I am, in part, because I see my body (e.g., hands, legs, arms, stomach, feet) as I move and experience specific sensations as a result of action. Research with adults suggests that self-knowledge partly emerges from visual, tactile, and proprioceptive information from our bodies. For example, people are more accurate at predicting a dart's landing position when watching video clips of themselves throwing the dart than when watching a clip of someone else tossing the dart (Knoblich & Flach, 2001). People even better recognize light-displays of their own movements than they do of those of other people, despite rarely seeing their entire bodies in movement (Beardworth & Buckner, 1981). Furthermore, people find it more difficult to identify their own hands, and their actions, in situations in which their hands are perceived as incongruent with their bodily orientation (van den Bos & Jeannerod, 2002). This research suggests that people are normally quite aware of their bodies and their past and potential future actions. We possess fairly detailed self-schemas that are rooted in our experiences of embodied possibilities.

One unusual experiment suggests how people's identification of their bodies depends crucially on intermodal correlation. Botvinik and Cohen (1998) had participants "seated with the left arm resting on a small table. A study screen was positioned beside the arm to hide it from the subject's view and a life-sized rubber model of a left hand and arm was placed on the table directly in front of the subject. The participants sat with eyes fixed on the artificial hand while we used two small paintbrushes to stroke the rubber hand and the subject's hidden hand, synchronizing the timing of the brushing as closely as possible" (Botvinik & Cohen, 1998: 766). After a short interval, participants had the distinct and unmistakable feeling that they sensed the stroking and tapping in the visible rubber hand, and not on the hand which, in fact, was being touched. Further tests revealed that if the experimenters asked participants, with eyes closed, to point to the left hand with the hidden hand, their pointing, after experience of the illusion, were displaced toward the rubber hand. Botvinik and Cohen argued that these results support the idea that our sense of our bodies as our own depends less on their differentiation from other objects and bodies than on their participation in specific forms of intermodal correlation. Thus, our tactile-kinesthetic sensations, and how they are correlated across modalities, provide a strong foundation for our sense of self.

The link between self and body need not imply that there must be a single self in the same way that each of us may possess, or is, a single body. Many scholars today acknowledge that there is not a single "self." Self is fragmented and, at best, provides the center of our "narrative gravity" (Dennett, 1992; Gergen, 1991). In fact, the complexity of our bodily experiences promotes an equally complex set of self-identities. People talk about their inner selves in different ways at different times, using a range of metaphorical concepts that arise from their varied bodily experiences in the physical and social world (Lakoff & Johnson, 1999). Metaphorical concepts express fundamental mental mappings by which knowledge from one domain (i.e., the target) is structured and understood by information from a dissimilar domain (i.e., the source). In many cases, these concepts reflect different kinds of embodied correlations, including (1) the correlation between body control and control of physical objects (e.g., SELF CONTROL IS OBJECT CONTROL – "After being knocked down, the boxer picked himself up off the canvas"), (2) the correlation between being in a certain normal location and experiencing a sense of control (e.g., SELF CONTROL IS BEING IN ONE'S NORMAL LOCATION – "I'm just beside myself with anger," "Peter is out of his mind"), (3) the correlation between self action and the movement of objects (e.g., CAUSING THE SELF TO ACT IS THE FORCED MOVEMENT OF AN OBJECT – "You're pushing yourself too hard," "I can't seem to get myself going"), (4) the correlation between our sense of self control and our control of unified containers (e.g., SELF CONTROL IS HAVING THE SELF TOGETHER AS A CONTAINER – "She is falling to pieces," "Pull yourself together"), and (5) the correlation between our sense of self and the search for things at particular locations (e.g., SELF AS AN ESSENCE THAT IS A FOUND OBJECT – "He is trying to find himself," "She went to India to look for her true self," "He found himself in writing").

These metaphorical ways of understanding the self are not consistent, because there is no single, monolithic self-concept. Yet these metaphors appear to be found in a variety of cultures, and capture important qualities of how we conceive of our inner lives, partly based on varying bodily experiences (Lakoff & Johnson, 1999). Cognitive scientists have, in fact, proposed that there are different levels of the self, each one rooted in different kinds of embodiments. For example, cognitive neuroscientist Antonio Damasio (1999) distinguishes between three kinds of self. The "proto self" is unconscious and constituted by "interconnected and temporarily coherent collection of neural patterns which represent the state of the organism" (Damasio, 1999: 154). Lower animals, even lobsters, possess a proto self. The "core self" is the nonverbal, or preverbal, subject of conscious experience. Dogs, cats, and human infants have core selves. The "autobiographical self," or "extended consciousness," is the record of one's life experiences and is usually thought to require a conceptual structure and maybe language.

All three kinds of self are closely rooted in the brain and body, with each level being built upon its predecessor (Damasio, 1999). The proto self requires a body that sends signals (via chemicals in the bloodstream) to the basal forebrain, hypothalamus, and brain stem, which causes the release of certain neurotransmitters in the central cortex, thalamus, and basal ganglia. These pathways provide the proper material to unconsciously represent different bodily states, including the body's relation to the environment. The core self requires a functioning proto self as well as the cingulate cortex, the thalamus, parts of the prefrontal cortex, and the superior colliculi. Once these different brain areas come into play, people can have a genuine subject of experience. The organism feels things, and feels itself feeling things. Autobiographical memories are stored in various sensory cortices and activated by convergence zones in the temporal and frontal higher cortices, as well as subcortical areas such as the amygdala, which together are important in experiencing and remembering how certain experiences feel and felt. Most generally, the emergence of self requires an organism with a particular kind of brain and to live in a world with other similarly embodied creatures.

Our sense of ourselves as persons that endure through physical (aging) and mental (beliefs, attitudes) changes is primarily based on our bodily interactions with the physical/cultural world. As James Gibson (1966, 1979) long argued, our perception of the sensory world is given to us directly by "affordances." An affordance is a resource that the environment offers an animal, such as surfaces that provide support, objects that can be manipulated, and substances that can be eaten, each of which is a property specified as stimulus information in animal-environment interactions. Each person/animal has a vast set of possibilities for action, based on the perception of affordances (e.g., chairs that can be sat on, streetcars that can be caught if running) that implicitly define who we are (White, 1999). Gibson defined the ecological self as follows: "Awareness of the persisting and changing environment (perception) is concurrent with the persisting and changing self (proprioception in any extended use of the term). This includes the body and its parts and all its activities from locomotion to thought, without any distinction between the activities called 'mental' and those called 'physical.' Oneself and one's body exist along with the environment, they are co-perceived" (1987: 418). Our self-concept is implicit in our perceptual, embodied interactions with the world, and our kinesthetic experiences of our own bodies (i.e., proprioception; see Chapter 3).

Our self-concepts depend, then, on the patterns of bodily actions we engage in on a daily basis. The sense of agency, as the causal basis for action, is perhaps the most convincing evidence for the "I" we experience as persons. For instance, I make a conscious decision to raise my right hand, and my body somehow responds accordingly. Much of the persistent belief that we are the "authors" of our actions is rooted in the systematic patterns of actions that appear to follow from our willful intentions.

But this belief about the link between agency and action may be based on a misinterpretation of brain and unconscious cognitive processes. Several lines of research suggest that the feeling that our conscious will serves as the causal basis for our actions may be illusory. For example, in an infamous study, Libet (1985) asked students to move their hands whenever they wished, while noting on a fast-moving analog clock when they made their decisions. The participants' EEGs were also concurrently measured. If willful bodily action is caused by a conscious decision, or will, then participants should indicate that they made their decisions to act prior to when brain processes executed the hand movement. In fact, the opposite was observed: the decision to move occurred about 350–400 milliseconds after relevant cerebral cortex activity began. One interpretation of this finding suggests that conscious decisions (i.e., sense of agency) do not cause human behaviors, at least for simple motor actions. Some scholars claim that Libet's findings, along with others, demonstrate that the concept of "free will" is an illusion (Wegner, 2002).

Many students, as well as cognitive scientists, are disturbed by the implications of Libet's work. Most people still maintain a belief in a concept of self-body dualism, at least to the extent that each person possesses a self that is the "pilot of one's ship." Yet people can be fooled into believing that their conscious wills are the causes of their actions, even when the true cause resides outside their brains. One study aimed to show this by applying transcranial magnetic stimulation (TMS) to one side of participants' brains by the motor area (Wegner & Wheatley, 1999). TMS induces motor neurons to fire so that people automatically move their limbs. These movements are involuntary, similar to the "knee jerk" that occurs when one's knee is tapped with a hammer. Participants in this study were subjected to TMS on one side of the brain and asked to make spontaneous limb movements. Interestingly, the participants believed that their conscious decisions were the cause of their "knee-jerk" reactions just as much when the true cause was the TMS as when they moved their limbs voluntarily. Results such as these call into question the simple idea that the conscious self is always the author of one's bodily action.

Chapter 8 explores some of the complex relations between neural activity, conscious will, and bodily action. For now, it appears that our feeling of ownership for our actions may be explained in terms of a matching of motor activity with sensory feedback, instead of any thought-then-action causal relationship. Both the thought and the action are due to a single, unconscious brain process with the thought of what is about to happen arising into consciousness a bit before the overt action is completed. Only when we reflect upon what has happened do we invoke a concept of agency to explain the reasons for our actions., even if we are often incorrect in our explanations as to why we behaved in a certain way (Wilson, 2002).

Individuals may claim ownership for their actions in the sense that actions arise from a complex interplay of brain processes, fast-acting cognitive mechanisms, and feelings of conscious awareness, all of which are experienced within the body. A central, even defining, aspect of our sense of self is our ability to predict our future actions. This predictive power is mistakenly attributed to some thought-to-action causal link, but is really an emergent property of brain, body, and world couplings. Our ability to predict our future actions explains, among other things, why it is difficult to tickle oneself. When trying to tickle ourselves, we can easily predict the direction of our movements, which greatly reduces the sensitivity to tactile stimuli compared to when they these are randomly applied by someone else. Many schizophrenics, who attribute the cause of their behaviors to outside sources, do not feel much difference between tickling themselves and being tickled by someone else (Blakemore, Wolpert, D., & Firth, 2000).

Characterizing the self as an emergent property of brain, body, and world interactions mostly assumes that each person has one brain and one body. But conjoined, or Siamese, twins offer an interesting challenge to this idea. Depending on how they are conjoined, these twins may share body space, various organs, and limbs, and experience areas of joint sensation and movement. Very few studies have examined twins' experience of body boundaries as this relates to the self/other distinction. For example, the first well-known pair, Chang and Eng, born in 1871, were joined together at the base of their chests by a band of cartilaginous tendon 5–6 inches long. The brothers had both regions of common sensitivity and areas of individual sensation (Murray, 2001). When touched on the middle of their band of union, both Chang and Eng felt the stimulus. But if a stimulus was moved even 1.2 inches toward one side, only one brother could still feel it. Another famous set of twins were the Tocci brothers, born in 1875. Each twin had a usable pair of arms. However, they were completely joined below the sixth rib, sharing a common abdomen, anus, and penis and one pair of legs. Each brother had control over the leg on his side of the body, but they were unable to walk.

One set of four-month-old conjoined twins were connected on the ventral surface between the umbilicus and sternum so that they always faced one another (Stern, 1985). One twin would often suck on the other's fingers, and vice versa, but they had no confusion as to which fingers belonged to whom. This suggests that each twin "knew" that one's own mouth sucking a finger and one's own fingers being sucked did not make a coherent self. Even with body fusion, the individual twins seemed to make distinctions between parts of their own bodies and those of the other twin.

However, many conjoined twins who were surgically separated as young children or adolescents report confusion as to whether they are the same person afterward (e.g., "Is it really me?" "Am I really myself?") (Separating conjoined twins is obviously a tremendous medical challenge. Yet surgeons actually construct, rather than merely separate, bodies, because there are no natural ways of making two bodies out of one that preserve each twin's self-identity and self-body relationship [Murray, 2001]).

It seems impossible for an individual to phenomenally feel from the inside part of another person's body. But cases of autositic-parasitic twins provide an exception to this idea (Murray, 2001). With autositic-parasitic twins, one twin dies at an early stage of embryonic development, but various portions of its body (parasitic) become attached to, and are sustained by, the surviving twin (autositic). Most twins with upper-body parasites give their "companion" a name and treat the parasite as a person (one parasite was even baptized). In the case of Laloo, born in 1874, the parasitic twin was attached to the lower part of his waist and had two arms and two legs and a penis, which had erections and discharged urine independently of Laloo's control. The parasite's "unruly behavior" suggests that an agency separate from that of the autositic twin was attributed to it. Laloo could, however, feel sensations whenever any part of the parasitic twin was touched.

These case studies raise more questions than they answer about how Siamese twins conceive of self-body relationships. One reasonable conclusion, though, is that the ways individuals know their body boundaries are actually contingencies that, although reliable for most of us, can lead to ambiguity between body and self for conjoined twins (Murray, 2001).

Most generally, understanding how brain, body, and world function to produce a sense of self requires that we view this interaction as part of a self-organized dynamic system. Brains operate at different levels, from the microscopic level of single neurons, to populations of neurons or cell assemblies, to levels at which mental functions are experienced from a first-person perspective. Higher and lower levels interact, and have causal influence, in both directions. Yet despite our feelings that this is the case, there is no single control center (i.e., the self) that oversees the operation of the different levels or their interaction. Self-organizing dynamic systems have a kind of permanency whose existence can only be understood from the inside (Flanagan, 2002). Thus, brain, body, and environment interaction gives rise to the sense of self that, again, has a feeling of some permanency.

What Do We Notice about Our Bodies?

What do adults ordinarily notice about their bodies? When I run uphill, I certainly feel the muscle tension in my legs, and the expansion of my lungs as I struggle to breathe. But I have little awareness of the hair on my head, the movement of my hands, the sensations in the pit of my stomach. Thus, the body does not appear to consciousness as a normal object of awareness as we actively engage with our surroundings.

Phenomenological philosophers have long struggled to characterize the felt sensations in mental life and bodily action (Husserl, 1977; Heiddeger, 1962; Merleau-Ponty, 1962; Sartre, 1956; Sheets-Johnstone, 1999). Contemporary Western cultures also wrestle with how to think about and describe bodily experience. We certainly have become obsessed with the care and appearance of the body. Much of this attention is with the body-as-object, or something that can looked at and desired, and not with the body-as-subject, or the first-person experience of one's body in action. Of course, most of us acknowledge that looking good on the outside makes us feel good on the inside! There is a significant trend, which remains quite active in California as a remnant of the "human potential movement," to develop practices that enhance one's felt understanding of one's body (e.g., massage, polarity therapy, progressive relaxation, rolfing, meditation, Vipassana meditation, yoga, biofeedback, the Feldenkrais method, autogenic training, the Alexander technique) (Marrone, 1990). Many of these techniques emphasize how each individual's sense of self is composed of a constellation of physical, emotional, and intellectual habits that can become limiting and restrictive. Various movement practices enable people to "get in touch with their bodies" in ways that most of us simply do not sense with appropriate attention in everyday life. This version of "embodied psychology" aims to develop a reciprocity of body and mind as part of psychotherapeutic healing processes.

Few systematic studies in cognitive science, however, have explored what people ordinarily notice about their bodies. An exception to this is one study that directly examined adults' intuitions of their daily embodied experiences (Pollio, Henley, & Thompson, 1997). Men and women responded at length to two questions: (1) "Could you tell me some times when you are aware of your body?" and (2) "Could you tell me of what you are aware of in that situation?" The first question was aimed at revealing the "whens" of bodily experience, and the second question the "whats" of bodily experience.

Participants' responses indicated that bodily experience tended to be focused on eight general situations:

i. Using the body (i.e., an awareness of the body when engaged in an activity or project);
ii. Sensing the body (i.e., an awareness of the body such as that felt when experiencing aches and pains, illness and fatigue, and various pleasures);
iii. Presenting the body (i.e., an awareness of the body as presented to other people, such as posture and mode of dress);
iv. Pregnancy and sexuality (i.e., the feelings associated with being pregnant, including nursing, and sexual intimacy and arousal);
v. Changes over time (i.e., an awareness of comparisons between a present experience of the body and past ones);
vi. Identity (i.e., an awareness of the meaning of some event, such as when a person is aware of his/her body "as a Christian");
vii. Awareness of others (i.e., an awareness of the presence or absence of others);
viii. Awareness of affect (i.e., an awareness of strong emotions as a major aspect of some situation).

The Pollio et al. interviews also revealed three major themes that reflect each person's unique mode of experiencing his/her body. Each theme included two specific subthemes:

1. Experiences of engagement
   a. Body in vitality
   b. Body in activity;
2. Experiences of corporeality
   a. Body as instrument
   b. Body as object;
3. Experiences of interpersonal meaning
   a. Body as appearance
   b. Body as expression of self.

Experiences of engagement occur when a person experiences his or her body as fully engaged in some project out in the world. Vitality refers to experiences in which the person is fully engaged in the world with little or no sense of the body-as-physical. Instead, there is a feeling of well-being and absorption in the world (e.g., "... the feeling of well-being, you go outside and take a deep breath and feel good all over"). Activity refers directly to the concrete movements a person is engaged in, in which there is a general awareness of the body as central to the experience (e.g., "In running I enjoy the feeling of the muscles burning, the tightness of the skin with the wind on it").

Experiences of corporeality arise as an awareness of the body-as-physical becomes present as an object in a world of objects or as a means for achieving goals. These experiences include both acting upon things and being acted upon by them. Instrument refers to experiencing the body as a tool for accomplishing things and as something that can be brought up in learning skillful performance (e.g., "In the early stages of learning how to dance, you have to think about the process of all these pieces"). Object refers to bodily limits, similar to the ways that objects have limits. Thus, the body can be impaired through illness, or may be seen in terms of possession and ownership. Furthermore, the body may call attention to itself and reorient a person back to the world (e.g., "I'm most aware of my body after I eat, aware and self-conscious of my belly").

Experiences of interpersonal meaning are those where the body is understood in terms of its social and symbolic meaning. People feel their bodies as they partake in the shared meanings of the everyday world. Expressions of the self refer to those instances where the body-as-self is highlighted, including aspects of lifestyle, character, and interpersonal stance (e.g., "I've always been hard on myself, seeing room for improvement. I guess I've fallen into the trap of the modern American male always trying to look like the model in *Esquire*"). Appearance refers to concrete ways that a person's body looks in the eyes of the self and to other people (e.g., "I try to dress in a way that calls attention away from my body and toward my face. Being fat means you have to try harder to just look okay").

The six subthemes identified above often blend together in different aspects of bodily experience. For example, "(when running) I'm often aware of my pace, the pace of my feet, and heartbeat and my breath. When I'm feeling at my peak, that's when I'm most aware of things working together." Another blend is when object, experience of self, vitality, and activity are combined: "When I'm doing what I want to be doing, there isn't a separation (between my body and me)... I perceive separatedness when I'm critical of my body or in pain. If I'm doing something well, I'm aware of being me... To be aware of my body... means that something isn't right."

This analysis of people's attention to their own bodies illustrates, once again, the reciprocity that exists between bodies and environment. People mostly notice their bodies in relational situations involving the environment and interacting with other persons.

Movement, Body Schemas, and Body Images

Movement is central to how we conceive of the relation between ourselves and our bodies. We do not feel subjective experiences to be specific brain states, but sensations of our bodies in action. Babies begin life by wiggling, stretching, opening and closing their mouths, swallowing, kicking, crying, reaching out to touch people and objects, and so on. In a very literal sense we kinesthetically grow into our bodies. Infants come to realize that different parts of their bodies are capable of specific movement (e.g., arms that extend, fingers that touch, spines that bend, knees that flex, mouths that open and shut, and so on). As infants make kinesthetic sense of their physical experiences, they progressively build more complex mental understandings having to do with containment, balance, weight, physical effort, and the consequences of their embodied actions upon the world. As the philosopher Edmund Husserl once observed, primal movement is "the mother of all cognition" (Husserl, 1980: 69).

What underlies people's abilities to move as they do and have any awareness of their bodies? People have a specific body sense that yields specific knowledge about their bodies. Various information systems yield information about the state and performance of the body. Among these systems are the following (Bermudez, Marcel, & Eilaan, 1995: 13):

(a) Information about pressure, temperature, and friction from receptors on the skin and beneath the surface.
(b) Information about the relative state of body signals from receptors in the joints, some sensitive to static position, some to dynamic information.
(c) Information about balance and posture from the vestibular system in the inner ear and the head/trunk dispositional system and information from pressure on any parts of the body that might be in contact with gravity-resisting surfaces.
(d) Information from skin stretch and bodily disposition and volume.
(e) Information from receptors in the internal organs about nutritional and other states relevant to homeostasis and well-being.
(f) Information about effort and muscular fatigue from muscles.
(g) Information about general fatigue from cerebral systems sensitive to blood composition.

These information systems work together in complex ways to produce both a "body schema" and a "body image." Unfortunately these terms have sometimes been used indiscriminately to refer to quite different types of bodily representations. Some of the ways the terms "body image" and "body schema" have been used include the following (Bermudez et al., 1995: 15):

(a) One's conscious experience of the body at a particular time.
(b) A changing nonconscious record of the momentary relative disposition of, and space occupied by, one's body parts.
(c) A nonconscious persisting representation of the structure and shape of one's body.
(d) A canonical representation of what bodies in general look or feel like.
(e) A knowledge of one's own specific appearance.

(f) Explicit conceptualizations of the body, acquired socially or academically (e.g., that one has a liver).
(g) Emotional attributions toward one's body, some of what are tacit and socially determined.
(h) Cultural symbolizations of the body.
(i) The neuronal vehicles for some of the contents referred to above.

These very different aspects of bodily representation can, however, be adequately distinguished from each other. "Body schema" is the way in which the body actively integrates its posture and position in the environment. We do not ordinarily sense our bodies making postural adjustments as we perceive objects and events and move about in the world. Body schemas allow us to walk adroitly without bumping into or tripping over things, to follow and locate objects, to perceive shape, distance, and duration, and to catch a ball with accuracy. These mundane events all take place independent of our conscious thoughts of the body.

Our felt sense of movement is regulated by our proprioceptive systems. Proprioception is neglected as an important embodied system, because it is not traditionally seen as an input system for presenting the world to the mind. Sir Charles Sherrington (1906) called this system the "sixth sense." The information proprioception provides comes from the nerve endings in muscles and joints, and partly also from those in the skin. The balance organ in the ear contributes information about one's posture and position in space. Nerve endings in the muscles give information about the amount and fluctuation of muscle tone and the length and tension of the muscles, and thus provides information about movement and the amount of force used. Nerve endings in the joints give information about the movement and position of the joints, and thus about movement and posture. Stretch receptors in the skin, especially in the face, give information about facial expressions and movement in speech and eating. The balance organ, together with information from the neck muscles, gives information about global posture and position with respect to the horizontal plane.

Sherrington emphasized how proprioception functions automatically and unconsciously and may operate when the brain is disconnected from the nervous system. All our movements and the maintenance of a posture require a subtle coordination of countless muscles and joints that make up our body schema. Without immediate feedback from the sensory nerves about what the muscles and joints are doing, all of our movements and even the maintenance of our posture would go totally awry. The body schema, the continually updated, nonconceptual, nonconscious information about the body provides the necessary feedback for the execution of both our gross motor programs and their fine tuning (Gallagher, 1995).

Take, for example, a simple bodily action like standing up straight. We have known how to do that since infancy, and need not bother consciously with the appropriate motor program to perform the action. Also, the fine tuning of this posture is provided for by the body schema. If our arms are slightly in front of the body, we have to lean back somewhat to compensate for the extra weight in front. If we carry something in front of us, we have to compensate more. The compensating just happens; we don't have to think about it. We don't even notice these small corrections, not in others and not in our own case. It is only when we see people with very large bellies or pregnant woman that we notice that they are leaning backward. All that information from the nerve endings in muscles and joints, together with the information from the balance organ, is needed. The body schema has to feed it to the motor program in time; otherwise we would fall over. But we don't have to be bothered with it. It all happens automatically, so that we have our hands literally free for other things. Of course this only goes for motor tasks that are not too complex, or that we have mastered some time ago. Acquiring new motor skills, such as learning to drive or play the violin, requires conscious effort and attention.

Our body schemas may be supramodal and used in comprehending body position information about both self and others. One study in support of this idea showed participants the successive positions of a model in either the same or different body positions (Reed & Farah, 1995). The participants' task was to move either their arms or their legs as they viewed the first picture. Participants better detected changes in the model's position when these changes were identical to the body movements made by the participants. Another study showed that the particular part of the participant's body being moved determined the participant's ability to detect changes in the model's body positions. People's body schemas appear to have internal organization, with different representations from different body parts. Using one part of the body schemas to monitor one's own movement automatically focuses attention on the corresponding parts of other bodies that we are watching.

One complex study employed a modified version of the "alien hand" paradigm to examine the contribution of body schemas to self-recognition (van den Bos & Jeannerod, 2002). A participant and experimenter sat at opposite ends of a table. Each person placed her right hand, which was gloved, on the table so that the hands faced each other. The participant's hand, however, was hidden under a screen with a mirror. A video camera filmed the mirror image that was displayed on the screen, which created the impression for the participant that she was looking directly at the table with the two hands.

Each trial began with the participant's and experimenter's hands in fists. A signal prompted the participant to move either the thumb or index finger. The experimenter moved the same finger as the participant (same-movement condition) or another finger (different-movement condition),

After 1 second, the screen was turned off and an arrow appeared pointing to the location of the screen where the hands had been displayed. The participant's task was to judge whether the hand she had seen at the location of the arrow was her own hand or the experimenter's.

There was one other important factor in this study. The image of the hand on the screen was also rotated in varying degrees or not rotated. When there was no rotation, the spatial orientation of the participant's own hand was consistent with the position of her body. When the image was rotated by 90 degrees, the orientation of the participant's, as well as the experimenter's, hand was incongruent with the participant's body orientation. In these two cases, both hands were seen as "alien." When the image was rotated 180 degrees, the experimenter's hand was congruent with the participant's body orientation, and the participant's hand was congruent with the experimenter's body orientation. This condition made it seem as if the experimenter's hand belonged to the participant's body, and the participant's own hand was seen as if it belonged to the experimenter.

Van den Bos and Jeannerod first examined the effect of action cues on self-recognition. The participants almost always recognized their own hands in the different-movement conditions, but made significantly more errors in recognizing their own hands when the experimenter performed the same finger movement. Thus, self-recognition becomes more difficult when fewer action cues were available.

Rotation of the image also affected participants' self-recognitions, but only in the same-movement condition. Thus, participants made the fewest (15%) errors when their hand orientations were congruent with their own body orientations, a higher degree of errors (24%) when the orientations of their hands were incongruent with body orientation (at 90 degrees rotation), and the most errors (35%) when the experimenter's hand was congruent with the participants' body orientations (180 degree rotation). The higher error rate in the 180 degree rotation condition shows that body schema clearly contributes to self-recognition, especially when other action cues are absent.

Studies like this reveal, again, that body schemas are integral to both how we move and recognizing who we are as unique persons. Not surprisingly, the environment affects people's intuitions about their bodies. People perceived their arm lengths to be greater when the outstretched arm approached a barrier (a wall) than when the arm was outstretched in an open space (a hallway) (Shontz, 1969). People also estimated arm length to be greater when they were instructed to point to objects (Shontz, 1969). When asked to estimate head width, people overestimated less when their faces were touched by someone else than when they were not touched. These findings demonstrate how the body's boundaries expand and contract in different contexts and tasks. Once again, there is no bodily perception without a world in which the body moves. Any change in the environment brings about some, even very slight, change in our experience of the body.

Body schemas are not isomorphic to, or can be explained by physiology. Our bodies react intelligently in response to the environment in complex ways that resist description by a single mechanism or reflex. We actively organize our embodied experience given practical concerns. My running across a field cannot be explained simply in terms of the physiological activity of my body (Gallagher, 1995). Instead, the pragmatic aim behind my movement (e.g., run to catch a ball in a game of baseball) explains my action, at the same time that the physical environment, my previous experience at catching balls, and even the rules of baseball shape the way I move my body. Thus, a person's individual experience, and the personal and cultural reasons for them, give rise to different body schemas that cannot be explained solely in biological terms.

Body image refers to conscious representations of the body, including how the body serves as an object of feelings and emotions, such as whether we experience ourselves as fat, thin, tired, and so on (Gallagher, 1995). People's subjective evaluations of their own bodies, along with their associated feelings and attitudes, have been extensively studied in terms of the relationship between body image and satisfaction with individual body parts, the relation of body image and eating disorders, and the relation of physical variables to body image (Fisher, 1990). A typical body image questionnaire asks participants to give ratings for 19 items, including self-perceptions of whether their bodies are healthy/unhealthy, physically attractive/unattractive, sources of pleasure/displeasure, something to be hidden/shown, calm/nervous, old/young, frail/robust, energetic/not energetic, and so on (Koleck, Bruchon-Schweitzer, Cousson-Gelie, Gillard, & Quintard, 2002). These questionnaires often find that body satisfaction is associated with sex, health, and current and future emotional adjustment.

There are important interactions between body schema and body image. For instance, the unconscious operation of the body schema influences significant aspects of our conscious experiences of the body. Some research demonstrates that changing how the body performs clearly affects how people perceive their bodies, but also colors people's perception of space and external objects. Thus, people's body size is consistently overestimated relative to their size estimates for other objects (Gardner, Martinez, & Sandoval, 1987). Various studies show that body schemas affect spatial perception and perception of objects. Changes in posture, mobility, physical ability, and other examples associated with the body schema imposed by abnormality, disease, or illness (e.g., obesity, rheumatoid arthritis, multiple sclerosis), or by temporary physical changes (such as pregnancy), affect perceptual, cognitive, and emotive aspects of body image. For example, degeneration of body function and changes in mobility lead to decreases in the senses both of body integrity and of strong body boundaries (Gardner et al., 1987). Various studies also show that exercise, dance, and other embodied practices affect people's emotional stances toward their body images (Asci, 2003).

Disordered Bodies

Neurological damage can have terrible effects on people's perceptions of their own bodies and of their bodily experiences. When people's perceptions of their bodies are disturbed, they suffer mental/emotional disarray. For example, people with cerebral palsy often experience involuntary movements of the limbs, and sometimes claim that a body part is not their own. Once again, the ability to move one's body intentionally with some sense of being able to predict what happens next seems critical to identification of oneself with one's body.

One of the most devastating disorders that a person can experience, apart from paralysis, is the loss of proprioception. Consider the famous case of Ian Waterman (Cole, 1995). Waterman fell sick at age 19, became very weak, and could not walk or maintain an upright position and his speech was slurred. He soon seemed to be paralyzed, but there was nothing wrong with his muscles or motor neurons. Even when lying in bed, Waterman could move his arms and legs in all directions. But he seemed to have no control over his movements and lost all sense of touch and proprioception from the neck down. All the large sensory nerves that send information from the periphery to the brain had been destroyed. Waterman was left with feelings of deep pain, of heat and cold, and of fatigue. But he did not have a single feeling of the position and posture of his body, or a feeling of touch on his skin. If he was not looking, Waterman could not say where his arms and legs were positioned.

Waterman eventually taught himself to sit up by consciously planning small action he needed to do. For instance, he first tried to use the muscles of his abdomen as if he were about to perform a sit-up. But when this plan did not work. Waterman realized that he needed to lift his head up first. When he did this and was first successful, Waterman was so pleased that he forgot to think about his movments and slumped backwards. Over many months of laborious practice, Waterman learned to sit up, eat, dress himself, write, and then even walk. Although his destroyed nerves never got better, he employed visual feedback to consciously plan each bodily movement. However, in the dark, Waterman could not see himself or his surroundings, and was as helpless as he was during the onset of his illness.

Waterman's ability to use the visual sense to substitute for muscle sense indicates that in sighted people the two senses may often be combined to allow judgments of movement. Deafferented patients such as Waterman (people whose sensory nerves leading from the periphery toward the brain do not function any more) have a different awareness of their bodies than we have, because we normally do not need to rely so heavily on vision for our proprioceptive behavior. Although these patients' body schemas are almost nonexistent, their body images remain remarkably intact because they have an awareness of how they look and how much space they occupy. These patients experience pain immediately as located within particular places within the frame of their body image. But their body images arise from their visual perception alone and not from proprioception.

One notable aspect of the disordered body is that people still feel body parts even after the part has been removed. One study of 300 amputees in prisoner-of-war camps during World War II showed that 98 percent experienced a "phantom limb," usually in the form of a pleasant tingling sensation (Henderson & Smyth, 1948). Some amputees, however, experience the missing limb as having pain.

There are various speculations about phantom limb experiences. Research with normal adults has shown that simply looking at a moving limb can create a sense of voluntary movement in the observer (Ramachandran & Blakeslee, 1998). People can even be fooled into thinking that someone else's hand, for example, was their own. One study had people don a glove, insert their hand into a box, and then on a signal, draw a line on a piece of paper (Nielsen, 1963). However, the participants did not know that the hand they saw in the box was actually a mirror reflection of another person's hand, also gloved and holding a pen in the exact place where they would expect their hand to be. When the signal was given, and the imposter hand drew a line that varied from the line the participant had been instructed to draw, participants typically adjusted their own arms to compensate for the observed arm's initial trajectory.

This "alien hand" procedure has been employed to study the experience of phantom limb movement (Ramachandran & Blakeslee, 1998). Individuals with a phantom arm placed both the phantom and their other real arm into a mirror box. They saw a reflection of the real arm in the place where the phantom would be if it were real. When the person moved the real arm voluntarily, he experienced the phantom arm as moving voluntarily as well. Thus, the visible hand guided the experience of the phantom. Even when an experimenter's arm appeared in place of the phantom, movement of that arm created the feeling that the phantom limb itself was moving. Studies such as this demonstrate that willful body movement can be experienced simply by watching any body move where one's body ought to be.

People's subjective experience of then disordered bodies show that body schemas are not equivalent to physiology (Gallagher, 1995). There is nothing in the physiology of an amputated leg that gives some patients the feel of their real legs before these were amputated. Instead, the missing limb remain part of the individual's body schema that continues to shape how that person moves and feels.

Understanding Other Bodies

When we see another person, we do not perceive his or her body as a mere physical thing, but rather as a living body like our own. There may be a deep connection between the mental representation of posture, the movement of one's own body, and the perception of posture and movement of other bodies. Ideomotor action refers to body movements that tend to arise in observers as they watch other people perform specific actions. For example, avid sports fans often report tensing their muscles and moving their arms and legs as they observe, say, a football game on television. Psychologists have debated the reasons for this kind of "ideomotor action" since the 19th century (Carpenter, 1874; James, 1890). Contemporary research suggest that simulation mechanisms provide the common code between perception and action, such that perceiving an action induces the production of a similar act, or the urge to act, in the observer (Knuf, Aschersleben, & Prinz, 2001; see Chapter 3). When we see someone perform an action, the same motor circuits that are activated when we perform such actions are concurrently activated (i.e., an "as-if-body" loop, Damasio, 1999, 2003). Because of this neural-sensation matching to a self-performed action, we understand other's movements as goal-directed actions. More generally, shared representations of perception and action may underlie social cognition and intersubjectivity (Gergely & Watson, 1999; Rochet, 2001; Trevarthen, 1977).

Understanding other people requires, among other things, the capacity to be empathetic. Empathy is not just understanding another person's particular experiences (sadness, joy, and so on), but is the experience of another as an embodied subject of experience like oneself. One recent theory of empathy suggests that attending to an object's state (e.g., looking at another person) automatically activates the subject's representations of the state, situation, and object, and that activation of these representations automatically primes or generate the associated automatic and somatic responses, unless inhibited (Preston & de Waal, 2002). According to this model, various phenomena such as emotional contagion, cognitive empathy, guilt, and helping are similar in that they rely on a perception-action mechanism (PAM).

Activating shared representations between perception and action is clearly an important element in the experience of empathy. But empathy is deeply grounded in the experience of our lived bodies, and this experience enables us to directly recognize others, not as bodies endowed with minds, but as persons like us (Gallese, Ferari, & Umilta, 2002). Other people's actions, sensations, and embodied experiences become meaningful to us, precisely because we share these with others. But how can such sharing of experience be possible?

One possibility is that the mechanism for this sharing of experience is simulation (Gallese et al., 2002). By modeling some behavior, our actions provide a simulated representation of the same process that can be used to produce it, on the one hand, and to decode it when performed by someone else, on the other. These "as if" simulation mechanisms may underlie a wide range of processes as diverse as action perception and imitation (as simulation of the observed action), emotion perception (as simulation of the perceived emotion), and mindreading. Simulation theory holds that we understand other's thoughts by pretending to be in their "mental shoes" and by using our own mind/body as a model for the minds of others (Gallese & Goldman, 1998). There are dedicated brain structures, called "mirror neurons," that underpin a direct, automatic, nonpredictive, and noninferential simulation mechanism, by means of which the observer would be able to recognize, understand, and imitate the behavior of others. Research suggests that a mirror matching system could be at the basis of our capacity to perceive in a meaningful way, not only the actions, but also the sensations and emotions of others (Gallese, 2001). For example, single-neuron recording experiments in humans have demonstrated that the same neurons become active when the subject either feels pain or observes others feeling pain (Hutchinson, Davis, Lozano, Troby, & Dostrovsky, 1999). Neuropsychological studies demonstrate that individuals with damage to the right somatosensory cortices, which are critical to understanding body maps, experience defects in emotion and feeling and in feeling empathy for others (Adolphs, Damasio, Tranel, Cooper, & Damasio, 2000). Thus, having some sense of our own bodily responses is an important part of understanding, and feeling appropriate emotion for, other people's experiences.

Bodies and Culture

People and their bodies move in physical environments imbued with culture. The body system (its anatomical structure, its orifices or entrances and exists, the substances it secretes, its position, etc.) offers insightful analysis for understanding cultural systems. "The physical experiences of the body, always modified by the social categories through which it is known, sustain a particular view of society" (Douglas, 1970: 93). Anthropologists have demonstrated in a variety of cultural settings how many elementary embodied experiences are shaped by local cultural knowledge and practice (see Csordas, 1994; Lambek & Strathern, 1998). The body is appreciated for its symbolic properties. People instill cultural meaning into bodily processes such as breathing, blushing, menstruation, birth, sex, crying, and laughing, and value the products of the body (e.g., blood, semen, sweat, tears, feces, urine, and saliva) differently in changing cultural contexts. More complex bodily experiences ranging from nerves (Low, 1994), rape (Winkler, 1994), AIDS (Martin, 1994), and pain and torture (Jackson, 1994; Scheper-Hughs & Lock, 1987), to name just a few, have been studied by anthropologists to explore the linkages between embodiment and cultural meaning. At the same time, anthropomorphism is a primary means by which small-scale societies use body parts, and their actions, to refer to an enormous range of houses, artifacts, animals, and plants (Tilley, 1994).

Much of the interest in cultural studies is not in embodiment per se, but the ways that attending to the body brings different cultural processes into focus (Lambek & Strathern, 1998). Rather than being a biological given, embodiment is a category of sociocultural analysis, often revealing complex dimensions of the interactions between bodies and personhood. Talk of embodiment is situated in reference to topics such as health and illness, kinship, modes of production and exchange, gender and age hierarchies, language practices, religious and political disciplines, jural rules, pervasive metaphors, spirit possession, historical experiences, and myths. People's bodies are more than surfaces for social inscription (i.e., the "body as text" metaphor), but incorporate cultural meanings and memories.

Culture does not just inform embodied experience; embodied experience is itself culturally constituted (Csordas, 1994; Maalej, 2004; Strathern, 1996). Many embodied experiences are rooted in social-cultural contexts (Quinn, 1991). For instance, the notion of CONTAINMENT (see Chapter 4), is based on one's own bodily experience of things going in and out of the body, and of our bodies going in and out of containers. But containment is not just a sensorimotor act, but an event full of anticipation, sometimes surprise, sometimes fear, sometimes joy, each of which is shaped by the presence of other objects and people that we interact with. Certain aspects of sensory perception are emergent and dependent on culture, which influences the embodiment of dispositions through everyday practice (Bordieu, 1977; Shore, 1996; Shweder, 1991; Strauss & Quinn, 1997).

Several ethnographic studies demonstrate that vision in many societies is not the central perceptual mode. Instead, the "lower" senses are central to the metaphoric organization of experience (see Chapter 4). This does not imply that people in various cultures have different physiologies, but only that they weigh sensory information differently in how they think about their experiences and the world around them. For instance, among the Songhay people of Mali and Niger, smell, taste, and sound contribute to the organization of their religious and philosophical experiences (Stoller, 1989). Songhay sorcerers and griots learn about power and history by "eating" it, ingesting odors and tastes, savoring textures and sounds. The stomach is considered the site of human personality and agency. Social relations are considered in terms of eating.

The Anlo-Ewe speaking people of West Africa do not emphasize strict distinctions between the five senses in the way that people from Western cultures seem to do (Geurts, 2002). In Anlo-Ewe cultural contexts, a discrete category demarking the five sensory systems is not tightly bounded or seen as a particularly meaningful way of classifying experience or theorizing about knowledge. Instead, in the Anlo-Ewe mind, sensations caused by stimuli from external objects are epistemologically related to sensations that arise from internal somatic modes (such as interoception, which governs balance, movement, and proprioception). The Anlo cultural tradition does not have a theory of the senses, but has a coherent and fairly complex theory of inner states which link sensations to emotions, dispositions, and vocations, referred to as "seselalame" (a feeling in the body or flesh).

Seselalame is a culturally elaborated way by which Anlo-Ewe read their own bodies while simultaneously understanding them in relation to objects, the environment, and the bodies of those around them. For instance, the Anlo-Ewe people greatly emphasize the proprioceptive quality of balance. They are openly encouraged to actively balance their own bodies as infants, they balance small bowls and pots on their heads, and they carry books and desks on their heads when walking to and from school. Adults perceive balance as a defining attribute of mature individuals and the human species more generally. But this attribute is not merely a physical characteristic of individuals, but a direct association between bodily sensations and who you are or who you may become. Thus, your character and your moral fortitude is established in the way you move. Thus, people are designated as moral or immoral through reference to the cultural categories that implicate and create sensory phenomena.

Among the Ongee, a hunting and gathering people of the Little Andaman Island in the Bay of Bengal, smell is the primary sensory medium through which the categories of time, space, and person are conceptualized (Howes, 2003). Odor, according to the Ongee, is the vital force that animates all living, organic beings. Newborns are said to possess little scent. Children acquire more olfactory strength as they get older. The odor that a person scatters about during the day is said to be gathered up during sleep by an inner spirit and returned to the body, making continued life possible. Death occurs when one loses one's odor, and once dead, a person becomes an inorganic spirit seeking out the odors of the living in order to be reborn. In these ways, the Ongee life cycle is conceived in terms of an olfactory progression.

Daily life is a constant game of olfactory hide-and-seek. Animals are killed to release their odors, while people try to hide their own odors from both other persons and animals. The Ongee speak of "to hunt" as "to release smell causing a flow of death." When walking, the Ongee try to step in the footsteps of the person in front to confuse personal odors, making it difficult for spirits to track them down. They also screen their odors with smoke. When they are traveling in single file, the leader will carry burning wood to cover the odors of all those walking behind. The Ongee also paint themselves with clay to inhibit smell emission. An Ongee with a painted body will declare, "The clay paint has been good! I feel that my smell is going slowly and in a zig-zag manner like the snake on the ground!" (Pandya, 11993: 137).

Space is understood by the Ongee in terms of the dynamic environmental flow of smells, and not as static physical dimensions. Thus, a village's space will expand or contract depending on the olfactory ambiance, as when strong-smelling substances such as pig's meat are present or the scent of seasonal flows wafts through the air. If asked to draw a map, an Ongee will depict a line of movement of scents from one place to another, rather than the locations of the places themselves. The Ongee measure time as a cycle of odors, or a "calendar of scents" (Radcliffe-Brown, 1964).

These few examples illustrate how different cultures attach different meanings to the uses of different bodily senses, including proprioception, and this affects the way each culture imagines and represents the world. What it means to be a person, and ideas about the kinds of persons that exist, are directly tied to the sense that a cultural group recognizes, attends to, and incorporates bodies into their ways of being in the world. The senses are ways of embodying social categories (Geurts, 2002). Sensory experience, which differs from physiological mechanisms, cannot, therefore, be defined universally, but is always deeply influenced by cultural variation.

Many cognitive scientists react negatively to anthropological claims about the cultural nature of bodily sensations. After all, people across cultures have similar biology, as well as highly similar bodily and social interactions that presumably reflect universal properties of embodiment. I agree with this sentiment, although I am quick to note that cognitive scientists still ignore how body experience is shaped by cultural practices that resist simple biological explanation. One way to embrace the role of cultural activity into a theory of embodied cognition is to recognize, and study, different levels of embodiment in thought, language, and action.

Levels of Embodiment

Cognitive scientists generally wish to uncover the neural and cognitive mechanisms that presumably subsume perception, thought, language, emotion, and consciousness. The essential link of bodies and persons does not imply that whole bodies are the only level at which to analyze and understand language and cognition. There are, in fact, three levels of embodiment: the neural level, the phenomenological conscious experience, and the cognitive unconscious (Lakoff & Johnson, 1999).

Neural embodiment concerns the structures that characterize concepts and cognitive operations at the neurophysiological level. Our concepts and experience are fundamentally embodied within the brain. Yet the neural level alone cannot explain the bodily basis of language and cognition. Brains do not simply receive input from the environment and provide output in the form of instructions to the body. Neural assemblies operate in relation to the entire body as it functions within concrete situations.

The cognitive unconscious consists of all the mental operations that structure and make possible conscious experience, including the understanding and use of language. The cognitive unconscious makes use of and guides the perceptual and motor aspects of our bodies, especially those that enter into basic-level and spatial-relation concepts. It includes all our unconscious knowledge and thought processes. The body is crucial at this level, because all of our cognitive mechanisms and structures are grounded in patterns of bodily experience and activity.

The phenomenological level is conscious, or accessible to consciousness. It consists of everything we can be aware of, especially our own mental states, our bodies, our environment, and our physical and social interactions. This is the level at which we feel experience, of the way things appear to us, and of qualia, that is, the distinctive qualities of experience such as the pain of a toothache, the taste of chocolate, the sound of a violin, or the redness of a ripe Bing cherry.

These three levels are not independent of one another. The details of the character of the cognitive unconscious and of conscious experience arise from the nature of neural structure. We would not have the spatial-relations concepts we have without topographic maps or orientation-sensitive cells. The neural level significantly determines, together with experience of the external world, what concepts can be and what language can be.

People are not just brains, or neural circuits. Neither are they mere bundles of qualitative experiences and patterns of bodily interactions. Nor are they just structures and operations of the cognitive unconscious. All three are present, and explanations at all three levels are necessary for an adequate account of the human mind. Not surprisingly, in my view, the three levels of embodiment together are constitutive of what it means for someone to be a human person with a particular identity and different cognitive abilities.

Conclusion

People's experiences of themselves as "persons" are clearly intimately related to their ordinary bodily experiences. Our senses of agency, ownership of our mental acts, unity, and continuity are tightly linked to the regularity of recurring body activities. None of this completely closes the mind-body gap, nor should what I describe here be seen as an attempt to reduce personhood to the body. Of course, the boundaries of the self and of personhood are not stable, but are shifting, permeable, and partly structured by social and environmental contingencies. But it is generally possible to conceive of personhood as an emergent property of interactions of the brain, body, and world. These dynamic couplings suggest that understanding the "self" and our sense of who we are as individual persons with controllable minds and bodies require special attention to these couplings, not just to brains, bodies, or world as separable entities. Appreciating that minds are related to whole persons, and that persons interact with each other and the environment, provides the key to unlocking the secrets of how perception, cognition, and language are thoroughly embodied. Let us continue now with this exploration of the embodied mind.

3

Perception and Action

Perception is the ability to derive meaning from sensory experience in order to guide adaptive behavior. Human perceptual experience is often thought to arise from the input of information from the world through the five senses to different regions of the brain. Most philosophers and psychologists argue that perception is an inferential process that occurs in a series of steps. We do not come into direct contact with the environment, but only some aspects of the environment impinge upon us. But traditional accounts of how we see, hear, smell, taste, and feel do not acknowledge the importance of the entire human body as it moves through the world and engages in intentional action. This neglect of the body in action has led to both simplified views of perceptual experience, and, ironically, overly complex mechanisms to account for how people perceive objects and events in the real world. My aim in this chapter is to explore the importance of embodied action in psychological accounts of human perceptual experience and action.

An Overview of Embodied Perception

An embodied view of perception assumes, as explained by biologist Humberto Maturana (1980: 5), that "Living systems are units of interactions; they exist in an environment. From a purely biological point of view, they cannot be understood independently of the part of the environment with which they interact, the niche; nor can the niche be defined independently of the living system that occupies it." Moreover, "when an observer claims that an organism exhibits perception, what he or she beholds is an organism that brings forth a world of actions through sensory motor correlations congruent with perturbation of the environment in which he or she sees it [the organism] to conserve its adaption" (Maturana, 1983: 60).

The idea of "bring[ing] forth a world of actions" emphasizes a person's bodily activity that abolishes a linear causal link between perception and action. As psychologist-philosopher John Dewey argued over 100 years ago in his famous critique of stimulus-response theories of behavior,

> We begin not with a sensory stimulus, but with a sensorimotor co-ordination, the optical-ocular.... In a certain sense, it is the movement which is primary, and the sensation which is secondary, this movement of body, head, and eye movements, determining the quality of what is experienced. In other words, the real beginning is with the act of seeing; it is looking, and not a sensation of light. (Dewey, 1896: 137–8)

All human activity involves embodied correlations. It is misleading to suggest that perception and action are discrete, independent processes that are causally related in a linear way. Consider one of Dewey's examples, where he argued that the quality of what is experienced depends on how we are already coordinated in some activity:

> If one is reading a book, if one is hunting, if one is watching in a dark place on a lovely night, if one is performing a chemical experiment; in each case, the noise has a very different psychical value; it is a different experience.... What provides the 'stimulus' is a whole act, a sensorimotor co-ordination, it is born from it as its matrix... the 'stimulus' arises out of this co-ordination; it is born from it as a matrix, it represents as it were an escape from it. Unless the sound activity had been present to some extent in the prior coordinates, it would be impossible for it now to come to prominence in consciousness.... We do not have first a sound and then activity of attention, unless sound is taken as mere neuron shock or physical event, not as conscious value. The conscious sensation of sound depends upon the motor response having already taken place. (Dewey, 1896: 140)

For Dewey, then, the meaning of any perceptual experience and the response arises together are part of the individual's "what I am doing now." This motto nicely captures the essence of embodied perception.

In more contemporary writings, Gibson (1966, 1979) argued that perceptual systems have evolved to facilitate our interaction with a real, three-dimensional world. Perception does not take place in the brain of the perceiver, but rather is an act of the whole animal, the act of perceptually guided exploration of the environment. The function of vision, for example, is to keep the perceiver in touch with the environment and to guide action, not to produce inner experiences and representations. At any given moment the environment affords a host of possibilities: I could grasp the object, sit on the chair, walk through the door. These are examples of affordances: relations of possibility between actor and animator (Gibson, 1966, 1979). Affordances enable animals to recognize what prey they may eat, what predators may possibly eat them, what trees may be climbed to escape danger, and so on. Imagine the color, texture, taste, and smell of a pineapple. These properties of the object are its affordances, which become variously salient given our particular interactions with pineapples. Our perception of affordances is relative to the perceiving object, so that, for example, in looking at a window one perceives not just an aperture, but an aperture that presents the possibility of one's looking through it (Bermudez, 1995). Perception and embodied action are, therefore, inseparable in the perception-action cycle (Neisser, 1976), in which exploration of the visual world, for example, is directed by anticipatory schemes for perceptual action.

Perception-action linkages are certainly constrained by the environment and can only be accurately described in terms of interactions of brain, body, and world. Most generally, meaningful perception arises as a result of structural couplings of the organism and its environment (Thompson, Palacios, & Varela, 2002; Varela, Thompson, & Rosch, 1991). Consider, as just one example, the case of color perception (Thompson et al., 2002). The traditional view suggests that the function of color vision is to recover from the retinal images reliable estimates of the invariant distal properties of specified surface reflectance (i.e., the percentage of light that a surface reflects at each wavelength). But an enactive approach suggests that different animals have different phenomenal color spaces and that color vision does not have the function of detecting any single type of environmental property. Color properties are enacted by the perceptuo-motor coupling of animals with their environments.

In fact, the "prespecified world" we find in, say, low-dimensional models of surface reflectances is actually the world as described in relation to the sensory-motor capacities of higher primates. It is reasonable to specify the world in advance when studying our own capacities or those of animals like us. But it is not legitimate to make this same move when studying animals different from us. For example, visual discrimination for birds is not a cyclopean image reconstructed, but a contextualized specification according to avian sensory-motor activity. This activity reveals what constitutes a relevant world for us, or any animal, not a reconstruction of the world as it appears visually to us.

The enactive view of color perception starts with two important facts (Thompson et al., 2002). First, many different animals (e.g., insects, fish, birds, and primates) living in diverse environment, all with extremely different neural apparatus, all possess color vision. Second, color vision nonetheless varies both in discriminality and sensitivity. These two observations suggest that there are important differences in phenomenal color spaces for different animals. Animals' different perceptual experience arises not only from their distinct neurophysiological make-up, but also from their evolutionary histories of environmental interactions. For example, bee color vision is shifted toward the ultraviolet, compared to other insect species, and bee color space includes novel hues. These facts can be explained by appealing to animal-environment coevolution. Bee color vision is sensitive to ultraviolet colors because it is advantageous for bees to detect flowers that have ultraviolet reflectances. Moreover, flowers have ultraviolet reflectances because it is advantageous from them to be seen by bees.

One of the colored objects that animals discriminate is other animals. Coloration affords an animal's visibility, both to cospecifics and to members of other species in its environment. It is not surprising that coloration is involved in camouflage and many kinds of visual recognition (e.g., species recognition, sexual recognition, and recognition of motivational states). Understanding the relation among color vision, animal coloration, visual recognition, and animal communication demands recognition of a broad range of physiological, ecological, and evolutionary considerations, ranging from the physiological functions of pigmentation, to coordinate inter- and intraspecies animal interactions, to the coevolution of various behavioral patterns. Most generally, there is a circular and reciprocal process of interaction in which the structure of the environment constrains the activity of the organism, and the activity of the organism shapes the environment (Odling-Smee, 1988). As Levins and Lewontin (1985) suggested, "the environment and the organism actively co-determine each other" (p. 89).

The Brain Alone Is Insufficient to Explain Embodied Perception

Understanding the embodied nature of perception requires looking beyond the brain, and into body-world interactions, when seeking causal explanations for perceptual experience. A traditional story told in most psychobiology textbooks is that the somatosensory region, including both subcortical and cortical neurons, specializes in processing somatic information. Primary sensory cortex has much in common with both primary auditory and primary visual cortex. First, tactile sense from the contralateral side of the body is represented in sensory cortex. Second, there is an orderly representation of one side of the body on the surface of the brain. This projection of the body onto the sensory cortex is called a "somatotopic map" and presents a picture called the "homunculus," or little man. The homunculus is sketched in Figure 3.1.

The empirical data used to construct the homunculus model were developed by Wilfred Penfield, a Canadian neurosurgeon, who was a pioneer in surgical removal of epileptic foci in the brain as a treatment for intractable epilepsy (Penfield & Roberts, 1958). He performed surgery on patients under local anesthesia so that the patient could communicate and move voluntarily Penfield would electrically stimulate the area thought responsible for the patient's epileptic seizures. When the areas of S1 were stimulated, patients often reported various tactile sensations in particular areas on the contralateral side of the body. This method allowed, Penfield to create a map of the projection of various parts of the body onto the brain.

The homunculus map looks completely different from an ordinary human body. The areas for the face, lips, and hands are massive when compared those for the feet, legs, and trunk. These larger areas of the human

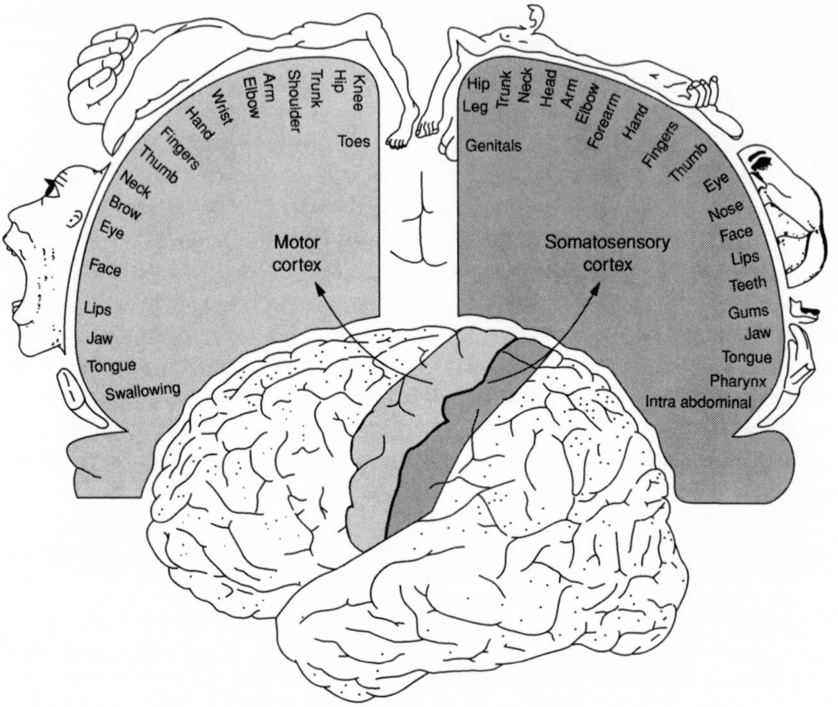

FIGURE 3.1. Human primary cortex. A view of the surface of the brain, showing the location of motor and sensory cortices.

primary sensory cortex corresponds to their increased tactile sensitivity in comparison to smaller areas of the cortex. For example, people can make much finer sensory discriminations with their fingertips and lips than when the stimuli are presented to their bellies or legs.

The discovery of somatosensory maps in the brain has led to the tendency in many disciplines to assume that matters of the body are best, and only, understood in terms of brain states and neural activity. Consider research showing that different areas of the monkey's brain (parietal cortex) become activated when specific areas on the monkey's hand have been touched (Merzenich et al., 1983). The internal tactile map discovered here is clearly analogous in that contiguous areas in the hand are represented as contiguous areas in the monkey's brain. These processes are presumably related because the nervous system physically connects the hand to the brain.

But, in fact, there is no single bundle of neurons that link every conceivable spot on the monkey's hand to a specific spot on the sensory map for the hand in the monkey's brain. This research has only shown that if you touch area X on the monkey's palm, area Y in the money's brain is activated. In this way, sensory maps only describe "what happens when" and not that "the hand is connected to the brain here" (Clancey, 1997). Showing the relation between parts of the body and parts of the brain does not tell us anything about "how processes involving nerve stimulation and neural activation are occurring within a single, connected physical system, the monkey's body" (Clancey, 1997: 83). Pictures of body parts and corresponding brain areas only portray a correlation of processes in one physically closed system (the monkey's nervous system) and should not be interpreted as showing that specific brain states alone contain sensory experience. The areas that are labeled P1, P2, and so on, encompassing neural patterns that categorize the activities of these areas, are not hardware that creates and sustain embodied activity, such as monkey hand sensations and movement.

In recent years, more detailed studies, using single-cell recordings, have shown that instead of one homunculus, there are four distinct somatotopic maps in primary sensory cortex (Nicolelis & Fanselow, 2002). These four maps differ in the kinds of stimuli that produce different responses (area 1, rapidly adapting skin receptors; area 2, deep pressure; area 3a, muscle stretch receptors; and area 3b, cutaneous stimulation of both transient and sustained sensations. Most importantly, this selectivity of different parts of the cortex is not fixed. Cells within any one map can respond to all the different kinds of stimulation so that the entire map can be dynamically reorganized, depending on injury and experience. "These changes strongly suggest that normal somatosensory cortex is subject to territorial competition, to a self-organizing force that can alter its topography" (Merzenich et al., 1983: 50).

None of this discussion, again, downplays the necessity of neural activity in the grounding of perceptual experience. Recent neuroimaging studies of a woman born without legs or forearms demonstrates that body parts can be represented in sensory and motor cortices even when these parts have not been physically present (Brugger, Regard, & Shiffrar, 2000). Human brains have clearly evolved to represent body parts. Yet we should, nonetheless, not assume a direct correspondence between a sensory/neural map and perceptual experience. Perception is not simply a matter of mapping stimulations with brain states (Clancey, 1997). Moreover, perception is not explained by somatosensory activities. Thus, if an irritant is injected into a nerve, this triggers a change in the activity of the nervous system. But most scholars would not call this change in activity a "perception" of the irritant. Perception can only be explained within the context of brain, body, and world interactions, and not by perturbations of neurons (Maturana, 1983).

A different reason to question whether perception is merely a mapping of sensory stimulation onto neural activity comes from recent neuroscientific research on odor perception. The neuroscientist Walter Freeman asked the following questions about perceptual experience: "Within a fraction of a second after the eyes, nose, ears, tongue, or skin is stimulated, one knows the object is familiar and whether it is desirable or dangerous. How does such recognition, which psychologists called preattentive perception, happen so accurately or quickly, even when the stimulus are complex and the context in which they arise varies?" (Freeman, 1991: 78). Freeman argues that these quick perceptions reflect self-organized processes involving the tendency of most collections of neurons throughout the cortex to shift quickly from one activity phase to another in response to even small inputs. This self-organized, chaotic activity is not solely, and simplistically, a brain or neural process, but reflects the more global dynamics of interactions of brain, body, and environment.

Freeman and associates applied this dynamical perspective to explain how trained rabbits recognize different smells (e.g., sawdust, banana) and behave in different ways (e.g., chewing or licking). Using an EEG, they recorded large-scale ionic currents of the olfactory bulb and the olfactory cortex in responses to different smells, both during and after training. The EEG recordings revealed bursts of activity when the rabbit was inhaling. The burst comprised synchronous waves of neural firings at each recording site. However, the amplitude modulation (AM) varied in a particular way across the olfactory bulb, and not just within a small set of neurons, for each type of smell. The contour map of amplitude was always the same for the same smell stimulus until the stimulus changed. When another smell was introduced, the contour maps of all the stimuli currently recognized changed to accommodate it, and the new pattern was stable until further smells were presented. For example, after the rabbit learned to recognize the banana smell, reexposure to sawdust led to the emergence of a new sawdust map. But each AM pattern is unique for each rabbit given its history, the shape of its body, the colors of its furs, and so on.

AM patterns correspond to affordances by which the rabbit "in-forms" itself about possible bodily interactions with an odorant, such as whether it is something that can be eaten or something that should be feared (i.e., a predator). But the patterns are not representations of odorants, or signals that specify the presence of food or danger, because it is impossible to match each AM with specific stimuli. The patterns are unique to the history of the animal, because of its past experiences, which shaped the synaptic connections in the bulb's neuropil. Freeman argued that the reentrant link between the bulb and the cortex constitutes a coupled system in that the activity of the bulb is modulated by the activity of the cortex.

Freeman and colleagues' computer model of the olfactory system, based on "ordinary differential equations, describes the dynamics of local pools of neurons." Experiments showed that the model described the EEG data, including both the bursts or neural activity and the properties of the contour maps of this activity. Freeman argued that the rapid bursts of neural activity along the rabbit's olfactory system in response to stimuli demonstrate that the olfactory system is a chaotic dynamical system. For example, the model predicted phase portraits of neural activity that most resembled strange attractors. Freeman speculated that perception in all sensory modalities involves repeated transitions between the strange attractors of the chaotic dynamical system of the brain, with each strange attractor representing a particular meaningful stimulus. "An act of perception is not the copying of an incoming stimulus. It is a step in a trajectory by which brains grow, recognize themselves, and reach into the environment to change to their own advantage" (1991: 85). Freeman's olfactory model does not explicitly show how odor recognition is tied to movement. But his empirical demonstration shows that odor recognition, like all sensory processing, depends on a structural coupling of perception and action as part of the brain, body, and world dynamical interaction. AM patterns reflect an early stage in intentional behavior, or affordances, by which an animal in-forms itself about whether to eat food or run from a predator given a specific odorant. But the AM patterns are not representations of odorants, because of the impossibility of matching these fluctuating, dynamic patterns with specific stimuli or with receptors that convey stimuli to the cortex. Instead, AM patterns are unique to an animal, arising out of past experiences, such as its movements (sniffing and licking), body shape, and color, which continuously shape and reshape how brains construct themselves.

My argument against the reduction of perception to neural activity does not at all imply that some areas of the brain may have evolved as part of specialized perceptual systems. I only claim, following Freeman and others, that perception is not solely located in brain activity, but must always be situated in terms of more complex dynamic couplings involving the whole body in action.

Moving the Body to Perceive

Perception cannot be understood without reference to action. People do not perceive the world statically, but by actively exploring the environment. For instance, if I move closer to the table in front of me, I see the textured lines in the wood surface better. If I turn my head, I distinctly hear the music playing softly on the stereo behind me. If I move over to the steaming cup of coffee on the counter, and lean over close by, I clearly smell the scent of coffee beans. Each bodily movement enables my sensory organs to do their work depending on my motivations and goals.

Movement is essential to perception. As my eyes move, the structure of the light around me (i.e., the optic array) changes and certain information previously unavailable (i.e., invariant information) now becomes present. The external structure is an ambient optic array that I manipulate when I move in it. When people merely touch an object, they understand little of what is perceived unless they move their hands and explore its contours and texture (Gibson, 1962; Steri, Spelke, & Rameix, 1993). By running their hands over "pictorially correct" raised surfaces, even the blind can understand many spatial representations of depth (Kennedy, Gabias, & Nicholls, 1991). Although our hands contain sensory transducers, the musculature with which we control movement allows us to explore objects in ways that make it easy to identify what is being felt. When we lift an object, this reveals something about its weight, rubbing our fingers across it tells us about its texture and overall shape, and squeezing it says something about its compressibility. To take a different example, without looking at a rod, people can determine its length by wielding it (Turvey, Solomon, & Burton, 1989). The body movement alone generates sufficient perceptual information to specify the rod's length.

Individuals possess strong associations between objects and the actions commonly carried out with them (Rosch et al., 1976), which reflects the fact that an object's function is intimately bound with the actions we direct to it. The affordances associated with objects are so strong that 3- and 4-year-old children may sometimes momentarily attempt to sit in toy chairs, get into toy cars, or slide down toy slides, despite the fact they are physically unable to do so given their size (DeLoache, Uttal, & Rosengren, 2004). Objects are viewed as part of the same basic-level category to the extent they can be used for some interactional purposes (see Chapter 4). These associations are not restricted to high-level actions, such as writing with a pen, but are also apparent at the microscopic level, such as in the hand shape required to grasp a pen (Klatzky, Loomis, Lederman, Wake, & Fujita, 1993). People apply various haptic tests to identify the different properties of objects. One study examined people's ability to identify common objects on the basis of touch alone (Klatzky, Lederman, & Metzger, 1985). Blindfolded participants handled 100 common objects, each easily identifiable by name, such as toothbrush, paper clip, onion, fork, and screwdriver. Approximately 96% of the identifications were correct, and 94% of these occurred within 5 seconds of handling the object. Touch depends quite obviously on awareness of the ways in which objects come into contact with one's body and affect one's body by giving rise to sensations. Indeed, a primary function of the cutaneous system is to employ stereotyped exploratory procedures (EPs), such as hand movements, to gain information about different kind of object properties (Lederman & Klatsky, 1990). An EP that applies pressure to an object, for instance, most appropriately conveys object hardness, whereas an EP employing lateral motion reveals aspects of object texture, and contour-following EP provides exact shape information.

Exploratory procedures are useful in identifying objects even when there is no body contact between person and objects (Gibson, 1968). For instance, we use sticks, rakes, screwdrivers, hammers, fishing rods, and tennis rackets to act upon other objects. We know that we are doing something to an object that has causal consequences even though we are not in direct bodily contact with the object in the way, for instance, that my fingers touch the coffee mug as I push it across the table. Empirical studies demonstrate that haptic exploration of objects using hand-held implements leads to reasonably accurate information about the objects (Bavac-Cikoja & Turvey, 1995; Lederman & Klatzky, 2003). These studies do not imply simply that action is important for perception, but that there is no perception without action.

Identifying People from Movement

People's moving bodies are a key clue to our identification of them as people, both generally and specifically. An elegant demonstration of this is found in research conducted by Johansson (1973). In one experiment, lights were placed at the major joints of a person dressed in black and photographed in the dark. Viewing the lights as stationary, observers reported seeing only random arrangements of dots. However, if the person to whom the lights were attached moved by walking, hopping, doing sit-ups, or any other familiar activity, observers immediately and unmistakenly saw a person engaged in that activity. If the lights stopped moving, they returned to what appeared to be a random assemblage. Observers can detect the sex, and even the identity, of a person walking to whom lights are attached (Cutting, Proffitt, & Kozlowski, 1978) and distinguish between an actor walking normally and walking with a limp (Johansson, 1975). Even facial expressions, which involve elastic transformation, can be perceived from the movement of a few point-lights (Bassili, 1978).

People are also better at identifying themselves from a point-light display of figures walking than they are at recognizing friends and colleagues (Beardsworth & Buckner, 1981). People appear to recognize something that they were already familiar with, namely, how their own gait would look. This effect cannot be attributed to perceptual learning alone, as people see the gaits of friends and colleagues more than they do their own gait. A strong possibility is that the production of movement can generate a corresponding quasi-perceptual representation.

In fact, perceptual judgments about human figures rely in part on the activation of one's own body representation. Behavioral evidence demonstrates that the recognition of handedness of a visually presented hand depends on a covert recruitment of sensorimotor processes that are constrained by the neural structures controlling the side of the hand to be recognized (Parsons & Fox, 1998). Different studies have examined people's ability to judge the weight of objects being lifted or carried by another person. People can extract weight information from videotapes (Valenti & Costall, 1997), point light displays (Runson & Frykolm, 1983), and static photographs (Valenti & Costall, 1997), and of objects being lifted or carried. One possible explanation for these results is that the perception of the muscular, postural, and movement cues involved in lifting and carrying recruits stored knowledge of how one's body responds to lifting and carrying. This recruited knowledge may then assist in perceptual judgments. Similarly, when apparent motion is induced by a stimulus pattern of two sequentially presented objects, the resulting motion follows the principle of the shortest path between two points. But when the two objects presented are human body shapes, the resulting motion does not always follow the principle of the shortest path (Heptulla-Chatterjee, Freyd, & Shiffrar, 1996; Shiffrar & Freyd, 1991). Instead, as if to automatically avoid impossible body movements, the motion takes longer paths and detours. Recent neuroimaging data, using PET, indicates motor system activity during perception of possible, but not impossible, human movement (Shiffrar & Pinto, 2002). Moreover, visual analysis of human movement differs from that of nonhuman movements, especially with slower rates of display, and when the visual signal is connected with an observer's internal representation of possible human movement.

Perceiving other people's activities often activates the brain's motor system (Stevens et al., 2000). Early studies showed shared mechanisms for action perception and action control in monkeys. "Mirror neurons" in monkey ventral premotor cortex are active both when a monkey observes a specific action, such as someone grasping a food item, and when the monkey performs the same kind of action (DiPelligrino et al., 1992; Gallese, 2000). Neurons in monkey premotor cortex discharge both when the animal performs a specific action and when it hears the corresponding action-related sound (Kohler, Keysers, Umilta, Fogassi, Gallese, & Rizzolatti, 2002).

Other studies show that there are shared motor representations for action, observation of another person's actions, and imitation and mental simulation of action (Decety & Grezes, 1999; Rossi et al., 2002). Even the presumed goal of an observed action is recognized by observers and activates related motor cortices (Gallese et al., 2002). A large meta-analysis revealed, for instance, that there are common activations sites in favor of a functional equivalence between execution (e.g., sequential finger movement vs. rest), simulation (e.g., motor simulations of grasping objects vs. observing objects), and observation (e.g., observing grasping vs. observing object). The most overlap in activation is observed in the supplemental motor area, the dorsal premotor cortex, the supramarginal gyrus, and the superior parietal lobe) (Grezes & Decety, 2001).

It is a mistake, however, to assume that perception of others in action is simply accomplished by the activation of shared motor representations in the brain. As noted in Chapter 2, people may understand the actions of others by engaging in a simulation of the same processes that can produce the other person's bodily actions. Beyond this possibility, there is clear evidence that our own physical actions, such as walking, running, coordinated finger action, and aspects of human speech, arise from the complex interactions of neural resources, bodily biomechanics, and external environmental structures. Perception of other people's bodily actions may also depend more on the dynamics of how certain movements are created from larger patterns of brain, body, and environmental interactions. For example, experiments in which participants perform a task using a hand-held pendulum show a frequency of oscillation that matches the resonant frequency of the whole wrist-pendulum system (Kugler & Turvey, 1987). The same effect occurs in swinging a golf club or tennis racket or in rocking a car to get it out of the snow (Hatsopoulos & Warren, 1996). In each case, proprioceptive information (from a musculoskeletal system with an intrinsic spring-like dynamics) couples neural systems to bodily and/or environmental resources in a way that creates a larger autonomous dynamical system. These findings do not support a traditional view of bodily action that assumes a central representation of the movement, which then generates the behavior.

Movement in Music Perception

Music perception is another domain in which perception is tightly associated with embodied movements, such as rhythmic gaits, breathing, and other locomotion phenomenon (Friberg & Sundberg, 1999; Friberg, Sundberg, & Fryden, 2000; Scruton, 1997). Shore and Repp (1995) highlight the important fact that musical motion is first and foremost audible human motion. They describe three levels of events awareness: the raw psychophysical perception of tone, the perception of abstract qualities of tone apart from their source, and the apprehension of environmental objects that give rise to sound events. This last level is the "ecological level" of perception where "the listener does not merely hear the sound of a galloping horse or bowing violin; rather, the listener hears a horse galloping and a violinist bowing" (Shore and Repp, 1995: 59). In this ecological framework, the source of perceived musical movement, especially self-motion, is critical to a listener's perceptual experiences, as is abundantly clear to listeners attending a live musical performance (Clarke, 2001). In this way, music perception involves an understanding of bodily motion – a kind of empathetic embodied cognition.

Behavioral studies demonstrate that musical structures have kinematic aspects that not only compel performers to modulate their tempo in specific ways, but also induces corresponding perceptual biases in musically trained listeners (Repp, 1998). Recent neurophysiological studies of music perception have emphasized the major role of body motion in music perception and production. Studies of brain-damaged patients with lesions located in various regions of the brain show that the rhythmic component of an auditory image cannot be activated without recruiting neural systems known to be involved in motor activity, especially the planning of motor sequences (Carroll-Phelan & Hampson, 1996). These neuropsychological data have allowed hypotheses about the induction of a sense of beat or pulse in terms of the so-called sensorimotor loop, which includes the posterior parietal lobe, premotor cortex, cerebrocerebellum, and basal ganglia, Under this perspective, a perceived rhythm is literally an imagined movement, even if the musculoskeletal system itself does not move (Todd, 1999). Thus, the act of listening to rhythmic music involves the same basic processes that generate bodily motion.

Perceiving Causality from Movement

All physical movement is caused by ensembles of forces in action. The visual perception of object motion is strongly influenced by this causality. Research on the visual perception of causality was initiated by the classic studies of Michotte (1963). Michotte examined whether and how people interpret the causality of object motion by asking subjects to describe simple films. Several of his studies focused on the interpretation of collisions. For example, Michotte proposed that people directly perceive "launching" when one moving object contacts a second stationary object that is set in motion after a brief delay. Participants invariably expect in these cases that the motion of X caused the subsequent motion of Y. More recent research indicates that observers can make fine discriminations between normal and physically impossible collisions (Kaiser & Profitt, 1987). Although Michotte argued that the perception of causality did not depend on experience, subsequent studies have suggested the opposite (Kaiser & Proffitt, 1984). For instance, practically all of the studies on perceiving causality assume that the visual system is the source of these perceptual judgments. But people's experiences of their own bodies in action, moving against objects, are surely a crucial factor as well. Michotte assumed that direct perception of causality could occur in a single event, such as in the collision of billiard balls, without the mediation of specific prior experience. In fact, Immanuel Kant (1787/1929) strongly argued that infants and young children could not learn causal relations without having some prior notion of causality. But embodied activity, including both the effect of whole bodies moving against one another and physical objects, and smaller events such as the effect of moving one's tongue and lips on one's mother's breast, may be fundamental to perceiving causality from movement (see Chapter 7).

Of course, we learn to reason causally through vision as well, such as when we see event 2 following event 1, and no event 2 is ever witnessed without event 1 first being seen. Yet vision is not the only sensory input into the acquisition of causation, as causality also fundamentally rests on haptic perception (White, 1999). Consider how I use my hands to push a mug across the surface of a table. Haptic perception teaches me about the proportions of the mug, such as its height, its hardness, its texture, and something of its size and shape. Understanding these specific properties of the mug is not critical, however, as my primary understanding of the event is my pushing the mug. My understanding of this fact arises from the interaction of the motor and sensory qualities of my pushing action. I may be mistaken about the height, weight, and volume of the mug, as well as even whether it is a mug, but I clearly recognize that I am the one pushing the object across the table. The correlation between my pushing and the information given by the haptic system enables me to state without doubt that I am pushing the mug. In this way, action upon objects haptically perceived meets all the conditions for causal realism (White, 1999). My judgment of a causal relation between my action and the mug moving is not just due to a spatio-temporal link between the action and the mug's eventual behavior. Yet I know that I am the cause of my mug's behavior, a fact that I understand directly from my perceptual/embodied experience.

Our ability to make causal inferences about the interaction of people with each other and objects does not depend on our understanding of an abstract rule or concept for causality. Instead, we draw causal inferences from our direct embodied experience with other people and objects, and perceive causality, even when mistaken, by applying our own embodied experience of how we act upon objects. We feel our hair move because the wind blows, we lose our balance because somebody forcefully knocks against us, and we feel our knees buckle slightly because a heavy object is placed upon our shoulders. In each case, we experience the mechanical action of other things acting upon us because of haptic perception, in the same way that we know that our movements are the cause of other objects moving when we act upon them.

Children acquire causal knowledge through their repeated direct perception of causal relations as they interact with objects and other people (see Chapter 7). Over time, this knowledge of causal relations can be used to interpret other events in which causal relations cannot be directly perceived through by our embodied experience. For instance, imagine that I see another person pushing a coffee mug across a table (White, 1999). My perception of the person's actions is different from what he or she perceives haptically, because I do not know his or her embodied experience in the way it is being perceived. Despite this incomplete information, I still infer a causal relation between the person's action and the movement of the mug based on my knowledge of causal relations in my own body movements when applied to other people and objects. I draw the causal inference about the event I witness because of my own understanding of embodied action and its effects in the world.

Perceiving Movement in Static Patterns

Even when viewing static visual objects or patterns, people tacitly recognize the presence of movement, at least some of which is tied to the human body in action. Studies reveal that people infer dynamic information about movement when perceiving static shapes, such as when reading handwriting and viewing pictures of the human body (Babcock & Freyd, 1988; Freyd & Pantzer, 1995; Freyd, Pantzer, & Cheng, 1988). For example, Kandel, Orliaguet, and Viviari (2000) showed participants the middle letter of a three-letter word as it was handwritten. The participants' task was to guess which of two letters would be the third letter. People were most accurate when the trajectories of the cursive handwriting were consistent with the movements used to write the words. Thus, people perceived handwriting displays based on the gestures that produced them, and not just the static features of which letters are most likely to follow one another. Other studies show that the velocity of a moving dot seems to be uniform if (and only if) it actually follows the law governing movement production (Viviani & Stucchi, 1992a,b; Viviani, Baud-Bovy & Redolfi, 1997). This suggests, once more, that production-related knowledge is implicitly involved in perceptual processing, as well as in perceiving causality.

Another instance of people inferring movement from static images is seen in the phenomenon of representational momentum (see Chapter 5). Our memory for the spatial location of an object is biased in the direction of the object's motion, even when the object is presented statically (Freyd, 1983). For example, when participants view a picture of a man jumping off a wall and are asked to remember the man's position, their memory for his position is systematically biased forward on the trajectory of his jump (Freyd & Finke, 1984). Thus, our memory for the location of a moving object, such as a person jumping, depends upon the spatio-temporal characteristics of the movement that caused the object to occupy that particular location (Freyd, 1987). Studies also show that seeing an object in motion facilitates people's recognition of new objects when these are oriented within the path of the first object's motion path (Kourtzi & Shiffrar, 1997). Moreover, parts of the same cortical areas involved in motion perception (e.g., medial temporal/medial superior temporal cortex) are activated during perception of photos representing implied motion, but not images that did not imply motion (Kourtzi & Kanwisher, 2000).

Our assumptions about the ways objects interact, and our bodily experiences of moving against objects, may also influence our perception of different object properties. For instance, the dent in a new car is something curved that calls attention to a force that may have acted on the object by virtue of its asymmetric shape. We do not see the dent in the car door as a static perceptual feature, but infer movement of the door's surface when it was contacted by some person or thing. Leyton (1992) outlined a grammar of the forces likely to have acted on an object to create different shapes. Perception of asymmetries and possible causal forces ties in nicely with the claim that perception involves not only what might be done to an object by acting upon it in a certain way, but what must have happened to an object to create the particular shape it has. Some of the ways people infer causal influences on static objects must be due to their own previous, and anticipated future, actions against objects and the effects that occur thereafter.

Are Perception and Action Separate Activities?

Psychologists traditionally assume that perception and action represent two different parts of the information processing system. Part of the evidence for the separation of perception and action comes from studies looking at dissociations of visual cognition and visually guided action (Stoerig & Cowey, 1997). For example, lesioned monkeys and human patients can perform visually guided actions without visual awareness (blindsight) (Humphrey, 1974; Weiskrantz, 1980). Blindsight is most easily observed in people who have patches of dead tissue in the primary visual cortex, creating a blind spot or scotoma. Although people with scotomas claim to have no visual awareness in their blind spot, they can report with almost 100% accuracy the direction an object moves across it, and can distinguish between horizontal and vertical lines. These participants typically suggest that they were just guessing, and are quite surprised when informed that their guesses were correct (Weiskrantz et al., 1974).

Blindsight effects have been noted in laboratory studies of people with normal vision (Heywood & Kentridge, 2000). Eye-movement studies show that people with normal brain functions do not perceive a gap in a target during saccades, but could still point to the new location of the same target (Bridgeman et al., 1979). Different studies examining perception of illusions indicate that the induced motion illusion (Bridgeman, Kirch, & Sperling, 1981) and Tichner's circles illusion (Aglioti, Goodale, & DeSouza, 1995) affect verbal reports, but not pointing responses. A similar dissociation is found with stationary stimuli, known as the Roelofs effect, in which participants are shown a target with a frame in complete darkness (Bridgeman, Peery, & Anand, 1997). Target and frame could be shifted asymmetrically to the left or right, and people often misperceive the target as going in the direction opposite the surroundings after it has been shifted. When there is no delay between stimulus exposure and the cue to either make a verbal response about the target's location or point to where the target has been, all ten participants evidenced the illusion in their verbal responses, but five did not do so when they gave pointing responses. In the 4- and 8-second delay conditions, however, this dissociation was not found, suggesting that the motor system has a very limited short-term memory. One possibility is that the two groups of participants (i.e., pointing vs. verbal report) did not necessarily follow different psychological laws, but switched from motor to cognitive modes at different delays after stimulus offset (Bridgeman, 2000).

Finally, other studies report a dissociation between perceptual and visuomotor processing for stimuli more distant than those studied in the laboratory (Proffitt, Creem, & Zosh, 2001). Participants judged the inclination or steepness of hills, both out of doors and in a simulated virtual environment. The angle judgment was obtained with three response measures – verbal estimates, adjustments of a representation of the hill's cross section, and haptic adjustments of a tilt board with an unseen hand. The first two measures yielded large overestimates of hill incline, whereas the latter judgments were close to veridical. These data suggest that there may be two pathways in the visual system, each of which accesses different internal maps of visual space.

Milner and Goodale (1995; following Ungerleider and Miskin, 1982) claimed that these assorted neuropsychological and experimental findings point to a functional distinction between major parts of the visual system, which have subsequently come to be dubbed the "what" and "where" systems. The ventral pathway, projecting from the primary visual cortex to the inferotemporal lobe, is referred to as the "what" system because of its concern with object recognition or pattern discrimination. The dorsal pathway, from the primary visual cortex to the posterior parietal cortex, in contrast, is referred to as the "where" system, because of its involvement in processing spatial placement of objects. These two systems are also described as the "cognitive" and "sensorimotor" visual systems (Paillard, 1987).

Many scholars, however, take issue with the supposed distinction between the "cognitive" and "sensorimotor" visual systems and present evidence in favor of an integrated view of perception and action. Under this view, perception and action may be two aspects of one and the same neural and psychological process (Möller, 1999). For example, participants in one study had objects placed in front of them which they had to pick up and place on a piece of paper (Creem & Proffitt, 2001). They did this alone, or while engaged in a semantic (pair-associated memory) or spatial imagery task. When participants were asked to pick up objects without a secondary task, they most often reached around to pick the objects up by their handles in a manner appropriate for use of the object. However, when the cognitive system was taxed by a concurrent semantic task, participants rarely picked up the objects appropriately. Yet there was little decrease in performance when the spatial imagery task was performed concurrently. A second study showed that when participants were presented with a purely visuospatial task (i.e., tracking a moving dot), the concurrent spatial imagery task interfered with grasping performance, but not the semantic task. In general, without the influence of the cognitive system, the visuomotor system cannot reach and grasp an object effectively. At least partial information from the semantic system is needed to grasp an object appropriately in a manner defined by its functional identity (e.g., grasping a spatula). These findings illustrate a necessary interaction between visual cognition and visually guided embodied action.

Other researchers have obtained significant effects of perceptual illusions on action, contrary to some earlier work (Franz, 2001). Thus, there is no difference in the size of the perceptual and grasp illusions if the perceptual and grasping tasks are appropriately matched (Franz et al., 2001). One possible resolution of the debate over whether perceptual illusions affect visually guided action is to be more precise about the locus of the illusions within the brain (Milner & Dyde, 2003). Unless the illusion really operates deep within the ventral stream (i.e., the "what" system), it is likely to influence activity in both the dorsal and ventral streams, thus not providing the best test of a perception and visuomotor dissociation.

Some other compelling evidence against a "what" and "where" distinction comes from studies with brain-damaged patients. For instance, patients with damage to the human homologue of the dorsal stream have difficulty reaching in the correct direction for objects placed in different positions in the visual field contralateral to their lesions. Patients with damage to this region of the cortex often show an inability to rotate their hands or open their fingers properly to grasp objects placed in front of them. But these patients can describe the orientation, size, shape, and relative spatial location of the very objects they are unable to grasp correctly (Goodale, et al., 1998). Patients with damage to the ventral stream show the opposite pattern of deficits (Goodale et al., 1998).

Goodale and Murphy (2000) suggest that one should not think about the dorsal stream as a system for spatial vision per se, but rather as a system for the visual control of skilled action. Both streams process information about the orientation, size, and shape of objects and about their spatial relations. Both streams are also subject to modulation by attention. But each stream deals with the incoming visual information in a different way. The ventral stream transforms visual information into perceptual representations that embody the enduring characteristics of objects and their spatial relations with each other. The visual transformations carried out in the dorsal stream, which utilize moment-to-moment information about the disposition of objects within egocentric frames of references, mediate the control of goal-directed acts.

Although visually controlled action involves neural pathways different from those underlying explicit perceptual judgments, leading to dissociations between perceptual and motor performance, perception and action may be similar to the extent that the tasks used to assess them depend on the same visual information (Smeets & Brenner, 1995; Vishton et al., 1999). For instance, information used in perceptual judgments of self-motion (i.e., retinal flow) is also used to control steering with a joystick (Li & Warren, 2002). Thus, perception and action are not different entities, but are two aspects of behavioral control (Kotchoubey, 2001). The dorsal system may be responsible for the fast modulation by optical information of action such as reaching and grasping (Green, 2001). The ventral system does not support perception, as distinct from action, but controls extended actions that unfold over longer time scales, thus drawing on optical information over larger spatial scales than simple, fast limb movements.

Perceptual scientists continue to debate the merits of the two-visual-systems hypothesis. But it seems clear that the original version suggesting a sharp separation of visual perception and visually guided action has been much weakened in recent years. One new proposal greatly diminishes the distinction between visual representation and the control of actions (Ellis & Tucker, 2000). According to this idea, the representation of a visual object includes not only description of its visual properties, but also encodings of actions relevant to that object. For instance, a mental representation of a wine glass is, at least in part, constituted by its making available reaching and grasping, and all the other things one has learned to do with a wine glass.

Research supporting this theory comes from studies on stimulus-response compatibility, where stimulus properties of objects quickly give rise to response codes (Simon, 1969, 1996). The Simon effect, for instance, involves responses that are made more quickly when the locations of stimulus and response correspond than when they do not, despite the fact that the location of the stimulus is not relevant to the task (Simon & Ruddell, 1967). For example, suppose that a left response is to be made to the letter H and a right response to the letter S. An H displayed to the left of fixation yields faster responses than the same stimulus displayed to the right of fixation. Many studies have explored S-R compatibility in regard to the impact of perception on action. Consider the following study (Brass et al., 2000). Participants were asked either to learn to respond differentially to nonspatial cues (e.g., a 1 or 2) or to respond by imitating one of two finger-movement stimulus cues. If the participants were presented with a 1, they were asked to respond with their index finger, and a 2 cued a response with the middle finger. In another condition, when participants saw a movie of an index finger, they were asked to move their index finger, and similarly for a movie of a middle finger. Seeing movies of actions to imitate as the stimulus sped up reaction times, as expected if perception and production of actions are linked. Moreover, being asked to respond to the movie of the index finger by moving one's own middle finger slowed down reaction times, an interference effect caused by stimulus-response incompatibility. A different experiment showed that the more a stimulus was similar to a required action, the faster people responded. These data illustrate the tight influence that perception has in forming motor movements.

Other studies show that even task-irrelevant spatial location information elicits a congruent spatial response code (Eimer, 1995). But location is not the only feature of a visual object that elicits action-related response properties, irrelevant of a goal. Action-related features, such as size, shape, and orientation, have similar effects. Tucker and Ellis (1998) presented pictures of objects to participants who judged whether they were shown in a normal or inverted vertical orientation. The participants responded accordingly by pressing a left or right key. The objects were also depicted in one of two horizontal orientations, differing in terms of which hand would be optimal to use in reaching and grasping the object in that orientation. For instance, a teapot could be presented with its handle to the viewer's left or right. Despite the irrelevance of horizontal orientation to the task, this variable influenced participants' key press responses. If the hand of response was the same as the optimal hand for reaching and grasping, implicit in the horizontal orientation, participants were faster and more accurate, compared to the incongruent case.

Further studies on the relevance of visual perception on motor programs investigated interference effects of distractors on a grasping movement (Castiello, 1996). In this study, distractors were task-relevant for a secondary, nonspatial task, but they interfered with the kinematics of the main grasping task. A different study examined whether a nonrelevant prime picture influenced the latency of a subsequent grasping movement (Craighero, Fadiga, Rizzolatti, & Umilta, 1999). There was a reduction in the grasping latency when the prime picture depicted the to-be-grasped object, but not when the prime depicted a different object. Thus, visual perception of an object affects the programming of a movement that immediately following the perception. These results have been interpreted as supporting the "premotor theory of attention" in which spatial attention is constrained by motor processes (e.g., saccadic eye movements, arm movements) (Rizzolatti, Riggio, & Sheliga, 1994).

Many studies, then, demonstrate that seeing an object affords actions associated with it. Smaller objects within arm's reach afford grasping, or more specifically, a particular kind of grasp. Features of an object such as its location, shape, and orientation will lead to activation of specific components of reaching and grasping actions. Particular directions of reach, particular hand shapes, and particular hands will be activated by the sight of an object within reach. These potentiated components of a grasping response are referred to as "micro-affordances" (Ellis & Tucker, 2000). Ellis and Tucker characterize these behavioral possibilities as dispositional properties of an observer's nervous system (also see Shepard, 1984). Under the "micro-affordance" view, grasping in general is not facilitated by an object (such as in Gibson's affordances), but a specific grasp appropriate to that object, in context, such as a particular shape of the hand, and a particular orientation of the wrist, and so on, is facilitated.

Another new theory has been proposed for understanding the links between perception and action or motor planning (Hommel et al., 2001). The "theory of event coding" (TEC) holds that cognitive representations of events (i.e., of any to-be-perceived-in-the-world incident in the distal environment) subserve not only representational functions (e.g., for perception, imagery, memory, and reasoning) but action-related functions as well (e.g., action planning and initiation). TEC claims that perceiving and action planning are functionally equivalent, because they are alternative ways of internally representing external events (or more precisely, interaction between the events and the perceiver/actor). Perceiving the world is a process of actually acquiring information about the perceiver-environment relationship, including movements of eyes, hands, feet, and body. The process of perceiving both presupposes and affords active behavior and performing an action both relies on and provides perceptual information. In this sense, perceptions, or stimulus codes, and actions, or response codes, both represent the results of, and the stimulus for, particular sensorimotor coordinations.

TEC argues that cross-talk between perception and action occurs at two levels – compensation and adaptation. Compensation refers to the fact that in order to interpret any change in the spatial distribution of signals at three receptive surfaces, animals must have a way to compensate for their own body movements. Thus, the system has to take into account the animal's body movements before it can use the sensory signal to recover the structure of the environmental layout (Bridgeman, 1983; Epstein, 1973; Shebilske, 1977). Adaptation refers to the flexibility of sensorimotor couplings and to the fact that perception can within certain limits be educated by action planning. For instance, studies of distorted vision have demonstrated that perception may teach action and action may teach perception at the same time (Redding & Wallace, 1997; Welch, 1978), again suggesting that commensurate or identical representations underlie both perception and action (Van der Heijden, Mussler, & Bridgeman, 1999; Wolff, 1999).

TEC's core concept is the "event code" that represents the distal features of an event. These distal features are not specific to a particular stimulus or response, but register sensory input for various sensory systems and modulate the activation of different motor systems. Thus, distal feature codes refer to not solely to single dimensions of color, size or shape, but to complex embodied possibilities, such as "sit-on-ableness." Even time and change might be represented by feature codes, so that events such as a "leftward motion" can be coded. Feature codes are not simply given but evolve and change though the perceiver's/actor's experience. For instance, a particular action may not always be coded as "left" or "right," but will be understood as, say, "left-of-body," "left-of-right index finger," and "left-handed."

Consider, for example, a person reaching for a bottle standing in front of him or her. One of the many possible ways to analyze this situation would be to conceive of the bottle as stimulus and of the reaching movement as a suitable response. A successful response clearly requires that several features of stimulus and action planning match. For instance, the internal distance of the hand should be identical to the perceived hand-bottle distance; the internal grasp should be identical to the bottle's perceived location. This matching task is easy because stimuli and to-be-performed responses share a large number of features. After all, action codes are already activated in the course of perceiving the stimulus.

Various evidence supports the predictions of the TEC. First, neurological findings on mirror-neurons suggest a population of neurons that fulfill both perceptual and action-planning functions (Rizzolati et al., 1990; see Chapters 5 and 6). These neurons may provide the neuroanatomical substrate of the common codes assumed for stimulus perception and action response.

Behavioral evidence consistent with TEC comes from various sources, including a dual task experiment in which participants briefly see a marked arrow while performing an already prepared, unspecific left or right keypress (Hommel, 1998). After the keypress, participants judged the direction of the arrow, which randomly pointed to the left or right side. Planning and performing a left- or right-hand keypress requires integrating a LEFT or RIGHT code, respectfully, into the corresponding action plan. If so, this interpreted code should be most available for processing and coding a LEFT or RIGHT arrow, so that people should be effectively blind to the arrow that points to the same side as a response. Consequently, left-pointing arrows appear during left-hand key presses in the way that right-pointing arrows appear during right-hand key presses. Thus, feature overlap between codes plan and stimulus should improve stroke processing. Indeed, this was what was found. In general, if the arrow pointed to the side of the response, it was about 10% less accurate than if the arrow direction and concurrent response did not match (Museeler & Hommmel, 1997).

A different set of studies examined action-perception transfer by having participants first make arm movements given verbal commands without visual feedback (Hecht, Vogt, & Prinz, 2001). The participants then made visual judgments of similar patterns. A separate group of participants performed the visual task first and then the motor one. The studies showed that there was transfer of both perception to action and action to perception. These findings are consistent with the claim that perception and action share a common representational code.

Other experimental paradigms offer data in support of TEC (Prinz, 1997). Induction paradigms, including spatial compatibility tasks and sensorimotor synchronization, show that certain visual stimuli induce particular actions by virtue of similarity. Interference paradigms showed mutual interference between the perception of ongoing events and the perception and control of ongoing action. Hecht et al. claim that these kinds of kinesthetic-visual transfer are most likely due to visuomotor-kinesthetic matching, which suggests that perception and action share common mechanisms, exactly what is predicted by TEC.

In general, there is emerging evidence that perception and action are deeply interrelated, and possibly share common neurological mechanisms. This work is clearly consistent with an embodied view of perception, as opposed to traditional accounts that sharply distinguish perception from embodied action.

Perception as Anticipated Embodied Interaction

One reason that many scholars argue against a strict divide between perception and action is that perceiving an object without touching it partly involves imagining how it may be physically manipulated (Newton, 1996; O'Regan, 1992). This perception-action coupling suggests that perceiving an object requires people to conjecture something that if pulled would bend, if thrown would knock something else aside, and if turned would reveal another side. I see an object and imagine how I might use it without doing so. For example, I understand the chair in the corner of the room as something I could potentially sit on or stand on or lift to ward off a snarling lion if I walked over to it. This idea can be extended to all objects and physical events in the world. Thus, I perceive the leaves covering my yard as something I could go rake up if I had the right tool to do so. In this way, perceiving something is not simply a visual experience, but involves nonvisual, sensory experiences such as smells, sounds, and movement of one's entire body, such as the feelings of readiness to take specific action upon the object. Under this view, perception is tightly linked to subjunctive thought processes (Ellis, 1995; Newton, 1996).

Consider how a person perceives an object by employing various elementary subjunctives (Newton, 1996). An object that reflects light uniformly will be seen as potentially hard and slick to the touch, whereas the warm and fuzzy blanket reflects light unevenly. To see that something is flat is to see it as giving rise to certain possibilities of sensorimotor contingency. To feel a surface as flat is precisely to perceive it as impeding or shaping one's possibilities of movement. Each case of perception involves someone imagining what it would feel like to touch an object, grasp it with the hands, turn it over, bite it, smell it, and so on. Developmental evidence shows that preschoolers can classify animate objects despite postural variation among them, primarily because the children could imagine ways that each object many be physically manipulated without altering its identity (Becker & Ward, 1991).

Object perception is not an event that happens to us; rather it is something that we do by looking at the object. Our looking at something is a goal-directed task that demands the coordination of head position and eye focus to bring the object into the visual field. To do this, the world is conceptualized in part as patterns of possible bodily interactions, or affordances (e.g., how we can move our hands and fingers, our legs and bodies, our eyes and ears, to deal with the world that presents itself). Under this perspective, eyes themselves do not see. But to see is to explore the environment by means of the exercise of one's visual apparatus (e.g., one's eyes). The activity of seeing thus depends on one's awareness (at least sometimes) of one's eye movements, also on head and body movements, and characteristic patterns of bodily sensations.

Are people aware of bodily possibilities when they see objects? A growing body of research has demonstrated that people readily perceive objects in terms of the possible bodily actions they afford. For instance, when observers are asked to view stairs of different heights and judge the one they could ascend in a normal fashion, they were consistent and accurate with respect to their actual stair-climbing abilities (i.e., judged climbing heights were a constant proportion of leg length) (Warren, 1984). Similar findings have been reported for people's judgments of sitting height (Marks et al., 1990), abilities to stand on or traverse different surfaces (Burton, 1992; Fitzpatrick et al., 1994), judgments of the capabilities of different people (Stoffregen et al., 1997), grasping of real objects (van Leeuwen, Smitsman, & van Leeuwen, 1994), catching fly balls (Oudejams, Michaels, Bakker, & Dohne, 1996), the use of tools (Wagman & Carello, 2001), climbing walls (Boschker, Bakker, & Michaels, 2002), and the design of virtual reality environments (Smets et al., 1995). The results of these studies are consistent with the idea that anticipated bodily interactions are a significant part of perceptual experience.

Sensorimotor Contingency Theory

Sensorimotor contingency theory is a new development that strongly embraces the importance of real and anticipated bodily movement in perceptual experience (Noe & O'Reagan, 2002; O'Regan & Noe, 2001; also see Churchland, Ramachandran, & Sejnowski, 1994 for a compatible perspective). The basic premise of this theory is similar to that of "interactive vision" idea in asserting that "visual experience is not something that happens in individuals. It is something they do" (Noe & O'Reagan, 2002: 567). Sensorimotor contingencies are a set of rules of interdependence between stimulation and movement. Perceivers learn to master the ways that visual information, for example, changes as a function of movement with respect to the environment. Visual experience is, therefore, a temporarily external pattern of skillful activity.

Consider the experience of driving a Porsche (Noe & O'Reagan, 2002). There is really no single feeling associated with driving a Porsche in the sense that there is no special bodily sensation that arises whenever someone is driving the car. Instead, the experience of Porsche driving is constituted by what a person does when he or she drives a Porsche, such as turning the wheel, shifting gears at different speeds, feeling the vehicle accelerate when the gas pedal is pressed, and even feeling the sensation of the wind blowing through one's hair if driving a convertible. A person's experience of driving a Porsche has no single defining sensation, but is grounded in knowledge of the sensorimotor contingencies governing the behavior of the car.

Seeing, in the sense of having a visual experience, is like Porsche driving. Thus, the experience of seeing is like that of driving in being constituted by all the things one does when one sees. Seeing a chair, again, involves that set of things that one can do with a chair, such as sitting on it, holding it up to fend off a snarling tiger, or even moving one's eyes around it to better appreciate the chair's red velvet covering. Each of these things can be done when you visually interact with the chair. Of course, there are sensations that arise from seeing a chair, such as feeling relieved; these alone do not define the fundamental elements of visual experience. They are just accidental add-ons to the activity of seeing an object in some specific situation.

One implication of sensorimotor contingency theory is that people should not generally be aware of all aspects of the environment before them. People will experience only those aspects of the world to which they are attending. In fact, as suggested above, there is good experimental evidence that people often fail to notice changes in the environment that are quite large and in full view. These "change-blindness" effects occur in circumstances as simple as making saccades to more complex events such as changing the person to whom one is talking (Levin & Simons, 1997; O'Regan, Resnick, & Clark, 1997; Resnick, O'Regan, & Clark, 1997; Simons & Chabris, 1999). For example, in one remarkable study, a person walking across a university campus was stopped by a person (the experimenter) holding a map who asked for directions to a specific location (Simons & Levin, 1997). During this conversation, two workmen carrying a door lengthwise walked between the subject and the person asking for directions. While the subject's vision was blocked by the door, one of the workmen carrying the door quickly switched places with the person originally asking for directions. Thus, in just a few seconds, the subject was now talking to a different person wearing different clothes. Only 50% of the subjects noticed any change had occurred when they were asked moments later.

A related phenomenon, called "inattentional blindness," occurs when participants are engaged in attention-intensive tasks and fail to notice when extraneous stimuli are presented (Mack & Rock, 1998). For example, people were asked to judge which of the horizontal and vertical lines of a briefly displayed cross was larger. In one condition, an extra, unexpected element was presented. Participants were asked whether they saw anything else besides the cross and were then given a recognition test to assess their perception of the extra element. Many participants failed to notice the extra element when they were just told to make judgments about the crossed lines. But when people were told to focus on anything else in the display, they rarely missed seeing the extra element. Thus, people's expectations about what they were seeing greatly influenced what they actually perceived.

None of these findings are consistent with any theory that supposes that people construct full-blown 3-dimensional representations of real-world environments. But the results are quite consistent with the idea that perception is a skill-based activity that fundamentally depends on eye, head, and body movements. To bring something into visual consciousness, one must do something (e.g., squint, lean forward, tilt toward the light, walk to a window) and not merely passively see. We experience only the things we specifically attend to, depending on our current needs and goals. The rest of the world is simply not present because of the lack of focused attention. Unattended portions of the world seem to be there only because we can direct our bodily attention to them in various ways when needed. Once we have done so, the richly detailed information becomes part of our conscious perception, as if the world had been there all along. Perception scientists debate whether change blindness and inattentional blindness are better explained as inattentional amnesia (Wolff, 1999), or active suppression (Tipper, 1985). Nonetheless, people rarely see everything out there in the world unless they move their bodies in different ways to attend to environmental information.

One provocative consequence of sensorimotor contingency theory is that there may be no need for "binding" in the visual system. Many perceptual scientists believe that the various visual subsystems for visual stimuli, must somehow be unified to explain coherent perceptual experience. For example, there may be particular cells (i.e., "grandmother" cells), or highly localized cortical regions (e.g., convergence zones) that combine information pertaining to specific percepts. Moreover, separate cortical areas that are concurrently activated during perceptual analysis may oscillate in synchrony, with the synchrony providing the coherence, or unity, to perceptual experience (Brecht, Singer, & Engel, 1998). Yet the fact that object features seem to be part of a single object does not demand that all these features must be "represented" in a unified way, whether it be in a single brain region, or in terms of various brain processes. Noe and O'Reagan argue that "what explains the conceptual unity of experience is the fact that experience is a thing one does, and one is doing with respect to conceptually unified external object" (Noe & O'Reagan, 2002: 585). Under this view, the classic problem of binding in perception may be dismissed as a pseudoproblem.

O'Reagan and Noe (2001) further argue that the senses cannot be individuated by their distinct qualitative characteristics (i.e., only eyes see, ears hear, and so on), but by different patterns of sensorimotor contingency by which they are governed. After all, it is possible to "see" the world through sensory systems other than vision. Consider one tactile vision substitution system (TVSS) (Bach-y-Rita, 1996; Kaczmarek & Bach-y-Rita, 1995). In TVSS, optical images picked up by a camera (worn on the head) are transduced in such a way as to activate an array of stimulators (vibrators or electrodes) in contact with the skin (e.g., the abdomen, the back thigh, or most recently, the tongue). Optical images in this way produce localized patterns of tactile sensation. After an initial period of training, both congenitally blind subjects and blindfolded normal participants were able to perceive some simple displays. These participants even reported that after some training, they ceased to experience tactile sensations when they used the TVSS device, and experienced objects as arrayed before them in three-dimensional space, just as captured by the camera. When the camera presented a rapidly approaching object, for instance, the rapid expansion of the TV object corresponded to expanding activity on the tactile grid, causing the person to immediately duck. Participants "learn to make perceptual judgments using visual means of analysis such as perspective parallax, looming, and zooming and depth judgments" (Bach-y-Rita, 1996: 91).

This kind of tactile perception enables participants to judge the shape, size, and number of objects and to perceive spatial relationships between them. With sufficient practice, participants are able to engage in tasks requiring skillful sensorimotor coordination (e.g., batting a ball or working on an assembly line). Participants must, however, be able to move the camera on their own. Enabling people to explore figures by sweeping the camera over a display results in vibration changes that are necessary for meaningful tactile images to be perceived. Of course, tactile vision is not nearly as effective as real vision. But the work on TVSS provides another example of the power of sensorimotor contingencies in perceptual processes.

A final source of evidence supporting the idea of sensorimotor contingencies in perception comes from a case study of a blind patient whose sight was attempted to be restored by surgical removal of cataracts (Gregory & Wallace, 1963). In fact, this surgery does not restore sight. One patient's experience was described in the following way: "He heard a voice coming from in front of him and to one side: he turned to the source of the sound and saw a "blur." He realized that this might be a face, Upon careful questioning, he seemed to think that he would not have known that this was a face if he had not previously heard the voice and known that voices come from faces" (Gregory & Wallace, 1963: 122). The patient acquired some form of visual sensation, or impression, but had not yet acquired the ability to see, presumably because newly acquired visual impressions were not yet integrated with patterns of sensorimotor contingency governing the occurrence of these sensations (Noe, 2004). Although surgery restores the mechanisms enabling visual sensations, it cannot restore the linkages between impressions and bodily movement required for correct vision. It should not be surprising, then, that blindness can result by simply severing visual areas connected to the motor areas (Nakamura & Mishkin, 1980). Even when the sensory apparatus and associated cortical regions for vision are intact, there is no vision without activation in the motor cortex. Case studies such as this support the general claim that perception of objects and space is based on a person's anticipation of the sensory consequences of actions that could be performed in a given situation.

Robotics

Traditional artificial intelligence (AI) models assume that intelligence is largely understood in terms of manipulating carefully constructed internal models of external reality. This has led to a quest for intelligent machines based on building models of the world from sensory data and the development of algorithms to "reason" about the world using these models. Most of the AI work tries to capture important aspects of high-level cognition, such as reasoning and language understanding. But people in a related branch of AI called "artificial life" (AL) have lowered their aim to develop machines that could exhibit insect-like intelligence. These scholars argue that the major part of natural intelligence is closely bound up with the generation of adaptive behavior in the harsh, unforgiving environment most animals inhabit.

Many of the new robots being constructed within AL are based on two fundamental principles: situatedness and embodiment (Brooks, 2002). "A situated creature or robot is one that is embedded in the world, and which does not deal with abstract descriptions, but through its sensors with the here and now of the world, which directly influence the behavior of the creature. An embodied creature or robot is one that has a physical body and experiences the world, at least in part, directly through the influence of the world on that body. A more specialized type of embodiment occurs when the full extent of the creature is contained with that body" (Brooks, 2002: 52–3).

Take, for example, a robot that moves around in the world by avoiding obstacles, finding doorways, and identifying objects, such as soda cans, that it can pick up. Traditional robots developed for this purpose see the world in order to get a full 3-dimensional model, and only then construct an internal plan for moving through the environment. Once this full-blown plan has been created, instructions are sent to the body as to what movements the robot should do. Thus, a high-level planner calls lower-level motor modules, when required, to act in particular ways.

On the other hand, more recent AL robots start by moving first, and use their own activity as a guide to understanding the environment. Brooks (1991) coined the slogan "the world is its own best model" to capture the essence of this idea. The overall behavior of the system is a result of various autonomous activities overriding each other, and not of the system as a whole making a global decision based on centrally held internal representations of the world. Each layer of the system is sensitive to specific parts of the environment. Although observers may interpret the robot's overall behavior as meaningful, there is no "meaning" programmed within the system, apart from the specific behaviors of its various parts in response to local environmental conditions (e.g., activity patterns that are bootstrapped by tight stimulus-response feedback loops, evolved to meet particular environmental constraints).

For instance, an early robot, "Genghis," was a big six-legged insect whose behavior was not organized in a single program, but in terms of fifty-one tiny parallel programs (Brooks, 2002). Three of these programs allowed Genghis to scramble around over rough terrains, mostly keeping its balance, and respond to obstacles in its way. The six pyroelectric sensors arrayed at the front of the robot allowed it to sense the presence of heat-emitting mammals. Whenever Genghis encountered a heat-emitting smell, it would chase the source of the smell over whatever terrain was in front of it. Of course, Genghis never knew the actual content of the heat-emitting smell, it just followed it. Genghis never planned ahead its trajectory or its every move. Its behavior is an emergent activity plan with a structure that lies at a level above that of its individual reflexes.

A later robot, known as "Herbert," moved around a laboratory environment and collected soda cans, not by detailed advance planning, but by very successfully using a collection of coarse sensors and simple, relatively independent, behavioral routines (Connell, 1989). Basic obstacle avoidance was controlled by a ring of ultrasonic sound sensors that brought the robot to a halt if an object was in front of it. General locomotion (randomly directed) was interrupted if Herbert's simple visual system detected a roughly table-like outline. At this point, a new routine kicked in and the table surface was swept using a laser. If the outline of a can was detected, the whole robot rotated until the can was centered in its field of vision. This physical action simplified the pick-up procedure by creating a standard action-frame in which the robot arm, equipped with simple touch sensors, gently skimmed the table surface ahead. Once a can was encountered, it could be grasped and collected and the robot then moved on.

Notice, again, that Herbert succeeds without using any conventional planning techniques and without creating and updating any detailed inner model of the environment. Herbert's world is composed of undifferentiated obstacles and rough table-like and can-like outlines. Within this world the robot also exploits its own bodily actions (rotating the torso to center the can in its field of view) to greatly simplify the computational problems involved in eventually reaching for the can. Herbert is thus a simple example of both a system that succeeds using minimal representational resources and one in which gross motor activity helps streamline the perceptual routines.

A different artificial life system, called "Creature," decomposed a situated system into a number of simple task-achieving behaviors, each of which links specific sensory and motor capacities so that it may interact independently and reactively with properties of the surrounding environment (Brooks, 1991). The robot's task-achieving behavior is not handled by explicit goal-directed planning, but by layered control that is achieved by building the lowest level task-achieving behavior, debugging its operation, then building another on this foundation, and so on. For example, the robot's real-world exploration can be built by starting with Level 0: "do not come into contact with other objects." Adding Level 1, "wander aimlessly," will produce moving around without hitting anything. With the addition of Level 2, "visit interesting places" (e.g., corridors of free space detected by sensors), the robot's behavior comes to look like exploration, without any goal or plan directed at that function. Preadaptive sensorimotor pairings between vision and reaching, or between manual contact and retrieval to the mouth, interact independently with the robot's experience of the environment to generate an illusion of hierarchically controlled sequencing and goal-directedness.

Another example of insect robotics is a society of robots designed to collect ore samples (Steele, 1994). These robots cooperate by dropping electronic bread samples along their travels, according to what they are sensing and doing. By dropping markers that meaningfully change the later behavior of the system, the robots use objects in the world to represent their interactive experience (see Chapter 5). The central idea is that descriptions of the patterns that the robots followed were not built in. Although the robots were designed to create a path, in order to pick up ore samples, the motion of the path was not represented as a plan inside the robot. The robots exhibited self-organized behavior simply by acting as individuals, reacting locally and following a hierarchy of rules for picking up ore samples. Steel's self-organization design was based on the idea that emergent structures will grow from the interaction of many elements and then decay again until an equilibrium state is reached. As he summarized, "We will design a system of interacting robots where equilibrium behavior consists in exploring the terrain around the vehicles. The presense of the rock samples constitutes a disturbance. The desired dissipative structure consists of spatial structure (i.e., a path) formed by the robots between the samples and the vehicle. This structure should spontaneously emerge when rock samples are present, it should enforce itself to maximimize performance and should disappear when all samples have been collected" (Steels, 1990: 182).

Both Brooks and Steele's robots are examples of structured coupling between the robot and aspects of the environment. For example, wall following, as in "Herbert," is continuously enhanced by ongoing obstacle avoidance and forward movement, and ongoing wall hugging enables doorway entry. Most generally, coordinated movement is accomplished efficiently and directly by layered automata where states relate what the program has just done and what it is sensing now. The recent work on robotics provides a kind of existence proof demonstrating the intricate links between perception and action in producing meaningful behavior. These robots show, similarly to the experimental work with human participants, that perception does not precede action, because action is integral to perceptual performance. At the same time, AL robots illustrate that it is not always possible to define meaningful action apart from how an organism interacts with the environment. For instance, Ghengis engages in a type of behavior that appears to be "chasing prey," but this phrase is only a convenient description of an emergent behavior, and not some internalized "mental" rule that the robot follows. "Chasing prey" emerges from actual embodied performance. High-level actions cannot, therefore, be reduced to simple sequences of movement, but may emerge from the interaction between the robot's various simple activities, or reflexes, and the particular environment to which it is adapted (e.g., Brook's subsumption architecture).

A very recent demonstration of an embodied agent more explicitly embraces ideas from dynamical systems theory (Beer, 2003). This agent is capable of visually discriminating between objects by catching circular objects and avoiding diamond-shaped ones. The agent's behavior was controlled through a dynamical "nervous system" that "evolved" for these purposes. A series of experiments showed that the agent foveated on and then scanned any object before either catching it or avoiding it, and made this discrimination primarily on the basis of the object's width. Quite importantly, the agent does not really know the differences between the different types of objects, because its ability to engage in categorical perception is not located within a single subsystem. Instead, the agent's adaptive behavior is a property of the entire coupled system (i.e., interactions of brain, body, and environment) that it was specifically selected for. Even if it may be possible to decompose the coupled brain, body, and environment systems to better understand how each participates in the overall behavior, it makes little sense to attribute simple cause and effect to these parts. As with any dynamical system, effects unfold in time to become causes, so that discrimination behavior really takes place on an extended transient of the entire coupled system (Beer, 2003: 236).

The lesson here for cognitive science is that description of what a person (or animal or mechanical object) does should not be reified as a naive intentional description, or assumed to be causally grounded in internal mental representations. Enactive systems, such as the AL robots, show how knowledge is embedded in a distributed fashion (body, sensors, actuators, nervous/control systems, etc.), or even partly in the environment. One may argue, nonetheless, that these robots are merely reactive, living in the "here and now of the world," and are truly not autonomous. Autonomous agents are situated and capable of learning from their experiences (and from evolutionary history) in ways that can be applied to solving new real-world problems.

Some cognitive scientists voice concern over whether it will be possible to scale up these reactive systems to model more complex cognitive behaviors (Clark, 1996; Ziemke, 1999). Some self-organized systems have tried to ground an agent's functions by connecting sensors and actuators to some central mechanism (e.g., a connectionist network or a classifier system). These systems allow the agent to adapt the central mechanisms on the basis of the robot's interaction with the environment. In this way, a self-organized autonomous agent may be grounded in experience (Beer, 1997, 2003). Of course, the robot's designers have a fundamental role in choosing a particular architecture (e.g., number of units, layers of a connectionist network), which makes these "autonomous" robots not so autonomous.

A different criticism of some AL robots is posed in terms of the "robot grounding" or "body grounding problem" (Sharkey & Ziemke, 1998). Despite embracing both embodiment and situatedness in designing enactive robots, most systems fail to capture the way bodily mechanisms are truly embedded in their environments. Biological self-organized agents are not designed and then inserted into some environment, because living organisms embody a long history of mutual specification and structural coupling throughout evolution and an organism's individual lifetime. Real bodies are rooted in the environment, and are not simply interfaces between internal controller and environment. Human bodies, to take one example, are tailored to perceive and act in a meaningful way because of the environments they inhabit. Thus, the embodied nature of current AL robots partly neglects the historical reality and environmental embodying of living bodies in which body, nervous system, and environment coevolve and are mutually determined (Ziemke, 1999). Perception and action are more tightly integrated in biological organisms than is necessarily the case with most AL robots (see Nolfi & Floreano, 2000 for further discussion of this issue).

A Dynamic Model of Intentional Action

Just as perception is traditionally thought to precede action, so too is action thought to originate in prior mental intentions. For instance, if your friend looked at you and purposefully yawned, you presume that she had some idea in mind that caused her to do as she did. But how can a thought or mental state provide the causal foundation for human action? Although we feel that a conscious choice underlies purposeful yawning, there must be some physical explanation for the yawn. As Aristotle famously argued, nothing can cause or move itself. Every physical event must result from some previous physical event (e.g., as efficient causes such as the movement that occurs when billiard balls strike one another), not from a mere conscious or mental act. But our ordinary experience, again, suggests that an intention to move our bodies results in our bodies actually moving in the ways they do. Contemporary philosophers, working on the topic of action theory, continue to struggle over how the mind both causes behavior and continuously monitors and directs its effects. Recent experimental results show that people mistakenly believe that their conscious will directs the timing of their motor actions when, in fact, the brain's action-readiness potential seem to cause one's conscious intention (Libet, 1985). Findings such as these are difficult to reconcile with traditional notions of intentional action.

Juarrero (1999) criticizes philosophers for failing to provide coherent answers to the question of what causes intentional behavior. She advances the idea that intentional behavior, and its causes, is best characterized as a fluid, dynamic process taking shape through the interactions between brains, bodies, and their environments. Juarrero adopts the perspective of complex dynamic systems theory as a "theory-constitutive metaphor" for reconceptualizing mental causation, particularly in terms of how philosophers think of the causes for intentional action. Juarrero's philosophical analysis has obvious, profound implications for cognitive science explanation of causation and human action.

One important implication of dynamical systems theory is that the intentions one feels to purposefully yawn, or raise one's hand to wave hello to a friend, result from a person's self-organizing tendency. This self-organizing structure embodies a tendency for someone to want to purposefully yawn even before the desire to perform the action reaches awareness. A concrete illustration of this point is seen in the developmental work of Thelen and Smith (1994). Thelen and Smith argued that motor development in infants is not a maturational processes determined by some hard-wired genetic code. Instead, motor development is a process of dynamical self-organization that arises from the infant's continuous interaction with its changing environment.

For example, two infants started out with different inherent dynamics for reaching. One infant, Gabriel, flailed wildly and repeatedly as she reached for an object, yet another infant, Hannah, was far less physically active and carefully assessed the situation before reaching. Both infants learned to successfully reach objects within a few weeks of one another. Yet this fact does not imply that there must be a preprogrammed pattern for intentional action that simply unfolds over time, as suggested by

Piaget (1975). Instead, each child generated different solutions for successful reaching. Thus, as a self-organizing system, the interaction of an infant's initial spontaneous dynamics and the environment facilitates each child's movement from equilibrium to a transformation that establishes second-order context-dependent constraints. These second-order constraints reshape, in different ways for each child, the springlike attractors for limb movements, allowing each child to successfully learn to reach for an object.

A dynamical account of intentional actions, such as your friend's yawn, starts with the idea that self-organized dynamical structures are globally stable even when there is disorder at lower levels. Yet a complex adaptive system, such as your friend, can be driven from equilibrium toward instability because of the interaction of external circumstances and the system's own internal dynamic processes. For example, feeling bored at a lecture can precipitate instability, not only at the neurological level, but at the cognitive and emotional levels as well. By forming an intention, say to yawn while looking over at another person, a cognitive phase change takes place that dissipates the disequilibrium. Beyond restoring dynamic equilibrium, the new intention's restructured contextual constraints reorganize the semantic space into a more differentiated and complex set of options. In this way, by formulating a prior intention, people avoid the need to consider and evaluate every logical and physical possibility for action. Thus, once your friend forms the intention to let you know of her belief about the lecture, that cognitive reorganization circumscribes your friend's yawning at you, rather than writing you a note, shaking her head, whispering to you, and so forth.

Conceptualizing action from a dynamical system perspective explains why people need not explicitly decide something each time they act. The person's current frame of mind automatically selects a subset from the unlimited other alternatives within her self-organized constraint-space. For instance, when your friend decides to inform you of her belief about the lecture, she does not need to explicitly formulate a decision or proximate intention about what to do. Her "choice" of yawning rather than doing something else (e.g., writing a note, talking aloud to you) can be "decided" by the interaction between her own dynamics and the environment as the process "moves downstream" (to use the dynamical language of moving through "landscapes"). For instance, your friend knows that her being in a lecture prevents her from saying something aloud, or perhaps even whispering. None of this, however, requires that she form an explicit intention requiring explicit deliberation. She can just decide to communicate her belief about the lecture and the environmental constraints take care of the fine-grained details of how this intention is manifested in real-world behavior.

A different phenomenological demonstration of how intentional action can be explained in dynamical terms is seen in David Sudnow's (1978) remarkable account of his own experiences leaning to play jazz improvisation on the piano. Sudnow began to master jazz improvisation by copying the sounds of jazz performers. But this proved to be extremely difficult because Sudnow was unable to precisely identify the notes and temporal values in these master performances. Even when Sudnow came close to making an exact description of a master's sounds, something still did not sound right. The difficulty was that the sounds did not provide the right information to guide his actions in moving his hands appropriately across the keyboard. A breakthrough occurred when an accomplished pianist urged Sudnow to produce a small number of simple scales and chord sequences that were characteristic of the jazz sound he wished to exhibit while playing.

Sudnow began to do this, patterning himself after the work of Jimmy Rowles. For instance, "There were these three diminished scales to begin with, each identified by reference to a theoretic system that related its use to four of the twelve dominant chords, so on my thinking there was a 'cognitive map,' each scale named by a starting place, each related to its class of chords" (Sudnow, 1978: 21). By repeatedly performing these scales, Sudnow came upon a remarkable result. "I recall playing one day, and finally as I set out into a next course of notes, after a lift-off had occurred, that I was expressively aiming for the sounds of these particular notes, that the sounds seemed to creep up into my fingers, that the depression of the keys realized a sound being prepared for on the way down" (Sudnow, 1978: 37). In other words, by engaging in a structured activity, reliable correlations emerged between the motor activities involved and the perceptual input deriving from interactions with a specific environment.

Sudnow correctly noted that the "knowledge" that emerged from his interactions with the piano was not explicit, context-free, musical knowledge. "As I found the next sounds coming up, as I set out into the course of notes, it was not as if I had learned about the keyboard so that looking down I could tell what a regarded note would sound like. I do not have that skill, nor do many musicians. I could tell because it was the next sound, because my hand was so engaged with the keyboard that it was given a setting of sounding places in its own configuration and potentialities" (Sudnow, 1978: 45). Thus, the situated, embodied activity of performing scales and chord sequences enabled Sudnow to become familiar with the attendant sounds and physical sensations and the correlations between them. Furthermore, Sudnow insisted that the same key, struck from different approaches with different intent, would give off a slightly different sound, because in performing it, he was "going for" that particular sound. A model for any note may have an objective classification, but that does not provide the dynamical basis of the sensorimotor mechanisms involved in making that sound happen.

In this way, intentions need not be viewed as independent mental events that cause behavior, but are best characterized as dynamic processes embedded in a physical, historical, and social world, including those of a person learning a skilled activity like playing jazz improvisation. Sudnow's phenomenological analysis of his learning suggests that skilled performance is not generated from a prior mental decision to act in a particular way that is independent of his ongoing piano-playing behavior. Instead, skilled human action may arise from how the individual's frame of mind automatically selects a subset of behaviors (i.e., hitting the right notes in the right way to produce the right sounds) from the unlimited alternatives within the self-organized constraint space that is defined by the person-environment interactions.

Conclusion

Perception is not a kind of information processing that samples, selects, or points out features of an independent object world. People do not first perceive to create a full-scale internal model of the world that is then used to generate appropriate action. Instead, perception involves bodily movements of various sorts and the anticipation of action when adapting to environmental situations. In this way, perception establishes a reciprocal relation in the physical coordination of the organism with the environment. This kind of body-world structural coupling is fundamentally grounded in self-movement. An embodied approach to perception and action sees these as dynamically intertwined, in that the physical properties of the real world are not entities to be statically perceived, but are opportunities for action.

Exactly how do perception and action interrelate? Many scholars talk of perception-action linkages in terms of "shared representations." But there is one functional scheme that provides a broader dynamical account for perception-action couplings. An overview of this is seen in Figure 3.2 (Viviani, 2002). This model includes two sets of hierarchically organized oscillators (or nonlinear resonators) that generate percepts and organize action. Each oscillator is tuned to respond maximally to just one category of stimuli, yet is flexible enough to respond to stimuli of different types, or stimuli that are incomplete or corrupt. The perceptual set is assumed to include a richer collection of resonant modes, or limit cycles, than the motor set. Thus, the behavior of the perceptual system converges toward certain basins of attraction more readily than is the case with the motor set. Each set has a full complement of within-set couplings, some of which are genetically determined, with others acquired from experience. These within-set couplings provide for the activation and organization of individual components in their respective domains. The perceptual mode that prevails at any moment depends on the sensory inflow, although the "winner" is

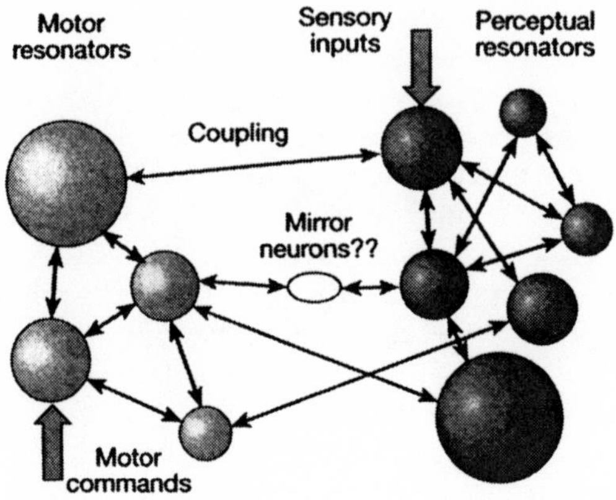

FIGURE 3.2. A functional scheme for describing motor–perceptual interactions; full description in the text.

strongly influenced by the couplings within the motor set. Through these couplings, resonant modes are induced in the motor oscillator even when there is no direct activation from any conscious will to move. There may even be no reason to assume any difference between perceptual and motor oscillators, because these may originate in the same physiological mechanism. Regardless of whether activation spreads from perception to action, or the other way, the end product is an integrated superordinate limit cycle, or basin of attraction. In fact, some familiar perceptual experience may be precluded in individuals in whom the motor set of oscillators are not functional. At the same time, suppressing perceptual resonance will alter motor functions, to some extent, both because some reafference would be missing, and because some global resonant modes would be unavailable.

This speculative proposal can account for several aspects of perception-action interaction, including mirror neurons, the role of anticipatory action in perception, why individuals with impaired motor cortex may suffer from vision problems despite having intact visual systems, and different empirical effects demonstrating the two-way influence of perception and action. Conceiving of perception and action as part of a dynamical system emphasizes the property that small changes in their parameters may result in abrupt (catastrophic) changes in the qualitative type of its attractors. This feature of dynamical systems provides a way of incorporating both continuity and discontinuity within the system and suggests ways of describing behavior in terms of striving for equilibrium as it unfolds in real-time. Most generally, this functional scheme explains many of the dynamical perception-action couplings that are at the very heart of embodied perception.

4

Concepts

A wonderful illustration of the importance of embodiment in ordinary concepts is evident in how Apache Indians in North America name the parts of automobiles (Basso, 1990). In the Couer d'Alene Indian language, the tires of a car or truck become "wrinkled feet," a reference to the pattern on their treads. The new knowledge of automobiles is likened to the old knowledge of the body. Basso has described an entire system of naming the parts of motorized vehicles in the language of the Western Apache of east-central Arizona. The Western Apache have extended the names for the body parts of humans and animals to refer to the parts of automobiles and pickup trucks. In this structural metaphor, the hood became the nose ("bichih"), the headlights became the eyes ("bidaa"), and the windshield became the forehead ("bita"). The term for the face ("binii") was extended to the whole area extending from the top of the windshield to the front bumper, so this term included the nose/hood and forehead/windshield as subparts. The front wheels became the hands and arms ("bigan"), and the rear wheels became the feet ("bikee"). All the items under the hood were classified as parts of the innards ("bibye"). Under the hood, the battery became the liver ("bizig"), the electrical wiring the veins ("bit qqs"), the gas tank the stomach ("bibid"), the distributor the heart ("bijii"), the radiator the lung ("bijii izole"), and the radiator hoses the intestines ("bich'i").

There is an underlying conceptual metaphor, MOTOR VEHICLES ARE HUMAN BODIES, which expresses correspondences between the parts of human beings and the parts of cars and trucks. In the MOTOR VEHICLES ARE HUMAN BODIES metaphor, the thing of which we speak (the motor vehicle), with its constituent parts and relations (its cognitive topology), is the target domain, whereas the thing with which we refer (human bodies), with its own constituent parts and relations, is the source domain. The naming of vehicle parts with the names of human body parts preserved the hierarchical cognitive structure of relationships among the parts so that both the car's body and the human body have "innards" that include, for instance, "liver."

Some scholars may argue that how people in one culture name parts of automobiles may not be the best place to find evidence of embodied concepts. But the Coeur d'Alene names for automobiles reveal a deep-seated cognitive imperative to make sense of the world in terms of our bodies (and in terms of embodied metaphor). By recognizing how parts of an automobile have a metaphorical relationship to human body parts (and functions), the Western Apache have created something new using their imaginative processes to the fullest. The Western Apache have in a sense reordered their experiences by looking at something differently than before. Yet this reordering of experience is not merely clichéd, or a one-shot mapping. Instead, there is a complex system of metaphorical correspondences that is grounded in people's ordinary experiences of their own bodies.

This chapter explores the importance of embodied experience in concepts and conceptual structure. I argue that significant aspects of both concrete and abstract concepts arise from, and continued to be structured in terms of, pervasive patterns of embodied activity. There is a growing literature from cognitive psychology and cognitive linguistics to support this contention. Much of this work is focused on inferring the existence of embodiment from the analysis of linguistic statements and how people interpret them (also see Chapters 5 and 6). Although traditional experimental psychologists are often skeptical about making claims about conceptual structures from analyses of how people speak, the linguistic evidence demands explanation within a more general psychological account of human conceptual systems. As will be seen, recognition of the body is central to the study and description of concepts.

Traditional Views of Concepts

The traditional view in psychology and philosophy argues that concepts are stored mental representations that enable people to identify objects and events in the real world. Classical theories assume that rules describe the objects in a category independent of situations (Bruner, Goodnow, & Austin, 1956). For example, a rule might attempt to capture the physical properties of chairs that are necessary and sufficient for membership apart from the contexts in which chairs appear. People presumably identify certain features or attributes of objects, such as "that object has four legs and barks," that match pre-existing summary representations in long-term memory, such as "A dog has four legs and barks." In this way, concepts and categories are defined by their relations to objects in the external world. Most theories of concepts also assume that there is a single amodal symbol to represent a property across different categories. For example, there must be a conceptual symbol for the property "red" that is the same attribute in concepts as different as apples, wine, and fire trucks. Amodal symbols are language-independent, context-independent, and disembodied.

Concepts are furthermore hierarchically organized in terms of their objective properties. "Chairs," for instance, fall into the middle level of the hierarchy with furniture as a superordinate level and specific chairs (e.g., rocking chairs) associated with the subordinate level. These "facts" presumably reflect the nature of things as they objectively exist in the world.

Psychological theories try to explain the process of identifying any instance as belonging to a particular category and the way conceptual information is structured in memory to facilitate understanding of these objects and events. A common method for uncovering the contents of any conceptual representation is to present participants with a word for some concept and have them verbally list features typically true of it. In property verification tasks, participants read the word for a concept and verbally say whether a second word specifies a property true of the concept (e.g., "bird" – "wings"). Psychologists generally assume that in completing these tasks, people access structured feature lists, propositions, frames, and semantic nets that contain only amodal features.

The example of a conceptual category judged best is called a "prototype." Categories are assumed to be mentally represented in terms of prototypes, with the degree of category membership being determined by the degree of similarity to the prototype. For example, sparrows are closer to the prototypical bird for Americans than are penguins or ostriches, and this makes it easier for people to verify statements such as "A sparrow is a bird" than to verify "A penguin is a bird" (Rosch, 1975; Rosch & Mervis, 1975). These empirical results are not due simply to some exemplars being more common than others, because even rare instances of a category may be closer to the prototype than more frequent examples. Thus, people rate rare items of furniture such as "love seat," "davenport," and "cedar chest" as being better exemplars of the category "furniture" than they do frequently encountered objects such as "refrigerator" (Rosch, 1975).

Problems with the Traditional View

There are several major problems with the traditional view of concepts. First, evidence shows that people represent certain properties quite differently in different contexts. For instance, the concept of "fire" is presumably an abstract representation that arises from all concrete instances of how fires are understood in specific contexts. Yet typicality judgments often vary as a function of context (Roth & Shoben, 1983). "Tea" is judged to be a more typical beverage than "milk" in the context of secretaries taking a break, but the opposite is true in the context of truck drivers taking a break. "Birds" that are typical from an American point of view, such as robins and eagles, are atypical from the point of view of an average Chinese citizen (Barsalou & Medin, 1986). These findings suggest that prototypes are closely tied to individual contexts and are not necessarily abstract representations that emerge from specific instances of any concept. To take another example, the property "red" is represented differently in apples, lettuce, potatoes, and wine (Halff, Ortony, & Anderson, 1976). People likely represent the same property locally in different contexts, rather than globally as a single symbol (i.e., the local form assumption) (Solomon & Barsalou, 2001).

Concepts are not direct reflections of things in nature, contrary to the traditional view. Concepts do not directly preserve aspects of the external objects they refer to, contrary to the assumption that concepts are amodal symbols. For example, certain cognitive categories in the middle of taxonomic hierarchies (i.e., basic-level categories) can be explained in terms of certain nonobjective properties. Empirical research has shown that the basic level is special for the following reasons (Lakoff, 1987):

(1) It is the highest level at which category members have similarly perceived overall shapes. For example, you can recognize a chair by its overall shape. But there is no overall shape that you can assign to a generalized piece of furniture such that you could recognize the category from the shape.
(2) It is the highest level at which a single mental image can represent the entire category. You can form a mental image of a chair. You can get mental images of opposing categories at this level, such as tables and beds. But you cannot get a mental image of a general piece of furniture that is not some particular piece of furniture, such as a table or bed.
(3) It is the highest level at which a person uses similar motor actions in interacting with category members. People have motor programs for interacting with objects at the basic level – interacting with chairs, tables, and beds. There are no motor programs for interacting with generalized pieces of furniture.
(4) It is the level at which most of our knowledge is organized. Think of all that you know about cars versus all that you know about vehicles. You know a handful of things about vehicles, but a huge number of things about cars. It is at the basic level that most of our useful information and knowledge is organized.

These observations explain why the basic level of categories has priority over the superordinate and subordinate levels. Most generally, the basic level is the level at which people interact optimally with their environment, given the kinds of bodies and brains that they have and the environments they inhabit. For example, to decide that a particular couch belongs to the category "things that can fit through the front doorway," a good strategy is to manipulate an analog representation of the couch's shape in relation to an analog representation of the doorway (Barsalou, 2001).

Representations that preserve perceptual properties, as suggested above, are often more efficient than purely symbolic representations, because they do not require external constructs to ensure proper inferences (Barsalou, 1999a). These facts can only be explained in terms of human embodiment and raise serious doubts about whether prototypes are abstract, pre-existing conceptual representations.

A related problem for the traditional view of concepts is that prototype theory assumes that category membership is determined by whether some candidate is sufficiently similar to the prototype, or a set of already represented examples, where similarity is based on matches and mismatches of independent, equally abstract features. Yet similarity does not explain many kinds of prototype effects. Thus, goal-derived categories, such as "foods to eat while on a diet" and "things to take on a camping trip," reveal the same typicality effects as do other categories (Barsalou, 1983, 1985, 1989, 1991). The basis for these effects is not similarity to some prototype, but rather similarity to an ideal. For instance, typicality ratings for the category of "foods to eat while on a diet" are determined by real-world knowledge such as how clearly each example conforms to the ideal of zero calories. This real-world knowledge, including temporary analog representations, is used to reason about or explain properties of concepts, not simply to match them to some pre-existing, abstract prototype. Even though categories such as "things to take on a camping trip" have prototypic structure, such a structure does not exist in advance because the category is "ad hoc" and not conventional (Barsalou, 1990).

In fact, there are many ways in which prototypes may be formed (Rosch, 1999). Some may be based on statistical frequencies, such as the mean or number (for family resemblance structures) of various attributes. Others appear to be ideals made salient by factors such as physiology (good color, good form), social structure (president, teacher), goals (ideal foods to eat on a diet), formal structures (multiples of ten in the decimal system), and individual experience (the first learned, the most recently encountered, or one made salient because it is especially meaningful, emotional, or interesting). Prototypes are not summary abstractions based on a few defining attributes, but are rich, imagistic, sensory, full-bodied mental events.

One reason cognitive scientists mistakenly believe that concepts must be pre-existing mental structures is that they commit the "effects = structures" fallacy (Gibbs, 1994; Gibbs & Matlock, 2000; Lakoff, 1987). This fallacy reflects the belief that the goodness-of-example ratings, for example, obtained in psychological experiments are a direct reflection of degree of category membership. But the "effects = structures" interpretation cannot account for many of the types of data reviewed above, especially the problems of complex categorization (Gibbs, 1994). In fact, many kinds of prototype effects can be explained by other principles (e.g., metaphoric and metonymic reasoning) that do not assume that the effects obtained in experiments reflect the structure of pre-existing knowledge. For example, many instances of complex categorization have prototype effects that are grounded in reference-point reasoning that reflects cases where a part of some category stands for the entire, more complex category (Lakoff, 1987). Thus, the prototypical case of a "housewife mother" is used to reason about the more complex category of "mother," because of the salience of nurturance to the concept of mother. Other instances of mothers, such as "unwed mothers," "surrogate mothers," "stage mothers," and so on, are all derived from the central, prototypical case. But this process of part-for-whole reasoning creates the less prototypical instances in the moment of thinking, and they are not simply read off an enduring conceptual map in long-term memory.

Much research points to the flexibility of concepts, which is difficult to reconcile with traditional views of concepts as abstract, disembodied symbols. One set of studies asked people to provide definitions for categories, such as bachelor, bird, and chair (Barsalou, 1995). An analysis of the overlap in the features participants provided for a given category revealed that on average only 47% of the features in one person's definitions for a category existed in another person's definition. A great deal of flexibility also exists within individuals when they are asked to provide definitions for concepts. When participants in the above study returned 2 weeks later and defined the same categories again, only 66% of the features noted in the first session were produced again in the second session. These results indicate that that substantial flexibility exists in how a person conceptualizes the same category on different occasions (Barsalou, 1995).

The significant flexibility shown by many experiments on defining categories arises not from differences in knowledge, but from differences in the retrieval of this knowledge from long-term memory. On different occasions, different individuals retrieve different subsets of features from their extensive knowledge of a category. In the same way, an individual may retrieve different aspects of his or her knowledge of a category on different occasions. For instance, the statement "The Christmas bird fed 12 people" makes encyclopedic information about turkeys and geese most accessible, whereas seabirds would be most accessible given a statement such as "The bird followed the boat out to sea."

Our ordinary experience with objects in the real world does not demand that we classify them. For example, my interactions with beds involve sleeping in them, moving them, and making them up, as well as, under special circumstances such as being in a psychology experiment, classifying them as belonging to the category of "furniture" (Murphy, 2002; Ross, 1999). People may certainly learn a good deal about beds from interacting with them in different ways that surely influence their concepts for "beds." One set of studies had people categorize patients based on their symptoms and then prescribe appropriate medicines based on these symptoms (Ross, 1990). The symptoms that were most critical to the prescriptions were as important as the symptoms themselves when people categorized the patients into different groups. Thus, what people learn from their interactions with items is incorporated into their concepts, and consequently affects categorization. Not surprisingly, other work shows that people who actually work with category members (e.g., tree experts) develop representations that reflect their interactions with objects (Medin et al., 1997). This is why, for example, biologists and laypersons have different concepts of tree types.

These studies on the effect of category use on categorization tasks illustrate how people's rich interactions with the world shape knowledge acquisition and representation. Psychologists conducting these studies discuss people's "interactions with the world" as a kind of "background knowledge." But some of these studies may reflect something of people's embodied understanding of objects and events, and not simply their abstract knowledge or beliefs.

Consider one set of experiments in which people were shown pictures of people performing actions on objects (Pazzani, 1997). Each picture depicted an adult or child doing an action on an uninflated balloon that was either large or small, and either yellow or purple. The action required was either to drop the balloon in a cup of water or to stretch it. Participants had to learn one of two types of categories, disjunctive and conjunctive. The disjunctive category was based on the rule "the person must be an adult OR the action must be stretching the balloon." The conjunctive category was defined by the rule "the color must be yellow AND the balloon must be small." Earlier research indicated that conjunctive categories are easier to learn than disjunctive ones (Bruner, Goodnow, & Austin, 1956). But participants here were also instructed either to learn "Category Alpha" or to identify those balloons that would inflate. "Category Alpha" instructions presumably would not activate people's background knowledge about balloons, but the second task should prompt participants to think about inflating balloons. In fact, when people received the "Category Alpha" instructions, they found the conjunctive category easier to learn than the disjunctive one. But when given the inflate instructions, participants learned disjunctive categories much faster, even more easily than did the Alpha people learning conjunctive categories.

This pattern of data demonstrates the strong effect that background knowledge (i.e., about balloon inflation) can have on category learning. Yet people probably do not have stored, declarative knowledge about the exact properties associated with balloon inflation. Alternatively, being instructed to identify which balloons most easily inflate prompts people to run embodied simulations about inflation given each balloon. My claim is that discussions of background knowledge effects on category learning may, in some cases, show the importance of embodied simulations, rather than the activation of prestored, abstract, declarative knowledge, in making categorization judgments.

These observations suggest that concepts are temporary constructions in working memory, based on embodied simulations, and not stable structures stored in long-term memory. One possibility is that concepts may be defined as statistical patterns in sensory-motor systems that take different forms in different context. Human conceptual systems evolved to support embodied action in the environment. Let us consider this idea in more detail.

Perceptual Symbols

A significant new goal in cognitive science is to establish how perceptual processes guide the construction of concrete and abstract concepts. The best example of this work is the development of the theory of "perceptual symbol systems" (Barsalou, 1999a, 2003). Perceptual symbols are derived from the representations generated from perceptual input systems, but are acquired by performing operations on perceptual representations and are similar to these operations. Thus, perceptual symbols are schematic, yet maintain some of the structure of the perceptual representations from which they were derived. Unlike amodal concepts, perceptual symbols are nonarbitrary, given their similarity to the objects they represent.

Perceptual symbols are also multimodal and include information from the five senses, along with proprioceptive and kinesthetic information. Perceptual symbols are not necessarily conscious images, but are unconscious states of perceptual systems specified neurally (Barsalou, 2003). For instance, the representation of a chair might be specified as a configuration of neurons active in the visual system, rather than as a conscious mental image. These perceptual representations are not necessarily holistic, but can reflect selective aspects of a perceptual state extracted via selective attention and stored in long-term memory (see sensorimotor contingency theory in Chapter 3). Thus, selective attention might focus on the form of an object, storing only its shape in memory, and not its color, texture, position, size, and so forth. This schematic extraction process not only operates on sensory states, but also works on internal mental events, extracting aspects of representation states, motivational states, and emotions. When there is no sensory input, activation of the conjunctive neurons partially re-enact, or reinstantiate, the earlier visual stimuli. These re-enactments, or simulations, are specific skills that serve as the foundational mechanism for providing context-specific representations of a category. Perhaps the most interesting aspect of perceptual symbol theory is the idea that conceptual processing involves sensorimotor simulations. Under this view, concepts are not understood and stored as abstract, disembodied symbols, because crucial elements of relevant perceptual and sensorimotor information are used in conceptual processing.

In fact, empirical evidence supports the claims of perceptual systems theory. First, evidence from cognitive neuroscience suggests that concepts are grounded in sensory-motor regions of the brain (Damasio, 1989; Damasio & Damasio, 1994; Gainotti et al., 1995; Martin, Ungerleider, & Haxby, 2000; Martin et al., 1996; Pulvermueller, 1999; Rosler, Heil, & Hennighausen, 1995; Tranel, Damasio, & Damasio, 1997; Warrington & Shallice, 1984). For example, functional imagery studies demonstrate that processing man-made objects activates the left ventral premotor cortex (Gerlach, Law, & Paulson, 2002; Grafton, Fadiga, Arbib, & Rizzolatti, 1997; Martin et al., 1996). Comprehension of man-made objects may therefore depend on motor-based knowledge of object utilization (action knowledge). In one case study, for example, patients with semantic dementia were better able to name objects when they also demonstrated, or mimed, the object's use than when simply asked to name the object alone (Coccia et al., 2004). Other neuroimagining studies show that action knowledge is important for the processing of manipulatable objects in general, regardless of whether these are man-made (articles of clothing) or not (fruits/vegetables) (Gerlach et al., 2002). This latter finding is contrary to theories that maintain that concepts are represented in taxonomic categories, but is congruent with perceptual symbol theory, in which categories differ in the weight they put on different forms of knowledge in varying tasks.

One challenge for psychological theories of concepts concerns productivity, or the ability to combine representations to form more complex structures. Traditional theories have difficulty explaining how concepts may be combined in natural ways. For instance, A and B may be easily blended together, but X and Y cannot. People's understanding of how concepts mesh together in the real world also constrains their conceptual understanding of events. Consider the expressions "The lamp is above the table" and "The table is below the lamp" (Solomon, 1997). These different sentences express different schematic images. For "The lamp is above the table," our embodied understanding of "above" is a schematic image having a top and a bottom region where our attention is focused on the top. For "The table is below the lamp," our understanding of "below" also contains a top and bottom regions, but, this time, our attention is focused on the bottom. These different construals of the relationship between the "lamp" and "table" are created by meshing types from memory with tokens from the perceived environment. Under this view, we create different propositional construals by determining which pattern of action from memory can be used to mesh with extant properties of the environment (Barsalou, 1999b; Glenberg, 1997).

Perceptual systems theory assumes that concepts can be combined according to the constraints by which objects can be physically manipulated in the world (Barsalou, in press). One study in support of this idea examined the features participants reported for noun phrases in which the same modifier (e.g., "half") revealed the insides of an object (e.g., "half watermelon"), or kept the insides of an object hidden (e.g., "half smile") (Wu & Barsalou, 2001). Participants produced more internal features (e.g., red, seeds) when describing noun phrases revealing the insides of an object than for noun phrases that kept the insides occluded. These findings support the idea that participants mentally simulate how concepts ("half" with "watermelon" or "smile") might be combined in the real world when they are asked to describe the features of different objects.

A different series of studies on conceptual combinations examined the role of perceptual similarity in categorization judgments (Solomon & Barsalou, 2001). These studies manipulated perceptual similarity across different tests. One participant, for example, first verified the concept-property pair "PONY-mane," and later either "HORSE-mane" or "LION-mane." If people perceptually simulate the concept to verify the property, then they should be faster to verify the "HORSE-mane" sequence than the "LION-mane" sequence, because horse manes are more similar to pony manes than are lion manes. This is exactly what happened. When participants process the "HORSE-mane" pair, they are reminded of the earlier pair involving manes, which either facilitates or inhibits priming depending on the type of mane suggested. These findings demonstrate how people performing verification tasks perceptually simulate a concept, and do not simply activate its abstract features.

Another set of studies showed that verifying a property in the auditory modality (e.g., "BLENDER-loud") is slower after verifying a property in a different modality (e.g., "CRANBERRY-tart") than after verifying a property in the same modality (e.g., "LEAVES-rustling") (Pecher, Zeelenberg, & Barsalou, 2003). Thus, switching modalities in conceptual processing takes effort, which is clearly contrary to the idea that conceptual knowledge is represented in an amodal manner.

Perceptual symbols theory assumes that even when participants receive nonpictorial materials and are not asked to use imagery, they nevertheless perform perceptual simulations spontaneously. Concepts arise as on-the-fly simulations of events (Barsalou, 2002, 2003). In standard categorization tasks, for example, people first simulate referents of the concept perceptually and then scan their simulations to produce the required information (e.g., list the features of "chairs"). Participants' responses in typical categorization tasks do not, therefore, reflect the pure amodal contents of some pre-existing, taxonomic mental representation. This conclusion is consistent with related work showing that when people are shown an object to be categorized, they are often reminded of a superficially similar object. Once reminded, they try to come up with an abstract description of the category that encompasses both objects (Ross, Perkins, & Tenpenny, 1990).

Another implication of perceptual symbol theory is that if a conceptualization attempts to simulate a perceptual experience, then it should typically simulate a situation, because situations are intrinsic parts of perceptual experience. For instance, imagining a chair in a living room evokes a very different chair than imagining a chair in a jet. One study nicely illustrates how people imagine themselves in concrete situations to produce exemplars of concepts (Vallee-Tourangeau, Anthony, & Austin, 1998). Participants generated exemplars from common taxonomic categories, such as furniture and fruits, and from ad hoc categories such as "things dogs chase" and "reasons for going on a holiday." Afterward, participants described the strategies they used in generating these examples.

Several kinds of strategies were reported. "Experiential mediation" involved retrieving an autobiographical memory of a situation that contained individuals from the target category, and then reporting the category to which this individual belonged. When generating types of fruit, for example, participants first retrieved a memory of a grocery store, scanned across it, and reported the types of fruit present in the produce section. "Semantic mediation," on the other hand, involved first retrieving a detached taxonomy that contained the target category and then reporting its subcategories. Thus, when generating examples of fruit, people first retrieved the fruit taxonomy and then reported subtypes, such as tropical fruit, dried fruit, and citrus fruit.

Analysis of participants' self-reported strategies showed that people used "experiential mediation" about three times as often as "semantic mediation" for both common taxonomic and ad hoc categories. It is not surprising that situations are important for ad hoc categories, given that these categories arise out of goal-directed activity in specific contexts. Much more surprising is that concrete situations were reported just as often for common taxonomic categories, suggesting that they, too, are organized around situations.

In general, research related to perceptual symbol theory suggests a new view of concepts that explains the perceptual grounding for the creation and retrieval of conceptual knowledge (see Barsalou, 2001). A conceptualization of a category typically includes background information based partly on people's embodied simulations or acting in life-like situations. This re-enactment or simulation is not necessarily complete. But each conceptualization represents a category in a way that is relevant to the background situation, such that different conceptualizations represent the category differently. In this way, perceptual symbols theory suggests how concepts arise in the moment from a tight coupling of cognitive and motoric processes.

Finally, perceptual symbols are involved with the representation of abstract concepts. Concepts such as truth, beauty, and virtue are not understood as single images, and each may have multiple representations in different contexts. The concept of "beauty" may involve our ability to perceptually identify instances by their appearance and the internal states, such as emotional feelings, that they produce in us. Abstract conceptual relations may be characterized as the manipulation of perceptual symbols. For instance, consider the idea of a "counterfactual" (Prinz & Barsalou, 2002). A counterfactual thought is a way of forming perceptual simulations. You can have a counterfactual thought if you form a simulation representing some nonactual state of affairs, P, and you are disposed, upon doing so, to add a representation of another state of affairs, Q, to your representation. This is a way of representing the fact that Q could not have occurred if P had been the case. Counterfactual thought need not, then, depend on specific images, but is one way of engaging in a kind of perceptual simulation.

Explaining abstract concepts and how they arise in the mind remains one of the greatest challenges for cognitive science. Perceptual symbols are on the right track, for the most part, in describing how abstract concepts may have multiple realizations, as is the case for all conceptual processing. Moreover, this view also correctly claims that abstract ideas have a perceptual, perhaps embodied, basis. As we will now see, the growing belief that concepts are tied to perceptual symbols is most dramatically voiced in cognitive linguistics.

Image Schemas and the Metaphorical Nature of Abstract Concepts

Cognitive linguistics embraces the important idea that linguistic structures are related to, and motivated by, human conceptual knowledge, bodily experience, and the communicative functions of discourse. Unlike generative linguists, cognitive linguists explicitly look for language-mind and language-mind-body linkages in their descriptions of linguistic structure and linguistic behavior. A key part of this work claims that many of our concepts are grounded in, and structured by, various patterns of our perceptual interactions, bodily actions, and manipulations of objects (Johnson, 1987; Lakoff, 1987; Lakoff & Johnson, 1999; Talmy, 1988, 2000). Specific patterns of force dynamics underlie our embodied understandings of abstract concepts (Talmy, 1988, 2000). Forces are viewed as physical, embodied entities (an agonist) acting in competition against other forces (an antagonist), with each entity having varying strengths and tendencies. We understand these entities primarily from our own bodily experiences such as pushing and being pushed, moving objects, and feeling the forces acting within our bodies as we move about the environment. These patterns are experiential gestalts, called "image schemas," that emerge throughout sensorimotor activity as we manipulate objects, orient ourselves spatially and temporally, and direct our perceptual focus for various purposes.

Image schemas can generally be defined as dynamic analog representations of spatial relations and movements in space. Even though image schemas are derived from perceptual and motor processes, they are not themselves sensorimotor processes. Instead, image schemas are "primary means by which we construct or constitute order and are not mere passive receptacles into which experience is poured" (Johnson, 1987: 30). In this way, image schemas are different from the notion of schemata traditionally used in cognitive science, which is of abstract conceptual and propositional event structures (see Rumelhart, 1980). By contrast, image schemas are imaginative, nonpropositional structures that organize experience at the level of bodily perception and movement. Image schemas exist across all perceptual modalities, something that must hold for there to be any sensorimotor coordination in our experience. As such, image schemas are at once visual, auditory, kinesthetic, and tactile. At the same time, image schemas are more abstract than ordinary visual mental images and consist of dynamic spatial patterns that underlie the spatial relations and movement found in actual concrete images.

Studies in cognitive linguistics suggest that at least two dozen different image schemas and several image schema transformations appear regularly in people's everyday thinking, reasoning, and imagination (Johnson, 1987; Lakoff, 1987). Among these are the schematic structures of CONTAINER, BALANCE, SOURCE-PATH-GOAL, PATH, CYCLE, ATTRACTION, CENTER-PERIPHERY, and LINK. These image schemas cover a wide range of experiential structures that are pervasive in experience, have internal structure, underlie literal meanings, and can be metaphorically elaborated to provide for our understanding of more abstract conceptual domains.

Consider the SOURCE-PATH-GOAL schema. This schema first develops as we learn to focus our eyes and track forms as they move throughout our visual field. From such experiences, a recurring pattern becomes manifest in tracking a trajectory from point A to another point B. Later on, as we move our bodies in the real world, ranging from experiences of reaching for objects to moving our entire bodies from one location to another, more varied SOURCE-PATH-GOAL experiences become salient. Although SOURCE-PATH-GOAL experiences may vary considerably (e.g., many objects, shapes, types of paths traveled), the emergent image-schematic structure of SOURCE-PATH-GOAL supports literal meanings, such as seen in "He walked across the room to the door," and can be metaphorically projected onto more abstract domains of understanding and reasoning (Johnson, 1987). This metaphorical mapping preserves the structural characteristics or the cognitive topology of the source domain (Lakoff, 1990). Thus, the SOURCE-PATH-GOAL schema gives rise to conceptual metaphors such as PURPOSES ARE DESTINATIONS, which preserve the main structural characteristics of the source domain (i.e., SOURCE-PATH-GOAL).

English is replete with conventional expressions that illustrate this underlying metaphorical conceptualization. For instance, we start off to get our Ph.D.s, but along the way we get sidetracked or led astray, and are diverted from our original goal. We try to get back on the right path and to keep the end in view as we move along. Eventually we may come a long way and reach our goal (Johnson, 1993). It is simply not an arbitrary fact of English that we talk about our lives and careers in terms of sources, paths, and goals; rather, we metaphorically conceptualize our experiences through very basic, bodily experiences in the world that are abstracted to form higher-level metaphoric thought. This way of talking about experience shows how the PURPOSES ARE DESTINATIONS metaphor, resulting from a very basic image-schematic structure, is constitutive of our understanding of intentional action.

Some creative instantiations of the SOURCE-PATH-GOAL schema are seen in poetry. Consider an excerpt from a poem, by the Chilean poet Pablo Neruda, titled "Ode and Burgeonings" (Neruda, 1972):

> My wild girl, we have had
> to regain time
> and march backward, in the distance
> of our lives, kiss after kiss,
> gathering from one place what we gave
> without joy, discovering in another
> the secret road
> that gradually brought your feet
> closer to mine.

This is one of Neruda's great love poems. Speaking of love seems to stretch the limits of language, one reason that we appreciate the works of poets who find expression for such experiences. The above lines illustrate unique, poetic instantiations of how we metaphorically conceptualize our love experiences partly in terms of journeys motivated by the SOURCE-PATH-GOAL image schema. The poet talks about going "backward, in the distance" (i.e., the path) of his love relationship with the "wild girl," stopping at those places that "we gave without joy" to find "the secret road" that brought true unity and happiness. Although these phrases are novel, they are related in metaphorical ways to mundane expressions people often use to talk about love and love relationships. For instance, consider the following list of conventional expressions:

> "Look how far we've come."
> "It's been a long, bumpy road."
> "We're at a crossroads."
> "We may have to go our separate ways."
> "Our marriage is on the rocks."
> "We're spinning our wheels."

These (and other) conventional expressions cluster together under one of the basic metaphorical systems of understanding: LOVE IS A JOURNEY (Lakoff & Johnson, 1980). This conceptual metaphor involves a tight mapping according to which entities in the domain of love (e.g., the lovers, their common goals, the love relationship, etc.) correspond systematically to entities in the domain of a journey (e.g., the traveler, the vehicle, destinations, etc.). Various correspondences arise when we think of love as a journey. Among these are the ideas that the person in love is a traveler, the goal of ultimate love is a destination, the means for achieving love are routes, the difficulties one experiences in love are obstacles to travel, and the progress in a love relationship is the distance traveled.

It is not an arbitrary matter to speak of love relationships as being at crossroads, on the rocks, or having been on a long, bumpy road. Instead, we understand that each of these expressions is appropriate to use in talking about love relationships precisely because of our common metaphorical transformation whereby love is conceptualized as being like a physical journey and our understanding of journeys is closely linked to the SOURCE-PATH-GOAL image schema. This discussion of the SOURCE-PATH-GOAL schema shows that there are direct connections between recurring bodily experiences, metaphorically understood abstract concepts, and both conventional and creative language that refers to these abstract concepts.

Another illustration of an image schema and how its internal structure is projected onto new abstract domain via metaphor is seen by considering the BALANCE schema (Johnson, 1987). The idea of balance is something that is learned "with our bodies and not by grasping a set of rules" (Johnson, 1987: 74). Balancing is such a pervasive part of our bodily experience that we are seldom aware of its presence in everyday life. We come to know the meaning of balance through the closely related experiences of bodily equilibrium or loss of equilibrium. For example, a baby stands, wobbles, and drops to the floor. It tries again and again, as it learns how to maintain a balanced erect posture. A young boy struggles to stay up on a two-wheeled bicycle as he learns to keep his balance while riding down the street. Each of us has experienced occasions when we have too much acid in our stomachs, when our hands get cold, our heads feel too hot, our bladders feel distended, our sinuses become swollen, and our mouths feel dry. In these and numerous other ways we learn the meanings of lack of balance or equilibrium. We respond to imbalance and disequilibrium by warming our hands, giving moisture to our mouths, draining our bladders, and so forth until we feel balanced once again. Our BALANCE image schema emerges, then, through our experiences of bodily equilibriums and disequilibrium and of maintaining our bodily systems and functions in states of equilibrium.

Our BALANCE image schema, to continue with this example, supports understanding of literal expressions such as "He balanced the weight on his shoulder" and is metaphorically elaborated in a large number of abstract domains of experience (e.g., psychological states, legal relationships, formal systems) (Johnson, 1991). In the cases of bodily and visual balance, there seems to be one basic scheme consisting of a point or axis around which forces and weights must be distributed so that they counteract or balance off one another. Our experience of bodily balance and the perception of balance is connected to our understanding of balanced personalities, balanced views, balanced systems, balanced equilibrium, the balance of power, the balance of justice, and so on. In each of these examples, the mental or the abstract concept of balance is understood and experienced in terms of our physical understanding of balance. Image schemas have internal logic or structure that determine the roles these schemas can play in structuring various concepts and in patterns of reasoning. It is not the case that a large number of unrelated concepts (for the systematic, psychological, moral, legal, and mathematical domains) all just happen to make use of the same word "balance" and related terms (Johnson, 1991). Rather, we use the same word for all these domains because they are structurally related by the same sort of underlying image schemas, and are metaphorically elaborated from them.

Consider now the pervasive bodily experience of MOMENTUM. We experience visual momentum when we see heavy moving things continue to move even when encountering other objects. We experience kinesthetic momentum both when we are the object that the heavy moving thing encounters and when we are the heavy moving thing. We experience auditory momentum both as a correlate of visual and kinesthetic momentum and independently, as when thunder builds up to a crescendo. We even experience internal momentum as when certain bodily functions build up such that they cannot be stopped. We abstract out of all of these similar experiences those aspects of form that they have in common or that are similar, which we refer to through language as momentum.

The MOMENTUM image schema serves as the embodied basis for several abstract, metaphorical concepts. Consider the following utterances:

"I was bowled over by that idea."
"We have too much momentum to withdraw from the election race."
"I got carried away by what I was doing."
"Once he gets rolling, you'll never be able to stop him talking."

These utterances reflect how the image schema for MOMENTUM allows discussion of very abstract domains of cognition, such as political support, control, arguments, and talking about physical objects moving with momentum. Imagine, for example, what it looks like for someone to be bowled over by an idea. This does not make literal or physical sense given that ideas are only abstract entities. Yet most people readily imagine a scene in which some physical force hits a person who is standing, thus causing that person to fall over as the physical force continues passing over the person's prone body. Many people appear to base their imagistic understandings of statements such as "I was bowled over by that idea" based on their own embodied experiences of being running into, and sometimes run over, by other people or objects.

Finally, consider the embodied roots of another salient image schema, STRAIGHT (Cienki, 1998). The term "straight" is employed in many physical and abstract ways. For instance:

> "The straight edge of the table."
> "Stand up straight."
> "I can't think straight."
> "It rained for three days straight."
> "Tell it to me straight."
> "Let me get this straight."
> "He's not straight, but gay."
> "I couldn't keep a straight face."

Why do we use "straight" in these rather different ways? The concept of straight has an important role in our sensory experience. Research shows that collinearity of points or elements in a visual pattern has an important role in visual perception (Foster, 1982). For example, classic Gestalt studies on empirical grouping, visual detection in moving fields, visual acuity in movement, visual texture discrimination, and visual discrimination of briefly presented dot figures all show that perception of straightness is a fundamental property of how we see and make sense of visual events. Straight lines are more easily and quickly seen then curved lines. Horizontal and vertical straight lines are especially more easily perceived than are oblique straight lines (Attneave & Olson, 1967). These findings partly explain why one's form of reference can be a form of gestalt (e.g., "The straight edge of the table") or can be an orientation, such as vertical (e.g., "The picture on the wall is not straight") (Zubin & Choi, 1984).

Beyond the importance of straightness in visual perception, people experience a positive correlation between straightness and things being in order. For instance, people waiting for an event, such buying a ticket to a movie, usually stand in such a way as to form a straight line. There is also a strong relationship between straightness and perceived solidness. Objects that are curved and soft, such as clothes, do not form solid containers in the way that objects with straight lines do, such as boxes.

Image schemas do not simply exist as single entities, but are often linked together to form very natural relationships through different "image schema transformations." Image schema transformations have been shown to play a special role in linking perception and reason. Among the most important image schema transformations are the following (Lakoff, 1987: 443):

(a) "Path-focus to end-point focus": Follow, in imagination, the path of a moving object, and then focus on the point where it comes to rest, or where it will come to rest.
(b) "Multiplex to mass": Imagine a group of several objects. Move away (in your mind) from the group until the cluster of individuals start

to become a single homogeneous mass. Now move back down to the point where the mass turns once again into a cluster.

(c) "Following a trajectory": As we perceive a continuously moving object, we can mentally trace the path it has traversed or the trajectory it is about to traverse.

(d) "Superimposition": Imagine a large sphere and a small cube. Increase the size of the cube until the sphere can fit inside it. Now reduce the size of the cube and put it within the sphere.

Each image schema transformation reflects important aspects of our visual, auditory, or kinesthetic bodily experience. To illustrate, consider how these transformations might apply to our earlier example of the image schema for balance or equilibrium. A situation where several of these transformations interact with the balance image schema is that of handling a group of animals. In order to successfully control and navigate a large number of animals, cattle or sheep perhaps, one needs to maintain the cohesiveness of the group. If a portion of the herd begins to drift apart from the whole, an instance of the multiplex to mass transformation, equilibrium has been lost and action must be taken to restore it. Such a corrective action requires that the path of the drifters be ascertained, following a trajectory, and that their destination be determined and "headed off," path-focus to end-point focus. There are many examples such as this that illustrate the role of image schemas and different transformations in structuring our understanding of real-world phenomena.

This discussion of image schemas and metaphor runs contrary to the popular view that there is some abstract similarity existing between literal and metaphorical concepts, such as our understanding of difficulty in terms of heavy physical weights (Murphy, 1996). There is not an objectively similar set of attributes for concepts such as difficulty and physical weight, nor are there similar features that connect "sunny dispositions," "bright words," and "radiant smiles." Conceptual metaphor theory demonstrates, alternatively, that concepts from different domains are related to one another by virtue of how people are physically constituted, their cognitive abilities, and their interactions with the world.

These developments on the importance of image schemas in structuring abstract concepts have led scholars, in several disciplines, to examine the embodied nature of various abstract ideas and events. Presented below are several extended examples of research that provides additional support for the prominence of image schemas and metaphors in structuring abstract concepts.

Thinking

Metaphor plays an essential role in how people conceive, and talk about, thinking. Cognitive linguistic studies demonstrate that there is an extensive subsystem of metaphors for mind, centered on the idea that THE MIND IS A BODY (Lakoff & Johnson, 1999; Sweetser, 1990). The mapping of the body onto mind gives rise to the following submetaphors:

THINKING IS PHYSICAL FUNCTIONING
IDEAS ARE ENTITIES WITH AN INDEPENDENT EXISTENCE
THINKING OF AN IDEA IS FUNCTIONING PHYSICALLY WITH RESPECT TO AN INDEPENDENTLY EXISTING ENTITY

More specifically, there are four extensive special cases of this metaphor such that thinking is understood as four different kinds of physical functioning: moving, perceiving, manipulating objects, and eating (Lakoff & Johnson, 1999). Consider first the idea that THINKING IS MOVING. This metaphor gives rise to a complex set of mappings:

THINKING IS MOVING (e.g., "My mind was racing")
IDEAS ARE LOCATIONS (e.g., "How did you reach that conclusion?")
REASON IS A FORCE (e.g., "He was forced to accept the plan")
RATIONAL THOUGHT IS MOTION THAT IS DIRECT, DELIBERATE, STEP-BY-STEP, AND IN ACCORD WITH THE FORCE OF REASON (e.g., "Don't skip any steps in figuring out how to solve that problem")
BEING UNABLE TO THINK IS BEING UNABLE TO MOVE (e.g., "I'm stuck")
A LINE OF THOUGHT IS A PATH (e.g., "You should pursue that line of thought")
THINKING ABOUT X IS MOVING IN THE AREA AROUND X (e.g., "I've been pursuing this topic for some time")
COMMUNICATING IS GUIDING (e.g., "He led me to that new idea")
UNDERSTANDING IS FOLLOWING (e.g., "I follow what you are saying")
RETHINKING IS GOING OVER THE PATH AGAIN (e.g., "I need to go back and consider that again")

The metaphor THINKING IS PERCEIVING also has a complex set of mappings, including the following:

THINKING IS PERCEIVING (e.g., "I am trying to see what you are saying")
IDEAS ARE THINGS PERCEIVED (e.g., "The idea became clear")
KNOWING IS SEEING (e.g., "I finally see what you are saying")
ATTEMPTING TO GAIN KNOWLEDGE IS SEARCHING (e.g., "I am looking for the right plan")
AN AID TO KNOWING IS A LIGHT SOURCE (e.g., "He shed light on the new theory")
BEING IGNORANT IS BEING UNABLE TO SEE (e.g., "She has blinders on")

DECEPTION IS PURPOSEFULLY IMPEDING VISION (e.g., "He put up a smokescreen")
DIRECTING ATTENTION IS POINTING (e.g., "Let me point out the benefits of this plan")
BEING RECEPTIVE IS HEARING (e.g., "He is deaf to what you are saying")
AGREEING IS SMELLING (e.g., "Something doesn't smell right about this theory")
PERSONAL PREFERENCE IS TASTE (e.g., "That is a sweet idea")

Manipulating objects is another bodily action used to understand thinking. This THINKING IS OBJECT MANIPULATION metaphor has many mappings, including the following:

THINKING IS OBJECT MANIPULATION (e.g., "Let's toss around some ideas")
IDEAS ARE MANIPULABLE OBJECTS (e.g., "Let's reshape that idea")
COMMUNICATING IS SENDING (e.g., "We exchanged ideas")
UNDERSTANDING IS GRASPING (e.g., "She easily grasped the difficult concept")
INABILITY TO UNDERSTAND IS INABILITY TO GRASP (e.g., "The idea is hard to get hold of")
THE STRUCTURE OF AN IDEA IS THE STRUCTURE OF AN OBJECT (e.g., "That idea has many sides to it")
ANALYZING IDEAS IS TAKING APART OBJECTS (e.g., "He tore apart the argument")

The final embodied metaphor for thinking is ACQUIRING IDEAS IS EATING. Its entailments include the following:

ACCEPTING IDEAS IS EATING (e.g., "He swallowed that idea whole")
INTEREST IN IDEAS IS APPETITE FOR FOOD (e.g., "He has an appetite for learning")
GOOD IDEAS ARE HEALTHFUL FOOD (e.g., "That is a savory idea")
DISTURBING IDEAS ARE DISGUSTING FOODS (e.g., "That idea is shit")
UNAPPEALING IDEAS ARE FLAVORLESS FOODS (e.g., "That is a bland theory")
CONSIDERING IS CHEWING (e.g., "Let's chew on that idea for a bit")
ACCEPTING IS SWALLOWING (e.g., "I can't swallow that idea")
FULLY COMPREHENDING IS DISGESTING (e.g., "That's too much for me to digest")
COMMUNICATING IS FEEDING (e.g., "He was fed several new ideas")

These four metaphors are extremely common in discourse and demonstrate how abstract concepts can be made concrete through comparison to bodily action. But these metaphors are not special to English speakers; linguistic analyses have shown that these same metaphors are also found in Chinese (Yu, 2003). Consider just a few examples of these metaphors (original expression, literal translation, and colloquial meaning):

THINKING IS MOVING
"si-lu" (thinking route/path) "train of thought"
"yun-tou zhuan- xiang" (dizzy-head, losing direction) "confused and disoriented"
"fan-si" (reverse-think) "engage in introspection, self-examination"
"zhui-su" (chase-trace) "trace back to, recall"

THINKING IS PERCEIVING/SEEING
"kan-fa" (see-method) "a way of looking at things"
"kan-chuan" (see-penetrate) "see through something"
"kan-di" (see-low) "look down on, belittle"
"kan-qing" (see-light) "underestimate"

THINKING IS OBJECT MANIPULATION
"sixiang jiaoliu" (exchange of thoughts/ideas) "exchange of ideas"
"pao zai nao hou" (toss at brain back) "ignore idea"
"wa-kong xinsi" (dig-empty thoughts/ideas) "rack one's brain"
"sixiang geda" (thought knot) "a hang-up on one's mind"

ACQUIRING IDEAS IS EATING
"chen-fu guannian" (stale-rotten idea/concept) "an outworn idea"
"sou zhuyi" (spoiled ideas/suggestions) "a lousy idea, a stupid suggestion"
"ru-ji shi-ke" (like-hungry) "acquiring ideas with great eagerness"
"sou-chang gua-du" (search-intestines) "search intently for an idea"

It is not surprising that thinking is conceptualized in embodied ways across cultures because of the prominence that moving, perceiving, manipulating objects, and eating have in people's everyday lives. As Yu (2003: 162) concludes, "The fact that distinct languages show metaphors in a systematic way supports the cognitive status of these metaphors as primarily conceptual, rooted in common human experiences" (also see Neumann, 2001).

Linguistic Action

Abstract concepts such as truth, ideas, justice, and friendship are also talked about in concrete ways, as if they are items that can be physically manipulated. For example, in his poem "Ultimately" (Hemingway, 1960), Ernest

Hemingway writes of truth as if it is something physical that can actually be spit out:

> He tried to spit out the truth;
> Dry-mouthed at first,
> He drooled and clobbered in the end;
> Truth dribbling his chin.

Our understanding of truth as something that can be spit out, in the above case with great difficulty for the person trying to speak honestly, is dependent on some recognition of a metaphorical idea (e.g., truth as a substance that can be ingested and regurgitated when needed). Again, there is an essential tacit connection between human embodiment, especially embodied action, and how we think about different physical and nonphysical concepts. Writers elaborate on these body-based metaphorical concepts in new, creative ways that ordinary readers understand given their own embodied experiences.

The excerpt from Hemingway's poem, shown above, indicates one instance of how people refer to linguistic action (e.g., speaking about the truth) in terms of associations to bodily actions (e.g., spitting out something that has been ingested). Experiences of the body in action, especially those related to oral and head activities and their related body parts, provide a critical source domain for structuring a variety of speech events. For example, one analysis of 175 body-part metaphors in a large corpus showed that body parts and bodily functions are essential source domains for characterizing people's description of talk (Goossens et al., 1995). There are several ways in which people's understanding of human embodiment is metaphorically projected to structure linguistic action.

The first way involves body parts that play a role in speaking, but that are put to a different use (e.g., eating and breathing). For instance, phrases such as "feed" and "force/ram/thrust something down someone's throat" depicts specific interactions between two people in which the speaker transmits something to a listener, and the listener obtains the information by eating it.

A second group characterizes speaking as eating (or part of the process of eating), such as "chew the fat" or "chew the rag" (i.e., "to chat or complain"). Given that both fat and rags can be chewed a long time, with little nutritional value coming from these activities, these idiomatic phrases express the idea of talking about something a long time with little new information to be gained from the experience.

The phrase "eat one's words" (i.e., to admit that one has said something in error) illustrates a different metaphor through linguistic action. By referring to the directionality of eating (i.e., ingesting), compared with the directionality of speaking (i.e., exteriorizing), these idioms express the idea that the speaker's words were somehow destroyed by making them go back to the place from which they arose. This hypothetical action renders the speaker's utterance mute because it no longer has the originally intended effect upon the audience.

On the other hand, the term "regurgitate" (i.e., to report what one has already heard or learned) depicts the same direction of action as does speech and expresses the idea that the speaker has once ingested some idea, but not quite digested it completely (like people with food or liquid) so that it can indeed be thrown up and out of the body.

The experience of breathing underlies many metaphorical phrases for linguistic action, in part because breathing is very much a part of speaking (e.g., "He breathed words of love into her ear"). The phrase "waste one's breath" characterizes the air one breathes as a valuable resource, one that is essential to proper bodily functioning, which should not be expended needlessly. To "cough up" something is to remove a substance (blood, phlegm) that causes bodily, and often breathing, discomfort. When a speaker "chokes back" something, he or she attempts to prevent something from escaping the body, thus expressing the idea of someone exerting great control over what he or she has started to say.

The metaphor "spit out" reflects the idea that the speaker has something of value in the body, which through effort he or she is able to gather up (like spit or phlegm) and say (or expectorate).

Various expressions for linguistic action center on the movement of the visible speech organs. "Keeping one's mouth shut," "opening one's lips," and "closed lipped" describe positions of the mouth and lips to stand for either the presence or absence of speech. Saying something "tongue in cheek" or "to lie through one's teeth" also express different types of linguistic actions (e.g., in gesture, lie) in which contours of the face and mouth metaphorically structure our understanding of what a speaker is communicating.

The bodily posture and experience of listeners captures something about how linguistic actions are understood. When someone "turns a deaf ear" or when something "goes in one ear and out the other," it is clear that the listener is not dedicating the right body part of successful communication.

Beyond the embodied character of linguistic actions, many aspects of nonverbal communication rest on bodily actions. "Patting someone on the back," "bringing/bending the knee to someone," and "tipping someone the wink" are each physical actions that reflect an individual's appreciation, respect, or friendship with another. These nonverbal actions sometimes co-occur with speech, but can also stand alone. "To pat oneself on the back" is a difficult, even ridiculous action to perform, one reason that it expresses the unacceptability of praising oneself.

Our sensory apparatus also plays an important role in various aspects of our metaphorical conceptualization of speaking. For instance, the metaphor "sniff" (i.e., to say something in a complaining manner) rests on the embodied experience that the act of perceiving something with our noses is often accompanied by a special noise (i.e., sniffing). The sniffing noise represents that a person has perceived something of value, which gets transferred to the idea that a listener has understood something of substance. Sniffing noises are often made when something objectionable is smelled and this gets mapped into the domain of linguistic communication to express the idea that the listener has just comprehended an unpleasant idea.

Both people and animals "poke their noses into things," which characterizes the positioning of the body in preparation to smelling something (i.e., dogs into holes in the ground, people into pots on the stove). The metaphorical saying that "he poked his nose into other people's business" suggests that a person has positioned himself to obtain, usually hidden, information. In a related way, "one puts out feelers" as preparation to perceiving something, which metaphorically is understood in the speech domain as putting oneself in a position to obtain information.

Violent physical action provides a rich source domain for characterizing many kinds of linguistic actions. The sport of boxing, in particular, provides the embodied actions underlying many linguistic concepts such as "pulling one's punches," "sparring," or "beating someone to the punch." In "pulling one's punch," speakers soften the impact of what they say for listeners. When speakers "spar" with listeners, the interaction is less serious, more playful, than is a full-fledged fight. And when speakers "beat someone to the punch," they make a point or argument before their listeners do.

A different set of violent actions used to conceptualize linguistic actions include "rap someone over the knuckles" and "box someone's ear." In both cases, the focus in on the painful sensation the listener experiences as a result of what speakers say. Other violent metaphors include "butt out," "kick someone around" (e.g., Richard Nixon's famous statement in 1962 to the press "You won't have Nixon to kick around anymore"), "tear apart," and "choke off." These idiomatic phrases reflect different aspects of situations where one person, the speaker, uses authority over another, with some expressions, such as "tear apart" and "choke off," highlighting the extreme nature of the speaker's actions.

Metaphors such as "make the fur fly," "back-bite," "snap at," "bite someone's head off," and "jump down someone's throat" take as their source domain different violent actions seen in the animal world, especially denoting the arbitrary, unnecessarily hostile, nature of the action given the situation. Describing speakers' linguistic actions using any of these phrases strongly implies that the person is overreacting to something another individual has said or done. A completely different type of violent action motivates "eat your heart out" and "cut off your nose to spite your face." Both metaphors express the tremendous self-inflicted pain a person experiences by his or her own action.

Several metaphors for linguistic action focus on restricted movement. "Tongue tied," "hold your tongue," and "bite your tongue" all refer to the silent consequences of being unable to speak, mostly through self-control. Somewhat related are phrases where some object is clumsily handled, such as "fumble," or where one's actions are awkward, as in "heavy-handed" or "left-handed compliment." When a speaker successfully exchanges information with another, often in cases where a speaker offers a reward to someone else in exchange for something, he or she "hands it to someone."

A particularly interesting metaphor is "shoot one's mouth off." This phrase views speaking in terms of clumsily handling a gun, which accidentally causes it to fire. When a speaker "shoots off his mouth," he wastes a bullet and draws unwanted attention, implying that the person does not really know what he is doing or talking about. On the other hand, speakers who pay excessive attention to what they are saying "split hairs," thereby communicating ideas that are trivial or off the point of the conversation or argument.

The embodied experience of walking motivates various speech actions, with different parts of walking movements being tied to specific ways of speaking. When someone "backtracks" while speaking, he or she reverses directions on the path he or she initially started out on to correct what has already been stated. A different error arises when someone "puts his foot in his mouth," indicating via the metaphor of a serious mishandling of the body when walking that a grave mistake has been made in saying what was just previously said.

There are different degrees of intensity in making speech acts. For instance, a warning or rebuke may be mild or strong. The degree of emphasis is particularly salient in some metaphors. For instance, in the metaphor "raise one's eyebrows" (meaning "express surprise or displeasure"), the speech act must be mild as the embodied action is quite slight. Duration is important in "chew the fat" (a high value in duration) and "go in one ear and out the other" (which implies a very brief duration).

The metaphorical structuring of linguistic action via significant patterns of embodied experience is, of course, tied to image schemas. For instance, the image schema BALANCE (i.e., a symmetrical arrangement of forces around a point or axis) motivates various phrases referring to a person's attempt to restore equilibrium of the body (and mind). When people say "get something off my chest," they describe a forceful action to remove an impediment that causes imbalance. Speakers who get something off their chests remove oppressive forces by merely talking to an appropriate person, often the person most responsible for placing the burden or impediment on the speaker. "Getting something off one's chest," just like "blowing off steam" and "coughing something up," restores a sense of balance or well-being to an individual.

The image schema CONTAINMENT underlies many metaphorical concepts related to our understanding of linguistic action. For instance, our mouths, like our bodies, are experienced as containers, such that when the container is open, linguistic action is possible, and when it is closed, there is only silence. To be "closed-lipped" reflects the silent, closed container, and when one "bites one's lip," the closing of the mouth and lips is done quickly with great force. When people "lie through their teeth," the container is perceived as a hiding place where true information resides, but the container is somewhat defective and we can see through the speaker's shameless attempt to lie about something when the truth can partly be seen. Some metaphors talk of entering the mouth container, as when "one puts words in someone's mouth" or "forces/rams/thrusts something down someone's throat," with the more forceful entry into the container reflecting greater intensity of the speaker's linguistic action.

Embodied CONTAINMENT also refers to cases where objects, or information, are removed from the mouth or head of a speaker, as in "He took the words right out of my mouth" and "pick someone's brains," both of which imply that the speaker is a person possessing some valuable object's) worth stealing.

The importance of the PATH image schema is seen in the metaphors based on walking, such as "backtrack," where the directionality of movement along some path must be reversed. PATH also is relevant to cases of reversed motion, as in the eating metaphors of "eat one's words" and "eat crow," which are specific instances of the general idea of "taking back one's words" (i.e., moving words back along the conduit path on which a speaker first send them).

The image schema of FORCE is central to many of the metaphors based on violent bodily actions noted above. In most of these instances, the force is noticeable because of its extreme nature (e.g., "bite someone's head off" and "snap at someone").

These selected examples clearly illustrate how image schemas connect the domains of embodied action with the domain of linguistic action. Most generally, this examination of metaphor and linguistic action reveals how people use their intuitive phenomenological sense of their bodies to make sense of, and structure, more abstract conceptual domains.

Grammar and Spatial Concepts

Another place to find embodiment in concepts is in the study of numerical systems across languages. Although speakers do not ordinarily understand the embodied character of the numerals in their language, a closer look at many numeral systems reveals that the linguistic labels for numerals are not arbitrary, but are often, in some languages particularly, motivated by embodied experience.

A good illustration of the embodied character of some numeral systems is Mamuo, a central African Niko-Saharan language (Heine, 1997). The first five numerals, 1 through 5, are etymologically opaque, as there appears to be no explanation for the words that refer to them. But the terms for the rest of the numerals are motivated by reference to body parts. Numerals in Mamuo are divided into quinary blocks, based on the five fingers of the human hand. Thus, 5 constitutes the basic numeral and counting starts over with each block of five entities. A second numeral base is 20, which reflects the total number of fingers and toes, which results in a vigesimal system (i.e., a system having 20 as its primary numerical base).

The body-part model for numerals in Mamuo is not unique to this language but is found in most languages of the world. The human hand is the most widely used model for structuring numeral systems, with the numeral 5 constituting the smallest recurrent base number (i.e., the number from which counting begins again) in languages throughout the world (Majewicz, 1981). Even the decimal system in English, for instance, relates to embodiment in terms of the numbers of fingers on our two hands (i.e., a system based on 10). Some languages appear to have numeral systems unrelated to the body-part model. But embodiment still plays a role in many cases. Thus, in Sotho, the verb for "jump" denotes the numeral 6. Why might the verb "jump" be related to 6? The motivation for this is that one must "jump over from one hand to the other" in counting upward from 5 to 6. This embodied action of jumping to the other hand stands for the actual numeral 6.

Some languages never explicitly mention the word "hand" in reference to any numerals, but, once again, there is an implicit relationship between the hand and numerals. For example, speakers of Api, a language of the New Hebrides, do not say anything explicit about the hand in their numerals for 6 through 9, because hand in implicit in the morpheme for "new." Thus, six ("otai"), is "new one," seven ("oluao") is "new two," eight ("otolu") is "new three," and nine ("ovari") is "new four," whereas ten ("luc luna") is "two hands."

A spectacular example of how body parts motivate numeral systems is seen in parts of New Guinea, where there are linguistic terms only for the first five numerals, but speakers can refer gesturally to numerals as high as 20 by using the fingers on one hand, then going up to the wrist, elbow, the upper arm, and around back to the other hand (Greenberg, 1978). Counting is not the only arithmetical operation motivated by embodied experience. Some language multiply by "two hands and two fingers," "two hands and three fingers," and so on (Stampe, 1976).

Many languages describe spatial orientation in terms of body parts. In Yucatec, a Mayan language of Mexico, the body-part term for back ("paach") denotes "behind," front ("tian") refers to "in front of," eye ("eich") denotes "inside," and marrow ("tu' u'") is used to talk of "in"

(Goldap, 1992; Stolz, 1994). This mapping of body part to spatial orientation is one of the source domains used in the experience of reference points. Other models include environmental landmarks and dynamic concepts. But the body-part model (i.e., the body in its most upright position) is clearly the most widely used in conceptualizing space.

The human body pervades the most significant model for talking about spatial orientation. But animal bodies also serve as structural templates for talking about and expressing spatial relations (i.e., the zoomorphic model). Chalcatango Mixtec have different terms for "human back" and "animal back," which shapes the ways different objects are conceptualized (Brugman & McCauley, 1986). For example, a table is conceived of as an animal whose back is the table top and whose belly is the table's underside. The top of a wall is described by the name of an animal back. Despite such examples of animal backs being used to refer to inanimate objects, no language conceptualizes of spatial relations in terms only of the zoomorphic model.

Cross-linguistic research demonstrates the pervasiveness of the human body in referring to spatial concepts (Heine, 1997). Consider some examples from the following set of prepositions:

The spatial concept "up" is described in terms of human body parts, especially by reference to the human hand. In 87% of all African and 61% of all Oceanic languages that used body parts for "up" terms, such as "above," "up," and "over," the word "hand" is grammaticized for this specific purpose.

The spatial concept of "down" is most widely described in both African and Oceanic languages using environmental landmarks (e.g., "earth" and "ground"). However, body parts still play an important role in both language families in talking about "down" concepts. In African, "buttocks" and "anus" are frequently mentioned and are seen in 85% of all languages that have a grammaticized morpheme for "down." Oceanic languages refer to either "foot" or "leg" as the primary (59%) body part in grammaticized morphemes for "down."

The concept of "front" is most frequently conceptualized in terms of the human face in 53% of the African and 72% of the Oceanic languages examined, with "eye" and then "breast" also being widely seen in African languages. Environmental landmarks are rarely seen in linguistic expressions about "front."

The concept of "back" is, not surprisingly, discussed in terms of the human back, as seen in 78% of the African and 95% of the Oceanic languages. "Buttocks" and "anus" are body parts widely seen in African expressions for the "back" concept. Once again, environmental landmarks are virtually absent as source domains for the "back" concept.

Spatial definitions are seen in how African and Oceanic languages refer to the spatial concept of "in." The "belly/stomach" body part accounts for 92% of African expressions, with far fewer expressions referring to other body parts such as "palm" (of hand) and "heart." But Oceanic languages use a variety of body parts relatively equally in talk of "in," including "tooth," "body-skin," "heart," "liver," and "bowels."

The body's extremities (e.g., hand or arm) are rarely referred to in talking about the spatial concepts of "up," "down," "front," "back," and "in" (Heine, 1989). Why might the extremities provide so little of the source domains in conceptualizing these spatial orientations? A good possibility is that our experience of the body's extremities simply does not facilitate an understanding of these particular spatial concepts. But the concepts of "left" and "right" refer to the extremities (i.e., "hand" to talk of left-right spatial orientation (Werner, 1904)). The location of the hand in relation to the rest of the body makes the hand more appropriate for the expression of "left" and "right" than it does for "up" and "down." On the other hand, it is curious that the body parts "nose" and "knee-cap" are not used in speaking of "front."

One linguistic proposal argues that the following scale underlies the world's languages in referring to spatial locations: down – up – in – front – back (Heine, Ulrike, & Hunnemeyer, 1991). Under this view, if any one of the five concepts is conceived of in terms of a body-part word, then none of the concepts to its right may be derived from some nonembodied source, such as environmental landmarks. Consequently, it is unlikely that a body-part term, such as "buttocks," would be used to talk of "down," and a landmark term for either "up," "in," "front," or "back." Similarly, the body-part model would not be used in talking of "back" or "front" if described in terms of environmental landmarks.

A relevant distinction in mapping body parts is that the upper half of the body plays a larger role in conceptualizing of spatial orientation than does the body's lower half. This may be due to the upper body being perceptually more differentiated and more salient for speakers wishing to talk about spatial concepts. For any given language, then, it seems more likely to call one's toes "fingers of the foot" than to call one's fingers "toes of the hand." Many East and Southeast Asian languages refer to the anklebone as "foot-eye," yet eyes are not described as "anklebones of the head" (Matisoff, 1978; Schladt, 1997).

The human body also provides a framework for talking about many kinds of abstract, schematic notions. Thus, reference to "top end" or "top" are done in terms of the head, "bottom end" in terms of the buttocks or foot, "opening" or "edge" in terms of the mouth, and "narrow sections" is understood as the neck or wrist. Different languages refer to objects in different ways according to this general body-part to abstract-schematic set of relations. Thus, in Tzeltal, objects such as knives, pots, leaves, feathers, and plants have conceptual properties arising from different body parts (Levinson, 1994).

Political Ideas

We have long been accustomed to the metaphor of the "body politic" ever since the work of philosopher Thomas Hobbes. The "body politic" metaphor is mostly thought to operate at a general level, but new research reveals the depth of this embodied experience in structuring political ideas. One analysis of the debates in the United States in 1990 over the Gulf War showed that several image schemas enabled people to reason about international politics (Beer, 2001). Balance is a central term in international relations. "Balance of power" expresses the shared wisdom of foreign policy. The terms "balance" and its cognates occur in the debate a total of 107 times. In the case of "balance," we come to understand more clearly an entire complex of related application. Representative Peter Fazio (D-Oregon) uses "balance" to lay out the national pieces of the Gulf region and attempts to structure the forces of that region on a very complex board: "If we think about what is the long-term effect here, we have embraced Iraq to counter Iran. Now we are embracing Syria to counter Iraq. After we decapitated Iraq in this war, if that is what happens, what then is next in the region? How do we instill a new government in Iraq? How do we balance the forces in the region? Will we have to occupy Iraq? Will we have to defend Iraq against Syria or Turkey or Iran in the near future in order to gain so-called or restore so-called balance in the region?" (CR, H-132).

Blockage includes many semantically related terms such as block, blockage, blockaded, blockading, blockages, blocked, blocking, and blocks. Related words are embargo, force, intervention, penetration, and sanctions. "Blockage" itself appears relatively infrequently, but "blockade" is used 69 times. In the case of the Gulf War, blockage is seen in the form of an economic embargo that is a major alternative strategic option. "Embargo" and its cognates appear 260 times. Opposite terms, such as "unblockage" or its distant cognates "liberation" and "free," appear 167 times. "Penetration" is the opposite of blockage in another dimension. When liberation relieves or dissolves the blockage, penetration pierces it. "Penetration" was used infrequently, but the notion of "intervene" was used 374 times. "Intervention," like "blockage," is a standard means of foreign policy and is densely connected in the theory and practice of international relations.

Center-periphery has wide play in international political economy. "Center" emerges as the key term in this dyad, appearing 37 times compared with "periphery's" 3. "Center" evokes a very clear circular spatial grid. Indeed, as Sen. Steven Symms (R-Idaho) used "center," he conjured up an image of a spider – Saddam Hussein – sitting at the center of a web of domestic power: "The Iraqi dictator sits at the center of a web of state, party, military, and secret police organizations" (CR, S-380). When the web spreads outward beyond the national boundaries of Iraq, it entangles an ever-growing number of participants, including the international world of terrorism. However, as in a real web, control always remains at the center. Indeed, as Sen. Orrin Hatch (R-Utah) suggested: "We all know that the world's most vicious terrorists have taken up residence in

Baghdad... Terrorists are on the move, and weapons, and equipment are being put into place. Iraq stands at the center of three actions, providing the crucial support – false passports, sophisticated equipment, vast sums of money – that only a state sponsor of terror has available" (CR, S-385). Senator Daniel Akaka (D-Hawaii) invoked the schema of center to describe contemplated actions against Saddam Hussein: "Following Iraq's illegal takeover of Kuwait, the United Nations has adopted 12 resolutions over the past months in an attempt to resolve the crisis peacefully and without the use of force. The centerpiece of the UN initiatives was an agreement to apply economic sanctions against Iraq, which would result in its peaceful withdrawal from Kuwait" (CR, S-396).

"Periphery" is an opposite of "center" and its textual use illustrates another important dimension of bodily orientation. For example, Sen. Paul Sarbanes (D-Maryland) distinguishes between vital (or central) and peripheral components of the national interest: "Of course, we have interests in the Gulf. But it is essential to distinguish between peripheral interests and vital interests. Vital interests exist when our national security is truly at risk. Vital interests are those you kill and die for" (CR, S-154). In much the same way, peripheral elements of the human body – such as skin or even limbs – may be sacrificed in order to maintain the "center" of the body – the life essence, or "soul."

"Collection" shows up most frequently as "collective" and is used to refer to the individual leader or nation and common activities taken in concert by democratic societies. The American president acts as the collective representative of a democratic people, mobilizing and applying their united forces and strength. As Rep. Frank McCloskey (D-Indiana) pointed out, "Such power ultimately is not up to one man, but the collective wisdom of the people through their elected representative" (CR, H-152). Democratic judgment, conscience, and decision are collective. As Rep. Patricia Schroeder (D-Colorado) pointed out: "That is what this democratic principle is all about. This is not a country where we recognize that one person has all the wisdom. Every one of us has feet of clay, and the best judgment we can have is a lot of collective judgment in this wonderful Republic" (CR, H-153). Another representative, Rep. Henry Waxman (D-California), noted that America has a leadership role and "bears the brunt of our collective security burden" (CR, H-156).

"Compulsion" is used as a frame to distinguish between free and slave societies, the free American Self and the enslaved Other. One of the marks distinguishing the oppressive regime of Saddam Hussein is the use of compulsory labor. The theme of compulsion also enters the democratic debate in Congress. Senator Joseph Libermann (D-Connecticut) made it clear that he did not wish to create an unseemly compulsion of the president to go to war. Rather, he wanted Congress to share the collective responsibility for the actions that must be taken: "I make my choice today to support the

President of the United States, to give him not a compulsion to go to war, but an authorization to commit our troops to battle should he determine it necessary to protect our national security" (CR, S-376).

The network of political life is constructed through contact. The world of international relations is bound together through contact. As Sen. Trent Lott (R-Mississippi) noted: "The world is united – and I have to commend President Bush for the effort he has made through the United Nations and with personal diplomacy, personal contacts with leaders all over the world to bring the world together, unite against the aggression of one man, really, Saddam Hussein" (CR, S-376). The great issues of war and peace also depend on contact. During the Gulf War debate, Sen. Patrick Moynihan (D-New York) noted that "No battle plan ever survived contact with the enemy" (CR, S-394). Likewise, Sen. Hank Brown (R-Colorado) evinced belief in contacts by stating his hope "that economic sanctions and diplomatic contacts would convince Saddam to restore Kuwaiti sovereignty" (CR, S-396).

"Container" obviously translates into "containment," one of the major orienting terms of postwar international relations. The Gulf War debate evokes new nuances. Iraq is a container that contains Kuwait, and Kuwait is a container that contains significant territory and oil. As Sen. Symms reported: "According to maps distributed to Iraqi embassies, this territorial enclave consists of Kuwait's Northern Province which contains approximately one-third of Kuwait's territory, and one-fifth of its oil" (CR, S-380).

"Containment," in contrast to "container," suggests a state of being rather than an actual object. As Sen. Kerry (D-Massachusetts) pointed out: "We sustained our fight against the Soviets for 40 years after Stalin took over Eastern Europe. We contained Stalinism, and in time, an isolated and decaying Soviet Union has been going through a process of caving in" (CR, S-249). The proposed strategy of containment took on a more economic flavor. As Senator Sarbanes spoke of the Iraqi case, the assumption of those who supported a sanctions policy was that over time "as the bite of these economic sanctions were felt and the punitive containment – the embargo, the blockage, the use of force to make the sanctions effective through the blockade – as that bite (became) stronger and stronger with the passage of time, it would over time lead to his departure from Kuwait" (CR, S-151). Finally, the *New York Times* talked of the wider political and military containment when mentioning what would happen if economic containment was not effective: "the conflict would then become regionally destabilizing, on a scale that is difficult precisely to define but that could become also impossible to contain" (CR, S-155).

This discussion demonstrates how many key political concepts can be traced back to bodily referents. Attraction is connected to alliance, balance to the balance of power, physical blockage to blockade, center-periphery to core and marginal interests, collection to collective interests as well as collective defense and security, compulsion to the use of force and coercion, contact to diplomatic discourse and military friction, and container to containment.

Mathematical Concepts

Mathematics is reputed to be the ideal case of disembodied thought. On the surface, mathematics seems to reflect highly abstract, transcendental ideas. But recent studies suggest that mathematical concepts are formed by two fundamental types of embodied metaphors: grounding metaphors and linking metaphors (Lakoff & Nunez, 2000). Grounding metaphors situate mathematical ideas in everyday embodied experience. For instance, grounding metaphors allow us to conceptualize arithmetic operations in terms of forming collections, constructing objects, or moving through space. These metaphor preserve image-schematic structures so that inferences about collecting, constructing, and moving are mapped onto the abstract domain of arithmetic.

Some of the most basic grounding metaphors are the following:

ARITHMETIC IS OBJECT COLLECTION

- numbers are collections of physical objects of uniform size
- the mathematical agent is the collector of objects
- the results of an arithmetic operation is a collection of objects
- the size of the number is the physical size ggvolume) of the collection
- equations are scales weighing collections that balance
- addition is putting collections together to form larger collections
- subtraction is taking smaller collections from larger ones to form other collections
- multiplication is the repeated addition of collections of the same size a given number of times
- division is the repeated dividing up of a given collection into as many smaller collections of a given size as possible
- zero is an empty collection

ARITHMETIC IS OBJECT CONSTRUCTION

- numbers are physical objects
- arithmetic operations are acts of object construction
- the results of an arithmetic operation is a constructed object
- the size of the number is the size of the object
- equations are scales weighing objects that balance
- addition is putting objects together with other objects to form larger objects
- subtraction is taking smaller objects from larger objects to form other objects

- multiplication is the repeated addition of objects of the same size a given number of times
- division is the repeated segmentation of a given object into as many objects of a given smaller size as possible
- zero is the absence of any object

Everyday talk about arithmetic reveals the constraining presence of these different governing metaphors, including "A trillion is a big number." "How many 5's are there in 20?" "There are four 5s in 23, and 3 left over." "How many times does 2 go into 10?" "If 10 is on one side of the equation and 7 is on the other, what do you have to add to 7 to balance the equation?"

Different linguistic examples distinguish the Object Collection metaphor from the Object Construction metaphor.

Object Collection:
"How many more than 5 is 8?"
"8 is 3 more than 5."

Object Construction:
"If you put 2 and 2 together, it makes 4."
"What is the product of 5 and 7?"
"Two is a small fraction of 248."

A different grounding metaphor is

ARITHMETIC IS MOTION
- numbers are located on a path
- the mathematical agent is a traveler along that path
- arithmetic operations are acts of moving along the path
- the result of an arithmetic operation is a location on the path
- zero is the origin (starting point)
- the smallest whole number (one) is a step forward from the origin
- the size of the number of the length of the trajectory from the origin to the location
- equations are routes to the same location
- addition of a given quantity is taking steps a given distance to the right (or forward)
- subtraction of a given quantity is taking steps a given direction to the left (or backward)
- multiplication is the repeated addition of quantities of the same size a given number of times
- division is the repeated segmentation of a path of a given length into as many smaller paths of a given length as possible

Once more, everyday language illustrates the ARITHMETIC IS MOTION metaphor, such as "How close are these two numbers?" "37 is far away from 189,712," "4.9 is almost 5," "The result is around 40," "Count up to 20 without skipping any numbers," "Count backward from 20," "Count to 100, starting at 20," and "Name all the numbers from 2 to 20." These examples show how embodied metaphors underlie systematic talk of arithmetic and arithmetic operations. Zero is not the same kind of thing as a number in the Object Collection and Object Construction metaphors, but is a number under the Motion metaphor. Thus, for the Object Collection and Construction metaphors, zero represents the absence of attributes, but under the Motion metaphor zero is a specific location in space. Lakoff and Nunez argue that the Collection and Construction metaphors are so basic that it took a long time for zero to be included as a number.

There are two related experiences that serve as the metaphorical basis for set theory: (1) grouping objects with conceptual containers, and (2) comparing the number of objects in two groupings. The source domain of the metaphor employs a container schema that specifies a bounded region of space, with an interior, a boundary, and an exterior. Objects within the boundary are in the container. Sets in mathematics are conceptualized as container schemas and the numbers of the sets are viewed as objects inside the container:

THE SETS-AS-CONTAINER-SCHEMA METAPHOR
- a set is a container schema
- a member of a set is an object in a container schema
- a subset of a set is a container-schema within a container-schema

This metaphor can easily be extended to metaphorically define unions, intersections, and complements. A different metaphor, the SETS ARE OBJECTS metaphor, makes it possible for objects to be set numbers. Although this metaphor shows how sets can be members of other sets, combining this metaphor with the SETS-AS-CONTAINER-SCHEMA metaphor illustrates why a set cannot be a member of itself. The reason is that the container-schema can not be inside itself.

My discussion here is limited to arithmetical metaphors. Lakoff and Nunez (2000) provide more extensive analyses of how embodied metaphors underlie many aspects of complex mathematics, including topics in logic, transfinite numbers, points at infinity, infinitesimals, and so on. They show how the basic cognitive mechanisms found throughout human conceptual systems (i.e., image schemas, conceptual metaphors, conceptual blends) are also part of where mathematics comes from. As they note, "Mathematics is not built into the universe. The portrait of mathematics has a human face." More importantly, mathematics comes into being because of the kinds of brains and bodies we possess. These are provocative, and certainly speculative ideas, on what is traditionally viewed as one of the most disembodied abstract concepts. Yet these analyses are quite consistent with the evidence described in this chapter on the embodied character of many concrete and abstract concepts.

Questions about Image Schemas

The fact that one can talk about different kinds of image schemas and different ways in which these can be transformed certainly suggests that image schemas are definable mental representations. But how are image schemas represented, given their cross-modal character? Where might image schemas be represented in the brain, given that they arise from recurring bodily experiences that cut across vision, audition, kinesthetic movement, and so on (i.e., are the SOURCE-PATH-GOAL and MOMENTUM schemas encoded in visual cortex or some other part of the brain)? The abstract, yet still definable, character of image schemas does not provide easy answers to these questions. At this point, linguists and psychologists should be cautious in making concrete claims about how and where image schemas might be mentally represented. Image schemas may best be understood as experiential gestalts that do not necessarily get encoded as explicit mental representations.

A different question concerns which aspects of recurring bodily experiences necessarily give rise to image schemas. For instance, like most people and animals, I regularly scratch itches on my skin. Does this mean that I must have a SCRATCH image schema? I do not believe that people have SCRATCH image schemas, primarily because these are not part of our cross-modal experience. However, scratching behavior helps restore bodily equilibrium and thus is part of the varied bodily experiences that give rise to a BALANCE schema. Most generally, the bodily behaviors that will give rise to image schemas are those that are recurring and help solve adaptive problems. Schemas such as BALANCE, SOURCE-PATH-GOAL, and MOMENTUM contribute to overall body schemas that help ensure human survival.

The emergent nature of image schemas as in-the-moment embodied simulations is best understood theoretically in terms of the complex interplay of brain, body, and world. Image schemas may be described as emergent properties, a kind of structural coupling between brain, body, and world, that arise from different "cycles of operation" constituting a person's life. Image schemas reflect a form of stability within cognitive systems. According to self-organization theory, order in a system arises around attractors that help create and hold stable patterns within the system. Attractors are preferred patterns, such that if the system is started from one state it will evolve until it arrives at the attractors and will stay there in the absence of other factors. An attractor can be a point (e.g., the center of a bowl containing a rolling ball), a regular path (e.g., a planetary orbit), a complex series of states (e.g., the metabolism of a cell), or an infinite sequence (called a strange attractor). A complex system will have many attractors and the study of self-organizing systems is focused on investigating the forms and dynamics of these attractors.

My suggestion is that image schemas are attractors within human self-organizing systems. Attractors, such as BALANCE, SOURCE-PATH-GOAL, RESISTANCE, VERTICALITY, and PATH reflect emerging points of stability in a system as it engages in real-world interaction. New, surprising patterns encountered in the environment throw a system into momentary chaos (e.g., the system goes out of BALANCE), until the system, through its self-assembly process, reorganizes and reaches a new stability (e.g., reaches a new state of equilibrium or BALANCE). The important point here is that attractors are not localized representations, but emerging patterns of entire systems in action (i.e., interplay of brain, body, and world). In this way, the stable properties of image schemas (e.g., the topographic structure of something like SOURCE-PATH-GOAL) are not separate from sensorimotor activity. Image schemas should not be reduced to sensorimotor activity, but it is a mistake to view image schemas as mental representations that are abstracted away from experience. One implication of this dynamical view is that each construal of an image schema will have a different profile depending on the overall state of the organism involved in some activity and past basins of attractions created within the system (i.e., past simulations of a particular behavioral modes such as BALANCE).

Question about Conceptual Metaphors

The cognitive linguistic research on conceptual metaphor has provided significant evidence on the embodied grounding of abstract thought. But there are several problems with the theory. First, conceptual metaphors appear to differ in the way they are experientially grounded (Grady, 1997, 1999). For instance, consider the well-known conceptual metaphor MORE IS UP (e.g., "Inflation is up this year"). It is easy to correlate having more of some objects or substance (i.e., quantity) with seeing the level of those objects or substance rise (i.e., verticality). But many conceptual metaphors do not suggest such straightforward experiential correlations. For instance, the well-known conceptual metaphors THEORIES ARE BUILDINGS and LOVE IS A JOURNEY do not seem to have the same kind of correlation in experience as seen in MORE IS UP. Thus, actual travel has little to do with the progress of relationships, and theories are not closely tied to the buildings in which people generate, discuss, and dismantle these ideas.

A related problem with conceptual metaphor theory is that it does not explain why certain source-to-target domain mappings are not likely to occur (Grady, 1997, 1999). For instance, a common way for people to think about the concepts of "theory" is in terms of the conceptual metaphor THEORIES ARE BUILDINGS. This conceptual metaphor motivates many meaningful linguistic expressions such as "The theory needs to be buttressed" or "The foundation for your theory is shaky." But some aspects of buildings are clearly not mapped onto the domain of theories, which is one reason why it sounds odd to say "The theory has no windows."

One problem that metaphor theorists have long struggled with is why some portions of a source domain get mapped onto a target domain, but not others. Consider the expression "This book is hard to digest." We readily recognize this expression as conveying something about the domain of thinking in terms of the domain of eating. Yet only certain aspects of what we know about eating get mapped into our understanding of thinking. Thus, we rarely hear people talk about their mouths in conventional expressions about thinking, but we do hear people say things such as "The author tried to bite off more than he could chew." What accounts for some expressions being acceptable and others not? What explains the "gaps" in metaphorical mapping processes?

Another problem for metaphor theory concerns how different conceptual metaphors relate to one another. Conceptual metaphors differ considerably. Some metaphors have greater detail and complexity in the kind of inferences they evoke. For instance, the conceptual metaphor MORE IS UP relates quantity to vertical elevation, as in "Gas prices are up this year" or "Inflation has stayed down over the last four years." This mapping of vertical elevation into quantity leads to a straightforward set of metaphorical mappings. Yet consider the conceptual metaphor LOVE IS A JOURNEY, as in "Our relationship is at a cross-roads" or "My marriage is on the rocks." In fact, LOVE IS A JOURNEY inherits the structure of, and elaborates on, the more general metaphorical idea of LONG-TERM PURPOSEFUL ACTIVITIES ARE JOURNEYS (Lakoff, 1993). Although these two metaphorical mappings seem logically related, it is difficult to determine which conceptual metaphors can be elaborated and are susceptible to being inherited.

A further challenge for metaphor theory is that some metaphors are equally appropriate to describe different conceptual domains. For instance, the word "feed" can be used to describe a professor's teaching style, as in "The professor spoon-feeds his students," as well as to talk about a completely different domain, as in "The minor leagues feed players into major league baseball." How may theorists account for this wide range of metaphorical uses to talk about abstract concepts?

A New View of Embodied Metaphor

An interesting solution to these problems suggests that conceptual metaphors are not the most basic level at which metaphorical mappings exist in human thought and experience. Grady (1997) argued that the strong correlation in everyday embodied experience leads to the creation of "primary" metaphors. Some of the most prominent primary metaphors are the following:

INTIMACY IS CLOSENESS (e.g., "We have a close relationship")
DIFFICULTIES ARE BURDENS (e.g., "She's weighed down by responsibilities")
AFFECTION IS WARMTH (e.g., "They greeted me warmly")
IMPORTANT IS BIG (e.g., "Tomorrow is a big day")
MORE IS UP (e.g., "Prices are high")
SIMILARITY IS CLOSENESS (e.g., "Those colors aren't the same, but they're close")
ORGANIZATION IS PHYSICAL STRUCTURE (e.g., "How do theories fit together?")
HELP IS SUPPORT (e.g., "Support your local charities")
TIME IS MOTION (e.g., "Time flies")
STATES ARE LOCATIONS (e.g., "I'm close to being in a depression")
CHANGE IS MOTION (e.g., "My health has gone from bad to worse")
PURPOSES ARE DESTINATIONS (e.g., "He'll be successful, but isn't there yet")
CAUSES ARE PHYSICAL FORCES (e.g., "They pushed the bill through Congress")
KNOWING IS SEEING (e.g., "I see what you mean")
UNDERSTANDING IS GRASPING (e.g., "I've never been able to grasp complex math")

These metaphorical correlations arise out of our embodied functioning in the world. In each case, the source domain of the metaphor comes from the body's sensorimotor system. A primary metaphor is metaphorical mapping for which there is an independent and direct experiential basis and independent linguistic evidence. A "compound" or "complex" metaphor, on the other hand, is a self-consistent metaphorical complex composed of more than one primary metaphor. Complex metaphors are created by blending primary metaphors and thereby fitting together small metaphorical pieces into larger metaphorical wholes.

For instance, consider the following three primitive metaphors: PERSISTING IS REMAINING ERECT, STRUCTURE IS PHYSICAL STRUCTURE, and INTERRELATED IS INTERWOVEN. These three primitives can be combined in different ways to give rise to compound metaphors that have traditionally been seen as conceptual metaphors. But the combination of these primitives allows metaphorical concepts without gaps. Thus, combining PERSISTING IS REMAINING ERECT with STRUCTURE IS PHYSICAL STRUCTURE provides for a compound THEORIES ARE BUILDINGS that nicely motivates the metaphorical inferences that theories need support and can collapse, and so on, without any mappings such as that theories need windows. In a similar way, the combination of STRUCTURE IS PHYSICAL STRUCTURE and INTERRELATED IS INTERWOVEN gives rise to a different metaphorical compound for theories, namely, THEORIES ARE FABRICS. This compound metaphor gives rise to the reasonable inferences that theories can unravel or may be woven together, without generating less likely entailments such as that theories are colorful in the way that some fabrics have colors.

This view of the embodied basis for metaphorical thought and language solves the "poverty of mapping" problem often noted for conceptual metaphor and other theories of metaphor (Grady, 1997). There is no need to posit specific mechanisms that override parts of source-to-target-domain mappings in primitive metaphors because of the positive correlation in embodied experience between the source and target domains (Grady, 1997). Moreover, the correlation between source and target domains may possibly be instantiated in the body via neural connections (Lakoff & Johnson, 1999). Under this view, neural connections in the brain may reflect how inferences from the sensorimotor source domain (i.e., verticality) are projected onto the subjective target (i.e., quantity).

Quite generally, metaphor is an extended consequence of topographic mappings, As in all topographic mappings, the structure of the source domain is preserved in the target domain because the neurons of the former map to (i.e., stimulate) the latter through reentrant signaling (or its equivalent). How do these connections form? Consider the MORE IS UP metaphor. In this mapping, the abstract domain of quantity or value correlates with the relative changes along the vertical axis of the spatial domain, as in "my stocks skyrocketed" and "his productivity is way up." These correlations occur by the neural networks characterizing each of these domains are coactivated in everyday experience, as when we pile more books on the desk and their height goes up or we add water to a container. If the mappings are connected by reentrant pathways, coactivation will strengthen the connections. Once those connections have formed, the relations in the source domain of verticality will be preserved by the mapping and therefore can form the basis of inferences in the target domain of quantity. If something shoots up, it is propelled quickly upward and in a very short time is much higher than before. Hence, the phrase "her fame skyrocketed" indicates a sudden and substantial increase in celebrity. Metaphor, then, is a neural mechanisms that enables networks used in sensorimotor activity also to serve as the substrates hat make abstract reason possible.

Is Cognitive Linguistic Evidence Relevant to the Study of Cognition?

As is the case with all scientific methods, there are limitations to the strategy of trying to infer something about conceptual structure from a systematic analysis of linguistic structure and behavior. The primary limitation is that shared by most linguistic research, namely the problem of making conclusions about phenomena based on the individual analyst's own intuitions. Many cognitive scientists believe that trying to infer aspects of conceptual knowledge from an analysis of systematic patterns of linguistic structure makes these theories appear post hoc. For instance, the claim that the systematicity in expressions such as "He's wasting our time," "I save an hour doing my paper on the computer," and "I can no longer invest that much energy into my marriage" is due to the presence of an independent, preexisting conceptual metaphor TIME IS MONEY provides only a motivated explanation for linguistic behavior. Cognitive scientists wish to predict behavior in advance according to the hypothetico-deductive method of scientific inference. What they seek is empirical, objective evidence that people's conceptual knowledge somehow predicts the existence of different linguistic behavior, not that people's linguistic behavior can be explained by positing theoretical entities such as conceptual metaphor. As argued by psychologist Sam Glucksberg, in his review of Koveceses' book *Metaphor and Emotion* (2000), "From the perspective of cognitive science, the cognitive linguistics program, as exemplified by scholars such as Kovecses, is overly (and, in my mind, unnecessarily) limited. It would benefit greatly from a deployment of convergent operations – that is, multiple methods to validate inferences drawn from linguistic evidence" (Glucksberg, 2002: 765).

This skepticism about the theoretical claims of cognitive linguists about the embodied, metaphorical nature of abstract concepts is surely reasonable. All scientific theories require the support of evidence obtained from convergent operations. But I strongly reject the implicit assumption that cognitive linguistic research stands outside of "cognitive science," which presumably possesses appropriate scientific methods to satisfactorily test important hypotheses about the human mind. First, the detailed analyses of how people talk about abstract concepts, only some of which have been described in this chapter, must be explained, and not merely dismissed out of hand, as is done by many psychologists and philosophers. The vast majority of studies in experimental psycholinguistics on metaphor comprehension focus on simple resemblance, or "A is like B," metaphors, such as "My lawyer is a shark," and ignore systematic conventional metaphors, such as those described above. However, cognitive linguistics has demonstrated the pervasiveness of conventional metaphors of varying types in speech and writing. This linguistic evidence must be explained by psycholinguists who propose general models of metaphor understanding.

Psychologists sometimes defend their neglect of embodied, conventional metaphors by arguing that some cognitive linguistic analyses are contrary to their own intuitions. Thus, psychologists voice skepticism about the intuitive, introspectionist methods of cognitive linguistics, but then justify their neglect of conventional metaphors because of their own intuitions! It would be far better, in my view, for psychologists and others to explicitly study embodied metaphors for abstract concepts according to accepted empirical methods and make decisions about cognitive linguistic claims based on these studies, and not simply to dismiss this work out of hand. Chapter 6 offers a more detailed discussion of some of this work, much of which is supportive of cognitive linguistic claims on embodied metaphors.

Apart from concerns about whether cognitive linguistic claims about abstract concepts are "psychologically real," there are some issues about cognitive linguistic research methods that should be further examined. For example, exactly what constitutes sufficient "systematicity" among conventional expressions to properly infer that these are motivated by some underlying conceptual metaphor? How does one determine the appropriate level of generality when identifying conceptual metaphors? Thus, is the appropriate source domain for the classic LIFE IS A JOURNEY metaphor really journeys, and not some other idea, such as travel, movement from one place to another, or physical movement of any sort? Furthermore, how do conceptual metaphors relate to one another within human conceptual systems? Cognitive linguists have various responses to some of these questions (see Gibbs, 1994; Grady, 1999; Kovecses, 2000b; Lakoff, 1990, 1993; Yu, 1999). But cognitive linguists need to provide more explicit criteria for identifying conceptual metaphors that scholars in other disciplines may employ in conducting their own empirical investigations on the possible embodied metaphorical nature of certain abstract concepts.

Conceptual metaphors as prototypical representations are assumed to exist as enduring knowledge structures in long-term memory and are essential to the content of everyday, abstract concepts. Yet cognitive psychologists are often skeptical of this claim, primarily because they doubt whether linguistic evidence alone can reveal much about human conceptual systems (Murphy, 1996). One instance of this skepticism about metaphors as conceptual prototypes is seen in the problem of multiple metaphors (Murphy, 1996; Gibbs, 1996). According to cognitive linguistics analyses, the concept of love, for example, can be understood through several different metaphors (e.g., LOVE IS A JOURNEY, LOVE IS INSANITY, LOVE IS AN OPPONENT, LOVE IS A VALUABLE COMMODITY). The entailments of these different metaphors vary in certain respects. Thus, LOVE IS A JOURNEY refers to the structure of a love relationship over time, whereas LOVE IS AN OPPONENT personifies love as an opponent against whom we often struggle. These different metaphors appear, at times, to be inconsistent with one another and it is unclear how to resolve such inconsistencies in the mental representation for our concept of love.

This argument preserves a view of concepts as monolithic entities that should be internally consistent. But the so-called problem of multiple metaphors for concepts can be easily handled if we view these prototypical concepts not as fixed, static structures, but as temporary representations that are dynamic and context-dependent. The LOVE IS A JOURNEY metaphor may better reflect a particular embodied conceptualization of love in certain situations, whereas LOVE IS AN OPPONENT may arise in forming a concept for love in other situations. These alternative ways of thinking about human concepts allow, and even encourage, the use of multiple metaphors to access different aspect of our rich, body-based knowledge about love to differentially conceptualize of these experiences at various moments of our experience. Each metaphoric construal of a concept in some context results in a concept that is independent as a temporary representation apart from embodied source domain information in long-term memory. My suggestion, then, is that conceptual metaphors may not preexist in the sense of continually structuring specific conceptual domains. But conceptual metaphors may be used to access different knowledge on different occasions as people immediately conceptualize some abstract target domain given a particular task. Conceptual metaphors may also simply emerge as the product of conceptualizing processes, rather than serve as the underlying cause of these processes (Gibbs, 1999b).

Chapter 6 reports the findings of some new experiments that should be especially comforting to cognitive psychologists seeking more objective evidence on the role of embodied conceptual metaphor in everyday language use. This new work provides a complementary way of doing cognitive linguistics that partially helps to eliminate the strict reliance on the individual analysts' own intuitions in assessing different kinds of linguistic phenomena. It also shows how motivated explanations of linguistic structure can be used to predict people's linguistic behavior in experimental situations.

Conclusion

Studies from cognitive psychology and cognitive linguistics paint a new view of concepts, one that is contrary to the traditional position in cognitive science in which concepts are abstract, disembodied, decontextualized, enduring mental representations. Both concrete and abstract concepts are temporary, dynamic, embodied, and situated representations. Moreover, concepts arise from acts of perceptual/embodied simulation and are not merely accessed as static representations in long-term memory. This embodied perspective explains why concepts are flexible, multimodal, and productive and give rise to explicit inferences as they are tuned to real-world contexts.

My advocacy of embodied simulation in the creation of concepts in context does not necessarily imply that the sensorimotor nature of conceptual processing is inherently nonrepresentational. After all, simulation processes operating to create specific concepts in context use various kinds of knowledge, including that about the body, that is represented. These simulations are not identical to the neural states that underlie perception, action, and cognition. But conceptual simulations surely involve brain processes in cooperation with the entire nervous system and body to create imaginative understandings of events, both when environmental information is present, and when it is not.

Metaphor is fundamental to conceptual processing. Abstract concepts are partly created from the metaphorical mapping of embodied source domains onto various target domains. In fact, abstract concepts would not exist in the ways that they do in ordinary cognition without body-based metaphor. Metaphor is not a way of accessing previously articulated abstract knowledge, but is inherent in the creation and maintenance of abstract construals in different situations. This position suggests, then, that human conceptual processing is deeply grounded in embodied metaphor, especially in regard to abstract understandings of experience.

5

Imagery, Memory, and Reasoning

The history of science reveals many notable examples of the power of embodied thought in creativity and imagination. Scientists frequently acknowledge that their great discoveries are brought about not through formal, purely analytic reasoning, but by "gut feelings" that take shape in the form of rich sensory images and bodily sensations. Albert Einstein, who always recognized his weakness in mathematics, described his creative process in the following way:

> The words of the language, as they are written or spoken, do not seem to play any role in my mechanisms of thought. The psychical entities which seem to serve as the elements in thought are certain signs and more or less clear images which can be voluntarily reproduced and combined.... The above mental entities are, in my case, of visual and some of muscular type. (Hadamard, 1945: 142–3)

Einstein's embodied thought processes took particular shape in one of his famous thought experiments where he pretended to be a photon moving at the speed of light. He first imagined what he saw and how he felt, and then became a second photon and imagined what he now experienced of the first photon.

Many scientists, like Einstein, have conceded that formal mathematics was useful for communicating their scientific discoveries, but that the locus of their original ideas was rooted in embodied possibilities. Another scientist, Cyril Stanley Smith, purposefully studied graphic arts to better develop his sense of the structure of metals. When he was developing alloys, Smith wrote "I certainly came to have a very strong feeling of natural understanding, a feeling of how I would behave if I were a certain alloy, a sense of hardness and softness and conductivity and fusability and deformability and brittleness – all in a curious internal and quite literally sensuous way" (Smith, 1981: 359). These embodied images were not incidental to Smith's creative work, for his research depended upon "aesthetic feeling for a balanced structure and a muscular feeling of the interfaces pulling against one another" (Smith, 1981: 359).

Similarly to scientific thinking, artistic creativity also involves imagined bodily sensations. One commentator on creativity in the arts suggested,

> To the pianist and sculptor, the instrumentalist, dancer, surgeon, and manual artisans, they [ideas] burst upon awareness in a kinesthetic form, feeling their way into varying types of muscular experience. Fingers "itch" to play, music "flows" from the hands, ideas "flow" from the pen. Movement expresses the "idea" of the dancer or orchestra conductor; the almost sensuous desire to model plastic form becomes compulsive in sculpture. (Hutchinson, 1959: 142)

Cognitive scientists rarely acknowledge the embodied nature of higher-order cognition. Gardner (1983) persuasively argued for the concept of kinesthetic thinking as one of the seven forms of multiple intelligence. But the tendency in cognitive science has been to view kinesthetic intelligence as a separate module of mind that does not necessarily interact with other aspects of mind and language. Yet there is an emerging literature in several areas of cognitive science that explicitly demonstrates direct links between higher-order cognition and embodied action, such that embodiment is essential to various cognitive functions. This chapter describes this work and its implications for theories of higher-order cognition.

Mental Imagery

The vast majority of scholarship on mental imagery within psychology, as well as many other disciplines, ignores the role that embodiment (e.g., people's subjective felt experiences of their bodies in action) may play in mental imagery activities. For instance, the classic empirical work on mental imagery investigates possible correspondences between mental imagery and visual perception (e.g., Finke, 1989). Following this trend, most contemporary cognitive psychology textbooks talk about mental imagery only in terms of visual perception (and, to a much lesser extent, audition). Although there are numerous studies examining people's kinesthetic and motor imagery, few scholars, until recently, searched for explicit links between kinesthetic activity and mental imagery. The recent work suggests that many aspects of visual and motor imagery share a common representational, and possibly neuropsychological, substrate. As Paivio (1986: 72) once noted, "all mental transformations engage motor processes that derive originally from active manipulation of the referent objects."

Imagining Human Movement

The embodied approach to mental imagery suggests that the long-noted equivalence between mental imagery and visual perception is not inaccurate, as long as one recognizes that visual perception is shaped by kinesthetic activity (see Chapter 3). My view of mental imagery is quite broad. Following Newton (1996), I use the term "image" to refer to any imaginary instance where one considers what it may be like to move one's body in a certain way or to think what it may be like to manipulate an object in different ways or what it must feel like to act upon an object in a certain manner, all without actually physically doing what we are currently thinking (Gibbs & Berg, 2002). For example, to entertain in our conscious minds the possible feeling that arises when we bend over to grab our left foot shows how people form proprioceptive mental images of an action. These mental images are not merely perceptual, but kinesthetic in the sense of entertaining what it is like to move our bodies in particular ways.

There is considerable research showing that our ability to imagine ourselves moving in certain ways subsequently influences our actual performance of those movements (a few recent studies include Corriss & Kose, 1998; Hanrahan, Tetreau, & Sarrazin, 1995; Hardy & Callow, 1999; Murphy, 1990; Smyth & Waller, 1998). A recent study, for example, showed that when participants had to copy figures, engaging in visual imagery benefited the drawing of overall form, whereas engaging in kinesthetic imagery facilitated fine-tuned movements of the two hands (Fery, 2003). Although there is much debate over which imagining techniques have the most measurable influence on learning and performance (see Ahsen, 1995), these empirical studies show, at the very least, that imagining our bodies moving has some relationship to subsequent real-life human action.

Ideomotor action refers to the fact that just thinking about an action can make people perform the action without any special influence of the will. Arnold (1946) found that the more vividly a person imaged a movement, the more it occurred. For instance, standing still and imagining falling over, by thinking about both what it would look like and what it would feel like, produces more teetering than does thinking about either the look or feel alone. Asking people to imagine bending their arms, without actually doing so, provokes movement-relevant electrical activity in the arms' biceps-brachial muscles (Jacobson, 1932). Once more, thinking about acting can produce movement without the feeling of doing.

Merely thinking about a kind of person can induce ideomotor mimicry of that person's behavior (Bargh, Chen, & Burrows, 1996). In one study, college students completed a scrambled-sentence task in which some words repeatedly mentioned the idea of aging (e.g., sentences containing the words "wrinkled," "gray," "retired," "wise," and "old"). Afterward, each participant's gait was secretly measured as he or she left the experiment room. People who earlier read words referring to the elderly in the scrambled-sentence task actually walked out of the room more slowly than did participants who were not presented with words referring to senior citizens. Postexperiment interviews suggested that participants were not consciously aware ofhaving been exposed to ideas about the elderly, or having walked slowly out of the experiment room. But reading words referring to characteristics of the elderly unconsciously prompted people to walk slowly. Interestingly, in a different experiment, when participants were told beforehand that the words mentioned in the sentences were expected by the experimenter to influence their behavior, they did not exhibit the same slowness in walking afterward. In this way, the cognitive influence on action seems to occur outside of participants' conscious will.

Many other studies have replicated and extended these original findings. One study asked college students to think about professors (Dijksterhuis & van Knippenberg, 1998). Afterward, the students gave more correct answers to questions from the game "Trivial Pursuit" than did participants who did not first think about professors. On the other hand, when participants were first asked to think about soccer hooligans (in a study conducted in Holland), they subsequently were inferior at answering "Trivial Pursuit" questions compared to control subjects. Related studies have also demonstrated that getting college students to think about old age can facilitate some loss of memory (Dijksterhuis, Bargh, & Miedema, 2001).

In each of the above studies, there is no mention of imagery in describing the locus of the experimental findings. Researchers simply assume that some kind of abstract knowledge is activated (e.g., when a person reads words such as "wrinkled," "gray," "wise," and "old") and integrated via symbolic mental processes. Yet participants may actually be creating rich mental images while engaged in tasks such as unscrambling words to form grammatical sentences. These mental images are not simply pictorial, but reflect complex interplay between image, somatic response, and meaning.

Much of the work on imagery focuses on people's deliberate imaginings of physical events. Imagining the location of objects around us also depends on kinesthetic action. For example, one study asked people to memorize the location of objects in a room (Presson & Montello, 1994). Afterward, the participants were blindfolded and asked to point to specific objects. People were quick and accurate in doing this. But when participants were then asked to imagine rotating 90 degrees and to point to specific objects again, they were slow and inaccurate. When participants were asked to actually rotate 90 degrees, when blindfolded, and to point to specific objects, they were just as fast and accurate as they were before rotating.

A similar set of results has been reported with children (Rieser & Rider, 1991). Five- and 9-year-old children were tested on their ability to imagine (when at home) their classrooms and to point to objects from various perspectives. When the perspective changes were accompanied by actually changing positions, 5-year-olds were correct in 100% of the trials, and the 9-year-olds 98% of the time. Yet when the children only imagined changing perspectives, the 5-year-olds were correct only 29% of the time and the 9-year-olds 27% of the time. A comparison group of adults showed that when actually changing positions, 100% of the their responses required less than 2 seconds, whereas when they imagined the perspective changes, only 29% of the responses required less than 2 seconds. Once more, important aspects of the imagination are shaped by bodily actions.

People also have the ability to imagine the environmental consequences of their actions. During tool use, people often change position, for example, when they use a wrench to turn a bolt. One set of studies specifically examined the idea that hand movements can facilitate imagery for object rotations but that the facilitation depends on people's model of the tool in some situation (Schwartz & Holton, 2000). Physically turning a block without vision reduced mental rotation times compared with imagining the same rotations without bodily movement. A second study showed that pulling a string from a spool facilitated participants' mental rotation of an object sitting on the spool. Overall, people's imagistic transformations are not dependent on the objective, geometric characteristics of an action. But people's imagistic abilities are dependent on their subjective modeling of the tools that mediate motor action and the environmental consequences of that action, and how they can transfer that understanding to new situations.

These representative findings illustrate the importance of embodied action in how people learn over time to mentally imagine their locations, and the locations of objects, in the world around them. Thus, imagining the location of objects in space, a task that many cognitive psychologists view as purely cognitive and divorced from the body, is strongly influenced by body movements. In general, these data support the idea that mental imagery for different real-world events incorporates embodied information.

Several studies have suggested that the mental representations of overt and covert actions are to a large degree "functionally equivalent" (Hall, Bernoties, & Schmidt, 1995; Vogt, 1995). For instance, there is a close relationship between the time needed to mentally rotate a hand or fist in line with the same orientation as a target picture, and the time needed to physically perform the same rotations (Parsons, 1987b, 1994). Moreover, imagined representations of the human body in motion are limited by the same biomechanical factors that constrain real movements (Kourtzi & Shiffrar, 1999).

Planning movements, and not just moving covertly or overtly, is the common element underlying embodied action and mental imagery performance (Salway & Logie, 1995). For example, Johnson (2000) reports the findings from a series of studies showing that motor imagery, or mentally simulated actions, is essential in people's prospective judgments of the awkwardness in prehension (e.g., people's judgments for executing different hand movements with a dowel). People appear to think ahead about their embodied movements not by activating a completed motor plan, but by planning the simulated action.

People often overestimate their physical abilities when they mentally simulate their possible future actions (Landau, Libkuman, & Wildman, 2002). In one study, a group of participants mentally simulated lifting a heavy object (a refrigerator) and then estimated how much weight they could lift. A different group of people estimated the weight they could lift without first engaging in the mental simulation exercise. People who mentally simulated lifting a heavy object reported being able to lift more weight than did participants in the no-simulation condition. Follow-up studies showed that people who mentally simulated an event, such as lifting a 100-lb. weight, many times beforehand reported that they could lift more weight than did participants who completed fewer simulations. Furthermore, people who simulated lifting a larger amount of weight estimated that they could lift more weight than did people who imagined lifting a smaller amount of weight. These findings nicely illustrate how even brief mental simulations of embodied activities shape people's abilities to predict future physical performance.

Predicting the outcome of a future action seems to require some ability to internally represent a model of the situation and then draw a conclusion on the basis of these representational structures. One study investigated whether people's verbal reports about imagined actions can be explained without appeal to representational structures (van Rooij, Bongers, & Haselager, 2002). While standing in one spot, participants were handed rods of different lengths that they then held at an upward 45-degree angle. The participants' task was simply to say whether or not they could use the rod to touch a distant object. Across the series of trials, the rods presented to participants either increased in length and then decreased, decreased in length and then increased, or were of random lengths.

Determining whether a rod can reach an object involves assessing information on the rod's length and one's own bodily abilities (i.e., one's posture, ability to lean forward with feet planted on one spot, arm length, and so on). A traditional representational account would argue that participants must calculate via some internal standard a comparison between the representations of the rod's length, the postural possibilities, and the estimated distance to the object. Successful imagined action, therefore, is based on mental calculations that transform these different, separate representations.

A dynamical systems account, however, maintains that a person's behavior is best described at the level of the whole embodied system, as a self-organizing pattern, emerging from the interaction among subsystems. As with all dynamical accounts of human performance, the emphasis here is on the temporal dynamics of the participants' behaviors across the different trials of the experiment. Differential equations are used to show how different potential functions capture the long-term dynamics underlying the participants' performance. These potential functions describe an attractor landscape, which, at different times for a participant, reflects relatively stable and unstable states of behavior. Van Rooij et al. tested a specific two-attractor space model that made specific predictions about the relative frequencies of different dynamical patterns, once more, across different sequences of trials in the experiment (i.e., presentation of rods from shortest to longest length, longest to shortest length, and rods of varying lengths presented randomly).

In fact, the results of van Rooij et al. (2002) showed that several dynamic patterns explained the participants' performance. Participants tended to give the same categorical responses in the random sequence condition. This assimilative effect is consistent with the dynamical view that the system tends to cling to the state it resides in. Second, there was an inverse relationship between rod length and probability of "yes" responses. This contrastive effect was enhanced when the coupled sequence ran from shorter to longer rods rather than the opposite, exactly what is expected because the multistable region is relatively large here. Finally, three dynamic patterns of hysteresis, critical boundary, and enhanced contrast were all observed, to different extents, in each participant's behavior throughout the trials in the experiment. Most generally, these data are consistent with a dynamical account in which the participants' imagined actions arise from the interplay between a control parameter (a parameter that leads the system through various dynamical patterns) and a collective variable governing the entire system. These parameters are not represented internally, but provide an "imagining landscape" that is an emergent property of the entire embodied system. Van Rooij et al. argue that it is difficult to imagine how a traditional representational theory could explain the dynamical patterns observed in participants' task-behaviors, given the complexity of having to integrate different internal mechanisms that are usually postulated for each finding (i.e., the problem of integrating hysteresis and enhanced contrast within a single mechanism). Nonetheless, the complex patterns in participants' performance can be explained within a more general dynamical model of self-organizing behavior. For the present purposes, a dynamical model also gives proper acknowledgment to the body's role in cognitive behavior, such as that used to momentarily imagine different human actions. This work, more generally, demonstrates how a dynamical model of human behavior can scale up to explain higher-order cognitive behavior.

Motoric Processes in Mental Imagery

It may not be terribly surprisingly that people are able to mentally imagine their bodies in action, and sometimes use their specific embodied experiences when imagining physical events in the real world. But some very interesting studies have more directly explored the links between motor processes and visual mental imagery abilities. For example, the transformation of mental images, as done in the classic Cooper and

Shepard (1982) task, depends on motor processes (Wexler et al., 1998; Wohlschlager & Wohlschlager, 1998). "Visuomotor anticipation is the engine that drive mental rotation" (Wexler et al., 1998: 79). Similar mechanisms may underlie both visual image transformation and the production/control of embodied movements.

Wexler et al. (1998) examined the relationship between mental rotation and motor processes by asking participants to rotate a hand-held joystick in a direction either in congruence or in opposition to the direction of simultaneous rotation of a mental image. Prior to the main experimental task, participants practiced the joystick rotation task. A visual tunnel prevented participants from seeing their hands as they manipulated the joystick. Participants practiced rotating the joystick at one of two specific speeds (45 or 90 degrees/second) in both clockwise and counterclockwise directions until they were adept at the task.

During the main experiment, participants simultaneously performed both a mental imagery rotation task and the motor rotation task. The mental rotation task used two-dimensional block drawings. One figure was presented at the top of a display for 5 seconds. Immediately afterward, an arrow was briefly displayed indicating where a second figure would appear. The second figure then appeared and was either a rotation (of varying degrees) of the original figure or a rotation of a mirror reflection (flipped 180 degrees on its vertical axis) of the original figure. The participants had to indicate whether the second figure was identical to the first (and simply rotated) or a mirror image of the first figure. When performing the motor task, participants were instructed to begin rotating the joystick (in the specified direction and at the proper speed) at the same time as the onset of the initial figure in the mental rotation task. The joystick rotation continued until the participant made a response in the mental rotation task.

The main finding in this study was that "clockwise motor rotation facilitates clockwise mental rotation and hinders counterclockwise mental rotation, and vice-versa for counterclockwise motor rotation" (Wexler et al., 1998: 86). Mental rotation was faster when it was in the same direction as the motor rotation than when the two rotations were in opposite directions. The speed of the motor rotation also influenced the speed of the mental rotation. People typically perform faster with practice across trials in a mental rotation task. Yet in this study, people who completed a first session of trials with a fast motor rotation speed followed by a second session with a slow motor rotation speed did not perform in this manner. Mental rotation speed decreased slightly for these participants in the second session compared to the first, indicating a tight link between mental and motor rotation speeds. In general, Wexler et al.'s (1998) results support the idea of a tight, dynamic relation between mental and motor rotation.

Another source of evidence on the link between mental imagery and motoric processes comes from studies showing that spontaneous eye-movements occur during visual imagery that closely reflect the content and spatial arrangement of the original visual scene (Brandt & Stark, 1997; Laeng & Teodorescu, 2002). Eye movements appear to have a significant, functional role in the process of mental imagery and may specifically be important in activating and arranging parts of a complex scene into their proper location.

One reason that mental imagery must involve aspects of kinesthetic experience is the fact that the congenitally blind are quite capable of forming imagistic representations (Zimler & Keenan, 1983). Different experimental studies indicate that congenitally blind participants exhibit typical mental rotation, mental scanning, and size/inspection time effects (Carpenter & Eisenberg, 1978; Marmor & Zaback, 1976). The strength of these effects is somewhat diminished and they are slower overall than those obtained with sighted individuals, but the pattern of results is similar for both sighted and congenitally blind people. This array of empirical findings for congenitally blind participants is clearly due to these individuals' tactile/kinesthetic, or haptic, imagery, given that blind participants are unable to complete purely visual tasks (Arditi, Holtzman, & Kosslyn, 1988). Blind persons' haptic understanding of objects and spatial relations arises from their active, exploratory physical movements. Most generally, both blind and sighted individuals' haptic abilities are constrained by a complex coordination between tactile senses, proprioception, and the involvement of motor cortex. The large range of imagery evidence for the blind clearly rejects the idea that mental images are necessarily amodally visual or amodally spatial (Intos-Peterson & Roskos-Ewoldsen, 1984).

These findings suggest that there is no reason to believe a visual representation is necessary for mental imagery. There may be two anatomically distinct cortical systems for dealing with visual representations (one involved in representing the appearance of objects, the other to represent the location of objects in space) (Farah et al., 1988). One neurological case study showed that a patient with brain damage from an automobile accident suffered from several deficits in visual recognition, but performed normally on most spatial mental imagery tasks (Farah et al., 1988).

Many neuropsychological studies support the claim that basic processes underlying embodied action are activated even in the absence of physical movement. For instance, brain-imaging studies, especially using positron emission tomography (PET), demonstrate that the activation of sensorimotor cortex occurs even in the absence of physical movement when people are engaged in a variety of mental tasks, ranging from judging the meaningfulness of imaginal movements to using different mnemonic strategies (Decety et al., 1994). Other PET studies found that particular areas of cortex are activated not only when people imagine themselves making different body movements, but also when people speak the name of a tool (Martin et al., 1996). Visual discrimination between mirror-reversed forms, such as a pair of hands, results in the strong activation of frontal motor cortex, both when people imagine the hand movements and when they physically perform them (Parsons et al., 1995). Frontal motor cortex is even activated when someone observes another person move his or her own hands (Rizzolatti, Fogassi, & Galese, 1997; DiPelligrino et al., 1992). Lesions in parietal cortex severely interfere with people being able to anticipate the outcome of a motor action, as well as the ability to engage in mental imagery tasks (Georgopoulos et al., 1989).

Neuroimaging studies have subsequently revealed that posterioparietal areas of the brain are activated when people mentally rotate pictures of multiarmed block-like objects (Kosslyn, DiGirolamo, & Thompson, 1998). Other brain areas (e.g., parts of the motor cortex) are also activated when people mentally rotate pictures of hands (Kosslyn et al., 1998). These findings suggest that people may rotate objects in mental images either by imagining the consequences of an external force or by imagining the consequences of manipulating an object with their own hands. Thus, mental rotation involves motor processes only when the forces involved are endogenous, and not when the rotating force is exogenous.

Most scholars now agree that the motor processes activated during perception and imagination are always a limited subset of those activated during overt movement (Ellis, 1995; Ramachandran & Hirstein, 1997). More generally, though, the various behavioral and neuroimagery findings highlight that motoric elements are recruited whenever the perceived or imagined object is conceptualized in action-oriented terms.

Several models have been proposed to account for people's ability to imagine, often correctly, how their bodies move in space and, more generally, the effect of motion on the behavior of objects. The most discussed model is "motor imagery theory" (Jeannerod, 1994, 1995). Under this view, imagery arises as the conscious experiences of an ongoing nonconscious premotor plan. As noted above, there is some dispute as to whether complete motor plans necessarily must exist for people to experience mental imagery (see Ito, 1999). The alternative "imagery as planning hypothesis" proposes that mental imagery is invoked when a person mentally transforms somatosensory representations in order to anticipate the result of upcoming movement in advance of its execution (Rosenbaum, 1991).

A "dynamic (depiction) model of imagery" acknowledges the importance of force dynamics in solving physical imagery tasks (Schwartz, 1999). Research supporting this view includes tasks studying self-motion (Parsons, 1987a, 1994), biological motion and friction (Hubbard, 1995), and momentum (Freyd & Johnson, 1987) and judging the behavior of water in tilting glasses (Schwartz, 1999). One computational instantiation of this view on how people represent context-specific dynamic information incorporates rate-based representation of physical properties such as friction, elasticity, and balance (Schwartz & Black, 1996), each of which we clearly experience with our bodies. This model captures, among other things, how people mentally imagine the speed and direction with which one object reacts to the movement of another. Not surprisingly, people conceptualize how objects react when moving against one another in very human terms. In his classic studies, Michotte (1963) observed that people described the collision of objects in terms of how humans act when they come into physical contacts (e.g., "A gave B a kick in the pants and sent him flying"). As will be argued below, many mental imagery phenomena, including how people imagine the movement of nonhuman objects, are understood directly via people's recurring embodied experiences.

One proposal that explicitly aims to explain the sensory-motor aspects of mental imagery is "perceptual activity theory" (Thomas, 1999). Under this view, mental imagery is not assumed to be the end product of perception (i.e., no inner picture or depiction of some stimuli is specifically created). However, mental imagery is intimately tied to the ongoing activity of perceptual/motor exploration of the environment. People have the phenomenological experience of having a mental image whenever a schema that is not directly relevant to the exploration of the present environment momentarily takes control of the body's exploratory apparatus.

Perceptual activity theory explains various traditional mental imagery findings (Thomas, 1999). Mental scanning parallels real-world visual scanning in that it takes longer to scan through a larger visual angle than a smaller one. When hand and eye movements are suppressed, the schema's failed attempt to initiate and control these movements will still result in a time course similar to real-world scanning. Size/inspection time effects occur such that smaller details in a visual scene take longer than to pick out in larger ones, in part because people must narrow their attentional focus or move closer to the target object to perceive smaller details. When people attempt to find smaller details in a mental image, the additional time to covertly move closer to the object or to narrow one's visual focus on the small details will also increase processing effort and time. Mental rotation effects, as suggested above, are tightly linked to motion processes so that our mental rotation of an object is similar to physically turning it in our hands (Kosslyn, 1994).

Finally, some scholars contend that conscious mental imagery enhances people's performance in a variety of perceptual-motor and cognitive tasks (Marks, 1999). In this view, mental imagery is again not the end product of a specific kind of cognitive processing, but provides the building blocks for thinking, problem solving, memory, and imagination, especially in regard to how people plan action. For instance, Newton (1996) claimed that intentional mental states are images of goal-directed action episodes that are created in response to external stimuli. Much of our conscious experience of sensorimotor imagery reflects these underlying mental states. Conscious imagery is consequently essential for the planning of human action (Marks, 1999), and embodied movement provides the roots for conscious experience (Sheets-Johnstone, 1998, see Chapter 9). For this reason, some scholars go so far as to suggest that people's conscious preparation of action and their imagery of this action are very difficult to distinguish (Rizzolati, 1994). In general, an increasing number of researchers now raise the possibility that motor imagery may not be separable from visual and auditory imagery (Klatzky, 1994).

Do Mental Images Arise from the Brain?

The previous section mentioned neuroimagining studies show that the motor cortex is activated during many mental rotation tasks. Correlating distinct brain regions with performance on different cognitive tasks may point to the neural mechanisms that underlie, for instance, mental imagery. In fact, Kosslyn (1994) claims that neuroscientific data resolve many of the traditional debates on the nature and function of mental imagery. Kosslyn, Thompson, Wraga, and Alpert (2001) recently published the results of another neuroimaging study testing the idea that distinct neural mechanisms underlie different ways of imagining object rotation. Participants in this study either first viewed an electric motor rotate an angular object, or actually rotated the object manually. Afterward, neuroimages were recorded as participants performed a rotation task in which they compared pairs of objects in different orientations. Participants were specifically instructed to imagine the object rotations as they had just seen the objects rotated (done by the electric motor or by their own hands). The results showed that the motor cortex was only activated in the condition in which participants imagined the rotation as a consequence of their own manual activity. Kosslyn et al. (2001) argued that these findings support the existence of qualitatively different ways of imagining object rotation, where each one can be adopted voluntarily depending on the task.

However, I resist drawing these conclusions, especially in simply reducing imagery to brain states and ignoring the rest of the body and bodily action. First, researchers posit the existence of different neural mechanisms given their interest in particular hypotheses, yet ignore other possible influences on people's successful performance on some experimental task. For example, Kosslyn et al. (2001) found activation of motor cortex only when participants first rotated an object, but not when they observed an electric motor rotate that same object. But they also found activations in many other brain areas for these different experimental conditions, including most conservatively areas 4, 6, 7, and 9 (as well as significant activation, according to more liberal statistical tests, in areas 18, 19, 37, 45/47, and 47). Why is activation in these areas not considered as evidence for multiple mechanisms operating during mental rotation tasks? Researchers too often focus their attention on data that seemingly support their hypotheses (e.g., the idea that there are distinct neural mechanisms responsible for mental rotation) and disregard alternative ways of explaining their data (e.g., might there be as many "mechanisms" involved in mental rotation as there are areas of brain activity?). To their credit, Kosslyn et al. (2001) comment "We recognize that some investigators may have specific hypotheses related to regions other than the ones for which we expected differences in activation" (p. 2522). Yet to claim that motoric mechanisms function only when people first manually rotate objects greatly simplifies the complexity of how brains, bodies, and the world interact during mental imagery.

More generally, there are several general and specific reasons to question whether mental imagery arises simply as the output of neural processes. First, the correlation between activation of certain brain areas and behavior on different experimental tasks should not be interpreted as evidence for distinct neural, or even cognitive, "mechanisms" of mind. Psychologists too often quickly rush to postulate the existence of distinct "mechanisms" based on different patterns of behavioral and brain-recording data. Yet different patterns of behavioral and brain data can almost as easily be understood as arising from distributed mental processes (Rumelhart & McClelland, 1986), holonomic processes (Pribram, 1991), or nonlinear dynamical interactions (Kelso, 1995; Port & van Gelder, 1995).

The problem with traditional imagery research in cognitive and neuropsychology is that it primarily conceives of mental images as internal mental representations that, perhaps, are rooted in distinct areas of the brain. But activating neural structures does not generate the experience of mental imagery, even for the relatively impoverished mental images studied by most cognitive psychologists. Mental images have a particular "feel" to them that is only meaningful in the context of kinesthetic experiences (Damasio, 1999). The search for the "holy grail" of mind in brain mechanisms conceals a subtle form of dualism where the body becomes the instrument for executing the brain's instructions. But as many scholars now argue, the particular brains we have, with their distinct neural organization, are shaped by the bodies we have and the actions we continue to perform in the real world (Freeman, 2000; Kelso, 1995; Lakoff & Johnson, 1999). Under this view, brains are not the sole underlying causal agents for imagistic experience. Mental imagery arises from neural and somatic activity that is understood by ongoing actions of the whole person.

The idea that mental imagery is a whole-person activity paints a different picture of the "mental simulation" perspective of mental imagery adopted by many cognitive and neuropsychologists. Following Berthoz (2000), I specifically argue that "simulation" should be replaced by the idea of "simulator." Consider, for a moment, a meteorologist creating a computer simulation of the path of a hurricane along the eastern seaboard of the United States. This simulation nicely maps various topological relationships of this weather system and may even be used to predict the behavior of real hurricanes. To some extent, computer simulations of cognition, including mental imagery processes, are similar to the meteorologist's simulations of the behavior of hurricanes – they capture relevant information about the formal characteristics of a set of operations that are carried out on particular representations.

A better notion of simulation is that of an actual "simulator" (Berthoz, 2000). Unlike a computer simulation of behavior (e.g., neural networks or any symbolic computing device), a simulator provides something close to what it actually feels like in a full-bodied manner to, say, fly an aircraft. Mental imagery, in our view, is a kind of simulator of action that is based on real-life actions and potential actions that a person may engage in. As a simulator, mental imagery provides a kinesthetic feel that is not simply the output of some abstract computational machine, but provides something of the full-bodied experiences that have textures and a felt sense of three-dimensional depth. The traditional focus in cognitive psychology on visual imagery, to the neglect of other sensory and kinesthetic domains, sometimes fools people into thinking that mental imagery is completely in the "mind's eye" without much engagement from the rest of the body.

But as Damasio (1994, 1999, 2003) has long argued, we have an ongoing awareness of our somatosensory systems. Noting that the brain continually receives feedback signals from the body's autonomic processes, Damasio suggests that this feedback provides us with a constant background awareness of our own bodies' somatosensory systems. This low level of awareness is akin to mood that colors our ordinary consciousness: "The background body sense is continuous, although one may hardly notice it, since it represents not a specific part of anything in the body but an overall state of most everything in it" (1994: 152). Although Damasio contends in his "somatic marker hypothesis" that people mark certain somatosensory sensations as positive or negative, depending on the context, these sensations are more complex and often attributed as properties of the object that may be the focus of our imagination. Our "markings" of these somatosensory sensations allow us to refer to something external to the body (e.g., as when comparing two objects in different orientations in a mental rotation task) and to refer to something that is embodied within us (as if the object has been introjected into our bodies). Mental imagery experiences often retain both these objective and subjective components.

Grush (2004) argued that simulation alone though motor planning, or mere activation of motor cortex, is insufficient to explain imagery. He advocates an "emulation theory" in which emulation of the musculoskeletal system is employed and imagery that is produced with the efferent motor center drives this emulation. By analogy, motor imagery is like a pilot sitting in a flight simulator, and the pilot's efferent commands (hand and foot movements) are translated into faux sensory information (instrument readings) by the flight simulator, which is essentially an emulation of an aircraft. This emulation theory of imagery, therefore, gives much greater emphasis to proprioception and kinesthetic action in the context of the entire body than does the simulation theory. The emulation represents objects and the environment as things engaged with in certain ways, as opposed to how they are considered apart from their role in the organism's environmental engagements.

How is it possible to describe this interaction of brains, bodies, and real-world objects/events during mental imagistic experiences as suggested by emulation theory? My view of mental imagery is that it can best be understood within an "enactive" approach to cognitive science. Once more, the most important feature of dynamical systems is that mental imagery arises as a generic feature of "emergence" in complex, self-organizing, systems. The nervous system, the body, and the environment are highly structured dynamical systems, coupled to each other at multiple levels. Emergence through self-organization has two directions (Thompson & Varela, 2001). First, there is local-to-global determination, or upward causation, as a result of which novel processes (e.g., unique imagistic experiences) emerge that have their own distinctive features, lifelines, and interaction with other aspects of thought and language. Second, there is global-to-local determinate, or downward causation, whereby global characteristics of a system govern local neural interactions. Conceiving of mental imagery as an emergent phenomenon suggests that it may have causal effects on substrate large-scale neural assemblies. This two-way causal interaction has not yet been demonstrated empirically for mental imagery per se, but various studies reveal similar reciprocal relationships between different conscious acts and neural events (Freeman, 2001; Thompson & Varela, 2001; see Chapter 8).

The relationship between neural dynamics and conscious mental imagery experience can be described in terms of the participation of neural processes in the "cycles of operation" that constitute a person's life. Three kinds of cycles are most relevant (Thompson & Varela, 2001): cycles of organismic regulation of the entire body, cycles of sensorimotor coupling between organism and environment, and cycles of intersubjective interaction, involving the recognition of the intentional meaning of actions and linguistic communication. Freeman (2000) nicely describes how these different cycles cooperate to produce "the biology of meaning." He noted, "A meaningful state is an activity pattern of the nervous system and body that has a particular focus in the state space of the organism, not in the physical space of the brain. As meaning changes, the focus changes, forming a trajectory that jumps, bobs, and weaves like the course of a firefly on a summer night. The elements of each dynamic state consist of the pulses and waves in the brain, the contraction of the muscles, the joint angles of the skeletal system, and the secretions of cells in the autonomic and neuroendocrine system. Meaning emerges from the whole of the synaptic connections among the neurons of the neuropil, the sensitivities of their trigger zones, determined by the neuromodulators, and to less extents the growth, form, and adaptations of the rest of the body. The skills of athletes, dancers, and musicians live not only in their synapses but also in their limbs, fingers, and torsos" (Freeman, 2000: 115).

My emphasis on a dynamical account of mental imagery is primarily motivated by a desire not simply to reduce mental imagery to states of neural activation. This does not deny, of course, the critical role that brains play in mental imagery, as well in other cognitive functions. But cognitive scientists need to recognize how imagery is accompanied by sensorimotor sensations, or whole "body-loops" (Damasio, 1994), which give imagistic experience its rich phenomenal quality. Dynamical accounts are suggestive of how people engaging in various actions may momentarily experience these meaningful, and indeed adaptive, imagistic states that are clearly embodied and not just locked within the brain.

Image Schemas and Mental Imagery

How do the recent empirical work and theories on the similarities between motoric and imagistic activity relate to broader views on human thought and language? In this section, I advance the idea that recent findings and theories on the kinesthetic nature of mental imagery fit in nicely with a rather different set of developments on the embodied foundation for thought and language (see Chapter 4). I describe these ideas and show how they specifically apply to traditional mental imagery findings and point to a more comprehensive view of the embodied grounding of higher-order cognition.

The possible relevance of cognitive psychology research on mental imagery to image schemas was first noted by Johnson (1987) and Lakoff (1987). They both described several studies on mental imagery that supported the idea that embodied image schemas and their transformations play an important role in cognitive functioning. Johnson (1987) suggested that the data from several studies on selective interference in mental imagery (Brooks, 1968; Segal & Fusella, 1970) provide evidence for image schemas. Thus, people seemed able to access certain modes of cognition, either recall of verbal information or visual imagery, through multiple channels, such as kinesthetic or verbal report. Moreover, both Lakoff and Johnson claimed that classic studies on mental rotation (e.g., Cooper & Shepard, 1982) also provide evidence in support of image schemas and their transformations. As Johnson (1987: 25) concluded from his discussion of the mental rotation data, "we can perform mental operations on image schemata that are analogs of spatial operations" (i.e., we rotate things quickly in our imagination because of our bodily experience of rotating things with our eyes, hands, and other body-parts). In other words, the empirical data suggest that image schemas have a kinesthetic character, as they are not tied to any single perceptual modality.

Does our ability to mentally rotate images truly reflect the operation of image schemas? To answer this question, one must be very clear about the differences between mental imagery as typically studied by cognitive psychologists and the idea of image schemas. Image schemas are presumably more abstract than ordinary images and consist of dynamic spatial patterns that underlie the spatial relations and movement found in actual concrete images. Mental images are traditionally viewed as temporary representations, whereas image schemas are permanent properties of embodied experience. Finally, image schemas are emergent properties of subjective felt bodily experience, whereas mental images are the result of more effortful cognitive processes. For example, research shows that some mental images can be generated by assembling the parts of the image one part at a time (see Finke, 1989).

Despite these differences, there are interesting similarities between mental images and image schemas that make the study of mental imagery especially relevant to our quest for the embodied foundations of mental imagery. One body of research that quite specifically points to the role of image schemas and their transformations in mental functioning comes from studies on representational momentum. The term representational momentum (RM) was coined by Freyd and Finke (1984) to refer to an internalized representation of physical momentum. A variety of experiments have studied different aspects of RM. The typical paradigm used to investigate RM consists of the presentation of a sequence of three static images, referred to as the inducing stimuli, of an object (usually a simple geographic shape or a dot) that appears to be moving linearly or rotating in one direction. A final target position of the image is then presented and participants are asked to determine whether this target image's position is the same as the third static image of the object. People's participation in a RM task involves their ability to follow in their imagination the path of a moving object and then focus on the point where it will come to rest (an example of the Path-focus to end-point focus image schema transformation).

The classic finding from RM studies is that participants' memory for the final position of an object undergoing implied motion is shifted toward the direction of the motion. For example, if participants watch an image of an object that appears to be rotating, and then have to remember the final position of the object, they will typically report that the object's final position was further along in the rotation than it actually was. The same sort of effect holds for linearly moving objects. The effect was first discovered for rotating objects (Freyd & Finke, 1984) and was later extended to linearly moving objects (Finke & Freyd, 1985; Hubbard & Bharacha, 1988), centripetal force and curvilinear impetus (Hubbard, 1996a), and spiral paths (Freyd & Jones, 1994). If participants watch an image of an object that appears to be moving along a linear path, and then have to remember this object's final position, they will report that the final position was further along the path than it actually was.

The RM effect is not due to apparent motion because increasing the amount of time between the presentations of the static images up to2 seconds still results in RM (Finke & Freyd, 1985). RM presumably "reflects the internalization in the visual system of the principles of physical momentum" (Kelly & Freyd, 1987: 369). Indeed, many characteristics of real-world physical momentum have been found in RM. For instance, the apparent velocity of the inducing stimuli affects RM (Freyd & Finke, 1985; Finke, Freyd & Shyi, 1986). Participants' memory for the final position of a quickly moving object is displaced further along in its path than if the object is moving slowly. Apparent acceleration of the inducing stimuli also affects RM in that objects that appear to be accelerating will produce a larger memory displacement (Finke, Freyd, & Shyi, 1986). Also, displacements that go beyond what one would expect in real-world momentum do not produce RM, (Finke & Freyd, 1985). If the target image of the object is in a position that corresponds to the "next" position in the sequence of inducing images, or is even further along in the path or rotation than the "next" position, the RM effect goes away.

Furthermore, memory displacement is greater for horizontal than for vertical motion (Hubbard & Bharacha, 1988). This may be a result of the predominance of horizontal motion in our environment. Gravity also affects RM (Hubbard & Bharacha, 1988). Objects moving downward are displaced more along their direction of motion than objects moving upward. If an object is moving horizontally and then disappears, participants consistently mark its vanishing point lower than it actually was. The same result occurs with ascending oblique motion. Interestingly, descending oblique motion usually produces displacement above the actual vanishing point. These results suggest internalized environmental constraints on momentum. What goes up must come down, what comes down comes down faster than what goes up, things moving linearly usually drop toward the ground, and that which drops at an angle usually ends up moving horizontally along the ground. It appears that RM is something more complicated than a simple representation of what an object's motion is like given that it has momentum.

Finally, and importantly, RM effects have been found not only for visual stimuli, but for auditory stimuli as well (Kelly & Freyd, 1987; Freyd, Kelly, & DeKay, 1990). Studies with musical pitch have demonstrated that a series of inducing tones either rising or falling in pitch, followed by a target tone either higher or lower in pitch than the third inducing tone, produces the same RM effects as with the studies using visual stimuli. This auditory RM appears not to be due simply to a correlation with visual RM, but rather seems only abstractly related to visual RM (Kelly & Freyd, 1987).

Many aspects of the data on visual and auditory RM can be explained in terms of image schemas and their transformations. First, the SOURCE-PATH-GOAL schema must underlie critical aspects of RM as a person observes an object move from a starting position along some path toward an imagined goal. The SOURCE-PATH-GOAL schema must be one of the most basic image schemas that arise from our bodily experience and perceptual interactions with the world (i.e., note all the actions where any part of a body moves to reach some physical object or location) (see Chapter 4). Besides the schema of SOURCE-PATH-GOAL, there may also be a specific schema for MOMENTUM. When we encounter the inducing stimuli in a RM task, either visual or auditory, a stored representation for momentum is not activated. Instead, we use the image schema for MOMENTUM, derived jointly by our minds, bodies and our environment, to expect the next stimuli to be further along in the path, rotation, or musical scale. Such an expectation would not occur using only the PATH image schema or FOLLONG-A-TRAJECTORY transformation. These may provide the direction that a moving or rotating object is about to traverse, but they cannot account for an expectation about the distance that the object will travel given that it has momentum. Yet a MOMENTUM schema accounts for specific, quantitative aspects of visual RM. Thus, our experience tells us that the faster something is moving, the more momentum it will have and thus the more distance it will travel when a stopping force is applied to it. Moreover, the notion of momentum as image schema also explains the cross modal aspects of RM. We abstract away from our experiences of seeing momentum, hearing momentum and feeling momentum those aspects that are shared or which are similar to one another. Thus, we get the same kinds of effects in auditory RM as in visual RM even though they are not always correlated in the environment (Kelly & Freyd, 1987).

The research on visual and auditory RM may also be used to speculate on how momentum can be created by image schema transformation, such as LANDMARK, PATH, BLOCKAGE, REMOVAL OF BLOCKAGE, and GOAL (see Johnson, 1987 for more discussion of the embodied evidence for these schemas). Image schema transformations like these would function in RM in the following way. First, we invoke the landmark image schema when we immediately attend to an object. As this object moves, we transform the landmark image schema into the path image schema in that our attention is now additionally focused upon the path of the landmark. This is known as the LANDMARK-PATH image schema transformation. We then invoke the BLOCKAGE image schema when the moving object disappears. This image schema is transformed into the REMOVAL OF BLOCKAGE image schema when the target stimulus appears. This transformation is known as the BLOCKAGE-REMOVAL image schema transformation. Finally, to determine the endpoint of the moving object given that it was a landmark moving along a path that encountered blockage, which was subsequently removed, we transform the PATH image schema into a MOMENTUM image schema, and then that into an endpoint focus or goal image schema. This gives us information about the likely position of the object given that it had not encountered any blockage.

People use the position provided by image schema transformations to compare to the target stimuli in a RM task. If there is a match between our expected position given by different image schema transformations and the target stimuli, we respond affirmatively. As the RM literature has shown, however, we are frequently mistaken in saying that target positions that are further along the path correctly indicate the position the object would have. This mistake is produced by the PATH-END-POINT FOCUS image schema transformation. This transformation gives us information about where the object should be given that it was moving at a certain speed, in a certain direction, and encountered blockage that was then removed. If we were instead relying only upon the information in memory on the actual position of the most recent image of the object, we would not make these errors.

In summary, although there are significant differences between mental imagery and image schemas, there is good evidence that spatial, kinesthetic, and visual representations exist for mental imagery. This conclusion is quite consistent with the idea that different modes of perceptual/bodily experience give rise to cognitive schemes that have analog-like properties. To the extent, then, that people's mental images reflect the operation of various modalities and kinesthetic properties of the body, the experimental findings on mental imagery support the idea that image schemas play a significant role in certain aspects of perception and cognition.

Memory

Memory has traditionally been studied as if it constituted a functionally separate storage device of mind containing information that is mostly represented in abstract, symbolic terms. There may be different memory systems, such as short-term and long-term memory, and varying contents, such as semantic and episodic information. But with the exception of some information that is "procedural" (e.g., knowledge about how to tie one's shoes), the traditional view is that memory is constituted by disembodied, abstract symbols.

Memory as Embodied Action

Much recent work suggests that memory and the process of remembering are partly based on embodied activity. Imagine yourself in your kitchen gathering the ingredients needed to bake a cake (Cole, Hood, & McDermott, 1997). You need not remember exactly where each ingredient presumably is kept in the cabinets around you because you can simply go to the cabinets and move through the contents inside until each necessary ingredient is located. The external world (i.e., the cabinet) may take the place of a fully detailed internally represented memory code for the ingredients and where they are located. The cabinet may even allow you not to retrieve in memory a detailed list of all the ingredients needed to make a cake. We know that whatever is needed will likely be found in the cabinet. It is not just the existence of the cabinet that allows these environmental structures to partly take over significant information processing. Rather, our movement through the cabinet, as we push some ingredients aside, enables us to figure out what is needed to bake the cake.

Of course, the kitchen cabinet may only serve as an external aid to memory, but not be part of the cognitive process of remembering. Yet drawing a rigid distinction between what is external and what is internal to remembering is less compelling, given that memory is composed of both internal representations and manipulation of environmental structures.

Consider the case of the expert bartender. Faced with multiple drink orders in a noisy and crowded environment, the expert mixes and dispenses drinks with amazing skill and accuracy. What is the basis of this expert performance? Does it all stem from finely tuned memory and motor skills? Studies comparing novice and expert bartenders show that expert skill involves a delicate interplay between internal and environmental factors (Beach, 1988). The experts select and array distinctively shaped glasses at the time of ordering. They then use these persistent cues to help recall and sequence the specific orders. Expert performance thus plummets in tests involving uniform glassware, whereas novice performance is unaffected by any such manipulations. The expert has learned to transform the working environment to simplify the task that confronts the body in action.

Our embodied experience clearly affords ease of remembering. One theory proposes that memory's primary function is to mesh the embodied conceptualization of projectible properties of the environment (e.g., a path or a cup) with embodied expressions that provide nonprojectible perceptions (Glenberg, 1997). This meshed conceptualization serves to control action in a three-dimensional environment. For example, people recalled objects in a room on the basis of the physical proximity of the objects to each other as the observer moved through the room, and not in terms of the semantic relatedness of the objects (Brewer, 1998). A different study had climbers reproduce on a scale model the locations and orientations of 23 holds of a climbing wall that each had just climbed (Boschker et al., 2002). Expert climbers correctly recalled more of the holds than did the novices. But the experts also focused on the functional aspects of the wall (i.e., its affordances), compared to novices who exclusively reported the structural, but not functional, aspects of the wall. People's memory for places is grounded in their embodied experience, as a perceptual symbolic form, and not in some abstract, amodal, schematic representation.

Another set of studies demonstrated this point by having participants read and memorize spatial layouts corresponding to scenarios viewed from particular perspectives (e.g., in a hotel scene, "To your left... you see a shimmering indoor fountain") (Bryant & Wright, 1999). Objects were located above, below, in front of, in back of, to the left of, and to the right of the participant in the imagined scene. After a scenario was imagined, the time it took participants to locate a particular object was measured. Given that the objects were equally well memorized, one might expect retrieval time to be independent of location. On the other hand, the time needed to locate an object might correspond to the degree of mental search one has to do to mentally find the object. But the results showed that the fastest responses were given to objects located on the head/foot axis, followed by the front/back axis, followed by the left/right axis. Participants used a "spatial framework" that was sensitive to environmental asymmetries (such as gravity) and bodily asymmetries (we generally look and attend to things in front of us). Retrieval processes are clearly shaped, in part, by constraints on embodied experiences.

Of course, environmental information can be suppressed so that conceptualization is guided by previous experiences, which is a conscious and effortful use of memory. Closing one's eyes or looking toward a blue sky is an action that helps to suppress the environment by eliminating projectible properties that normally interfere with thought processes. Research shows that people avert gaze when working on moderately difficult recollection tasks (but not easy ones) and that this behavior enhances accurate remembering (Glenberg, Schroeder, & Robertson, 1995). The ability to suppress environmental information contributes to prediction, the experience of remembering, and language comprehension.

Working Memory

Working memory is a type of short-term memory that functions as temporary storage for the information needed to accomplish particular tasks, including reasoning, problem solving, and language understanding. A classic model claims that there are three components to working memory: a phonological loop, a visuospatial sketchpad, and a central executive (Baddeley, 1986; Baddeley & Hitch, 1974). But several recent proposals suggest that working memory also reflects different embodied abilities (Carlson, 1997; Glenberg, 1997; Wilson, 2001).

Speaking is a bodily activity that, in different situations, may either facilitate or hinder memory of verbal material. For instance, search tasks involving speech disrupt short-term memory for verbal information (Baddeley, 1986). Of course, the serial nature of speaking is one reason that verbal rehearsal, either overt or covert, is particularly important when people must recall items in serial order (Healey, 1982). Other studies reveal that short-term memory span for verbal items depends on the time needed to pronounce the items. Thus, Chinese and English speakers have different memory spans, because of the different times needed to pronounce the same items in these different languages (Stigler, Lee, & Stevenson, 1986). Cross-linguistic differences are also found within individuals. In a study of Welsh-English bilinguals, memory span was found to be larger for English than for Welsh within the same participant sample (Ellis & Hennelly, 1980).

Differences in articulation rates can also account for the fairly extensive differences in memory span between sign and spoken languages. Deaf participants, who use American Sign Language, typically have memory spans of around four items, in contrast to the approximately seven items for oral speakers (Wilson & Emmory, 1997; Wilson, Iverson, & Emmorey, 2000). The difference in span appears to reflect differences in articulatory time for speakers and signers (Marschark, 1994).

Working memory for sequences of body postures and for sequences of spatial locomotion displays some of the same effects that characterize immediate memory for language. Thus, sensorimotor rehearsal in working memory is not restricted to spoken language. Experimental participants can enhance their short-term memory span for digits when they are taught to serially tap the appropriate fingers corresponding to different digits at the same time that they verbally rehearse the digits they hear (Reisberg, Rappaport, & O'Shaughnessy, 1984). Other studies show that eye movements during a task of copying block patterns reduces the load on working memory and facilitates fast, accurate performance (Ballard, Hayhoe, Pook, & Rao, 1997).

Many studies have explored the relation between overt movement and memory for information placed along an imaginary path. For example, Baddeley and Lieberman (1980) had participants imagine a four-by-four square matrix pattern. Participants were then required to imagine placing consecutive numbers in a series of adjacent squares following a path around the matrix. After the "number path" had been described, the participants were then asked to recall verbally the sequence of imagined movements required to reproduce the imagined path. In one experimental condition the participants were blindfolded and were given a flashlight with which they had to follow the motion of a swinging pendulum. A tone signaled whether the flashlight was shining on or off the pendulum. Therefore, participants were performing two distinct tasks concurrently – generating the mental image of a path and moving their arms back and forth in time with a metronome. The mental imagery task involved only auditory input and vocal recall, whereas the movement tasks involved auditory feedback from the tone and controlled tracking movement of the hand and arm. Neither task involved visual input.

Under these circumstances, participants' recall of the matrix paths was significantly impaired relative to that for performing the imagery task without concurrent movement. This interference seemed to be specific to the combination of the imagined path task and concurrent movement. When the imagined path task was concurrent with visual discrimination of patches of light, recall performance was unimpaired. In other words, the cognitive processes involved in mentally imaging a sequence of locations along a path appear to overlap with the cognitive processes involved in controlling arm movement. The fact that participants were blindfolded in the movement condition indicates that this overlap in processing resources is linked to spatial representations and movement control rather than relying solely on the visual system.

Other studies showed that recall of an imagined path was disrupted by concurrent arm movement (Quinn, 1994). For example, participants in one condition tapped areas on a table top in a random fashion. In a different condition, the experimenter held the participant's hand and moved it across the table top in a random fashion (i.e., the participants had no control over their movements). The results showed that random movement generated by the participant resulted in disruption of imagined path recall, but not when the experimenter generated the movement. When the experimenter held the participant's hand and moved it in a regular and predictable pattern, the dual task disruption reappeared. In summary, participants had difficulty recalling the imagined matrix path when they controlled their movements or could predict where their hand was going next. However, the participants had little difficulty recalling the imagined matrix path when they did not controlled their own movements. These results demonstrate how working memory may be disrupted by planning movements as well as by executing them.

There is also evidence that motor activity influences how people recall information from constructed mental images (Kosslyn et al., 1988). Participants were presented with a sequence of four contiguous segments of a visual matrix. Each segment contained an arrow indicating how the segment should be drawn. The participants' task was to combine the segments by physically drawing them as a single shape. Afterward, participants were shown individual segments of the matrix, and judged if each presented element was part of the overall figure. Response times to make these judgments from memory increased with serial position in the drawing. Thus, people took about 50% longer to respond "yes" to a given segment if it was the last segment in the matrix than if it was the first segment. Motor activity appears to influence the way people recall visual stimuli.

There may, however, be functional differences in working memory for purely visual and movement-based information. Various work supports the idea that temporary memory for visual information may be distinct from temporary memory for paths between objects or targeted movement sequences. Logie and Marchetti (1991) examined two contrasting memory tasks to test this possibility. One task involved presenting participants with a sequence of squares appearing one after another in different random locations on a computer screen. Participants' recognition memory was then measured for the sequence tested after a retention interval of 10 seconds during which the screen was blank. A second task presented participants with an array of squares each in a different hue of the same basic color (e.g., shades of blue). During the retention interval, participants either tapped out a regular pattern, or simply viewed random sequences of line drawings of objects in the same location. Analysis of the recognition scores showed that presentation of the line drawings disrupted retention of the color hues, but did not disrupt retention of the sequence of squares. In contrast, tapping out a pattern disrupted memory for the sequence of squares in different locations, but did not affect memory for color hues. These data suggest that a separation exists between a visual temporary memory system and a spatial movement-based memory system.

Some scholars argue that visuospatial working memory processes are part of a dynamic motor system, dubbed the "inner scribe," which is linked to a static visual store, called the "visual cache" (Logie, 1995; Logie & Pearson, 1997). In this view, the inner scribe is capable of redrawing the contents of the visual cache, which permits visual and spatial rehearsal, manipulation, and transformation of information within working memory. Some neuropsychological evidence is consistent with this idea. Farah et al. (1988) described a patient who had great difficulty with mental imagery tasks that involved judgments about visual appearance, such as "Which is darker blue, the sky or the sea?" However, the same patient had no difficulty with imagery tasks that involved mental actions such as imaging and recalling a path between targets. One computational model of visual memory appears to capture some of these very performative characteristics of visuospatial working memory (Kosslyn, 1987).

The research described in this section all points to the conclusion that working memory is at the very least partly related to motoric activity. Various bodily actions, including private speech, covert looking, and motoric activity, enhance short-term memory. Some of the evidence suggests a strong isomorphism between short-term memory performance and embodied action. Findings such as this reveal how working memory is more a collection of performative strategies (touching, speaking) than it is a separate, architectural component of mind. A sensorimotor account of working memory posits a rapid cycling of information between perceptual and motoric forms of coding (Wilson, 2001). The automaticity of translation between the two forms of coding suggests that isomorphism between perceptual and motoric representations confers processing advantages, even in the absence of overt perceptual and motoric activity.

Imagination Inflation

There is growing interest among memory researchers in how imagining an event alters autobiographical belief. For instance, when people are asked to rate the likelihood that they have experienced a set of events, and then later are asked to imagine a subset of these events, they will more likely report later on that they had actually experienced the events previously imagined (Garry & Polaschik, 2000). This false memory finding is known as "imagination inflation." Various studies have demonstrated that the more times someone imagines an event, the more likely he or she will be to say that he or she has indeed experienced the event (Goff & Roediger, 1998), although this result is not simply due to an increase in familiarity with an event. Of specific interest here are findings that visually imagining an event from a first-person (own) perspective leads to greater imagination inflation than imagining from a third-person (observer) perspective (Libby, 2003).

Most recently, studies have shown that false memories were more likely in cases when individuals were instructed to imagine events in great sensory detail (Thomas, Bulevich, & Loftus, 2003). In one study, participants sat at a table filled with numerous objects. They heard a series of statements (e.g., "flip a coin") and then had to perform or imagine performing the called-for actions. Several days later, when participants came back, they simply had to imagine performing various actions on objects, but without any objects in front of them. Finally, participants' memories were tested for what they did on the first day of the experiment. After even a few imaginings, people sometimes remembered performing actions that they had not performed. Not only did they falsely claim to have engaged in common actions (e.g., "roll the dice"), but also said that they had done rather bizarre or unusual actions (e.g., "kiss a plastic frog").

These different results suggest that people will have greater confusion between what they actually have experienced and what they merely imagined the more that they engaged in embodied simulations of the events during the imagination phase of the experiment. One possibility is that planting false memories is more successful to the extent that people engage in kinesthetic imagination of these events. This idea is ripe for further empirical study.

Memory for Language

A well-known finding from experimental psychology is that people remember words better when they read and say them aloud than when they only read them (Slamecka & Graf, 1978). This "generation effect" demonstrates that engaging the body, through speaking, leads to more durable memory for words. Research also shows that people incidentally recall the statements in a scripted dialogue better if participants enacted them than if they simply read them (Jarvella & Collas, 1974). Learning to consciously recall language may also be enhanced if people speak, rather than read, the material. The great acting coach Stanislavski (1936/1982) maintained that placing oneself into the situation of the character, and creating a history for a fictitious role, allows actors to give a more believable performance.

Actors are taught to envision themselves in the particular situations that their characters are facing and imagine themselves responding as the characters. Actors are also told to identify personal memories that evoke emotions similar to those supposedly experienced by their characters.

One study provided support for the importance of enactment in memory for discourse (Scott, Harris, & Rothe, 2001). Participants were told to read a 5-minute monologue and try to learn as much as they could about the character (they were not told to memorize the text). All participants then engaged in one of five different 30-minute activities. These were (1) a read-only activity where participants simply performed an unrelated distractor task, (2) a writing task where each person wrote out answers to five questions about the character voicing the monologue, (3) a collaborative discussion task where groups of participants discussed the five character questions, (4) an independent discussion task where only one person at a time responded to the same set of character questions, and (5) an improvisation task where the participants dramatized in small groups their reactions to the five questions.

After the 30-minute activities, the participants recalled the monologue they originally read. Participants in the improvisation group exhibited memory superior (based on the gist of their recalls) to that of people in any other condition. This finding demonstrates the value of embodied activity, where participants directly dramatized the action, in memory for dramatic monologues. Asking people to actively experience a character as a full person (with appropriate cognitive, affective, and emotional dimensions) leads to better memory than in conditions that still provoked high-level cognitive, but less embodied, involvement.

Performing activities that are compatible to the meanings of words is important in remembering language. People who were induced to nod while incidentally reading positive and negative adjectives were later on more likely to recognize positive adjectives, but participants who were induced to shake their heads were more likely to recognize negative words (Foster & Strack, 1996). Moreover, when people moved their heads in a manner that was compatible with the adjectives they read (e.g., nodding for positive adjectives), they were better able to perform a secondary task than when the words and head movements were incompatible. Once more, performing incompatible motor and cognitive task concurrently requires more cognitive capacity, which appears to hinder memory for words.

A different source of embodiment in memory for language is seen in recent studies on brain imagining. For instance, one PET study showed that remembering that vivid words had been paired with sounds at encoding activated auditory brain regions that were engaged during encoding (Nyberg et al., 2000). This finding suggests that memory for language includes modality-specific information, and does not simply involve accessing an amodal representation for words in memory.

In a related study, using fMRI, participants were first presented with word-sound or word-picture pairs (Wheeler, Peterson, & Buckner, 2000). Afterward, participants engaged in different tasks, including recalling the associated sound or picture given a word, or remembering whether a word was paired with a sound or picture. Brain imaging during the memory portion of the experiment revealed that regions of visual and auditory cortex were activated differentially during retrieval of pictures and words, respectively. Furthermore, the regions activated during retrieval were a subset of those activated during a separate perception task in which people viewed pictures or heard sounds. These data support the idea that retrieval or visual and auditory information associated with word learning, reactivates some of the same sensory region that was active during learning. Once again, embodied processes engaged in learning language appear to be encoded as part of the representation of language in memory.

Finally, many studies have investigated the benefits and costs associated with imagining embodied action when remembering linguistic statements. For instance, research shows that people's memory for verbal statements about embodied actions, such as "peeling potatoes" or "lighting a cigarette," are facilitated when people pretended to perform these actions without using real objects (Engelkamp, 1998). People also recall phrases that they have enacted better than they do phrases that they have watched other people enact (Hornstein & Mulligan, 2001). Moreover, phrases requiring interactions with objects are better recalled than enacted statements without objects.

Why are enacted statements most memorable? People who enact statements with an object are provided more detailed sensory information than are people who only pretend to perform the same action. During its execution, a person receives visual feedback on his or her own action. If real objects are involved in the task, then additional visual and tactile information is provided. Engelkamp and Zimmer (1984) demonstrated that when participants rate the similarity of pairs of action phrases, when they enact the first action phrase, rather than just hear it, their judgments of similarity to the second action phrase are faster than when both action phrases are only presented verbally. Thus, the enactment of the first phrase activates or primes the motoric information necessary for the subsequent comparison more effectively than does the verbal description of the action. Simply imagining the first action was not sufficient, however, to achieve the priming effect on similarity judgments (Engelkamp, 1998).

These various findings address several important issues about memory and language (Engelkamp, 1998). First, three kinds of information contribute to the recall of action phrases, namely the visual sensory information provided by observing one's own body movement required for the action, the visual sensory information from observing the physical objects involved in the actions, and the motoric or kinesthetic information from the movement. Second, visual sensory information from perceiving real objects improves memory, but it is not crucial for the enactment effect. Third, visual information from observing other people's actions does not enhance memory for action statements compared to enactment by the rememberer. Motoric or kinesthetic information appears to play the most critical role in remembering linguistic statements.

Reasoning

Assessing human intelligence often focuses on how people reason, make decisions, and solve problems. As is the case for mental imagery and memory, most cognitive scientists view human reasoning as a computational skill that requires altering abstract, symbolic representations from initial problem states to reach different goal states (e.g., means-ends analysis). People presumably solve problems via general reasoning strategies and domain-specific knowledge.

But consider the following reasoning problem. Imagine running across a large room from one wall to another (Schwartz, 1999). Now imagine doing the same activity, this time in waist-deep water. Although the spatial relations are identical in both cases, our imaginary feeling of the two situations is quite different. In fact, people take longer to imagine how long it takes to walk 30 yards carrying a heavy backpack than it does to walk the same distance without carrying anything (Decety, Jeannerod, & Problanc, 1989). Although this finding may simply be due to people's beliefs about the effect of carrying weight on their walking speed, other work shows that people always take longer to respond to the 30-yard question when told they are wearing a backpack, no matter what they actually believed (Finke & Freyd, 1985). In fact, 5-year-olds correctly modified the force needed to push an object off a table at different heights to make it land on a specific target despite their incorrect beliefs about where the object would land when they were asked beforehand (Krist, Fieberg, & Wilkening, 1993).

It is difficult to account for these findings in terms of abstract reasoning strategies that do not acknowledge the importance of embodied simulation in how people solve problems. In fact, studies show that people can solve a physical problem by simulated doing, which involves an imagined action that facilitates correct inferences even when people are unable to verbally articulate what they are doing (Schwartz & Black, 1999). For instance, people imagined that two beakers of water with identical heights but different widths were tilted at various angles. When people were explicitly asked about when the water would reach the top of both beakers, they did so incorrectly. However, when people closed their eyes and tilted the glasses until the imagined water reached the top, they did so correctly for both types of beaker. Simulated doing through imagery includes motor as well as visual components, and that motoric information is not always available to visual awareness or consciousness when solving real-world problems (Schwartz & Black, 1999).

How people move their bodies may even influence creative problem solving. A recent series of studies showed how arm flexion elicits a systematic processing strategy that facilitates creative insight (e.g., the ability to engage in contextual set-breaking, restructuring, and mental search), but arm extension impairs insight processes (Friedman & Foster, 2000). Furthermore, data from the same studies revealed that people solve more analogy problems when flexing their arms as opposed to extending them. These empirical findings are not due to participants' own affective states or moods that may arise from the activity of moving their arms in particular ways. Instead, motor actions, such as moving your arms in particular ways, influence cognitive processes associated with creative insight and problem solving. One possibility is that approach and avoidance motor actions not only elicit bodily signals that trigger differential processing strategies, but may also differentially activate the brain-based motivational system (Lang, 1995).

People often rely on environmental resources in an embodied manner when solving different problems. Participants with good imagistic capacities were asked in one study to observe and recall a drawing of an ambiguous picture (duck/rabbit) (Chambers & Reisberg, 1992). The drawing was flippable in that it could be viewed as either of two different things, though not at once. The participants had not seen the duck/rabbit picture before but were trained on related examples (Necker cubes, face/vase pictures) to ensure that they were familiar with the phenomenon in question. They were briefly shown the duck/rabbit, told to form a mental picture so that they could draw it later, and then asked to consult their mental image to seek an alternative interpretation for the two pictures. Participants were given hints that they should try to shift their visual fixation (e.g., from lower left to upper right). Finally, participants drew their images and tried to find alternative interpretations of their drawing.

Despite the fact that some of the participants were vivid imagers, none of the participants tested were able to recognize the alternative image of the stimuli (e.g., from duck to rabbit). In sharp contrast, all participants were able to find the alternate construal after they had made their own drawings. This pattern of findings shows how people's problem-solving capacities are significantly extended by the simple device of externalizing information via bodily activity (e.g., drawing the image from memory) and then confronting the external trace using on-line visual perception.

People employ various "complementary strategies" to alter the environment to enhance their reasoning abilities. These strategies include embodied actions, such as using one's hands to manipulate Scrabble pieces or to do complex arithmetic using pencil and paper, that help people improve their thinking and memory to solve problems. For example, when viewing an upside-down photograph, people do not try to mentally rotate the image in their heads, but physically turn the picture right side up. Thus, people physically alter the environment, rather than altering their mental abilities, to better identify what are looking at.

Complementary strategies clearly enhance people's problem-solving abilities. For instance, in one study, participants were shown two sets of 30 coins (i.e., different quarters, dimes, and nickels) and asked to calculate the amount in dollars and cents (Kirsh, 1995). People were faster and more accurate in determining the sum when they were allowed to touch the coins than when they were not allowed to use their hands. Touching the coins appears to help people remember intermediate sums, in the same way that writing down the intermediate sums facilitates solving complex multiplication problems.

A different study asked participants to find the sum of digits presented on dice-like markers (Cary & Carlson, 1999). When participants were permitted to handle the markers, every participant actually did so. But when participants were prohibited from touching the markers, they talked aloud far more than in the other condition. Talking provided a kind of environmental support for working memory when other resources such as touching the dice were unavailable. In a related way, abacus experts often solve mental arithmetic problems employing specific routines of physically manipulating the abacus (Hatano & Osawa, 1983; Miller & Stigler, 1991; Stigler, 1984). Finally, children who are allowed to gesture count more accurately than when they are prohibited from doing so (Alibali & DiRusso, 1999). Active gesture helps children both to keep track and to coordinate tagging the items and saying the number words. Observers who actively rotated three-dimensional novel objects on a computer screen later showed faster visual recognition of these objects than did people who passively observed the same sequences of images of these visual objects (Harman, Humphrey, & Goodale, 1999). People who engage in active rotation also were subsequently faster in a mental rotation task involving the studied objects (James, Humphrey, & Goodale, 2001).

People continuously use perceptual information from the environment to guide their actions and reduce cognitive effort in reasoning. One study examined this idea in the context of people's performance playing the computer game Tetris (Kirsh & Maglio, 1994). In Tetris, pieces, or zoids, enter the board from the top and the players have to decide whether to move them right or left or to rotate them. Physically rotating a piece can save considerable cognitive effort in placing the zoid in their appropriate place over that needed to do the rotation mentally. Overall, people took about 150 msec to physically rotate a zoid, whereas doing so mentally takes between 700 and 1500 msec. People clearly off-load the internal computations needed to place their zoid by physically doing the same transformation in the environment. Thus, people use their bodies and the world to save internal computations. In high-speed tasks, such as playing Tetris, the person and environment can be so tightly coupled that it is better to conceive of the two as constituting a single conceptual system rather than two independent systems (Kirsh, 1995).

People also create and employ tools when solving everyday tasks to explore the possible variations in their ideas when seen in the real world. Having tools available for doing this, and extenuating internal representations, makes this easy to do. The most intelligent use of space is to try out possibilities that are difficult to imagine using only internalized thought (Kirsh, 1995). Consider how one plays the board game of Scrabble. Finding the best set of words that can be created through combining the letters is easiest to do when the letters are shuffled around.

Making a complex recipe often involves the same sort of physical exploration. When participants were asked to prepare a recipe including 3/4 of 2/3 of a cup of cottage cheese, most people engaged in some embodied action using external resources, rather than figuring out the exact amount using arithmetic (Brown, Collins, & Duguid, 1989). For instance, one participant took 2/3 cup of the cheese, flattened it out into a uniformly thick circular disk on a utility board, and drew a cross on it with his finger to see the desired amount by discarding the quarter. Like most participants, this person never verified the procedure algorithmically through arithmetic (e.g., $3/4 \times 2/3 = 1/2$). Other studies show that when people employ external resources during problem solving (e.g., engaging in complex paper-folding tasks), they actively leave traces of the work, such as written notations, that facilitate their retracing their work later on (Shirouzu, Miyake, & Masukawa, 2002). In these ways, formal reasoning skills are not independent of people's ability to physically manipulate the external environment.

All these studies point to the possibility that the dynamic relations between embodied agents and the environment form a complex computational system (Hutchins, 1995; Suchman, 1987; Wilson, 2004). Embodied agents can inventively exploit facts about the physical environment to avoid explicit representations and reasoning (Agre & Chapman, 1987; Brooks, 1991). For example, Hutchins (1995) demonstrated how the cognitive processes involved in flying a plane or piloting a ship do not take place in the pilot's head, but are distributed throughout the cockpit, in the members of the crew, the control panel, and the manuals.

Another emerging literature on embodied reasoning concerns students' learning of physics. Solving physics problems generally requires that students understand and correctly apply abstract physical laws. But novice physics students' knowledge about physical phenomena is not a tightly connected, logically organized structure that might be properly called a theory. Instead, studies shows that physical knowledge is a set of loosely connected ideas about the world, abstracted from concrete experiences, that can be used to generate explanations in particular situations and in response to particular questions or cues (diSessa, 1993). These ideas, called "p-prims," are "phenomenological primitives," because they are self-evident to the holder, requiring no further explanation.

For example, students do not try to explain why you get more results when you expend more effort pushing a big rock, because there is nothing puzzling about this phenomenon. Students' preconceptual understanding of something like impetus is simply an invention particular to a small class of problems. Thus, when explaining the physics of tossing a ball, the action of one's hand on the ball is never described because it is entirely unproblematic from the student's point of view. A p-prim of "force as mover" describes and explains precisely the situation of tossing. In contrast, after the ball detaches from the hand, the situation is problematic. But why does the ball keep going upward until the peak of the trajectory even though gravity acts on the ball to go down? At the peak, the ball appears to stop, and it looks as if the forces are balancing. What is balancing the force of gravity? DiSessa claims that this kind of problem presents a conflict that forces students to invent a concept such as impetus to explain the continuous force that keeps the ball moving and balancing at the peak of its trajectory. In this way, naive physical theories are ad hoc explanations situatedly invented, rather than a product of some consistent theory or "representation" in the mind. In everyday life, people often communicate with each other about motion and force, not to explain these phenomena, but to coordinate their situated actions for collaboration. A person may say "Push it harder" or "Keep your strength for pulling," for example, without needing to articulate the meaning of force and motion.

To take another case, the question of why it is hotter in the summer may activate for students a p-prim connecting proximity and intensity. As students tacitly know from their own experiences, one is more strongly influenced by something the closer one is to it. Candles are hotter and brighter the closer you get to them, music is louder the closer you are to the speaker, the smell of garlic is more intense the closer you bring it to your nose. Simple activation of the idea "closer means stronger" with the p-prism "connecting proximity to intensity" allows students to understand why it is hotter in the summer than in the winter, because the sun is closer to the earth in summer.

Another problem students face concerns the idea that gravity holds a rolling ball onto the ground. One student explained this first by saying "gravity holds the ball right onto the surface," which indicates a misconception of gravity as a constraint, "holding the ball at a certain distance." One may characterize the student's mistaken idea as a piece of knowledge he could incorrectly apply in many situations. But the student's idea may alternatively be seen as involving the activation of one or more p-prims from what diSessa called the "constraint cluster," including "supporting," "guiding," and "clamping." Thus, the student's explanation is specific to the situation, and reflects an imaginative line of reasoning, because in the situation, the student's idea was not inconsistent with Newtonian reasoning. In this way, the student's primitive, embodied reasoning actually indicates the seeds of a more complex Newtonian understanding.

These few examples serve to illustrate the power of embodied thought, in the form of p-prisms, in how students learn to solve elementary physics problems. Learning to solve these physics problems eventually refines p-prims, but does not replace them (diSessa, 1993). Thus, embodied knowledge constitutes an enduring part of people's advanced reasoning about physical events.

Some cognitive scientists argue that experience with the physical world sometimes confuses students in reasoning about physics problems (Clement, 1987; McCloskey & Kohl, 1983). Yet teachers of young children often acknowledge the importance of allowing children to physically interact with materials when learning mathematics and science concepts. One case study clearly demonstrated how one child's direct kinesthetic experience supported her learning about the mathematics of motion (Wright, 2001). Karen is a third/fourth grader in an urban public school in the Boston area. Her teacher claimed that students' first-hand experiences of motion (e.g., running, walking, etc.) helped them understand mathematical concepts of motion. Analyses of Karen's work with a teacher shows three examples of how she used her body as a resource for learning mathematics. First, Karen used her body to produce different positive outcomes of a two-person race. Second, Karen used her hands in place of dropped objects to compare patterns of speed. In these two instances, Karen came to understand that any one motion (e.g., "run" or "walk") can have a variety of speeds, and that these differences (e.g., walk vs. walk slowly vs. run fast vs. moderately fast) predictably affect the outcomes of a race. Finally, Karen's enacting different motion types facilitated her correct interpretation of a data table. She recognized how distance affected varying speeds when time was held constant. All three cases showed how Karen used her body to enact motion types to conceptualize new representations about time and space. One mathematics and physics teacher reports that his students more easily learned ideas about space, time, and speed by his having them move their bodies in various ways (Liljedahl, 2001). Doing so enabled his students to connect static representations of motion directly to their own embodied actions.

Children are not the only people to use embodied activity in thinking about math and science concepts (see Chapter 7). A study of how physicists interpret graphs revealed that "scientists engaged in collaborative interpretive activity to transport themselves through talk and gesture into constructed visual representations through which they journey with their words and bodies" (Ochs, Jacoby, & Gonzales, 1994: 168). In general, studies like these show how physical enactment of different sorts is a critical resource in scientific reasoning.

Summary

Traditional views of higher-order cognition as computational processing on symbolic representations fail to capture the importance of embodiment in human thought. People's previous and current embodied actions serve as the grounding for various aspects of imagination, memory, and reasoning. On-line embodied processes emphasize overt sensorimotor activity to assist with cognitive tasks that interact with the immediate world. Off-line embodiment occurs when sensorimotor processes run covertly to assist with the representation and manipulation of information in the temporary absence of task relevant input or output. Both of these aspects of embodiment work to create an embodied model of mind that is not internal to people's heads, but is distributed as a "cognitive web" across brains, bodies, and world. This distributed, embodied view of cognition offers a vision of human thought that is far less internally computational and far more bodily extended into the real world of action than is traditionally understood in cognitive science. Once again, this claim does not imply that cognition never relies on disembodied, computational processes. Yet there is an ever-growing literature to support a view of imagery, memory, and reasoning as intimately tied to bodily activity, such that higher-order cognitive process are situated, embedded, and embodied.

6

Language and Communication

Communicating with others mostly requires that we move our bodies. When I speak to a friend, I move my lips, tongue, and vocal apparatus, along with various body parts not directly associated with speech, such as my eyes, hands, head, and torso. In some situations, I can effectively communicate some idea or belief simply by nodding my head or blinking my eyes. Even the absence of overt body movement can communicate, as when you stare blankly at me after I ask you a question. We interpret the lack of body movement as meaningful precisely because bodily motion normally communicates.

The traditional belief among many cognitive scientists is that meaning is an abstract entity divorced from bodily experience. Understanding language is assumed to require breaking down the physical information (e.g., speech sounds) into a language-independent medium that constitutes the "language of thought." The meaning of any sentence presumably can be represented as a complex proposition consisting of a predicate with several arguments. Longer texts are represented in associative networks of propositions (predicate-argument schemas) or as abstract mental models (Fletcher, 1994; Fletcher, van den Broek, & Arthur, 1996; Kintsch, 1988). More recent approaches to the semantics of words and sentences include powerful quantitative tools, such as hyperspace analog to language (HAL) or latent semantic analysis (LSA), both of which reduce the problem of meaning to a simple matter of computing word co-occurrence (Burgess, 2000; Burgess & Lund, 2000; Kintsch, 1998). The resulting high-dimensional semantic space of words can be used to predict several psychological effects, such as the acquisition of vocabulary in children, word categorization, sentence coherence, priming effects, meaning similarity, and learning difficulty of texts.

The primary problem with these different views of language, similar to those with the other topics covered in this book, is that they conceive of meaning, and human cognition more generally, in terms of abstract and disembodied symbols. Traditional views of language and communication ignore the fundamental problem of how meaning is grounded in ordinary experience (the "symbol grounding problem") (Harnad, 1990; Searle, 1980), especially in regard to how meaningful symbols relate to embodiment and real-world referents (Johnson, 1987). Although cognitive neurolinguists examine the neural basis for human linguistic abilities, most research on the links between language and brain functions do not properly acknowledge the importance of people's ordinary kinesthetic experiences. This neglect has seriously undermined scientific understanding of the relations between mind and body, and, more specifically, linguistic meaning, communication, and embodiment.

My aim in this chapter is to argue the case for embodiment in psychological theories of language and communication. I consider a range of hypotheses on the possible influence of embodied activity in language use, ranging from speech perception and the evolution of language to word meaning and discourse comprehension. The chapter also describes the significant work in cognitive science on gesture and its critical role in communication and cognition.

Time Course of Linguistic Communication

Embodied experience may influence linguistic communication at several levels. Each of these levels reflects how the body shapes communication at different time scales, ranging from slow-moving linguistic evolution to fast-moving aspects of immediate, online language production and comprehension. Consider the following hypotheses:

(1) Embodiment plays a role in the development of and change in the meanings of words and expressions over time, but does not motivate contemporary speakers' use and understanding of language.
(2) Embodiment motivates the linguistic meanings that have currency within linguistic communities, or may have some role in an idealized speakers/hearers' understanding of language. But embodied experience does not play any part in speakers' abilities to make sense of or process language.
(3) Embodiment motivates contemporary speakers' use and understanding of why various words and expressions mean what they do, but does not play any role in people's ordinary on-line production or comprehension of everyday language.
(4) Embodiment functions automatically and interactively in people's on-line use and understanding of linguistic meaning.

These hypotheses reflect a hierarchy of possibilities about the interaction of embodied experience with different aspects of language use and understanding. Because they relate to different time scales on which linguistic meaning occurs, each hypothesis requires appropriate methods to empirically study it, with certain disciplines being better able to provide evidence in support of these different possibilities. My essential claim is that debates about embodied language and communication will be best served by looking specifically for its effects on human performance at these differing levels, and not just arguing a priori that embodied experience plays little or no role in speaking, understanding, and communication.

Language Change

Embodiment has a clear role in how languages change, especially through the use of metaphoric reasoning. Many types of word meanings become extended from body concepts to conceive, and talk of, ideas from dissimilar domains, such as space and time (Geeraerts, 1997; Traugott & Dasher, 2002). For instance, Sweetser (1990) has shown how many polysemous words in Indo-European languages acquired their nonphysical meanings via metaphorical extensions from earlier acquired concrete, physical meanings, so that VISION/HEARING/TACTILE ACTS gets mapped onto ideas about INTELLECT. Thus, metaphorical mappings from the idea of visually seeing things to the idea of intellectually understanding things defines a pathway for semantic change. The presence of conceptual metaphors such as UNDERSTANDING IS SEEING not only explains how words change their meanings historically (i.e., why the physical sense of "see" regularly gets extended via metaphor at a later point to have a nonphysical meaning), but also motivates for contemporary speakers just why it is that polysemous words have the specific meanings they do (e.g., why it just makes sense to us to talk about understanding ideas using expressions such as "I clearly see the point you're making in this essay"). With few exceptions, words in Indo-European languages meaning "see" regularly acquire the meaning "know" at widely scattered times and places (see Andrews, 1995 for similar evidence from Russian).

A different instance of how bodily ideas/experiences drive semantic change through metaphor is seen in the development of modal verbs (Sweetser, 1990). Modal verbs, such as "must," "may," and "can," pertain to experiences of actuality, possibility, and necessity. Thus, we often represent our experience of things, event, and relations as being actual, possible, or necessary. We often feel ourselves able to act in certain ways ("can"), permitted to perform actions of our own choosing ("may"), and compelled by forces beyond our control ("must"). A pervasive embodied metaphor of THE MIND IS THE BODY drives the use of physical experiences to conceive of mental processes of reasoning as involving forces and barriers analogous to physical and social forces and obstacles. Consider the following examples (Gibbs, 1994: 160):

"You must move your foot, or the car will crush it."
(Physical necessity.)

"Sally can reach the fried eel for you."
(She is physically capable of reaching it.)

"Paul must get a job now."
(Paul is forced to get a job, although the compulsion is not physical.)

"You may now kiss the bride"
(No social barrier prevents you from kissing the bride)

The different root meanings of these modal verbs involve notions of force and obligation that are metaphorically extended from the bodily sense to describe more abstract ideas about mental processes. The historical evidence demonstrates that semantic change for many words, as seen here for modal verbs, is driven by embodied metaphor. Most generally, there are extensive mappings from perceptual/kinesthetic experiences onto cognitive processes, and later on ideas about verbal expression, that appear to drive semantic change in a wide variety of languages across different times and places (Koivisto-Alanko, 1998).

Speech Perception

How do listeners link speech and meaning? How do listeners learn to extract phonetic information from a complex speech array to identify individual words? Categorizing speech sounds is an enormously complex task. Environmental noises, including that from other speech, often interfere with the speech signal. Other factors, such as speaking rates and voice of the speaker(s) (i.e., high vs. low pitch), also complicate stable speech identification.

The traditional approach acknowledges the invariance problem by focusing on invariant acoustic functions used in phoneme identification (Stevens & Blumstein, 1981). The phonetic information in the speech signal is then compared with the identical abstract representations for phonemes in the mental lexicon. For example, the word "keep" is composed of three phonetic segments: an initial consonant (/k/), a medial vowel (/i/), and a final consonant (/p/). Each phonetic segment may be described in terms of a small set of distinctive features that recombine to form the set of segments in a given language.

But there are problems with this view. Primarily, there is not a complete set of invariant properties that can unambiguously identify all phonetic segments in the speech signal (Klatt, 1989). Many features contribute to this complexity in mapping. For example, when speakers talk, they do not produce the phonetic segments of a word sequentially, because the articulatory gestures for certain segments overlap with others. Coarticulation enables speakers to rapidly produce sequences of phonetic segments, but it complicates listeners' mappings of acoustic signals and phonetic structures.

One solution to the problem of a lack of invariance in the acoustic signal is to suggest that speech perception may be aligned with embodied articulation processes (Liberman et al., 1967). Although the relationship between acoustic stimuli and perception is quite complex, the link between articulation and perception is more direct. Sounds produced in similar ways but with varying acoustic representations are perceived in similar ways. For example, the acoustic cues for a [d] in a syllable onset differ depending on the vowel that follows, yet an articulatory description of [d] as an "alveolar constriction" is compatible in each environment. Speech decoding results in an abstract phoneme-based representation via a listener's own knowledge of the effects of coarticulation on his/her own productions. Anecdotal evidence suggests that producing speech silently facilitates students' leaning of new speech sounds. Trying to say new sounds encourages learners to attend to subtle motor processes that might otherwise be overshadowed by auditory sensations. This motor theory of speech perception maintains that listeners use their own internalized articulator motor patterns, encapsulated in a "specialized speech module," to interpret spoken language (Liberman, 1970; Liberman & Mattingly, 1989).

The motor theory was devised to explain how disparate acoustic stimuli could represent the same phoneme. The discontinuity in the acoustic stimulus for "got" and "gaze" provides a striking example in which the percepts are in accord with the articulatory maneuvers that make the sounds, rather than the acoustics of the sounds emitted. Another example is found in the interposition of brief silences in a spoken sentence. If a tape recording is made of the phrase "please say stop" and a silence of about 5 ms is inserted after "say," the phrase becomes "please say chop" (Dorman, Studdert-Kennedy, & Raphael, 1977). This makes sense given the articulatory gestures required to say "please say chop." Producing the sudden burst of sound for "chop" requires closing the airway briefly, thereby creating a brief silence.

Considerable evidence shows that perception of phonemes is accomplished not simply by analysis of the physical acoustic patterns but through their articulatory events, such as movements of the lips, tongue, and so on (Fowler, 1994; Liberman, 1996; Liberman & Whalen, 2000). For instance, Fowler (1987) analyzed findings from speech production and perception tasks and proposed that listeners "focus on acoustic change, because changing regions of the sound spectrum best reveal the gestural constituency of the talker's utterances." Not surprisingly, sign language users also focus on optical change (i.e., movement) because changing regions of the observer's visual field best indicate the gestural constituency of the signer's utterance. There is also evidence that children's own attempts at vocal articulation are governed to some extent by their visual observations of articulations patterns of others (Studdert-Kennedy, 1981). The child recognizes speech sounds as patterns of gestures and in attempting to represent them, often fails to produce the correct sound because of an error in timing.

Other evidence suggesting that speech is processed in terms of articulatory gestures is found in research on immediate serial recall. For example, the recency effect refers to people's superior performance in recalling the last few spoken items in a list of words. The suffix effect refers to the decrease in recall for the last few items when the list is followed by a single irrelevant syllable or word (thus, a reduction in the recency effect) (Nairne & Walters, 1983). Both the recency and suffix effects are significantly reduced for nonspeech stimuli, such as when people read printed words (known as the modality effect). Traditional theories claim that modality effects arise because the last few items are briefly held in an unprocessed form (i.e., their acoustic properties) that is then disrupted by hearing additional material (Surprenant, Pitt, & Crowder, 1993). But studies show that the recency and suffix effects occur for human speech stimuli, but are nonexistent for nonlinguistic sounds (Greene & Samuel, 1986). In fact, when people hear a list of words followed by an ambiguous suffix, and they think it is the sound of a trumpet, then the suffix effect disappears, but not when told that this same sound was the syllable "wa" (Ayres et al., 1979). These findings suggest that it is not sensory modality (hearing vs. reading) per se that guides speech perception. Instead, speech perception is organized around the fact that the auditory information was spoken speech, or even thought to be human speech, with articulatory gestures.

Another phenomenon demonstrating how phoneme perception is shaped by recognition of their articulation is the "McGurk effect" (Massaro, 1987; McGurk & MacDonald, 1976). Watching a speaker's mouth saying a syllable that conflicts with a heard syllable often changes what syllable is heard. For example, when participants hear the bilabial stop "ba" but see a speaker uttering the velar consonant "ga," they often report hearing the alveolar stop "da" that retains some of the phonetic features of the two sounds. Participants in these studies are not aware of this conflict between the two sources of information. The McGurk effect illustrates how listeners process phonemes not strictly in terms of acoustic properties, but by articulatory gestures as well. Listeners appear to use information about the way a sound is produced from both auditory and visual modes in the process of speech perception. Lachs and Pisoni (2004) proposed, in fact, that both visual and auditory displays of speech are organized by the same laws underlying articulatory events. Cross-modal matching between speech and vision (i.e., face and mouth movements) is achieved, under this view, by comparison to a common source of information about vocal tract activity.

The correspondence between sight and sound is also made by infants. If an 18- to 20-week-old infant is simultaneously shown two videos of the same face saying two different syllables, and hears one of the syllables through a loudspeaker placed directly between the two video screens, the child gazes longer at the video face corresponding to the audible signal (Kuhl & Meltzoff, 1987).

Within a broad perspective, each of the above findings is consistent with the idea that speech perception is linked with the articulatory gestures of speaking. The motor theory, more specifically, fails, nonetheless, to explain certain aspects of speech perception. First, there seem to be as many motor manifestations of a given consonant as there are acoustic signals (MacNeilage, 1975). Second, listeners are still able to perceive speech when they suffer from speech production (i.e., motor) difficulties. Third, very young infants appear able to recognize speech sounds easily, despite being poor speech articulators (Jusczyk, 1995). Finally, early studies show that nonhumans can learn to discriminate different speech sounds, an unlikely possibility if human speech production processes are involved in speech perception (Kuhl & Miller, 1975).

Because of these problems, a revised motor theory emphasized abstract, as opposed to real, phonetic gestures that can be detected through specialized processes (Liberman & Mattingly, 1985). Phonetic gestures, including movements such as rounding of the lips, raising the jaw, and so on, are invariant motor commands sent from the brain to the vocal tract. Under this view, the conversion from acoustic signals to intended phonetic gestures is rapidly and automatically processed by a phonetic module. This revised view suggests that the important thing may be the biological capacity for speech, even in the absence of experience with a functioning vocal apparatus. This relationship would not necessarily be disrupted by damage to the vocal tract. It is interesting, nonetheless, that electrical stimulation of certain sites in the human brain leads to the final gesture of speech and also affects the perception of phonemes (Ojemann & Mateer, 1979). Thus, electrical stimulation in the same location of the periSylvan area of the left hemisphere produces deficits in phoneme perception and oral gesture repetition.

This revision of the motor theory is, unfortunately, difficult to experimentally test, because the concept of gesture remains elusive, at both the underlying and surface levels of production. Some scholars question whether the evidence that phonetic gestures are processed necessarily implies that speech perception requires access to a speaker's motor system. For instance, Fowler's (1986; Fowler & Rosenblum, 1991) direct-realist theory claims that a unit of motor organization (i.e., the gesture) is fundamental to speech perception, but that phonetic gestures are distal events, and that speech perception involves recovery of distal events from proximal stimulation. Finally, some scholars claim that speech perception is not special, but shares underlying pattern recognition processes involved in all types of perception (Massaro, 1987).

But more recent research attempts to demonstrate how phonetic primitives are gestural, and not abstract features (Browman & Goldstein, 1995). Articulatory gestures are unified primitives characterizing phonological patterns, in addition to capturing something about the activity of the vocal tract articulators. More specifically, the lexicon is composed of dynamically specified gestures, where lexical items differ from one another in terms of these gestures and their organization. Once again, gestures are not the movements themselves, but abstract characteristics of the movements. Several dynamical models have been developed that implement phonetic gestures as fundamental couplings among the articulators and the gestural laryngeal characteristics of coarticulation (Kelso, 1995). These modeling efforts most generally illustrate how phonetic gestures can structure acoustic signals directly.

There is another body of literature that highlights the embodied nature of speech processing. Many studies now suggest that the speech signal includes not only phonetic and prosodic information, but also nonlinguistic or indexical information. Listeners can readily identify talkers, their physical and emotional states, their sexes, their regional dialects, and other qualities associated with speaking rates and the dynamics of articulation (Nygaard, Sommers, Mitchell, & Pisoni, 1994). Studies demonstrate that the mental lexicon may be an episodic or exemplar memory system in which each occurrence of a word leaves a detailed trace in memory (Goldinger, 1998; Nygaard, Sommers, Mitchell, & Pisoni, 1994; Remez, Fellowes, & Rubin, 1997). This indexical information, including information about the production of sounds, is encoded in memory along with the phonetic properties of speech. This recent research is consistent with the theory of perceptual symbols (Barsalou, 1999a) in that high-level symbols are represented in memory in terms of their perceptual properties and not in terms of their amodal form.

Gesture and Speech

People move their bodies when they speak. These movements are not accidental, but are often tightly linked to the communicative messages speakers wish to convey. Listeners take notice of these gestural movements and may infer different things about speakers and their messages as a result of what they see.

There are several views of the relationship between speech and gesture (Iverson & Thelen, 1999). One position maintains that speech and gesture are separate communicative systems, which occasionally become linked due to the cognitive demands associated with speech production (Butterworth & Beattie, 1978; Butterworth & Hadar, 1989; Hadar, 1989;

Hadar, Wenkert-Olenik, Krauss, & Soroker, 1998). Gesture serves to support speech production activities, for example, by compensating when speech is temporarily disrupted (e.g., by coughing) or when speakers are unable to put their thoughts into words. But gestures do not influence underlying speech production processes.

A second view holds that there are deep cognitive linkages between speech and gesture, presumably located at the physiological encoding stage (i.e., the stage at which words forms must be accessed from lexical memory) (Krauss, 1998; Krauss & Hadar, 1999). Gestures are especially useful, on this view, when speakers experience difficulty retrieving words, because the production of gesture activates relevant spatio-dynamic features of the concept (i.e., thought) that a speaker had in mind. The link between speech and gesture is limited, then, to a particular stage of speech production.

A third view of speech and gesture assumes that these communicative activities are grounded in common thought processes (Iverson & Thelen, 1999; McNeil, 1992). Speech and gesture have a strong reciprocal relationship through the entire process of speech production, ranging from phonological encoding up through producing syntax, semantics, and discourse. Even though speech and gesture may communicate different aspects of people's thoughts, the tight coupling of these activities suggests that any disruption in one (e.g., gesture) will have negative effects on the other (e.g., speech).

Several kinds of empirical evidence support the third view that speech and gesture are fundamentally grounded in the same underlying cognitive processes. First, when speakers momentarily hesitate, or stutter, their gestures tend to be held motionless until speech continues (Mayberry & Jacques, 2000). There are two hypotheses to explain this fact. The lexical retrieval hypothesis claims that gesture plays an active role in lexical access, particularly for words with spatial content (Butterworth & Hadar, 1989; Krauss, 1998). An alternative view, the information packaging hypothesis, suggests that gesture is involved in the conceptual planning of messages. Specifically, gesture helps speakers to package spatial information into verbalizable entities. Thus, gesture plays a role in speech production because it plays a role in the process of conceptualization.

One study comparing these two hypotheses had 5-year-olds engage in one of two tasks that required comparable lexical access but different information packaging (Alibali, Kita, & Young, 2000). In the explication task, children answered whether two items did or did not have the same quantity (Piagetian conservation). For the description task, children described how two items looked different. These two tasks elicited similar utterances (e.g., "This one is lower, and this one is higher"), but made different demands on children's conceptual packaging of spatial information. Thus, children in the explication task must consider multiple perceptual dimensions in justifying their judgments, something that is not required in the description task. Not surprisingly, children presented more substitute gestures (e.g., right hand moves from back to top of the glass), and used more nonredundant gestures in the explication task than in the description task. This finding is most consistent with the information packaging hypothesis. Although gestures may facilitate lexical retrieval, word finding is not the only place where gestures are involved in speech production. Gesture appears to play a critical role in the conceptualizing and planning of messages.

Neuropsychological research supports the idea that gesture and speech are tightly linked. First, hand and arm movements are represented in brain sites closely related to those responsible for movement of the vocal tract. Second, common brain mechanisms exist for language and sequential motor functions, specifically in the lateral periSylvan cortex of the dominant hemisphere (Ojemann, 1994). Stimulation of this brain region disrupts both oral facial movements and speech production (e.g., naming in reading). These findings raise the possibility that the tight temporal link between speech and gesture may be achieved because of spreading activation from the brain region responsible for speech production to that associated with hand and arm movements, and vice versa.

Studies also show that high levels of EEG activity are found in motor areas of the brain when people are asked to read silently, especially when the words are verbs (Pulvermueller, 1999). A PET study showed high activity in the left premotor cortex when people had to retrieve words for tools, but not words for other conceptual categories (e.g., animals) (Grafton et al., 1997). Verbs and tool names may exhibit the strongest brain activity in the motor cortex because people encode the motoric functions of these words as part of their semantic representations, which become activated when speakers attempt to retrieve their words from memory.

These data suggest that there may be a strong connection between the cerebellum and traditional language areas of the brain such as Broca's area. A different set of brain studies, employing fMRI, showed that there is some overlap between brain areas activated during language and motor tasks (Loring et al., 2000). In this experiment, right-handed participants performed several motor movements (e.g., random finger tapping, toe movement, complex finger tapping, copying displayed hand shapes) and a verb generation task. The results showed that there was significant activation throughout Broca's area during both the language task and each motor task, especially those that required hand movements. Most surprisingly, perhaps, is that evidence also suggests that Broca's area is activated when people just think about moving their hands (Tanaka & Inui, 2002). Recent functional brain imaging studies, more generally, have reported Broca's area activation during tasks outside the linguistic domain, including motor execution (Iacoboni, Woods, & Mazziotta, 1998), perception of others' actions (Decety et al., 1997), and mental simulation (Grafton et al., 1996). Contrary to the popular belief that Broca's area is only associated with certain aspects of language production, this area of the brain appears to be widely involved with any coherent sequence of body movements (Grezes & Decety, 2001; Rizzolatti & Arbib, 1996). Arbib (1998) specifically argue that Broca's area functions include representational capacities related to action/recognition of oro-facial and brachio-manusual based behavior.

Evidence of the tight coupling between speech and gesture also comes from research showing that impairment in some motor functions, such as the ability to move sequentially, also hurts language performance. For instance, a study of right-hemisphere damaged patients showed that they did significantly more poorly than left-hemisphere damaged patients in a copying hand movement task (e.g., closed fist, thump sideways on the table, slap palms on a table), in a task demonstrating the use of common objects, and in a task where people had to produce familiar gestures given a verbal command (e.g., show how to wave good-bye) (Kimura, 1973). This pattern of interferences suggests an overlap in cerebral representation of speaking and certain manual activities. Many researchers now agree that speech and gesture originated from the same neural system (Corballis, 1994).

These different lines of evidence from neuropsychology are generally very consistent with the idea that speech and gesture constitute a tightly coupled cognitive system (Iverson & Thelen, 1999). One proposal on the linkage between speech and gesture claims that the origins for this tight coupling occur in early development of motor and hand coordination (Iverson & Thelen, 1999). A great deal of hand-mouth contact occurs during infancy. Research with infants 9–15 months old shows that there are systematic relationships between types of hand actions and oral activity in face-to-face interaction (Fogel & Hannan, 1985). Although the manual and vocal system develop independently, they appear to influence each other to a significant degree, especially in the production of rhythmical movements (Butcher & Goldin-Meadow, 2000). Infants' first gestures tend to be produced without speech or with meaningless speech. Later on, when speech and gesture begin to occur, they are not tightly linked in time, with one preceding the other. Finally, speech-gesture synchrony emerges quite dramatically when infants simultaneously combine meaningful words with gesture.

Iverson and Thelen (1999) claim that speech and gesture momentarily activate and entrain one another as a coupled oscillator. At first, an infant's manual activity takes precedence, but through rhythmical activity, and later through gesture, manual behavior gradually entrains the speech production system. The initial basis to move hand and mouth together cascade with a single coupled connected system where the mental thought is manifested as movement. This initial activation increases as infants learn to vocally communicate through words and phrases, leading to a tight synchrony of speech and gesture. Eventually, every communicative act, either by speech or gesture, is remembered as an ensemble, including the proprioceptive consequence of that movement. This linkage of speech and gesture provides another example of the sensorimotor origins of thought and of the continual importance of embodied action in mental life.

A final, very different, example of the interaction of speech and gesture is seen in a study of the meaningful gestures used by the Plains Indians of the United States (Farnell, 1995). Among the Assinboine or Nakota people of northern Montana, storytellers use hand gestures that constitute a unique sign system, one that can be used independent of speech. This sign system, called Plains Sign Talk (PST), has for centuries been an intertribal lingua franca for Plains Indians speaking different languages. Although fluent sign talkers are not nearly as common today as they were one hundred years ago, various elders who learned PST when young, deaf families, and participants in ceremonial rituals have kept PST alive. For the Assinboine, PST is not merely a dramatic enhancement of the speaker's narrative, because all speech acts are simultaneously voiced and manual, with both the verbal and signed elements being considered aspects of "talking." As one teacher of PST commented when asked for the spoken equivalent of a signed utterance, "Like I just showed you."

The Assinboine philosophy of "being-in-the-world" makes body movement fundamental as a way of knowing. For the Assinboine, physical being is essential to the attainment of power. For example, prayer is a highly embodied activity where bodily suffering in the hot steam of a sweat lodge and from fasting and periods of isolation provides a significant pathway to seeking and giving power. Suffering is most intense when participants fast, dance, and endure the sun's heat during the sun dance ceremony. People only own their bodies and this makes bodily sacrifice the most meaningful way to obtain spiritual guidance and personal power. The act of dancing in the sun dance ceremony is itself prayer and not merely action that accompanies spoken prayer.

PST contrasts with American Sign Language (ASL) in significant ways. Signs referring to thoughts, minds, and intelligence in ASL center on the head, and signs for emotion and feelings are enacted near the heart and chest. ASL signs reflect folk ideas about the spatial locations of the entities and powers in the body within American society. But PSL sign for concepts such as "know" and "think" are enacted around the heart, and the sign for "doubt" is literally "being of two hearts." To say that someone has a good mind, a Nakota speaker will move a pinched index finger from the heart away from the body with the finger pointing straight ahead, followed by the sign for "good." The movement from the heart is important here, because the heart is not simply the location for the mind. Of course, hearts have little relevance to minds in most Western societies.

Seeing is a powerful metaphor for thinking in English, especially in reference to the end-product of thought. To say "I see what you mean" reflects the metaphorical idea that to perceive something is to correctly understand it. However, in PST, the active process part of the visual metaphor is emphasized rather than its end-product. Thus, talk of thinking refers to the action of looking, specifically looking from the heart. Unlike in English, where there are significant differences between thinking and feeling, PST incorporates the Assinboine folk idea that to know something is to "to know in one's heart," an idea that reduces the distinction between what one personally experiences and what one might objectively know to be true.

Even though the Assinboine primarily view thinking as an activity of looking from the heart, the head still plays a significant role in PST related to the sensory abilities of hearing, listening, seeing, looking, tasting, eating, drinking, and smelling. The individual signs for these center around the face and head near the respective organs. Beyond this, many names for individuals and tribes are performed near, or touching parts of, the face and other regions of the head. For instance, BLOOD (a part of the Blackfeet confederacy) is referred to in PST by a circular action of the fist on the cheek, SIOUX or ASSINBOINE is described by a flat hand moving across the throat referring to "cut throats," NEZ PERCÉ are signed as "pierced noses," CREE by fingers drawn along the side of the face, FLATHEAD by a flattened head, and KIOWA by a head cut at one side. These head- and face-oriented signs are highly metaphorical and work as the primary ways of identifying strangers.

This case study shows how a unique sign system, which can work independent of speech, reveals people's embodied understandings of the world and human events. The PST system also illustrates the importance of embodied metaphor in how people effectively conceptualize abstract ideas and events.

Body Movements and Discourse

Discourse analysts have long argued that embodied activity, such as eye gaze, gestures, and posture, is central in establishing speakers' goals in conversation. As Goodwin (1981: 125) noted, "Emergent displays thus integrate the bodies of the participants into the production of talk, and are important constitutive features of the conversation." There are many examples of how speakers and listeners coordinate their body positions to express different kinds of meaning. For example, one study demonstrated how students use gestures and bodily position vis-à-vis one another (and the teacher) in the construction of silence (Leander, 2002). One conversation in this analysis took place in a high school class in American history. The teacher, Sid, at the front of the room, began to review material from the previous day's class on Constitutional law, and then asked the class a question. The students were seated around the room with four white girls, including Chelle, seated in the back, and four African American students, including Shameen, Rod, and Trent, grouped in the front of the room.

SID: "Do women have full equal rights?"
ROD: "Yes, the."
SID: "And wh-what guaranteed them full and equal rights"
SHAMEEN: "19th Amendment?"
SID: "The 19th Amendment gave them the right to vote. What guaranteed them full and equal rights?"
CHELLE: (from the back of the room) "No we don't have equal rights"
ROBERT: "She says – we got somebody back here that says they don't have equal right."
SID: "They don't have equal rights?"
TRENT: "You're kidding. There was an amendment that did it."
ROBERT: "That's what she said, 'No, we don't' " (facing forward, pointing toward Chelle with thumb of left hand, over shoulder)
CHELLE: "We don't." (Chelle smiles as Robert looks back at her)
SID: "What, what are the laws that give women full and equal rights, from the Amendment to the Constitution?" (Kareena enters, sits in desk behind Robert, sitting up on knees)
SHAMEEN: "13th, 14th, and 15th?" (Ian gets up from seat, walks to back of room)
SID: "13th says all people are – no – 13th says you can't own a person, no slavery, as you'll find out. 14th says – what's the 14th? (holding hands up, palms pressed together) "Raise your hand." (Kareena moves from seat in front to seat in back)
SHAMEEN: "Ah-hah, I said it though."
SID: "14th says?"
SHAMEEN: "14th says that all people are created equal."
SID: "No."

The conversation reveals several ways that people reproduce the social structures through their routine embodied movements. For example, in the midst of Sid and Shameen's exchange, Robert reproduced Chelle's speech with "She says – we got somebody back here that says they don't have equal rights." By drawing attention to Chelle's backchannel comment, Robert brings himself and others into the exchange for several seconds, following which Sid and Shameen continue their questions and answers. But Robert's remark about Chelle's comment, although bringing it up front for class discussion, also marks an embodied alignment with the "we" of the class, because he maintained a face-forward position, and pointing over his shoulder with his thumb at Chelle and then looking back at her only briefly. The embodied positioning aligns Robert firmly with the normative ongoing class discussion, yet destabilizes the conversation by physically pointing to a dissenting voice. Inviting dissension while turning away from it is an important part of the silencing process. Thus, once can silence someone not just by closing off a particular speaker, but also by creating a silenced position in regard to a dominant one.

During Robert and Chelle's interaction, Kareena's entrance into the classroom and taking a seat illustrates how students negotiate their embodied positions with regard to how they view their social alignments in context. For instance, temporarily shifting where one sits can be related to shifting topics, the ideologies called up by them, and students' relations with one another. Kareena had originally entered the classroom and left her books in a seat in front of Trent. Yet when she re-entered the room during discussion, Kareena took a position in the back of the classroom, sitting on her knees at her desk, and observed the interaction. Eighteen seconds later, Kareena moved to the front of the room, retrieved her books, and took a seat behind Robert. This new seating allowed Kareena to align with the group of students in the back of the class, while avoiding the particular conversational focus of the entire classroom. In fact, Kareena demonstrates her new alignment with Chelle by "repositioning" herself in the class. Thus, students take positions with their bodies as well as in their speech. People's bodies are thus a valuable resource in marking their ideological views.

Much research in psycholinguistics demonstrates the importance of "common ground" between speakers and listeners in successful communication (Clark, 1996; Gibbs, 1999a). There are three primary sources for common ground (Clark, 1996). The first source is "linguistic co-presence," where the listener takes as common ground all of the conversation up to and including the utterance currently being interpreted. A second source for common ground is "physical co-presence," where the listener takes as common ground what he or she and the speaker are currently experiencing in terms of their immediate physical environment, including the actions and positioning of their own bodies. The final source of evidence is community membership. This includes information that is universally known in a community and can be represented by mental structures such as scripts (Schank & Abelson, 1976) or schemata (Rumelhart, 1980). Moreover, it also covers mutually known conventions governing the phonology, syntax, and semantics of the sentence uttered.

Normally, mutual knowledge is established by some combination of physical or linguistic co-presence and mutual knowledge based on community membership. But physical co-presence (i.e., sight, sound, touch) alone provides multiple resources for conversational grounding. One study of collaborative problem-solving (e.g., repairing a bicycle) showed that physical co-presence has several independent sources of visual information: (1) participants' hands and faces, (2) participants' behavior and actions, (3) focused task objects, and (4) the work environment in context (Kraut, Fussell, & Siegel, 2003). When people work side by side, they have all four sources of visual information available. Thus, participants can monitor each other's facial expressions and body orientations vis-à-vis task objects (e.g., the bicycle, its parts, tools for repairing it). Facial expressions and visible actions directed toward the task provide evidence of whether someone understands an instruction. In fact, research shows that when people work side by side, they perform the task of fixing a bicycle faster and using fewer utterances than when they are remotely linked by video and audio, or audio alone (Kraut et al., 2003).

There are major differences between visual co-presence, or just sharing a joint view, and full physical co-presence, in which spatial relations between people and task objects are monitored. For example, seeing another person's upper body allows a remote partner to observe that he or she is pointing at something. Yet having a spatially consistent view of both participants and task objects is needed to understand the precise target of a pointing gesture, as well as the targets of the partner's eye gaze. Several systems have been developed that provide participants with multiple cues as to, for example, where a person at a meeting is looking at any moment in time, or which object a hand gesture is aimed at (Luff et al., 2003; Stiefehagen, Yang, & Waibel, 2002).

Computer interface designers have attempted to build embodied interface agents to provide a higher bandwidth of communication than would otherwise be possible with a less embodied system. Unfortunately, many new interface agents do not provide much bodily information other than ornamental things such as redundant pointing gestures, a few facial expressions, a cocked head, and an external wardrobe. But one model of embodied conversation aims to exploit the affordances of the body to facilitate meaningful dialogue between interface agents and human users (Cassell et al., 2001). REA is an embodied, multimodal, real-time conversational agent that acts as a real estate salesperson while showing users around virtual houses. REA has a fully articulated graphical body, can sense the user passively through cameras and audio input, and is capable of speech with intonation, facial display, hand and eye movements, and gestural output. The system consists of a large projection screen in which REA is displayed, and which the user stands in front of. Various microphones capture speech input. Two cameras mounted on the top of the projector screen track the user's hand and head positions in space. One computer runs the graphics and conversation of REA, while a second manages the speech recognition and image processing.

The following provides an actual conversational interaction between a user, Tim, and REA (Cassell et al., 2001: 60):

Tim approaches REA.
REA notices and looks toward Tim and smiles.
Tim says, "Hello."
REA responds, "Hello, how can I help you?" with a hand wave.
Tim says, "I'm looking to buy a place near MIT."
REA says, "I have a house . . . " with a beat gesture to emphasize the new information "house."
Tim interrupts by beginning to gesture.
REA finishes her current utterance by saying "in Cambridge" and then gives up her turn.
Tim refines his house request.
REA finishes the house description and then continues.

Although REA is somewhat awkward in her conversational interactions, she converses as well as she can because of the system's ability to track the user's hand and head movements, infer the specific speech acts the user conveys, and use voice information to recognize when the other speaker's turn begins and ends. A future goal of this project is to allow REA to entrain, or increasingly adapt, her behaviors in synchrony with the user.

Word Meaning

Words are traditionally defined in terms of semantic features that are usually abstract and are thought to reflect different conceptual relations. Yet in recent years, scholars have argued that some aspects of word meanings arise from, and are mentally represented in terms of, perceptual/embodied experience. Consider the word "stand" in the following sentences:

"Please stand at attention."
"He wouldn't stand for such treatment."
"The clock stands on the mantle."
"The law still stands."
"He stands six foot five."
"The part stands for the whole."
"She had a one-night stand with a stranger."

These sentences represent just a few of the many senses of "stand" that are common in everyday speech and writing. Some of these senses refer to the physical act of standing (e.g., "Please stand at attention," "The clock stands on the mantle," "He stands six foot five"), whereas others have nonphysical, perhaps figurative, interpretations (e.g., "We stood accused of the crime," "The part stands for the whole," "He wouldn't stand for such treatment"). What are the principles that relate the meanings of polysemous words? For instance, what relates the different physical and nonphysical senses of "stand" in the examples noted above?

Some linguists in recent years have argued that many polysemous words resist being defined by a general, abstract, core sense (Brugman & Lakoff, 1988; Fillmore, 1982; Geeraerts, 1993; Sweetser, 1986). Cognitive linguists have suggested that the meanings of polysemous words can be characterized by metaphor, metonymy, and different kinds of image schemas (Lakoff, 1987; Johnson, 1987; Sweetser, 1990). Under this view, the lexical organization of polysemous words is not a repository of random, idiosyncratic information, but is structured by general cognitive principles that are systematic and recurrent throughout the lexicon. Most important, perhaps, is the claim that these principles arise from our phenomenological, embodied experience. One possibility is that bodily experience partly motivates people's intuitions as to why different senses of "stand" have the meanings they do.

Gibbs et al. (1994) attempted to experimentally show that the different senses of the polysemous word "stand" are motivated by different image schemas that arise from our bodily experience of standing. Their general aim was to empirically demonstrate that the meanings of the polysemous word "stand" are not arbitrary for native speakers, but are motivated by people's recurring bodily experiences in the real world.

As a first step toward understanding how image schemas partly motivate the meanings of the polysemous word "stand," a preliminary experiment sought to determine which image schemas best reflect people's recurring bodily experiences of standing. A group of participants were guided through a brief set of bodily exercises to get them to consciously think about their own physical experience of standing. For instance, participants were asked to stand up, to move around, bend over, to crunch, and to stretch out on their tiptoes. Having people actually engage in these bodily experiences facilitates participants' intuitive understanding of how their experience of standing related to many different possible image schemas. After this brief standing exercise, participants then read brief descriptions of 12 different image schemas that might possibly have some relationship to the experience of physical standing (e.g., VERTICALITY, BALANCE, RESISTANCE, ENABLEMENT, CENTER-PERIPHERY, LINKAGE). Finally, the participants rated the degree of relatedness of each image schema to their own embodied experiences of standing. The results of this first study showed that five image schemas are primary to people's bodily experiences of standing (i.e., BALANCE, VERTICALITY, CENTER-PERIPHERY, RESISTANCE, and LINKAGE).

A second experiment investigated people's judgments of similarity for different senses of "stand." The participants sorted 35 different senses of "stand" into five groups based on their similarity of meaning. An analysis of these groups revealed that participants did not categorize physical senses of "stand" separately from the nonphysical or figurative senses. For example, the physical idea of standing in "to stand at attention" was often grouped with the metaphorical senses of "stand" in "let the issue stand" and "to stand the test of time."

The third experiment in this series examined the relationship between the five image schemas for the physical experience of standing and the various senses of "stand" studied in Experiment 2. Once again, participants were first asked to stand up and focus on different aspects of their bodily experience of standing. As they did this, the participants were presented with verbal descriptions of the five image schemas BALANCE, VERTICALITY, CENTER-PERIPHERY, RESISTANCE, and LINKAGE. Afterwards, the participants were given a list of 32 senses of "stand" and asked to rate the degree of relatedness between each sense and the five image schemas.

The rating data from this third study allowed Gibbs et al. (1994) to construct an image schema profile for each of the 32 uses of "stand." Several interesting similarities emerged in the image schema profiles for some of the 32 senses of "stand." For example, "it stands to reason" and "as the matter now stands" both have the same image schema profile (in their rank-order of importance) of LINKAGE – BALANCE – CENTER/PERIPHERY – RESISTANCE – VERTICALITY. The expressions "don't stand for such treatment" and "to stand against great odds" are both characterized by the image schema profile RESISTANCE – CENTER/PERIPHERY – LINKAGE – BALANCE – VERTICALITY.

The primary goal of this study, though, was to assess whether the senses of "stand" seen as being similar in meaning in the second experiment were reliably predictable from the image schema profiles obtained in the third experiment. Statistical analyses showed that knowing the image schema profiles for different senses of "stand" allowed us to predict 79% of all the groupings of "stand" in Experiment 2. These data provide very strong support for the hypothesis that people's understandings of the meanings of "stand" are partly motivated by image schemas that arise from their bodily experiences of standing.

A fourth study showed that participants' sortings of "stand" in different groups cannot be explained simply in terms of their understanding of the contexts in which these words appeared. Thus, people did not sort phrases, such as "don't stand for such treatment" and "to stand against great odds," because these phrases refer to the same types of situations. Instead, it appears that people's similarity judgments are best attributed to their tacit understanding of how different patterns of image schemas motivate different uses of the polysemous word "stand."

These studies demonstrate that people make sense of different uses of "stand" because of their tacit understanding of several image schemas that arise partly from the ordinary bodily experience of standing. These image schemas, the most important of which are BALANCE, VERTICALITY, CENTER-PERIPHERY, RESISTANCE and LINKAGE, not only produce the grounding for many physical senses of "stand" (e.g., "he stands six- foot five," "stand in the way," and "stand at attention"), but also underlie people's understanding of complex, metaphorical uses (e.g., "the part stands for the whole," "as the matter now stands," and "the engine can't stand the constant wear"). People perceive different senses of "stand" as similar in meaning partly on the basis of the underlying image schema profile for each use of the word in context. Similar work shows the embodied basis of people's understandings of the various meanings of the preposition "on" (Beitel, Gibbs, & Sanders, 2000).

My argument about the meanings of several polysemous words does not imply that people judge similarity of meaning between two senses of a word only on the basis of image schemas. Many aspects of word meaning that have little to do directly with image schemas certainly play some role in people's understanding of word meaning and their judgments of similarity of meaning for different senses of a polysemous word. At the same time, this experimental research does not imply that people automatically access some specific pattern of image schemas each time they encounter a particular use of a word. The main conclusion, though, from the experimental work on "stand" and "on" is that people tacitly recognize some connection between these schematic bodily experiences and different aspects of linguistic meaning, including meanings that are highly abstract and/or metaphorical.

The work on image schemas and word meaning provides support for the idea that some aspects of meaning are grounded in contemporary speakers' embodied experience, which they can tacitly recognize under the right experimental conditions. But other psycholinguistic studies suggest that people may automatically infer perceptual/embodied characteristics of word meaning while reading or listening. Some research has found priming between words that refer to objects with similar perceptual characteristics (Schreuder, Flores d'Arcais, & Glazenborg, 1984). For instance, the words "orange" and "ball" are perceptually similar, because the objects have the same shape. The words "skipping rope" and "ball," on the other hand, are conceptually related, because the objects are both toys. Other word pairs are both perceptually and conceptually similar, such as "butter" and "ball." Finally, some word pairs are both perceptually and conceptually unrelated, such as "hoe" and "ball."

Several studies, employing tasks where participants either simply pronounce or give lexical decisions on target items (e.g., "ball"), demonstrated significant perceptual and conceptual priming effects. These priming effects were even stronger when the word pairs were both perceptually and conceptually related (e.g., "butter" and "ball") (Schreuder et al., 1987). More recent studies, however, suggest that perceptual priming is found only when participants are first alerted to an object's perceptual characteristics (e.g., does the word "ball" refer to an oblong object?) (Pecher, Zoelenberg, & Raajamadon, 1998). These studies on perceptual priming in word identification tasks generally suggest that the perceptual characteristics of objects, including those that objects afford, might be automatically activated in memory, but perhaps not for all cases, when concrete nouns are read.

One set of studies examined the idea that perceptual symbols are used in on-line language comprehension (Stanfield & Zwaan, 2001). Perceptual symbols are the residues of perceptual experience, stored as patterns of activation, in the brain. Unlike amodal representations, perceptual symbols bear an analogue relationship with their real-world references. Participants in these studies were presented with sentences such as "He hammered the nail into the wall" and "He hammered the nail into the floor." After reading a specific sentence, participants saw a picture depicting the object mentioned in the sentence (e.g., the nail). This picture presented the object either in a horizontal or in a vertical orientation, thus creating a match or mismatch with the orientation of the object implied by the sentence. In fact, responses were significantly quicker when there was a match between the implied orientation and the picture than when these were mismatched. These results support the idea that people activate and manipulate perceptual symbols when understanding the context-specific meanings of words during utterance interpretation.

A follow-up set of studies extended the previous findings to the representation of an object's shape in sentence comprehension (Zwaan, Stanfield, & Yaley, 2002). For example, participants saw the sentence "The ranger saw the eagle in the sky" followed by a picture of an eagle with either folded or outstretched wings. Not surprisingly, people gave faster recognition judgments to the eagle when the picture matched the shape implied by the sentence. A second study showed the same findings using a naming task that did not involve people matching the picture with the previous sentence. Once more, the results support the hypothesis that people activate perceptual symbols of referents for words during language interpretation.

Research shows that people translate words and sentences into a flow of events comparable to normal perceptual experiences. For instance, researchers argue that the words in which events are represented in language reflect their chronological order (i.e., the iconicity assumption; Dowty, 1986). Understanding the word "crossing" in "crossing the river" demands that readers track the spatial evaluation over time of some target, or trajector, which starts at one side and ends up at the other. Because the trajector cannot be represented at both sides at one time, readers must create a dynamic representation that captures the temporal perceptual character of the phrase's meaning.

Experiments show that people create dynamic, temporal representations as part of their understanding of word meaning. Zwaan (1996) demonstrated that time shifts in narratives increase processing time. Thus, people reading the phrase "An hour later" after some event take longer to process this phrase than when a minor time shift is implied, such as with the phrase "A moment later." These findings are consistent with the "iconicity assumption," not only in that events are assumed to occur in chronological order, but also occur contiguously. Other data indicates that continuing actions in sentences are more activated in memory than are events not continuing. Thus, people are faster to say that "walked" is a word after reading the pair of sentences "Teresa walked onto the stage. A moment later she collapsed" than they did having first read the sentences "Teresa walked onto the stage. An hour later she collapsed." Related studies show that embodied actions that continue remain more activated than events that have been discontinued. Thus, people were slower to judge that "kicking" was a word after reading "Steve stopped kicking the soccer ball" than after reading "Steve was kicking the soccer ball" (Carreiras et al., 1997). These findings, again, show how people's construal of events, based on their embodied understandings, play an important role in the processing and representation in memory of words in linguistic expressions.

Very recent work indicates that schematic images are recruited during immediate processing of verbs (Richardson et al., 2003). A norming study first showed that participants were generally consistent in pairing four different pictures that reflect various schematic images (e.g., a circle, a square, an arrow looking up, down, left, or right) with different concrete and abstract verbs (e.g., "push," "lift," "argue," "respect"). A second norming study had participants create their own schematic images for verbs in a simple computer-based drawing environment. Once more, there was good consistency in the spatial shapes people thought best described the meanings of the different verbs. These findings show that people have regular intuitions about the spatial representations underlying different verbs, even abstract ones.

Additional studies showed that verbs activate underlying spatial representations during online language comprehension. For instance, in one study, participants heard a sentence (e.g., "The girl hopes for a pony") with two pictures presented sequentially in the center of the computer screen. The two pictures reflected different images of the main and object nouns in either vertical or horizontal position. Afterwards, participants were tested on their memory for the pictures in a speeded recognition task. As predicted, people recognized the pictures faster when they were oriented along the same axis of the associated verb. Verb comprehension appears to activate schematic images that act as scaffolds for visual memory of the pictures. The pictures that were encoded as oriented similarly to the verbs' meanings were identified faster during the memory tests.

These results suggest that verb meanings are actively linked with perceptual mechanisms that influence online comprehension and memory. One possibility is that different perceptual and motor experiences become associated with verbs, which are activated as part of people's perceptual-motor simulations of the sentence during understanding (Barsalou, 2001).

Different experiments demonstrate that embodied action influences immediate symbolic, or semantic, judgments for simple linguistic statements. In these studies, participants were first asked to make hand shapes corresponding to verbal descriptions such as "pinch" and "clench" (Klatzky et al., 1989). Following this, the participants made speeded judgments on the sensibleness of phrases such as "aim a dart" (sensible) or "close a nail" (not sensible). Embodied action relevant to the phrases facilitated people's speeded verifications of these phrases. For instance, the hand shape for "pinch" speeded the sensibleness judgments for "throw a dart" but not "throw a punch." Interestingly, when participants were asked to make verbal responses (but not hand shapes) to the nonverbal prime (e.g., the word "pinch" when shown the nonverbal signal for pinch), the priming effect was eliminated. Sensibleness judgments, like online comprehension, require a type of mental simulation using an embodied, motoric medium.

Image Schemas and Utterance Interpretation

Image schemas are cognitive representations that arise from people's recurring embodied experiences (see Chapter 4). The empirical findings from cognitive psychology (see Chapter 5) correspond to some of the inferences people appear to draw when understanding different sentences that metaphorically refer to momentum. Consider the following utterances.

"I was bowled over by that idea."
"We have too much momentum to withdraw from the election race."
"I got carried away by what I was doing."
"We better quit arguing before it picks up too much momentum and we can't stop."
"Once he gets rolling, you'll never be able to stop him talking."

These utterances reflect how the image schema for MOMENTUM allows discussion of very abstract domains of cognition, such as political support, control, arguments, and talking in terms of physical objects moving with momentum. We may be able to predict important aspects of the inferences people draw when understanding these sentences, given what is known about representational momentum from cognitive psychological research (see Chapter 5).

One of the findings from representational momentum research is that people behave as if an apparently moving object continues to move even after encountering an obstacle. Essentially, the moving object appears to carry the obstacle along with it rather than deflecting off it or stopping.

When understanding the sentence "I was bowled over by that idea," people should infer that the idea was important and that the speaker was convinced by the idea. This follows from one of the characteristics of moving objects – the bigger objects are, the more momentum they have when moving. Accordingly, a big object encountering an obstacle should result in that obstacle being carried along with the big object. Applying the conceptual metaphor IDEAS ARE OBJECTS, one should infer when reading or hearing "I was bowled over by that idea" that the person encountering an important (big) idea would be convinced (carried along) by that idea.

Another result from the research on representational momentum is that objects moving with momentum are perceived as being unable to stop immediately. Even if a force is applied to stop the object, it will continue for some distance before coming to rest. One might infer from this situation that if reaching a particular destination is desired, then the more momentum an object has the better are the chances for the object to reach the destination. We can apply this knowledge, along with the conceptual metaphor ACCOMPLISHMENTS ARE MOVEMENTS, to the sentence "We have too much momentum to withdraw from the election race" to infer that the candidate in the election race has a good chance (much momentum) to win the election, and therefore should not attempt to withdraw (stop).

A related finding from representational momentum research is that an object with unchecked momentum will move a long distance, perhaps even overshooting some desired destination. This situation gives rise to the inferences drawn when comprehending "I got carried away by what I was doing." Specifically, a person doing something without monitoring the time involved or the resources devoted to doing it (an object moving with unchecked momentum) might devote too much time or too many resources to the task (overshoot the desired destination).

A different aspect of the representational momentum research concerns the apparent speed and acceleration of the moving object. This factor affects the perceived amount of momentum that an object will have. Applying this finding to the sentence "Once he gets rolling, you'll never get him to stop talking" leads to the inference that interrupting (stopping) the person early in the conversation (when speed is low) will be easier than interrupting him later (when speed is high). This result also applies to the sentence "You had better stop the argument now before it picks up too much momentum and we can't stop it." The inference here might be that arguments start off fairly innocuously (with low speed), but as they progress, things may be said that are unretractable (high speed). For both sentences, we understand that the talking or argument should be stopped as early as possible.

There is no experimental evidence to support these speculative ideas. But this discussion illustrates important possibilities about how image schemas may underlie various aspects of the rather subtle inference patterns associated with the meanings of utterances.

Embodied Metaphor in Figurative Language Interpretation

Many experiments, however, illustrate how image schemas serve as the source domains in different metaphorical concepts and partly account for the rich meanings of a wide range of linguistic phenomena, including idioms, conventional expressions, and novel metaphors (Gibbs, 2002). Consider the idiom "spill the beans." Try to form a mental image for this phrase and then ask yourself the following questions. Where are the beans before they are spilled? How big is the container? Are the beans cooked or uncooked? Is the spilling accidental or intentional? Where are the beans once they've been spilled? Are the beans in a nice, neat pile? Where are the beans supposed to be? After the beans are spilled, are they easy to retrieve?

Most people have definite responses to these questions about their mental images for idioms (Gibbs & O'Brien, 1990). They generally say that the beans were in some pot that is about the size of a person's head, the beans are uncooked, the spilling of the beans is accidental, and the spilled beans are all over a floor and are difficult to retrieve. This consistency in people's intuitions about their mental images is quite puzzling if one assumes that the meanings of idioms are arbitrarily determined. People's descriptions about their mental images for idioms reveal some of the embodied metaphorical knowledge that motivates the meanings of idiomatic phrases. One study examined people's mental images for groups of idioms with similar figurative meanings, such as about revelation (e.g., "spill the beans," "let the cat out of the bag," "blow the lid off"), anger (e.g., "blow your stack," "hit the ceiling," "flip your lid"), insanity (e.g., "go off your rocker," "lose your marbles," "bounce off the walls"), secretiveness (e.g., "keep it under your hat," "button your lips," "keep in the dark"), and exerting control (e.g., "crack the whip," "lay down the law," "call the shots") (Gibbs & O'Brien, 1990). Participants were asked to describe their mental images for these idioms and to answer questions about the causes, intentionality, and manner of actions in their mental images for these phrases.

Overall, participants' descriptions of their mental images were remarkably consistent for different idioms with similar figurative meanings. The general schemas underlying people's images were not simply representative of the idioms' figurative meanings, but captured more specific aspects of the kinesthetic events with the images. For example, the anger idioms such as "flip your lid" and "hit the ceiling" all refer to the concept of "getting angry," but participants specifically imagined for these phrases some force causing a container to release pressure in a violent manner. There is nothing in the surface forms of these different idioms to tightly constrain the images participants reported. After all, lids can be flipped and ceilings can be hit in a wide variety of ways, caused by many different circumstances. But the participants' protocols in this study revealed little variation in the general events that took place in their images for idioms with similar meanings.

Participants' responses to the questions about the causes and consequences of the actions described in their images were also highly consistent. Consider the most frequent responses to the probe questions for the anger idioms (e.g., "blow your stack," "flip your lid," "hit the ceiling"). When imagining anger idioms, people reported that pressure (i.e., stress or frustration) causes the action, that one has little control over the pressure once it builds, that its violent release is done unintentionally (e.g., the blowing of the stack) and that once the release has taken place (i.e., once the ceiling has been hit, the lid flipped, the stack blown), it is difficult to reverse the action.

Similar findings have been found for mental imagery of proverbs (Gibbs, Strom, & Spivey-Knowlton, 1997). For instance, people imagine the phrase "A rolling stone gathers no moss" in particular ways, in part because of the metaphorical idea that LIFE IS A JOURNEY, which is grounded in the image schema of SOURCE-PATH-GOAL. Thus, people are limited in the kinds of images they create for idioms and proverbs because of very specific embodied knowledge that helps structure their metaphorical understanding of various concepts (Gibbs & O'Brien, 1990). For example, people's images for the anger idioms are based on folk conceptions of certain physical events. That is, people use their embodied knowledge about the behavior of heated fluid in containers (e.g., the bodies as containers and bodily fluids within them) and map this knowledge onto the target domain of anger to help them conceptualize in more concrete terms what is understood about the concept of anger. Various specific entailments result from these general metaphorical mappings, ones that provide specific insight into people's consistent responses about the causes, intentionality, manner, and consequences of the activities described by stacks blowing, lids flipping, ceilings being hit and so on. It appears, then, that the embodied metaphorical ways in which people partially conceptualize experiences actually provide part of the motivation for why speakers have consistent mental images and specific knowledge about these images for idioms and proverbs with similar figurative meanings.

Embodied Action in Metaphor Processing

A new line of research investigated the possible influence of bodily action on people's speeded processing of simple metaphoric phrases (i.e., hypothesis 4 above). Phrases such as "stamp out a feeling," "push an issue," "sniff out the truth," and "cough up a secret" all denote physical actions upon abstract items. Wilson and Gibbs (2005) hypothesized that if abstract concepts are indeed understood as items that can be acted upon by the body, then performing a related action should facilitate making a sensibleness judgment for a figurative phrase that mentions this action. For example, if participants first move their leg as if to kick something, and then read "kick around the idea," they should verify that this phrase is meaningful faster than when they first performed an unrelated body action.

Participants were first taught to perform various specific bodily actions given different nonlinguistic cues. The sixteen bodily actions were throw, stamp, tear, push, swallow, sniff out, cough, spit out, poke nose, grasp, shake off, put finger, chew, stand, stretch, and shake. The participants learned these actions by watching a videotape of an actor performing these actions after showing a distinct icon before each event. Participants then had to demonstrate perfect memory for the different actions given their respective cues. Following this, participants were individually seated in front of a computer screen. The experiment consisted of a series of trials where an icon flashed on the screen, prompting the participant to perform the appropriate bodily action. After this was done, a string of words appeared on the screen and participants had to judge as quickly as possible whether that word string was "sensible."

Half of the word strings were sensible and half were not. The sensible phrases were all conventional metaphoric phrases referring to an embodied action on some abstract concept. In the experiment, some of the bodily actions participants first performed were relevant to the following verbal phrases (e.g., the motor action kick was followed by "kick around the idea"), and some were not (e.g., the motor action chew was followed by "kick around the idea"). A third type of trial involved no prime at all (i.e., participants did not perform any bodily action before seeing the word string).

Participants made sensibleness judgments more quickly to the metaphorical phrases that matched the preceding action than to the phrases that did not match the earlier movement. People were also faster in responding to the metaphor phrases after having performed a relevant body moment than when they did not move at all. A control study, where people simply had to provide a word that best described each action, showed that these priming effects were not just due to prior lexical associations between the primes and targets. In short, performing an action facilitates understanding of a figurative phrase containing that action word, just as it does for literal phrases. People do not understand the nonliteral meanings of these figurative phrases as a matter of convention. Instead, people actually understand "toss out a plan," for instance, in terms of physically tossing something (i.e., the plan is viewed as a physical object). In this way, processing metaphoric meaning involves some imaginative understanding of the body's role in structuring abstract concepts.

Desire as Hunger: A Case Study in Embodied Metaphor

A different research project on embodied action in metaphorical meaning looked at people's interpretations of metaphorical expressions about human desires (Gibbs, Lima, & Francuzo, 2004). Consider the following last lines from the book titled *Holy Hunger: A Memoir of Desire* (Bullitt-Jones, 1999), in which the author summarizes her spiritual journey after the death of her father:

In my case, I hungered, I yearned for something – or Someone – that would really fill me up, fill up my life, give me something to live for, something larger than the ordinary of everyday but found there, nevertheless, in the turning of the days and the seasons, the rising and the setting of the sun, in the sheer gift of being alive.

By the time my father died, I knew I was on my way. I had set my course. I knew that whatever my life was about, it was about desire, the desire beyond all desire, the desire for God. It was about learning to listen to my deepest hunger and to let this hunger guide me, as a ship steers at night by the stars.

These few lines poetically describe how even the most abstract desires, such as the need for spiritual fulfillment, are often conceptualized in terms of felt embodied experiences, such as those associated with hunger. The metaphorical mapping of hunger onto desire is frequently found in talk of various kinds of desires, including lust and the desires for both concrete objects and abstract ideas/events. Thus, American English speakers often talk of abstract desires in terms of hunger:

He hungers for recognition.
He hungers for adventure.
He had a hunger for power.
He hungers for revenge.

Asserting this metaphorical relationship is not just a conventional or arbitrary way of speaking about desire, because there appear to be rich, systematic correspondences between feeling hunger and feeling different aspects of desire. Gibbs et al. (in press) investigated whether university students in two cultures, the United States and Brazil, metaphorically understand different desires in terms of their embodied experiences of hunger. They first examined people's embodied experiences of hunger, apart from their understanding of hunger in talk of desire. Some bodily experiences of hunger should be far more prominent than others across both American English and Brazilian Portuguese speakers. If hunger and desire are highly correlated, and if people metaphorically make sense of their desires partly in terms of hunger, then these more prominent parts of their hunger experiences should be invariantly mapped onto their different concepts for desire. Thus, people should subsequently view certain ways of talking about desires in terms of specific hunger experiences more acceptable than less prominent aspects of feeling hunger.

A first study presented American and Brazilian college students with three types of symptoms that may possibly result from a person being hungry (these were translated into Brazilian Portuguese for the Brazilian participants). "Local" symptoms referred to specific parts of the body, "general" symptoms referred to whole body experiences, and "behavioral" symptoms referred to various behaviors that may result as a consequence of a person being hungry. Each of these three symptoms included items that we presumed may be closely related to the experience of being hungry, items possibly related, and items not at all related to hunger. An analysis of these ratings showed that English and Portuguese speakers gave similar ratings to the different items. For example, the two groups of participants agreed that strong effects of hunger on the human body include the stomach grumbling, thought of food making one's mouth water, having a stomachache, and having a headache (local symptoms); feeling discomfort, becoming weak, becoming dizzy, getting annoyed, and having an appetite (general symptoms); and the person feeling out of balance, becoming emotionally fragile, and becoming very anxious (behavior symptoms). The two groups of participants also agreed on those items that were not related to their hunger experiences. Examples of these items include the following: the knees swell, the feet hurt, the hands itch, and the fingers snap (local symptoms); one wants to run, does not wish to see anyone, becomes talkative, and gets a fever (general symptoms); and the person behaves normally and the person can work well (behavior symptoms). Overall, these findings indicate significant regularities in people's embodied experiences of hunger, at least as suggested by speakers from these two different cultures.

A second study examined whether people's folk knowledge about hunger is correlated with their understandings of difference experiences of desire. To do this, English and Portuguese speakers from the same populations sampled in the first study were asked to give their intuitions about two types of questions. The first set of questions focused on how people's bodies felt when experiencing three types of desire: love, lust, and the desire for things other than human beings, such as fame, adventure, money, and so on (the "other" category). Participants were asked to read each question and then rate the relevance of various bodily experiences (e.g., becomes dizzy, weak, annoyed, talkative) when that person was in love, in lust, or experiencing some other desire.

The second set of questions focused on people's intuitions about the acceptability of different ways of linguistically expressing desire. Similarly to the body questions, half of the items were constructed from bodily experiences strongly (or highly) rated for hunger as shown in the first study, with the other half coming from weakly (or low) rated hunger items. These linguistic questions were posed for three types of desire (i.e., love, lust, and other), as was the case for the body questions. The participants' task was simply to read each statement (e.g., "My whole body aches for you," "I have a strong headache for knowledge," "My hands are itching for you,"

"My knees ache for information about my ancestry") and rate whether it was an acceptable way of talking in their respective language.

An analysis of the mean ratings showed that the findings for both the Body and Linguistic questions are generally consistent across English and Portuguese for the three types of symptoms for the three types of desire (love, lust, other). For instance, in regard to students' ratings of the acceptability of different linguistic expressions, both the American and Brazilian students viewed "I have a great appetite for money" and "I have a stomach pain for my old way of life" as being reasonable, acceptable ways of talking about different desires. But they also rated expressions such as "I became talkative for adventure" and "My knees swell for information about my ancestry" as being unacceptable ways of talking about desire.

Overall, then, the findings showed how knowing something about people's embodied experiences of hunger allows scholars to empirically predict which aspects of desire will and will not be thought of, and talked about, in terms of our complex embodied understandings of hunger. This evidence is generally consistent across two different languages and cultural communities. People use their knowledge of their bodily experiences/actions as the primary source of metaphorical meaning and understanding.

Understanding Time Expressions

One of the topics that has generated significant debate in discussions of embodied metaphor is language about time. Time, like most abstract domains, can be described by more than one metaphor. In English, two separate metaphors are used to sequence events in time (Lakoff & Johnson, 1980). The first is the ego-moving metaphor in which the ego or observer's movement progresses along the time-line toward the future (e.g., "We're coming up on Christmas"). The second is the time-moving metaphor in which a person is standing and the time-line is conceived as a river or a conveyer-belt in which events are moving from the future to the past (e.g., "Christmas is coming up").

These two metaphors lend to different assignments of the front and back in the time line. In the ego-moving metaphor, front is assigned to a future or later event (e.g., "The revolution is before us"; the revolution is a later or future event and is said to be before because it is further along the observer's direction of motion). When an observer moves along a path, objects are ordered according to the direction of motion of the observer. In the time-moving metaphor, front is assigned to a past or earlier event (e.g., "The revolution was over before breakfast"; the revolution is the earlier event, and is said to be before because it is further along in the direction of motion of time). Once again, an analogous system exists for ordinary objects in space. When objects without intrinsic fronts are moving, they are assigned fronts based on the direction of motion.

Are ego-moving and time-moving expressions understood through different conceptual schemes? A common argument in the debate on time is that linguistic metaphors play no causal role in shaping abstract domains (Murphy, 1996). One study that tested this idea provided participants with a block of temporal statements that either were consistent with one scheme, or switched between ego-moving and time-moving schemes (Gentner, Imai, & Boroditsky, 2002). For each statement (e.g., "Christmas is six days before New Year's Day"), participants were given a time-line of events (e.g., past...New Year's Day...future), and had to place an event (e.g., Christmas) on the time-line. Participants took more time to do this when the temporal statements switched between the two metaphors.

A different study on understanding time expressions asked people at an airport (Chicago O'Hare) a priming question in either the ego-moving form (e.g., "Is Boston ahead or behind in time?") or the time-moving form (e.g., "Is it earlier or later in Boston than it is here?") (Gentner et al., 2002). After answering, the participants were asked the target question "So should I turn my watch forward or back?" which was consistent with the ego-moving form. The experimenter measured response times to the target question with a stopwatch disguised as a wristwatch. Once again, response times for consistently primed questions were shorter than for inconsistently primed questions. Switching schemas caused an increase in processing time. These results suggest that two distinct conceptual schemes are involved in sequencing events in time.

Additional evidence on embodied metaphor in understanding temporal statements comes from a study in which participants answered blocks of questions about days of the week phrased in either the ego-moving metaphor (e.g., "We passed the deadline two days ago") or the time-moving metaphor (e.g., "The deadline passed two days ago") (McGlone & Harding, 1998). For each statement, participants indicated the day of the week on which the event in question has occurred or would occur. At the end of each block, participants read an ambiguous temporal statement such as "The meeting originally scheduled for next Wednesday has been moved forward two days" and were asked to perform the same task. The "move-forward" statement is ambiguous because it could be interpreted using one or the other schema to yield different answers. Participants in the ego-moving condition tended to disambiguate the "moved forward" statement in an ego-moving-consistent manner (thought the meeting was on Friday), whereas participants in the time-moving condition tended to disambiguate in a time-moving-consistent manner (thought the meeting was on Monday). These studies provide strong evidence for the psychological reality of two distinct globally consistent schemas for sequencing events in time.

Some scholars suggest that even if languages differ in the metaphors they use to describe abstract domains, speakers of these languages should not differ in their mental representations of these domains (Murphy, 1996). Recent evidence suggests that this is not the case (Boroditsky, 2001). English and Mandarin speakers talk about time differently. English speakers use predominately horizontal terms to talk about time, whereas Mandarin speakers use both horizontal and vertical terms. A metaphorical structuring account would predict that Mandarin speakers would be more likely to rely on vertical spatial schemas when thinking about time than English speakers.

This is indeed what was observed. When answering true/false questions about time (e.g., "March comes earlier than April"), Mandarin speakers were faster after vertical spatial primes than after horizontal spatial primes. This result implies that Mandarin speakers were relying on vertical representations of time to answer the time questions. The reverse was true for the English speakers. English speakers were faster answering the questions after horizontal spatial primes than after vertical spatial primes. This difference is particularly striking because both groups performed the task in English, and all of the Mandarin speakers had had at least 10 years of speaking English. Further, English speakers who were briefly trained to talk about time using vertical metaphors produced results that were statistically indistinguishable from those of Mandarin speakers. This is strong evidence that embodied metaphorical concepts play an important role in shaping abstract thought.

People's understanding of time is not necessarily based on online sensorimotor activity, but rather on people's representations of and thoughts about their past and present spatial experiences. Support for this claim comes from several experiments in which people in different settings were asked a question about time (Boroditsky & Ramscar, 2002). For instance, students waiting in line at a cafe were given the statement "Next Wednesday's meeting has been moved forward two days" and then asked "What day is the meeting that has been rescheduled?" Students who were farther along in line (i.e., who had thus experienced more forward spatial motion) were more likely to say that the meeting had been moved to Friday. Similarly, people riding a train were presented with the same ambiguous statement and question about the rescheduled meeting. Passengers who were at the end of their journeys reported that the meeting was moved to Friday significantly more than did people in the middle of their journeys. Although both groups of passengers were experiencing the same physical experience of sitting in a moving train, they thought differently about their journeys and consequently responded differently to the rescheduled meeting question. These findings, along with others, suggest that it is how people think about spatial motion, and not the physical experience itself, that influences their thoughts about temporal events.

How people think about motion through space also influences their comprehension of fictive motion sentences, such as "The road runs along the coast." Although fictive motion expressions communicate no explicit motion (i.e., roads do not literally run), people may understand these statements in terms of implicit, imaginary sensations of movement (Talmy, 1996). Experimental studies show this is true (Matlock, 2004). Participants read stories about protagonists traveling through spatial regions and then made speeded decisions about whether a fictive motion statement related to the story. Reading times in different experiments were faster when sentences followed stories depicting short distances, fast motion, and uncluttered terrains. People gave faster positive decisions to statements containing fast verbs, such as "The road runs along the coast," than to expressions with slower verbs, such as "The road meandered along the coast." None of these differences were found in control studies examining comprehension of nonfictive motion spatial sentences, suggesting that the fictive motion effects are not due to lexical priming.

Overall, these studies imply that embodied simulation is critical to processing fictive motion. Thus, people interpret the meanings of fictive motion statements by "replaying" the movement, reconstructing a mental enactment of movement implicit in the sentence. People are not aware of these simulations, and so fictive motion processing is not dependent on deliberate thought about motion. These psycholinguistic studies provide additional support for the general claim that language is closely tied to imagination that is grounded in ordinary embodied action.

In general, the experimental work on understanding linguistic statements about time shows how people conceive of time in embodied, metaphorical ways. These data directly contradict the view that metaphorical talk of time emerges from abstract similarities between space and time (Jackendoff & Aron, 1991).

Embodied Metaphors in American Sign Language

Another example of contemporary research on how bodily action shapes utterance interpretation comes from the study of American Sign Language (ASL). A common conceptual metaphor with embodied roots in American English and other languages is COMMUNICATION IS SENDING AND RECEIVING OBJECTS. This conceptual metaphor underlies speakers' use and understanding of linguistic expressions such as "We tossed some ideas back and forth" and "His meaning went right over my head." In each case, ideas correspond to objects and the act of communicating corresponds to the sending and receiving of these objects.

Recent work on ASL demonstrates that a similar conceptual metaphor underlies ideas about communication in ASL (Taub, 2001; Wilcox, 2001). ASL signers generally exploit signing space to schematically represent spatial relations, time, order, and aspects of conceptual structure

(Emmorey, 2002). When signers describe spatial relations, there is a structural analogy between the form of a construction and aspects of the described scene. Specifically, physical elements in ASL (the hands) map to physical elements within the scene (objects), movements of the hands map to the motion of referent objects, and locations in signing space map to physical locations within the scene. Through metaphorical mappings, signers can extend the use of classifier constructions and signing space to describe abstract concepts and relations.

However, the conceptual metaphors in ASL are different from those in spoken language, because they involve a double mapping (Taub, 2001). First, there is a metaphorical mapping from a concrete, embodied source domain to an abstract target domain (e.g., objects that can be grasped and passed to others are mapped onto ideas/thoughts/concepts). Second, there is an iconic mapping from the concrete domain to the linguistic domain (e.g., cylindrical objects map to cylindrical handshapes).

For example, similarly to English speakers, ASL signers use the communicating-as-sending metaphor. For both speakers and signers, the discourses of communicating ideas and throwing objects are linked, whereby an idea corresponds to an object, and telling or explaining the idea corresponds to throwing the object to someone. But unlike spoken English, ASL has an additional iconic mapping between the concrete domain (objects) and the articulators (the hands). Consider the English statement "I didn't get through to him" in reference to a speaker trying to get a listener to understand some idea or belief. In ASL, the equivalent sign (paraphrased as THINK-BOUNCE) indicates a failure to communicate and consists of an iconic depiction of a projectile bouncing off a wall (the dominant handshape moves from the head and bounces off the nondominant hand). Thus, ASL has two levels of human movement in the sign referring to failure to communicate.

ASL exhibits double mappings in many conceptual domains. For example, the metaphorical mapping between power and height (e.g., power is up) has an additional iconic mapping between height and signing space. Thus, authority figures are associated with higher locations in signing space, and less powerful people are associated with lower locations. This nicely illustrates how bodily action helps to articulate abstract ideas such as our conceptualization of people in authority. Similarly, signers use the "intimacy is proximity" metaphor to associate known or preferred objects/people with locations near the body and less preferred objects/people with locations away from the body.

Taub also argues that some signs (e.g., THINK-PENETRATE) are fully motivated by a single metaphor, whereas other signs are only partially motivated, motivated by several metaphors simultaneously, or are motivated by both metaphorical and pure iconicity. For example, the sign for SAD consists of a downward motion of both spread fingered hands, palms in, in front of the face. The signer builds on the mapping of the up-down scale onto emotion, where negative emotions have downward movements (e.g., "I'm feeling down today").

The sign for THRILL employs both the metaphors in sad and happy and adds a third. Thus, the upward movement for HAPPY EMOTIONS ARE UP begins at the center of the chest, where THE LOCUS OF EMOTION IS THE CHEST, and includes the open-8 handshape, which is motivated by the metaphor FEELING IS TOUCHING.

Finally, the sign for EXCITE incorporates both metaphor and iconicity. EXCITE uses the same three metaphors as THRILL but differs in meaning from THRILL in that rather than having both hands move upward in a single, long rapid stroke, the two hands alternate making short upward movements at the chest. Thus, whereas the sign for THRILL represents a brief, rapid experience, the sign for EXCITED represents the experience of an ongoing state.

Another metaphor that is structured in terms of movement around the body is time (Wilcox, 2001). Time in ASL is expressed in relation to the "time line," with each time sign running along an imaginary line through the body. The signer's body represents present time, and areas in the front and back of the body represent future and past, respectively (see Emmorey, 2002 for a different model of time in ASL). Time signs such as NOW, WILL, and ONE-DAY-PAST have relative locations on the line that agree with the temporal message, even though their specific locations are not to scale. Most generally, ASL represents time as a perceptual experience in terms of spatial path and temporal unidirectionality. Thus, time is perceived as running from past (back) to future (front). The front and back of a human body correspond to the body's daily movements of running ahead into the future and stepping back into the past.

As in spoken language, the container schema is also prevalent in ASL. For example, the idea of a person being knowledgeable is expressed by signers by the use of the C handshape at the front of the forehead. The sign demonstrates that the mind could be visualized as a full container. A signer can convey the idea of incomplete understanding, or a momentary lapse in thought, by collapsing the handshape. But the container metaphor in ASL is more than a simple ontological metaphor describing an abstract entity. Understanding metaphorical mappings convey abstract connections within the interior of the container. These mappings are organized by different image schema, such as SOURCE-PATH-GOAL, LINK, PART-WHOLE, CENTER-PERIPHERY, and FRONT-BACK. These image schemas underlie the source domains in many complex metaphors. For instance, the FRONT-BACK schemas refer to ideas such as "It's in the back of my mind somewhere." Deaf people know that the brain's activities are specialized in different regions, but they typically use the forehead area in making signs such as remember, understand, memorize, think, imagine, idea, puzzle, and hypothesize, among many others.

One example of taking ideas out of one's mind concerns a signer who was attempting to write a book detailing all the jokes and folklore he has remembered from talking with deaf persons all over the world (Wilcox, 2001). The sign for "pool-ideas-into-book" began with the signer having both fists close to his forehead and then throwing them outward and downward toward his lap area, with fingers splayed out, into the place where a book might be written or read. Thus, the ideas are taken from the mind as a container and put into a different container or book.

ASL has the metaphor IDEAS IN EXISTENCE ARE STRAIGHT. Entities in the world that are erect and straight tend to be objects that persist. Living objects that are alive have integrity and stand tall, whereas dead trees, flowers, and even people topple over. These experiential events serve as the source domain for understanding abstract mental processes. Thus, ideas, thoughts, or understanding can be metaphorically viewed as living things. When referring to the process of abstract thoughts, and coherent ideas, ASL has the G classifier handshape in which the index finger is extended upright and pointed near the forehead. This icon of the straight finger serves as a metaphor for physical life or existence.

Not surprisingly, there is an equally pervasive countermetaphorical mapping that IDEAS NOT FULLY IN EXISTENCE ARE BENT. This metaphor is based on the experience of entities not in existence being difficult to see. Thus, when an idea metaphorically disappears from view, by signers bending or flexing their index finger, it is permanently gone. ASL signs that evoke IDEAS NOT FULLY IN EXISTENCE ARE BENT include weak-minded, dreams, and mull-over, with each sign articulated with bent fingers. Most generally, thought corresponds to our experiences of watching living things come into being or crumbling away – with the bending or straightening of a finger mirroring life.

Finally, the conceptual metaphor IDEAS ARE OBJECTS TO BE GRASPED is represented by a handshape with simultaneous iconic and metaphoric representations. Thus, a fully closed fist handshape is used in the sign to represent someone reaching out to grab objects as in "Ryan scooped up the jewels with one hand." This same classifier is employed in cases like "I will take grandmother with me," even if we don't literally grab people in taking them somewhere. Not surprisingly, the same sign can be used metaphorically as when signing "Hang onto that idea." This particular handshape maps the grasping of an object in such a way that it cannot escape onto the intellectual process of permanently holding onto an idea in memory.

Linguistic analyses such as these show how spoken and signed language share many of the same schematic mappings between embodied experiences/actions and more abstract conceptual domains. There is no empirical evidence as yet demonstrating that embodied metaphors are accessed, or activated, during comprehension of ASL. But the above linguistic analysis suggests that this is a likely possibility, and should be a topic for future experimental work.

Neural Theory of Language

The empirical work illustrating the importance of embodied experience in linguistic understanding has focused mostly on behavioral and neuropsychological evidence. But there are also recent developments in cognitive science on the neural basis for language interpretation. The neural theory of language (NTL) is an interdisciplinary project at the University of California, Berkeley devoted to understanding how neural structures of the human brain shape thought and language and influence language learning and understanding (Feldman & Narayanan, 2004). These studies attempt to define the representations and computations used to link brain functions, including those related to emotion and social cognition, with language use. A general assumption, based on neuroscientific work, is that there should not be brain areas that are specialized for language, and that language processing should not be confined to only a few select regions of the brain.

An early NTL project provided a neural model for learning spatial relations terms in the world's languages (Regier, 1996). For example, English has several concrete and abstract spatial terms, such as prepositions that can be used to express both spatial and nonspatial meanings, as in "I'm in a depression," "Prices went up," and "He's beside himself." These nonspatial uses of spatial relations arise from systematic conceptual metaphors that preserve the spatial logic of the source domain (see Chapter 4). Previous linguistics work showed that many elementary spatial relations are topographical in nature (Talmy, 2000). To build a neural model for spatial relations, Regier adopted ideas from several aspects of cognitive neuroscience. First, topographical maps of the visual field were used to compute image schemas that also were topological. Second, orientation-sensitive cell assemblies were used to compute the orientational aspects of spatial concepts that rely on bodily orientation (e.g., above). Third, center-sensitive receptor fields were employed to characterize concepts such as contact. Finally, a filling-in architecture was used to deal with notions such as containment.

Regier's model was tested in the following way. A few simple figures (squares, circles, triangles) were presented with various spatial relations, both static and moving (e.g., "in," "on," "through," "above"), in a simple computer model of a retina (n × m pixels). One figure served as Landmark and the other as Trajector (e.g., if the circle is under the square, the square is the Landmark and the circle is Trajector). The model's task was to learn the spatial-relations system of a language and the spatial-relations terms, so that the system could provide the right name for new spatial configurations presented on the computer screen. A difficult challenge here was to learn these spatial-relations terms without any feedback about when the system was incorrect.

In fact, Regier's model was extremely good at learning these spatial terms, and even accurately displayed prototype effects without being trained on prototypes. One implication of the work is that conceptual and linguistic categories may be formed using perceptual apparatus from the visual system. Thus, conceptual categories of spatial relation are created based on the brain's structure and our bodily experience of spatial relations.

A different model within the NTL framework, called KARMA (knowledge-based action representations for metaphor and aspect), characterized metaphoric reasoning about events (Narayanan, 1997). Many narratives describe abstract plans and events in terms of spatial motion and manipulations. For example, read the following brief newspaper story about European economics (Narayanan, 1997: 1):

> Britain was deep in recession while Germany was flourishing three years ago. France kept moving steadily long after Germany had fallen into recession. But now France is plunging deeper while the German economy continues to struggle. Britain has been taking small steps toward stimulating its economy by cutting interest rates, and has finally started to emerge from recession.

Narayanan's basic hypothesis was that people understand this narrative from their knowledge of embodied metaphors, including those related to moving steadily, falling, taking small steps, plunging deeper, struggling, and starting to emerge. These embodied metaphors function to project features of spatial motion and manipulation onto abstract plans and processes. Representational structures, called "x-schemas," encode embodied metaphors in a way that retains their dynamic and highly responsive real-time nature to reason about abstract events.

Narayanan's computational model included a detailed account of how any motor schema may be modeled in the form of Petri nets that are reducible to structured connectionist neural networks. The x-schema representation reflects low-level motor synergies that perform motor control and connects motor actions to produce complex motor sequences. These motor events, actions, and processes are invariantly projected onto more abstract domains to link physical and economic domains, such as ACTION IS MOTION, A RECESSION IS A HOLE, and MORE IS UP. Neural models use the physical language in the news story to activate a mental simulation of physical action, using control structures (with actual motor action assumed to be inhibited). The results showed that this computational model drew the same inferences people do when reading a wide variety of newspaper stories about economics. For instance, the system drew inference related to goals (their accomplishment, modification, subsystem, concordance, or thwarting), aspect (temporal structure of events), frame-based inferences, perspectival inferences, and inferences about communicative intent. In general, Narayanan's system shows how the same structured neural network used to control high-level motor schemas also operates during abstract reasoning about economic events.

A second part of Narayanan's work focused on aspect, or the linguistic devices that speakers use to direct listeners' attention to the internal temporal characteristics of a situation. For instance, the verb "tap" is inherently iterative and suggests repeated actions, "pick up" has a purpose and a final state, "run" has no inherent final state, "slip" is nonvolitional, and "walk" is durative (it takes an extent of time). English has different lexical, morphological, and grammatical means of specifying aspect. The English progressive construction ("be + V-ing"), for instance, enables speakers to focus on the ongoing nature of an underlying process that has been started, yet not completed. The past-perfect construction ("has V-ed") gives speakers the ability to specify consequences of a situation, as when someone has completed some action. Different aspectual verbs, such as "tap," "walk," and "run," also denote temporal characteristics of situations.

Narayanan (1997) built a computer model to illustrate the semantics of aspects in terms of embodied action within a neural system. This model showed how aspectual expressions in language are linked to schematic processes that recur in sensorimotor control, such as inception, interruption termination, iteration, enabling, completion, force, and effort. Consider "Jack walked to the store." Walking involves specific enabling conditions (e.g., an upright position, a visual/kinesthetic test indicating a steady ground) and specific resources (e.g., energy) and may have a specific goal (e.g., getting to the store). These features interact with the controller, which results in specific meaning inferences. Thus, when a listener hears "John walked to the store," he or she is likely to infer that Jack got to the store. The statement "John was walking to the store" does not imply that John actually arrived at the store. Most theories of aspects are unable to deal with this "imperfect paradox," but Narayanan's model illustrates how the difference between these two sentences arises from the constraint that in one case (e.g., "John walked to the store") the result is obtained only if the goal (of reaching the store) is reached. In the case of "John was walking to the store," no such constraint exists and the result occurs only after John gets to the store. In a similar way, Narayanan's model gives statements such as "He is rubbing ointment" and "He is coughing," iterative readings, because of the inherently iterative nature of activities like "rubbing" and "coughing." The dynamic, highly responsive nature of x-schemas enables Narayanan's computational model to make real-time defeasible inferences associated with understanding aspect.

One other neural model was developed for learning the verbs of hand motion (Bailey, 1998). English has a large number of verbs associated with different hand motions, including "push," "pull," "shove," "wave," "pinch," "yank," "slap," "clutch," "hold," rub," "squeeze," and "fling." Each verb denotes a slightly different embodied action. Other languages have their own special collection of verbs for hand motion. For instance, in

Farsi "zadan" denotes many different kinds of object manipulation with quick motion. Tamil's "thallu" and "ilu" are equivalent to "push" and "pull" in English, but refer to ballistic actions, rather than to a smooth continuous movement. In Cantonese "meet" refers to both pinching and tearing, and suggest forceful manipulation by two fingers, but is also appropriate to use when referring to tearing large items when two full grasps are employed. Spanish has three separate words for "push," with "pulsar" referring to poking or using a single finger to push a button, "presionar" referring to applying pressure to something, and "empujar" meaning to push open a door, or push another person, usually employing two hands.

Human bodies provide the conceptual basis for defining the range of meanings associated with each verb for hand motion in any language. People do not have direct access to complex neural networks that coordinate their actions. But how does this work? Bailey created a computational model to simulate the acquisition of verb semantics for hand action. The first step was to adapt a computational model of the body, named "Jack," that could carry out arm movements correctly. This was done by creating a set of modified Petri nets that were mapped onto a structured connectionst network. The resulting neural model embodied a collection of motor synergies which are low-level self-controlled motor actions such as tightening a grip, extending a finger, releasing a grip, pivoting a wrist, and so on. These synergies were coordinated to provide a mechanism for executing motor schemas in real time, given different environmental conditions.

Another computational mechanism enabled Bailey to model the relationship between low-level motor synergies and the feature structures for different verbs. For example, suppose that the program learned that the word "shove" involves using the slide-executing schema with high force and short duration. This information, in which schemas and parameters define the word, serves as part of its stored definition. Bailey trained the model in English and several other languages by presenting the system with 165 labeled examples of actions corresponding to 15 English verbs and 18 word senses.

The model possessed sufficient computational-to-neural local mappings to correctly learn verbs for hand motion so that the system could recognize the action, name it correctly, and perform the appropriate hand motions given a specific verb (for English, and to a lesser extent Hebrew, Farsi, and Russian). Although the model was not perfect (it performed at about the 80% level on both tasks), Bailey's model demonstrates how the conceptual role of distinguishing between different verbs for hand motion is grounded in the sensorimotor system.

These results are intriguing, although the researchers involved with this project note that the findings are presented as "existence proofs" rather than as models of real neural structures operating in real time. Yet as existence proofs, these studies suggest some of the complex ways that brains, bodies, and world interact to provide the grounding for linguistic meaning.

Embodied Construction Grammar

Embodied construction grammar (Bergan & Chang, in press) follows the basic tenets of mainstream construction grammar (Goldberg, 1995; Kay & Fillmore, 1999), and cognitive grammar (Langacker, 1991) in assuming that all linguistic knowledge, at all levels, can be characterized as pairings of form and meaning, called "constructions." Understanding utterances, quite broadly, involves internal activation of "embodied schemes," along with the mental simulation of these representations in context to generate a rich set of inferences. Constructions are important in this account because they provide the interface between phonological and conceptual knowledge, thereby evoking embodied semantic structures.

Consider the expression "Mary tossed me a drink." A constructional analysis presumes that the active ditransitive argument structure imposes an interpretation in which one entity takes some action that causes another entity to receive something. Although the verb "toss" may be seen in many argument structures, its appearance in "Mary tossed me a drink" is permissible only if its meaning can be recognized as contributing to a transfer event. The word "tossed" evokes a specific physical action that also denotes tense and aspect information related to the larger event in which it is involved. Prototypically, the TOSS schema represents knowledge about a low-energy hand action that causes an entity to move through the air. More specifically, the TOSS schema helps profile the role of the Force-Motion schema within the active ditransitive construction. Thus, the action of tossing profiles a forceful action on an entity that causes its resulting motion, including a tosser (agent) and the tossed object (the object). Constructions are not deterministic, but fit a specific utterance and context to some degree, with the result of processing being the best-fitting set of constructions.

This brief overview of constructional analysis provides the first step in determining the meaning of the utterance "Mary tossed me a drink." The meaning arises from the simulation of grounded semantic structures as characterized by the constructional analysis. First, executing schemas, or x-schemas, are used for executing and perceiving an action and brought to bear in understanding larger abstract action. For example, the TOSS schema evoked by "tossed" enters the tossing-execution schema, which is the explicit, grounded representation of the semantic pattern used by an agent (or tosser) to perform a tossing action. This scheme specifically captures a sequence of actions that are related to tossing an object, including possibly preparatory actions (e.g., grasping the object and moving it into a suitable starting position) and the arm movement necessary to launch the object. Subsidiary actions that move the object along a suitable path with low force are also included. This execution scheme for tossing may also specify other conditions that possibly hold at different stages of the event, such as that the tossed object must be in the agent's hand before the action takes place, and that the object will be flying toward some target afterward.

In general, constructions, such as the active ditransitive, enable listeners to access detailed dynamic knowledge that characterize rich embodied structures merely by specifying a limited set of parameters. One important result of this analysis is that x-schemas provide significant inferential power to evoke detailed meanings for any utterance. For instance, part of the inferences associated with understanding "Mary tossed me a drink" refer to aspects of the chronological stages inherent in the event-level transfer scheme and the action-level tossing scheme, such as the following:

SPEAKER does not have drink
Mary exerts force via TOSS
DRINK in reach of Mary
DRINK in hand of Mary
Mary launched DRINK toward SPEAKER
Mary exerts energy (force-amount = low)
DRINK flying toward SPEAKER
DRINK not in hand of Mary
Mary causes SPEAKER to receive DRINK
SPEAKER has received DRINK

This analysis of embodied action schemas can also specify a rich set of inferential meaning evoked by metaphorical utterances such as "Mary tossed the *Enquirer* a juicy tidbit." This expression emphasizes the same construction as in "Mary tossed me a drink," including the active ditransitive construction. But for the metaphorical expression, "the *Enquirer*" cannot be a literal recipient within the TRANSFER schema. A solution to this problem is to construct a metaphorical map that allows a target domain involving Communication to be structured in terms of a corresponding source domain of Object-Transfer, which enables "the *Enquirer*" to be construed as a suitable recipient. Once this mapping occurs, this links to the inference that the object transfer may be metaphorical as well, belonging to the domain of information, and not food, interpretations of "juicy" and "tidbit." Moreover, both the overall event and the means by which it take places can be understood as a verbal act of transfer, as opposed to physical.

Most generally, embodied construction grammar is a simulation-based model of language understanding. Critical to this perspective is the idea that motor action may be simulated and applied to understanding of various aspects of language (Bergan & Chang, in press; Feldman & Narayanan, 2004).

Embodied Text Understanding

Readers use their embodied abilities to immediately create construals of the different perspectives, and shifts of perspective, of the objects and actions described by language (MacWhinney, 1998). Consider the sentence "As far as the eye could see, stalks of corn were bending as waves under the battering force of a surging curtain of rain" (MacWhinney, 1998). How might readers construct a meaningful interpretation of this sentence? One could argue that readers comprehend this sentence by simply creating a picture of a heavy rain pouring down on a large corn field. But this characterization underdetermines the embodied richness of what people normally understand from this sentence. A more embodied view of understanding claims that readers adopt different perspectives to make sense of the complex actions described in the sentence. Readers might first adopt the perspective of "the eye" and imagine scanning the scene from the foreground to the horizon. This spatial perspective provides an interpretation of the phrase "As far as the eye can see." The spatial perspective required to imagine "stalks of corn" necessitates a shift from our point of view, as readers understand the corn stalks to be a distributed figure located across the vast ground. Readers next view the stalks as bending, which arises from the secondary spatial perspective suggested by "under the battering force," and then elaborate upon the shift of perspective to the "surging curtains of rain." Each perspective shift, therefore, is guided by specific words, such as "as far as" and "under." In general, people's embodied comprehension of this sentence requires a shift across four perspectives: "eyes," "stalks of corn," "battering force," and "curtains of rain." Note that the syntactic form of the sentence, emphasizing "corn" as the subject responding to an external force, shapes the dynamic character of sentence processing as a series of embodied perspective shifts.

Consider now a different sentence, this one with a metaphorical content: "Casting furtive glances at the seamstress, he wormed his way into her heart" (MacWhinney, 1998). Readers first adopt the perspective of the implied subject and imagine him, or her, casting glances at the seamstress. After this, readers shift to the subject's embodied action of worming (i.e., moving as if a worm), yet soon recognize that the action here is not literal but metaphorical in the sense of the subject trying to place himself inside the seamstress's heart. Even here, readers soon comprehend that by metaphorically inserting himself into the seamstress' heart, he has really placed himself closer to the seamstress' emotions and affections. The embodied action of worming, again, suggests a slow, deliberate process of becoming emotionally closer to the seamstress, which she implicitly accepts, allowing the suitor to enter into her affections. The different spatial perspectives readers adopt as they comprehend the sentence give rise to a rich, embodied interpretation.

This approach to language understanding argues that people create meaningful construals by simulating how the objects and actions depicted in language relate to embodied possibilities. Thus, people use their embodied experiences to "soft-assemble" meaning, rather than merely activate pre-existing abstract, conceptual representations.

Empirical research indicates that readers use spatial perspectives to construct mental models of narrative texts. One study asked participants to first memorize the layout of unnamed rooms in a building, along with objects in the rooms (Morrow, Bower, & Greenspan, 1989). Afterwards, participants read a story describing a person's movements throughout the building. At various points when reading the story, participants were asked to judge the location of specific objects. The results showed that people were quicker to make these judgments when the objects were located in rooms visited by the protagonist. Thus, participants constructed a spatial model of the narrative by adopting the embodied perspective of the person in the story, and not by simply creating an objective sketch of the rooms and the objects in them.

Other work provides evidence of spatial indexing and motor participation in a variety of language comprehension and memory task (Richardson & Spivey, 2000; Spivey & Geng, 2002). For example, when participants are facing a blank screen (or have their eyes closed) and are listening to a scene description that contains spatiotemporal dynamics in one particular direction, their eye movements tend toward that direction more so that any other (Spivey & Geng, 2001). Furthermore, when people attempt to recall semantic properties of a visual object or of a spoken factoid that was previously presented in a particular location of the computer screen, they tend to fixate on that (now empty) location in the display (Richardson & Spivey, 2000). Spatial information seems closely tied to a range of mental representations, even those for which the spatial properties are arbitrary or irrelevant, such as a random factoid delivered by a talking head in a particular corner of the computer screen.

Readers construct mental models for narrative by adopting the perspective of the protagonist. Participants in one study read texts describing a protagonist and a target item, such as a jogger and sweatshirt (Glenberg, Meyer, & Lindem, 1987). The protagonist and target item in one experimental condition were spatially linked (e.g., the jogger put on the sweatshirt before jogging), whereas in a different condition, the two were dissociated (e.g., the jogger took off the sweatshirt before jogging). After reading the main part of the story, participants judged whether they earlier read the word "sweatshirt." People were faster to make this judgment in the linked, or associated, condition than when the protagonist and target were dissociated. Thus, readers appear to create mental models for narrative in which spatial information (e.g., the location of the sweatshirt) is tied to the story's characters and their embodied actions.

Research also shows that readers construct fairly elaborate, embodied microworlds when comprehending literary stories (Zwaan, Magliano, &

Graesser, 1995). One study had college students read short literary stories to determine whether readers automatically imagine different possible dimensions of the microworld, including information about the characters, temporality, spatiality, causality, and intentionality (i.e., the characters' goals and plans). Examination of the time needed to read portions of these stories revealed increased reading times for sentences when a new character entered the microworld, when there was a significant gap in the story's timeline (e.g., flashforwards and flashbacks), when the spatial setting changed, when a story action was not causally related to the prior context, and when a character generated a new plan or goal. These data support the idea that readers actually "flesh out" important embodied characters of the stories they read, which takes varying amounts of cognitive effort.

Other empirical findings also show that people assume the perspective of the protagonist when reading narratives. Thus, participants in one study were faster to pronounce the single word "sat" having just read "After standing through the three-hour debate, the tired speaker walked over to his chair" than when they had just read "The tired speaker moved the chair that was in his way and walked to the podium to continue the three-hour debate" (Keefe & McDaniel, 1993; O'Brien & Albrecht, 1992). Notice, again, how different aspects of an object's (e.g., chair's) affordances become prominent depending on the type of body action the protagonist was likely to perform (i.e., sitting). Readers' creation of embodied representations not only influences their understanding of a protagonist's actions, but also shapes their understanding of the orientation of objects (Sanford & Moxy, 1995).

Finally, a specific type of embodied knowledge that is useful in text processing is "scripts" (Schank & Abelson, 1976). Scripts consist of well-learned scenarios describing structured embodied situations in everyday life. Many studies show that readers automatically infer appropriate script-related actions when these are not explicitly stated (Abbott, Black, & Smith, 1985; Bower, Black, & Turner, 1979; Gibbs & Tenney, 1980; Graesser et al., 1980). Other experiments reveal that prior activation of script-based knowledge provides readers with a highly available set of causal connections that can facilitate sentence-by-sentence integration (Bower et al., 1979; Garrod & Sanford, 1985; Sanford & Garrod, 1981; Seifert, Robertson, & Black, 1985; Sharkey & Sharkey, 1987).

One difficulty with the idea of script-based narrative understanding is that these categorizations are often too rigid to accommodate variations from what may be typically expected. For example, we do not usually have a "walking in nature and having a personal revelation" script. A solution to this problem assumes that scripts "do not exist in memory as precompiled chunks" (Schank, 1982: 16). Instead, the different parts of a script may be reconstructed depending on the context.

There are two kinds of high-level processing mechanisms that allow us to create the right script at the right time during text understanding: memory organization packets (MOPs) and thematic organization packets (TOPs) (Downing, 2000; Schank, 1982). MOPs are processing structures that allow people to relate new information with existing expectations to generate reasonable predictions about future events. TOPs are related to MOPs, but are specifically abstractions that allow people to establish connections between different events and discover similarities between them. Thus, reading "West Side Story" may remind us of "Romeo and Juliet" because of the similarity between their goals (e.g., mutual goal pursuit), conditions (e.g., outside opposition), and specific features (e.g., young lovers, false report of death). In this way, TOPs are not static memory representations of abstract prototypical categories, but are processing capabilities that allow readers to be creative in their understandings of events, such as those encountered in literary texts.

One analysis of the American novel *Catch-22* (Heller, 1961) demonstrates the power of MOPs and TOPs to provide coherence to disparate texts (Downing, 2000). *Catch-22* is the story of an American bombardier squadron during World War II on an imaginary island, Pianosa, off the coast of Italy. The novel describes, often quite humorously, the contradictions and absurdities of war and America's military-industrial power in the twentieth century. Consider one excerpt from the novel:

> Sharing a tent with a man who was crazy wasn't easy, but Nately didn't care. He was crazy, too, and had gone every free day to work on the officers' club that Yossarian had not helped build. Actually, there were many officers' clubs that Yossarian had not helped build, but he was proudest of the one on Pianosa. It was a sturdy and complex monument to his powers of determination. Yossarian never went there to help until it was finished – then he went there often, so pleased was he with the large, fine, rambling, shingled building. It was truly a splendid structure, and Yossarian throbbed with a mighty sense of accomplishment each time he gazed at it and reflected that none of the work that had gone into it was his. (Heller, 1964: 28)

This excerpt illustrates an incompatibility between two MOPS: "help build officer club" and "refuse to cooperate." But Nately simultaneously holds both these conflicting beliefs and does so with great pride. This contradiction differs from our usual expectation that people feel pride when they actually do something to achieve a goal. But readers resolve this contradiction by creating a meta-MOP "Pride" where the prototype and the expectations usually associated with it are not fulfilled. In this way, readers "soft-assemble" a new concept with its own prototypical structure.

This analysis does not, however, explain why readers perceive this passage from Heller's novel as funny and informative. But TOPs are useful for this purpose, because they establish connections between apparently unconnected schemas. Thus, readers of the above passage must draw a novel connection between two war situations: one where an officers' club is built, another where cooperation with the enemy takes place. Readers do this by creating an analogy between competing with the enemy and cooperating in the building of an officer's club. Both events are then perceived as thematically related and negative. This analogy between the enemy and the higher officers reflects a parallelism that is recurrent in the novel and is explicitly pointed out by Yossarian when he says "The enemy is anybody who is going to get you killed, no matter what side he's on."

The incongruity of this analogy helps account for the humorous nature of Yossarian's predicament. Although cooperating with the enemy is a very serious matter, or to put it in other words, it is something important; building an officers' club, by comparison, is a trivial matter. Understanding this specific theme is representative of a broader theme repeated throughout the novel, where trivial situations reveal a more dramatic background.

This discussion of one portion of the novel *Catch-22* (offered by Downing, 2000) demonstrates the adaptive character of many aspects of text understanding. Skilled readers do not comprehend texts by simply activating pre-existing prototypes in the form of scripts. Instead, prototypical understandings arise as the products of dynamic and embodied meaning construction processes (in this case through the interaction of MOPs and TOPs).

There are other reasons to doubt whether people activate pre-stored prototypical knowledge, such as scripts, when understanding texts. Most prototype event sequences (e.g., the events that occur at a restaurant) are typically part of common knowledge within a given culture. However, routinized sequences of events can also be quite idiosyncratic. For example, my friend John regularly gets up at 5:30 a.m., drinks a glass of tomato juice, puts out the cat, and goes jogging. When he finishes running, John puts on the coffee, shaves, brushes his teeth, and sits down to read 17th-century English poetry. Although John engages in this sequence of events each day, the sequence is unlikely to be performed by anyone but him (Colcombe & Wyer, 2001).

Do people form person-specific prototypes that are then used to comprehend new experiences that exemplify them? One may believe that prototypes for the self's and well-known others' actions may be the most enduring scripts, given that they are continually embodied in everyday life. But as argued in Chapter 4, prototypes need not necessarily be pre-existing mental representations that get activated to facilitate processing of related events. In fact, research shows that when individuals read descriptions of events that pertain to themselves or to a familiar other (i.e., a parent or roommate), they do not activate a prototypical representation of the behavior in interpreting these events (Colcomb & Wyer, 2001). This is true regardless of whether the sequence is similar to one that they personally experience or observe on a daily basis, or whether it exemplifies a more general prototype of the events that occur in a particular type of situation (e.g., cashing a check). Thus, even if prototypical sequences of embodied actions (i.e., a script) exist in memory and are used to comprehend the behavior of unfamiliar persons, individuals do not apply these when comprehending events that pertain to themselves or someone with whom they are familiar. These recent research findings suggest, at the very least, that people do not necessarily form abstract representations for the most familiar event sequences they experience in daily life. People may alternatively create prototypical scenarios on the fly as part of the embodied simulations they engage in during discourse processing.

A Case Study: The Indexical Hypothesis

The claim that embodiment underlies people's understanding of language is nicely developed in the "indexical hypothesis" (Glenberg, 1997, 1999; Glenberg & Robertson, 2000). This view assumes that three major steps occur when language is understood in context. First, words and phrases are indexed to objects in the environment or to perceptual symbols in long-term memory. Second, the affordance structures (i.e., the possible actions that can be done to an object by a person) are derived for each object in the situation. Third, the listener must combine or "mesh" the affordances according to the constraints on embodied possibilities in the real world. For instance, the affordances of a chair include those of sitting on it, or using it to hold off a snarling lion, but they cannot ordinarily be meshed with the goal of propelling oneself across a room. This constraint on the meshing of embodied affordances predicts that people will have an easier time understanding the sentence "Art used the chair to defend himself against the snarling lion" than interpreting the sentence "Art used the chair to propel himself across the room."

One empirical test of the indexical hypothesis asked people to judge the meaningfulness of afforded (i.e., with coherent mesh) and nonafforded (i.e., those without coherent mesh) sentences, such as those shown above. The results, not surprisingly, showed that people judged the afforded sentences to be significantly more sensible than the nonafforded ones. Furthermore, a second study measured the speed with which people read these two types of sentences. This study showed that nonafforded sentences took significantly longer to comprehend than the afforded ones. These psycholinguistic findings highlight the importance perceptual, embodied information when people combine conceptual representations during ordinary language understanding.

Consider the sentence "John scratched his back with a floppy disk." One might object that we understand this sentence, but not the sentence "John scratched his back with thread," because of background knowledge. Glenberg and Robertson (2000) demonstrated that this background knowledge cannot be pre-stored propositions from which relations (e.g., a disk can be used for back-scratching) are inferred by a formal process. First, understanding the experimental sentences did not seem to depend on having had experiences similar to those described by the sentences (e.g., experience using a disk to scratch one's back). The stimuli used by Glenberg and Robertson (2000) described novel situations (e.g., in another scenario a person uses an upright vacuum cleaner as a coat tree) with which the readers were unlikely to have had experience. Second, associative relations between concepts that mesh such as floppy disk and back-scratching are no stronger from the associative relations between concepts that did not mesh, such as thread and back-scratching. Nonetheless, readers would readily reject the sensibleness of sentences formed from nonmeshing concepts. Third, people required about the same time to read and understand sentences that supposedly required formal inferences as sentences that did not (e.g., She used the back scratcher to scratch her back). Fourth, understanding innovative denominal verbs (e.g., to crutch) for which there can be no pre-stored propositional knowledge because the verbs were used for the first time in the experiment. Thus, although background knowledge must be used in understanding, the background knowledge appears to be very flexible rather than pre-stored. This flexibility is provided by perceptual symbols from which new affordances can be derived to potentially mesh, under the guidance of syntax.

Language at many levels consists of instructions for constructing an embodied mental simulation of what the language is about (that is, an embodied mental model). Thus, noun phrases are instructions for retrieving (indexing) representations from which affordances can be derived (Glenberg & Robertson, 2000), verbs of manner are instructions for retrieving motor programs or plans that can potentially select and act on those affordances, verb-argument constructions (e.g., the double object construction) provide a general framework (e.g., transfer) that must be accomplished when simulating the effect of the verb (Kaschak & Glenberg, 2000), and temporal adverbs provide instructions for controlling the manner in which multiple models are combined. Thus, "while" is an instruction to mesh or simulate how two actions can be performed simultaneously, "after" is an instruction to simulate the current clause and then the next, and "before" is an instruction to simulate the first clause, simulate the second clause, and then to check that the simulation of the first clause (temporally second event) will mesh with the end-state of the simulation of the second clause (temporally first event). This general approach considers language as instructions for constructing simulations.

There appear to be limits, however, on the extent to which embodied experience constrains text comprehension. One set of studies investigated the type of inferences people construct when reading (Graesser, Singer, &

Trabasso, 1994). Although readers easily draw inferences about why actors/events take place, and why the writer included something in a text, people do not necessarily draw inferences about how some action/event occurred. For example, when readers saw "The cook tripped the butler," they immediately inferred something about why the cook did what he did (e.g., for "revenge"), but readers did not draw specific embodied inferences about how an event occurred (e.g., the cook used his "foot" to do the tripping). Readers construct embodied representations for text only to the extent those inferences enable them to understand the plot and the writer's rationale for including something in the text. Narrative texts might be easier to understand than expository ones, precisely because the events in narratives are more action-driven and embodied allowing them to track protagonists' goals, than are seen in expository writing. These psycholinguistic studies provide additional evidence that people's construals of meaning are constrained by their recognition of embodied possibilities alluded to by texts.

Conclusion

A common theme in cognitive science is that language understanding is a modular activity with little interaction with conceptual and experiential knowledge, especially during the early stages of processing. Even if contextual information is employed to assist appropriate understanding of what speakers/writers mean, this knowledge is assumed to be represented in an abstract, disembodied format (e.g., list of propositions). This chapter presents a variety of empirical research that points to an opposite conclusion. Embodied activity plays a role in a least some aspects of language evolution, the processing of speech and word meaning, how people understand why various words and phrases have the meanings they do, and people's immediate comprehension of verbal expressions and written discourse. As was seen in Chapter 5 for aspects of higher-order cognition, embodied activity shapes parts of on-line communication and the off-line knowledge that is accessed during linguistic processing.

A significant part of embodied activity subserves simulation processes that operate during language understanding. In fact, language understanding within real-world communicative contexts may be best described as a kind of embodied simulation, rather than the activation of pre-existing, disembodied, symbolic knowledge. None of this implies that all aspects of language and communication, including some body movements used to express meaning, are rooted in embodiment. But there is sufficient evidence to suggest that many aspects of language and communication arise from, and continue to be guided by, bodily experience.

7

Cognitive Development

Developmental psychologists have long debated the role of early embodied action in cognitive development. Since Piaget's (1952, 1954) writings on how sensorimotor activity underlies different aspects of cognitive growth, psychologists have considered ways of linking patterns that emerge from young children's bodily and perceptual experience with later intellectual development. Many psychologists now argue that children's acquisition of significant conceptual abilities is rooted in innately given knowledge, whereas others emphasize the child's active looking and listening skills. Yet neither of these positions gives appropriate attention to the child's self-generated movements and felt sensations in learning to perceive, think, and engage in intelligent behavior. Scholars such as Dewey (1934) and Montessori (1914) earlier emphasized the importance of "learning by doing,"but there has not been enough concern with how kinesthetic action serves as the potential building block for conceptual development. This chapter describes ideas and empirical evidence in support of the embodied grounding for cognitive development.

Piaget's Contribution

Jean Piaget's seminal investigations of child development assumed that growth is a form of individual adaptation to the environment. Even small infants exhibit intelligent behavior, not by thinking, but by acting physically in the world (Piaget, 1952). Two principles of biological adaptation, assimilation and accommodation, provide the mechanism for development of intelligent action. Assimilation refers to the process by which infants use their existing abilities when responding to environmental challenges. Accommodation refers to the process of changing one's existing abilities to adaptively deal with some task or situation. Most actions involve some combination of assimilation and accommodation. For instance, between 6 and 12 months, infants learn to eat solid foods. The child begins to assimilate the food by employing the tongue and lip action it uses for breast-feeding. But these movements are inadequate for dealing with soft, solid foods, and infants must then coordinate their tongue movements in new ways to accommodate their own actions to the shape of the food, including, at times, the shapes of spoons. Both assimilation and accommodation are necessary parts of how the child learns to act in the real world.

Piaget's theory of intellectual development posited a first stage of sensorimotor development that occurs in the child's first two years of life. The sensorimotor stage is rooted in the infant's embodied exploration of the environment, or specifically, infants' growing understanding of their bodies and how their bodies relate to objects and other people in the world (Piaget & Inhelder, 1969).

The sensorimotor stage is divided into six substages:

(1) Reflex schemes (0–1 months): inborn reflexes, such as sucking, looking, and crying, establish the infant's first connections with the world.
(2) Primary circular reactions (1–4 months): repeated actions (circular) induce coordination within the infant's own body, such as coordination of muscles in the mouth to suck on the thumb, where the initial occurrence happen by chance.
(3) Secondary circular reactions (4–8 months): repeated actions involve coordination between the infant's action and the environment, such as kicking to make a hanging mobile move, a discovery that happens by chance.
(4) Coordination of secondary circular reactions (8–12 months): goal-directed actions not motivated by chance occur, such as using one hand to hold an object while the other hand explores it.
(5) Tertiary circular reactions (12–18 months): familiar secondary reactions are used to make new things happen, such as when the child explores how different objects fall from his or her high-chair, which involves trial-and-error problem solving.
(6) Invention of new means through mental combination (18–24 months): the ability to think before acting by representing actions as mental images or symbols emerges, a process of problem solving without trial and error.

Piaget's theory was developed from his observations of his own young children. For example, evidence for substage 3, secondary circular reactions, is seen in the following observations of 4-month-old Laurent: "At 4 months 15 days, with another doll hanging in front of him, Laurent tries to grasp it, then shakes himself to make it swing, knocks it accidentally, and then tries simply to hit it. At 4 months 18 days, Laurent hit my hands without trying to grasp them, but he started by simply waving his arms around, and only afterwards went on to hit my hands. The next day, finally, Laurent immediately hits a doll hanging in front of him" (Piaget, 1952: 167–8).

Piaget interpreted this sequence of events as evidence of infants using their own actions to create interesting effects in the world. This example also illustrates how disequilibrium serves as the primary catalyst of development. Whenever assimilation and accommodation processes fall short of adaptation, the experience of disequilibrium forces the child to discover new ways of knowing the world. But most importantly, an infant's early skills and knowledge, or schemes, that start out as sensorimotor actions serve as the foundation for later conceptual schemes, involving ideas, concepts, and thoughts. The cognitive operations used in manipulating symbolic representations share a formal structure with sensorimotor activity that is governed by the laws of physics. The logic inherent in coordination of action is presumably reconstructed at the level of internal thought, ultimately enabling objective logico-mathematical knowledge. Thus, as the infant develops, overt actions give way to internal actions on "images of abstract objects and their displacements" (Piaget, 1954: 4). Piaget assumed, therefore, that the child's embodied activities are a necessary component in coming to know the world, but higher-order forms of thought become divorced from earlier sensorimotor behaviors as they become "interiorized."

Recent Studies on Physical Reasoning

Many of Piaget's original observations on sensorimotor development have been more rigorously studied by developmental psychologists over the past few decades. This research suggests that young infants are capable of sophisticated physical reasoning about objects and their properties, far beyond that observed by Piaget. A main complaint motivating this work is that Piaget confused an infant's motor competence with its conceptual abilities. Of course, this criticism assumes that what is conceptual may have little to do with what is motoric, or more fully embodied, about young children's concepts. The question here is whether this new evidence from developmental psychology demonstrates that sensorimotor activity is not a prerequisite for cognitive development.

Consider the case of object permanence. Object permanence refers to the child's understanding that objects continue to exist even when they are hidden from view. Piaget assessed this ability by examining young children's searching behavior. For example, when a toy is shown to an infant (ages 0 to 4 months) and then hidden under a cushion, the baby fails to seek out the object. Piaget assumed that objects for these babies were not differentiated from their own bodily actions. In the next stage of object permanence, infants begin to search for partially hidden, but not fully hidden objects. Later on, infants can search for fully hidden objects, but only if objects are hidden in the same spatial location on repeated trials.

Thus, if the toy is hidden under a different cushion in full view of the child, the infant will search for the toy under the cushion where it had been hidden on previous trials. This "A-not-B" error occurs between 8 and 12 months of age. Eventually, children move into a stage in which the A-not-B error disappears and then can correctly search new locations for objects (when they change from A to B). Nonetheless, infants are still unable to search for an object under different cushions without first observing the object being hidden. Finally, in stage 6 of object permanence, around 15 to 18 months, infants systematically search for hidden objects until they are located.

One difficulty with Piaget's observational studies is that the object concept is measured through analysis of infants' searching behavior. But infants may possess some object concept, and recognize that objects are different from their own actions, before they can successfully reach for objects. One reason for babies making A-not-B errors in object permanence tasks is that they fail to inhibit a predominant action tendency to search for the object under the cushion where it was first, but is not now, hidden (Diamond, 1991; Reiser, Doxey, McCarrell, & Brooks, 1982). This suggests that babies may have some early object concept, but give misleading evidence of a lack of this concept because of their tendency to reach into the place where the object was first hidden.

Significant research using methods that do not require babies to reach for objects suggests that babies may understand a good deal about the existence of objects. For example, 5-month-old infants in one study sat in front of a screen that rotated through 180 degrees toward and away from the baby (Baillargeon, Spelke, & Wasserman, 1985). After the baby habituated to this event, a box was placed in the path of the screen at the far end of the apparatus. When the screen began its 180-degree rotation, it gradually occluded the block, and when it reached 90 degrees, the entire box was hidden. At this point, babies were shown one of two critical events. "Possible events" were those in which the screen rotated until it had passed through 180 degrees, when it stopped, having apparently made contact with the box. "Impossible events" were those in which the screen rotated until it had passed through the full 180-degree rotation, apparently having moved right through where the box was located. Although the full 180-degree rotation was familiar to the babies, they spent more time looking at the impossible event than the possible one. This result suggests that even 5-month-olds understand something about object permanence, because they seem surprised that the screen could pass through the box in the impossible event.

One difficulty with Baillargeon et al.'s (1985) study is that the experimental task may lead babies to form a strong perceptual expectation that the rotating screen will stop. This expectation may not require that the infant form a representation of the occluded object. Some scholars claim that infants may have some knowledge about the continued existence of occluded objects, but may not set up representations of individual objects until around 1 year of age.

To test this idea, Xu and Carey (1996) compared 10-month-old babies' reactions to two occluding conditions, a property-kind condition and a spatio-temporal condition. In the first case, infants sat in front of a screen, and a truck was brought out from the right side and then returned behind it. Similarly, a toy kitten was brought out from the left side of the screen, and then moved behind it. Babies habituated to these repeated events. The screen was then removed and either one or two of the toys appeared. For the spatio-temporal condition, the same sequence of events occurred, but this time the truck and kitten were brought out simultaneously from behind the screen. Finally, a baseline condition simply measured infants' looking times for one or two objects that were not occluded.

Analysis of babies' looking times showed that they stared longer at the two-object outcome in the baseline and property-kind conditions, but looked longer at the single-object outcome in the spatio-temporal condition. This pattern of data indicated that infants generally prefer looking at two objects, but could overcome this preference in the spatio-temporal condition. Xu and Carey argued that the 10-month-olds were unable to perceptually distinguish between the toy and kitten to recognize that there were two different objects hidden behind the screen. Thus, young infants may only possess a generalized understanding of objects. Only later will infants be able to represent the specific identities of objects.

This work is representative of studies examining infants' physical reasoning in that children's sensorimotor behavior and experience is assumed to play a minimal role in how they come to acquire conceptual knowledge about objects and their properties. In fact, eliminating the child's reaching in standard object permanence tasks is seen as a good way of removing motor behavior from the assessment of conceptual knowledge. Not surprisingly, perhaps, there are criticisms of studies employing the preferential looking method, particularly in regard to whether these measures adequately assess infants' cognitive, as opposed to purely perceptual, capacities (Bogartz & Shinsky, 1998; Haith, 1997).

But a large number of habituation-dishabituation studies demonstrate that young infants recognize many other object properties and the rules governing their behavior. Thus, 3-to-4-month-olds are sensitive to object substance and different physical limits on object motion, such as that one solid object cannot move through another, and that an object much larger than an opening cannot pass through it (Spelke et al., 1992). Babies at this age also recognize something about the effect of gravity and will look surprised when a moving object stops in midair without support (Sitskoorn & Smitsman, 1995). Even 2 $^1/_2$-month-old babies expect a stationary object to move when a moving object collides with it (ref). Babies 3 $^1/_2$ months old recognize when an object is compressible or not (e.g., a sponge vs. a wooden block) or when it is taller or shorter than the height of a screen (Baillargeon, 1987a, 1987b). By 5–6 months of age, infants know that a larger moving object can cause a stationary object to travel further (Baillargeon, 1994. Beginning around 6 months of age, infants recognize that one object placed on top of another will fall unless a larger portion of its bottom surface contacts the lower object (Baillargeon, 1994 Baillargeon, Needham, & DeVos, 1992).

Habituation studies also show that young infants not only may understand something about objects and their properties, but also may represent spatial relations between objects. For instance, in once study, 5.5-month-olds were habituated to displays of a tall rabbit and a short rabbit passing around a screen and appearing on the other side (Baillargeon & Graber, 1997). Infants were then shown the same display except that a window had been cut off the top part of the screen. If a tall rabbit has traveled the area behind the screen, then it should appear in the window. In fact, when the short rabbit passed behind the modified screen, infants continued to habituate. However, when the tall rabbit passed behind the modified screen without appearing in the window (an improbable event), infants dishabituated (i.e., showed longer looking times) Infants presumably developed expectations that an object moving in a visible trajectory would appear when it was briefly occluded.

A control group of babies were treated identically except that before the experiment began they briefly saw two rabbits standing on either side of the screen. These infants did not dishabituate to the impossible event. Infants seemingly understood the display in terms of a rabbit passing behind the screen and stopping, while another rabbit appeared at the other side. Later work showed that 3 1/2-month-old infants behave in the same manner (Baillargeon & DeVos, 1991). Thus, very young infants appear to be able to represent spatial relations. Finally, different studies reveal that 10-month-old babies can remember the location of objects when they are out of sight for as long as 70 seconds (Baillargeon, DeVos, & Graham, 1989). And when watching a blue ball disappear behind a screen with a red ball appearing on the other side, 10-month-olds infer that the first object launched the second object behind the partition (Cohen & Oakes, 1993).

The studies mentioned here, again, represent only a few of the dozens of experiments showing that young infants have significantly more sophisticated knowledge about objects and their properties than claimed by Piaget. There is an emerging body of work, however, showing that older children, between 2 and 3 years of age, lack aspects of this knowledge. For instance, in a task where 2- and 3-year-olds had to find a ball after watching it roll behind a screen and stop, toddlers under 3 years old performed no better than would have been expected if they were simply guessing at the ball's location (Berthier et al., 2000). Follow-up studies provided the children with more visual information about the ball's trajectory by replacing the opaque window screen with a transparent one (Butler, Berthier, & Clifton, 2002). This additional visual information did not help the 2-year-olds, but did assist the 2 ½-year-old toddlers to some degree. Finally, even when the children were given a full view of the ball's trajectory until it came to rest against a wall, the majority of 2-year-olds still could not find the ball. Analysis of the children's gaze showed that if they looked at the ball as the screen was lowered and then fixated on it until the door opened, they were correct almost 90% of the time.

These findings suggest that toddlers do not have knowledge of continuity and solidity in the way that younger infants appear to have it, at least as measured by habituation tasks when children look longer at impossible events. One possibility is that toddlers' problems in the search task require them to predict where the ball should be, something that is not measured in typical habituation studies. Moreover, the toddlers in the above studies had to coordinate their predictions with the appropriate actions of reaching out for the ball at the right spots. It appears then, that 3 to 4-month-olds can reason about an object's motion being constrained by continuity and solidarity, as demonstrated by habituation studies, but they cannot yet reason about after-the-fact incongruous events (Keen, 2003). Infants' perceptual recognition of impossible events in habituation studies may reflect just one small part of young children's eventual ability to make predictions about objects and events in the real world.

Three Theories of Cognitive Development: Does Experience Matter?

The question, again, remains whether success on any of the experimental tasks described above depends on sensorimotor experience. Piaget may have drastically underestimated infants' concepts and physical reasoning skills, but this does not necessarily imply that embodied experience has little role in very early conceptual development. Some psychologists argue that very young babies possess considerable knowledge about objects before they have attained the capacity to physically manipulate them around the age of 6 months. This suggests to these scholars that infants' developing physical reasoning skills must be based on innate, modular knowledge, which becomes more elaborate as children come into contact with different aspects of the physical world (Leslie, 1994; Spelke, 1988, 1990, 1991). Under this view, infants are born with substantial beliefs about how objects move in continuous paths and do not change shape or pass through one another, based on unchanging, possibly innate, principles such as cohesion, boundedness, and rigidity (Spelke, 1994; Spelke & Newport, 1998). These initial perceptually based descriptions of concepts are gradually refined as the child learns to attend to relevant features of the environment. Some of these early concepts may be modular in being informationally encapsulated from other kinds of physical and spatial knowledge (e.g., a geometric spatial module; see Herner & Spelke, 1994, but also see Newcombe, 2002 for evidence refuting this proposal).

A slightly different perspective on conceptual development claims that the infant is endowed with certain domain-specific biases (rather than modules), which in interaction with the external environment become progressively modularized, or specialized to acquire knowledge as development proceeds (Karmiloff-Smith, 1992). Although infants (like older children) use domain-general processes, such as representational redescription, to recode sensorimotor input into accessible formats across a variety of domains, it is unlikely that there are domain-general stages of change such as proposed by Piaget. Thus, infants possess at birth the primitive forms of knowledge that are present in adults, with development occurring in a gradual, continuous manner (Case, 1992; Karmiloff-Smith, 1992).

A third perspective on the development of infants' physical reasoning claims that children do not have innate beliefs about objects. Instead, infants come into the world with highly constrained mechanisms that guide their reasoning about objects (Baillargeon, 1994, 1995, 2000). Infants first learn preliminary aspects of a concept in an all-or-none manner that capture its essence, and later on begin to identify discrete and continuous variables relevant to the concept to form a more elaborate conceptual representation.

Some of Baillargeon's studies described above provide evidence in support of this claim. Infants' reasoning about support, collision, and unveiling relations shows how initial concepts are revised over time to provide more elaborated concepts. Thus, the concept of support is first understood in an all-or-none manner as contact or no contact. With greater perceptual experience, primarily through looking, infants incorporate discrete (e.g., locus of support) and continuous (e.g., amount of support) information. Baillargeon and colleagues claim that this acquisition sequence is not due to the gradual unfolding of some innate belief about support, but arises from constrained learning mechanisms, such that infants make appropriate generalizations about objects and their behaviors in an ordered manner. For example, infants recognize that a small object cannot pass through a gapless opening before understanding that a large object cannot pass through a small gap. An innate-belief view of conceptual development would have predicted that infants should understand both possibilities at the same time, because of some core principle of penetrability.

Under Baillargeon's view, children acquire important conceptual schemes, such as object permanence, through perceptual means, such as by looking and listening, rather than through acting on the world. Consider the case of a 3-month-old infant who realizes that an object will fall when released midair and stop fully when it hits the ground. The child may initially understand this physical act because she repeatedly sees adults drop things off tables and throw clothes in hampers. Only when the child can independently put objects on surfaces and see how they may fall off if the surface is not sufficiently supported will the child acquire a full mastery of the concept.

Most generally, infants infer the rules of how objects behave once they have experienced many opportunities of watching objects move, collide, fall, and so forth. These visual experiences are initially constrained by a learning mechanism that is dedicated to acquiring event-general expectations (e.g., a general principle covering all occlusion, containment, and covering events), which later on develops into a mechanism enabling event-specific expectations (i.e., different principles about occlusion, containment, and covering events, respectively) (Baillargeon, 2004). In fact, exposing infants to different contrastive information about physical events, such as those pertaining to height, appear to benefit 9 1/2-month-old infants' detection of violations of specific principles (Wang, Baillargeon, & Brueckner, 2004). Overall, this position places primary emphasis on the child's looking skills as the key ingredient in successful differentiated physical reasoning.

The Importance of Embodied Action in Physical Reasoning

Each of the above theories of cognitive development gives little attention to the role of full-bodied sensorimotor activity in how the child learns to reason about the physical world. Spelke (1998) correctly argues that the simple fact that behavior on some task has changed over time does not necessarily imply that experience is the cause of that development. Various maturational processes, perhaps triggered by the environment, may drive behavioral change and development overall, apart from any particular experiences the child has looking at or manipulating objects. Yet appeals to nativist accounts of cognitive development still ignore fundamental knowledge (including deeply nonrepresentational information) that children acquire from their bodily experiences in interaction with the physical and cultural world.

I agree wholeheartedly with Spelke (1998) when she suggests four guidelines for investigators studying cognitive development, one of which states that "All accounts of the findings of infant studies require evidence. In particular, those who would explain infant's performance by appealing to sensory or motor processes must provide evidence for these processes, on a par with those who would explain infant's performance in terms of perceptual or cognitive processes" (Spelke, 1998: 41). But scholars who embrace the idea that concepts are acquired through nonsensory or disembodied processes must also share in the burden of having to explicitly seek out an embodied alternative as part of their experimental work.

The fact that infants are not adept at manipulating objects until around 6 months old misses the obvious point that infants still have many complex bodily interactions with objects (e.g., touching them, being placed on and inside of them, having their mouths on them). Newborns will often bring objects placed in their hands up to their mouths for oral contact (Lew & Butterworth, 1997). This kind of oral exploration enables infants to learn important qualities of objects, such as their solidity, boundedness, and rigidity, properties that are widely assumed to be innately given. Other studies show that newborns' hand and arm movements are far from random. In one study of hand and arm movement, newborns were presented with three conditions: a person facing them, a ball moving slowly in front of them, and a control condition with neither a person or ball (Roseblad & von Hofsten, 1994). These newborns more often flexed their fingers and moved their hands in the social condition (i.e., a person facing them) than in the other two conditions. When newborns saw the rolling ball, they were more likely to extend their fingers (as if to anticipate a grasp), to move their thumbs and index fingers (as if to grasp), and to extend their arms forward (as if to reach). A different study indicated that newborns resisted when adults attempted to manipulate their arms and could visually follow the movements of their arms if they could see them (van der Meer, van der Weel, & Lee, 1995). Finally, newborns presented with an object in different locations directed more arm and hand movements in the direction of the object (Bloch, 1990). These different results together suggest that even if very young infants cannot actually reach or grasp, they can engage in motor activities that are adaptive to the social and physical environment.

Although 2- and 3-month-old infants' initial exploration of an object tends to be oral, 4- and 5-month-old infants tend to examine objects visually (Rochat, 1989). Yet infants who had 2-week enrichment experiences of wearing sticky mittens (i.e., mittens with palms that stick to the edges of objects and allow infants to pick them up) later on showed more object engagement than did inexperienced peers (Needham, Barrett, & Peterson, 2002). Thus, experience with acting on objects may be critical to increasing infants' engagements with objects and developing their object exploration skills.

As infants grow and experience direct contact with objects, not just with their hands, they learn a great deal about notions such as support, continuity, and boundedness directly from their kinesthetic experiences – for example, infants' self-produced locomotion and their reactions to the deep side of a visual cliff (Bertenthal, Campos, & Barrett, 1984; Bertenthal et al., 1994). Infants who had early experiences with self-produced locomotion (either their own naturally acquired experiences or artificially acquired experiences using an infant walker) exhibited wariness toward the deep side of the cliff (as described by an increase in heart rate or sudden avoidance of the deep side), compared to infants who did not have locomotion experience. Self-produced locomotion does not necessarily lead infants to fear heights when they first learn to walk, because infants may have to relearn the consequence of deep slopes for each domain of movement (e.g., crawling vs. walking) (Adolph, 1997, 2000; Clearfield, 2000). Being able to walk also increases social interactions. Thus, an upright infant is more likely to be able to look, vocalize, and smile at adults (Gufstafson, 1984). Finally, infants with more locomotion experience, through either crawling or assisted walking, are more likely to persist in searches for hidden objects (as examined in object permanence tasks) (Bai & Bertenthal, 1992; Bertenthal et al., 1984; Kermoian & Campos, 1988). The development of walking also assists blind infants' search for hidden objects (Bigelow, 1992).

Other studies observing a link between infants' leg movements and the movements of a hanging mobile provide additional support for the claim that producing actions with observable effects on objects is highly reinforcing for young infants (Rovee-Collier & Hayne, 2000). Infants who exemplify more active exploration strategies (exploring more, switching more between oral and visual modalities of exploration) are also better able to segregate a visual display into its component parts, compared to infants with much less active exploration strategies (Needham, 2001).

The above studies demonstrate important links between infants' perceptual, cognitive, and action-based abilities. None of these results imply that sensorimotor processing alone may be responsible for children's understanding of physical events. But, at the very least, the evidence suggests that sensorimotor experience contributes to children's understanding of objects and their behaviors. Infants' earliest concepts of objects are tied not just to their visual experiences, but to noting how objects change in different circumstances, both when that change occurs through the infant's own movements and when infants move around objects when carried around by adults (Bloom, 1993). For instance, a blanket appears when the baby is being put down to rest and disappears when it is picked up for feeding or playing. Thus, infants' theories of objects must arise partly from their embodied actions in relation to objects. It is unsurprising, then, that children's first words express something about objects that move (e.g., "ball") (Bloom, 1993). "Both conceptual categories and eventual linguistic categories build on an infant's nascent theories about objects, motion, space, and causality, and these theories originate in the early experiences that come about with movement and change in location" (Bloom, 1993: 86).

One possibility is that the movement of objects resembles certain aspects of an infant's own tactile-kinesthetic actions. In this regard, there are two broad types of onset of motion, self-instigated motion and caused motion. Adults think of biological motion as having certain rhythmic, but unpredictable, characteristics, whereas mechanical motion is thought of as undeviating, unless the moving object is deflected in some way. Infants' concentrated attention on moving objects may easily lead them to analyze the animate trajectories of objects in motion.

Very young infants, in fact, are sensitive to the difference between something starting to move on its own and something being pushed or otherwise made to move (Leslie, 1988). Self-motion is the start of an independent trajectory where no other object or trajectory is involved. Noticing that dogs bob up and down as well as follow irregular paths when they move is one example of this. When 1- to 2-year-olds played with little models of a variety of animals and vehicles, they often responded to the animals by making them hop along the table, but made the vehicles scoot in a straight line (Mandler, Bauer, & McDonough, 1991). Thus, very young children appear to understand differences in the movement of animate and inanimate objects.

Perceived differences in motion patterns can be used to ground infants' early understanding of the distinction between animate and inanimate objects (Premack, 1990; Mandler, 1992). Self-propelled, irregularly moving things tend to be animate, and contact-propelled, smoothly moving things tend to be inanimate. However, the animate/inanimate distinction may arise from a belief, not bodily information, about whether an object has the right source of energy (internal vs. external) and is made of the right kind of stuff to initiate its own actions (Gelman, Durgin, & Kaufman, 1995). Thus, preschoolers can make judgments related to animacy based on still pictures of animate-like versus nonanimate-like objects. But this finding may be due to infants' understandings of how various shapes relate to animate action (i.e., perception of curvilinear contours, faces). People often infer dynamic, sometimes embodied, information from static percepts (see Chapter 3). Features are important in the perception of objects and their behaviors because these are correlated with dynamic information that children experience from their own bodies and from watching others.

Perceptual Meaning Analysis: Mandler's Theory

My earlier brief review of three broad theories of cognitive development suggested that few approaches appropriately acknowledge infants' sensorimotor abilities in their physical reasoning skills. One theory that embraces a slightly more embodied view of children's cognitive development maintains that infants' capacity to abstract certain kinds of information from perceptual displays develops concurrently with sensorimotor skills, rather than being a subsequent development (Mandler, 1992, 2004). Early concept formation does not depend on physical interactions with objects, but instead arises from independent analyses of certain perceptual experiences. Innate perceptual mechanisms begin very early on to generate abstract, nonpropositional images that are "simplified and condensed relationships of spatial structure" (Mandler, 1992: 591–2). Thus, the process of perceptual analysis extracts various aspects of the spatial structure of objects and their movements in space, usually from visual experience, although touch, audition, and one's own movements are also included. Perceptual meaning analysis redescribes the spatial and movement structure of perceptual displays to, once more, to analogic representations, or image schemas, that compose the primitives of an accessible conceptual system (see Chapter 4). One possibility is that image schemas underlie many concepts acquired early in a child's life, such as animacy, inanimacy, agency, containment, and support relations (Mandler, 2004).

As described in Chapter 4, image schemas are not images in the sense of necessarily having detailed information about object movement such as speed and direction. Unlike visual images, for example, image schemas are not usually conscious, and are best thought of as topographical representations that can be complex, despite their primitive nature (e.g., a CONTAINMENT schema consists of a boundary plus an inside and outside). Although image schemas may be temporary constructions, created on the fly as part of people's embodied simulations, Mandler (1992, 2004) maintains the more traditional view that image schemas are permanent representations in memory. Nonetheless, let me now explore more fully the idea that image schemas underlie aspects of young children's concepts.

Consider first the idea that various image schemas underlie young children's understanding of animacy. The contingency of animate movement not only involves such factors as one animate object following another, as described by the image schema LINKED PATHS, but also involves avoiding barriers and making sudden shifts in acceleration. Adults are sensitive to all of these aspects of animate movement (Stewart, 1983), but it is not yet known whether infants are responsive to such movement, even though they appear to be perceptually salient. Nor has anyone considered how factors such as barrier avoidance might be represented in image-schema form (Mandler, 1992). Several FORCE schemas, such as BLOCKAGE and DIVERSION, may be useful in describing barrier avoidance, but these schemas need to be further differentiated to account for animate and inanimate trajectories. One might represent animate and inanimate differences in response to blockage as a trajectory that shifts direction before contacting a barrier versus one that runs into a barrier and then either stops or bounces off from it (Mandler, 1992).

Studies of babies' understanding of causality may reveal how FORCE and CAUSED-MOTION schemas shape understanding of causality. Imagine a film clip of one ball rolling out from behind a screen from the right and striking a second ball situated in the middle of the screen, followed by the second ball rolling off the screen to the left. When watching this film, observers experience the first ball as having caused the movement of the second. Now imagine the same event with a brief delay between the time the first ball strikes and the time the second ball moves. The delay removes the appearance of a causal relation. But now imagine seeing a third film clip, which is just a copy of the first film clip played in reverse. Now a ball moves in from the left, strikes the ball in the middle, and causes it to roll off to the right. Aside from the direction of movement, the third clip has exactly the same contiguity and successive relations as the first. Just like the first film clip, we see this clip as causal. The change in direction makes an important difference, however. In the first clip, people perceive the ball on the left as the agent with causal powers that are transfixed to the ball in the center of the screen. In the third clip, the ball on the right is the causal agent.

Even 6-month-old infants are sensitive to causal relationships (Leslie & Keeble, 1987). When infants watch the second clip, played fast forward and then in reverse, they do not get very excited by the reversal. When they see the first clip played forward and then in reverse (like the third clip), they get very excited by the reversal. The first reversal is perceived as a change in the locus of causal power, but the second reversal is not thus perceived. These findings suggest to some that contiguity and succession are insufficient to explain how we think about causation (Leslie & Keeble, 1987). In addition to concepts of spatial and temporal properties, infants have an innate concept of causal power. Spatial and temporal properties are guides to attributing causal power, but they are not constitutive of causal powers. Under this view, casual power cannot be identified with any perceptual representations.

The main problem with this conclusion about causality is that it neglects the infant's understanding of its own body as both source and recipient of causal forces. Infants and young children, similarly to adults, manipulate objects and feel the pushing and pulling of objects that make contact with them. In these situations, characteristic kinesthetic and somatosensory experiences are specifically felt, and infants may use such experiences to ground their early notions of causal powers. They may project characteristic embodied experiences onto perceived objects.

For example, the pattern of contiguity and succession that children see when billiard balls collide are most significantly similar to the patterns produced by seeing their own interactions with objects. Thus, part of infants' ability to recognize causal relations may be due to image schemas like FORCE that is derived through somatosensory and kinesthetic experiences, and projected onto inanimate objects when they act as causes. One suggestion is that infants' understanding of contingent interactions among objects is also preceded by their analysis of the reciprocal give-and-take occurring during adult-infant turn-taking (Mandler, 2004; Murray & Trevarthen, 1985), which is certainly an embodied activity.

Several LINK schemas may also structure young children's understanding of causal relations between animate and inanimate objects. A LINK is established as the children regularly encounter one event followed by another, such as seeing that a spoon always falls to the floor when pushed off the side of the highchair. Of course, the ability to know that one has moved oneself, as opposed to being moved by someone or something else, gives rise to the SELF-MOTION schema, which also surely is critical to the perception of many causal events involving animate and inanimate objects. Different studies with 7-month-olds show that they look longer at object movements that begin without being compelled by contact with another object (Spelke et al., 1995). In this way, infants may acquire some of their understanding of objects and the circumstances in which they move from their own felt understandings of their bodily experiences. These image schemas provide enough information to understand what a concept of "starting to move" is like without the more detailed perceptual analysis that characterizes each perceptual event (Mandler, 2004). Furthermore, studies reveal that infants as young as 3 months of age can distinguish between correct and incorrect human actions (Bertenthal, 1993), suggesting that concepts of animacy are rooted in image schemas like SELF-MOTION.

CONTAINMENT is another image schema that is critical to cognitive development. Some concept of containment seems to be responsible for the better performance 9-month-old infants show on object-hiding tasks when the occluder consists of an upright container, rather than an inverted container or a screen (Freeman, Lloyd, & Sinha, 1980; Lloyd, Sinha, & Freeman, 1981). These infants already appear to have a concept of containers as places where things disappear and reappear. Image schemas may explain some of these data. For example, the CONTAINMENT schema has three structural elements (interior, boundary, and exterior) that primarily arise from two sources: (1) perceptual analysis of the differentiation of figure from ground, that is, seeing objects as bounded and having an inside that is separate from the outside (Spelke, 1988), and (2) perceptual analysis of objects going into and out of containers. The list of containment relations that babies experience is long. Babies eat and drink, spit things out, watch their bodies being clothed and unclothed, are taken in and out of cribs and rooms, and so on.

An infant's understanding of opening and closing is also related to the development of containment. Piaget (1952) documented in detail the actions 9- to 12-month-old infants performed while they were learning to imitate acts that they could not see themselves perform, such as blinking. Before infants accomplished the correct action, they sometimes opened and closed their mouths, opened and closed their hands, or covered and uncovered their eyes with a pillow. Piaget's observations testify to the perceptual analysis in which the infants were engaging and their analogical understanding of the structure of the behavior they were trying to reproduce. Such understanding seems a clear case of an image schema of the spatial movement involved when anything opens or closes, regardless of the particulars of the thing itself.

Although bodily experience may be the basis for understanding of containment, it is not obvious that bodily experience per se is required for perceptual analysis to take place (Mandler, 1992). Infants have many opportunities to analyze simple, easily visible containers such as bottles, cups, and dishes and the acts of containment that make things disappear into and reappear out of them. Indeed, it might be easier to analyze the sight of milk going in and out of a cup than milk going into or out of one's mouth. Nevertheless, whichever way the analysis of containment gets started, one would expect the notion of food as something that is taken into the mouth to be an early conceptualization.

Another aspect that seems to be involved in an early concept of a container is that of support. True containers not only envelop things but support them as well. Infants as young as 3 months are surprised when support relations between objects are violated (Needham & Baillargeon, 1993). Infants 5 1/2 months old are surprised when containers without bottoms appear to hold things (Kolstad, 1991). Similarly, 9-month-old infants could judge whether a block could be supported by a box open at the top only when they were able to compare the widths of the block and the box in a single glance as one was lowered into the other (Sitskoorn & Smitsman, 1991). Finally, Baillargeon (1993) demonstrated that 12 1/2-month-old infants could determine whether a cloth cover with a small protuberance could hide a small tiger toy only when they were able to compare the size of the protuberance directly with that of the toy. These findings suggest that the notions of containment and support may be closely related from an early age. A primitive image-schema of SUPPORT might require only a representation of contact between two objects in the vertical dimension (Mandler, 1992).

One could argue that development of the notion of object permanence can be thought of as the development of several different image schemas and the workings of transformations between them. Following Mandler (1992), the transformations LANDMARK, to BLOCKAGE, to REMOVAL OF BLOCKAGE, and finally back to LANDMARK underlie the demonstration of object permanence in the 4 1/2-month-olds. The reason the 3 1/2-month-olds do not exhibit object permanence is that they either have not developed one or more of these image schemas or are not yet capable of transforming them. The specific explanation requires more specific tests to determine which is true, but we suspect it has to do with blockage and removal of blockage. This follows from the fact that 3 1/2-month-old infants can already focus on individual objects and thus appear to have developed the image schema for LANDMARK.

Finally, consider the concept of agency. A traditional belief is that infants learn agency from observing the effects of their actions on the world (Gibson, 1988). An infant discovers his or her own agency by observing that his or her solitary movements bring about desired consequences, such as keeping a picture in focus rather than out of focus (Kalnins & Bruner, 1973).

But this view of how agency develops does not properly acknowledge a child's kinesthetic activity (Sheets-Johnstone, 1999). For example, very early in a young infant's life, the simple act of moving its lips, tongue, and mouth on its mother's breast directly exposes the child to its own causal powers. Numerous other body actions, such as chewing, swallowing, and bending and extending fingers, provide infants with a tactile-kinesthetic sense of agency. This understanding of agency is not an awareness derived from just seeing our efforts in the world, but rather is rooted in our own tactile-kinesthetic experiences. Of course, young children, like adults, do not engage in activity for no purpose, but aim to achieve specific goals (e.g., touching objects, obtaining food). Developmental studies show that 5-month-old infants begin to distinguish between goal-directed actions and those that occur accidentally (Woodward, 1999). By 9 months of age, babies appear to be able to understand something about the paths along which objects will travel (Gergely et al., 1995). These findings are consistent with the idea that an image schema of SOURCE-PATH-GOAL, along with ANIMACY and SELF-MOTION, help infants reason about the behavior of moving objects. Once more, recurring aspects of infants' using their bodies and parts of their bodies, ranging from moving their eyes to gaze at specific objects to moving their whole bodies to reach people and objects, provide part of the foundation for more complex physical reasoning skills.

Object Permanence Again

I started my discussion of recent cognitive development work by focusing on experimental studies of object permanence. These studies aimed to explore when and how infants acquire the object concept and reason about the behavior of objects. I was critical of these studies for not exploring the importance of the child's own actions, such as its reaching behavior, in theoretical accounts of concept acquisition.

But there are several newer studies that have attempted to model the child's performance on object permanence tasks, specifically investigating infants' A-not-B errors. For example, Munakata et al. (1997) developed a connectionist model to address developmental decalage between infants' success on the object concept search task when assessed by reaching and success when assessed by looking preferences, an advance that occurs several months earlier. The traditional explanation of successes and failure in search tasks are principle-based – that is, early successes imply an all-or-nothing knowledge of principles (e.g., object permanence) and failures are attributed to ancillary deficits (e.g., means-end abilities). Munataka et al. argued that the principle-based approach leads, for example, to the premature inference that 3 $^1/_2$-month-old infants who look longer at the "impossible" disappearing event (see Baillargeon, 1993) have knowledge of object permanence.

They propose an alternative "adaptive processes" account of the acquisition of the object concept in which knowledge is graded in nature rather than all-or-none, evolves with experience, and is embedded in specific processes underlying overt bodily behavior. The adaptive processes approach attributes success to the ability to represent occluded objects, which in terms depends on the connection among many relevant neurons, an ability that is acquired through a process of strengthening these connections. Failures occur because different behaviors require different degrees of development in the relevant underlying processing system and resulting internal representations.

This connectionist model shows how an infant could gradually learn to represent occluded objects over time, thus accounting for successes and failure without assuming principles and ancillary deficits on the object search tasks. Thelen et al. (2001) propose a dynamical alternative to Munakata et al.'s (1997) Hebbian network model of the A-not-B task. Dynamic systems psychologists view development in terms of the infant's active engagement with the environment through movement, rather than depending on theoretical constraints or neurological programs. As Esther Thelen and Linda Smith argue, "Development does not happen because internal maturational processes tell the system how to develop. Rather, development happens through and because of the activity of the system itself" (Thelen & Smith, 1994: 305). Under this view, cognition is structured in movement activity. A young child's ability to integrate information from across different sensory modalities is not a result of development, but the very basis from which development emerges. Development is seen as an emergent property of the whole system and can only be understood in terms of the complex interaction of psychological, biological, and physical components. A key feature of dynamic systems is that they are self-organizing – they arrive at new states simply through their own functioning, without specification from the environment or determination from within. With a continuous change in one or more control parameters (akin to but not equivalent to independent variables), new states may emerge spontaneously as a function of nonlinear interactions between the systems' components.

Quite importantly, the development of behavior that appears to be discontinuous or disorderly at the performance level may arise from underlying processes that themselves are continuous and orderly (e.g., an infant's vocabulary acquisition or first steps), which is a key feature of all self-organizing systems. Dynamic systems theory is good at interpreting multiple levels of performance (e.g., infants are competent at the perceptual level when assessed by visual preference, but not when assessed by reaching). A dynamical systems view of the A-not-B error claims that this behavior is not specific to any particular point in development, but may arise in different situations in which children produce goal-directed actions to remembered locations. More specifically, the error is attributed to the interaction of many factors. These include visual and attentional processes that function in the perception of objects, motor processes used in planning and executing hand and arm movements toward a target location, short-term memory processes active in maintaining task-related information when relevant perceptual cues are absent, and long-term memory processes that maintain results from past actions.

In a typical A-not-B experiment, infants start by locating the hidden object under location A over repeated trials, which produces a relatively stable long-term memory of the A location. At the start of the first B trial, infants plan a movement toward the B location to retrieve the object. However, in the absence of appropriate perceptual cues that specify that the object is in the B location when the object is hidden, the motor plan to reach toward B decays, especially over longer time intervals. After several seconds, a plan to move to A, which has been strongly established from previous trials, begins to dominate and the infant consequently makes the A-not-B error by reaching for the object in the A location.

Several experiments tested this theory by having 2-year-olds first see and then find a toy at the A location over several trials. When the toy was then hidden at the B location, the toddler's search was biased toward the direction of A. The magnitude of the pull toward A depended on the number of times the toy had been previously hidden at that location. Furthermore, the longer the children had to wait before reaching for the toy at the B location, the more likely they were to make a response toward A. The bias toward location A was also present even when the A trials, both during training and in the main experimental task, varied over an 8-inch region. Finally, shifts in the babies' position and visual perception influenced the probability of making the A-not-B error. When 8- to 10-month-olds stood up on the B trials, they significantly reduced their A-not-B errors (Smith et al., 1999). These results are consistent with the dynamical claim that the error arises from an interaction of four factors: the graded nature of spatial memory, the sequence of events in the task, the limited xx location in the task space, and the delay in the B task.

The dynamical approach to development is significant because it embraces the idea that cognition is connected to bodily action. A child's new abilities emerge through the dynamic indeterminacy of self-organization. Unlike most theories, the dynamical perspective explains development in terms of multiple causes and connections and acknowledges that even small, unexpected factors may critically shape the course of development. Moreover, dynamical systems theories recognize the importance of studying the whole system (i.e., the child) in understanding development, and not assuming that cognitive growth is based on the acquisition of isolated competences. Although dynamical systems theory has been most successful in describing motor and perceptual development (Bertenthal &

Pinto, 1993; Butterworth, 1993; Goldfield, 1993; Thelen, 2000; Thelen & Smith, 1994; van Geert, 1991), there is an increasing body of work showing how emotional and personality development may also be characterized in dynamical terms (Granott & Paziale, 2002). This work is clearly consistent with my "embodiment premise" by explicitly looking for the possible roles that embodied activity has in human development.

Children with Physical Handicaps

One challenge to the idea that sensorimotor experience is critical to cognitive growth comes from the study of physically handicapped individuals. Although sensorimotor activity may provide part of the input for perceptual systems, high-level symbolic thought may still arise in its absence. As one group of scholars argued, "Since motor movements are not assumed to play an important role in their conceptual abilities, there is no reason to believe that motorically impaired children need be differentially disadvantaged in the development of these early foundations of thought, unless additional damage to non-motor areas of the brain have occurred" (Berko et al., 1992: 229).

In fact, some studies report research consistent with the idea that motor experience is not crucial for intellectual development. This includes studies looking at academic achievement in children who are congenital amputees (Clarke & French, 1978), object permanence in children with severe quadriplegic cerebral palsy (Eagle, 1985), stage 6 object permanence and intersubjectivity in one 3-year-old child with congenital upper and lower limb deformities (Kopp & Shaperman, 1973), and cognitive gains in psychometric measures in thalidomide children with at least one partial limb (Gouin-Decarie, 1969).

But many studies have been interpreted as supporting the view that motor experience is crucial for cognitive development. Consider the development of motion. First, crawling allows different kinds of interaction with the environment than are possible with the nonmobile infant, and crawling experience is well established as the cause of transition in spatial location coding (Campos et al., 2000). Studies with children whose vision was obscured by congenital cataracts, and who underwent operations to remove them at different ages, show how crucial normal expectable input can be to the development of normal vision (Mauer et al., 1999). Adventitiously blind individuals perform better at distance judgments than congenitally blind children, suggesting the importance of expectable early experience for basic spatial functioning (Reiser, Lockman, & Pick, 1980). Severely motorically handicapped groups are delayed in their complex spatial relation and planning skills (McDonnell, 1988; Rothman, 1987). Moreover, nonambulatory children with cerebral palsy showed more significant deficiencies than did children with three unaffected limbs (McDonnell, 1988; Rothman, 1987).

Children with cerebral palsy may, of course, have other neurological impairments.

Determining which of these alternative views on sensorimotor experience and cognitive development is correct is a tricky problem. There are several methodological issues with most studies of cognitive development in the physically handicapped, including the diversity of procedures used, yielding data that are incommensurable across studies, and the fact that performance on some conceptual tasks is facilitated by bimanual manipulations of the objects and so forth. Thus, differences in the results between limb-deficient and nonhandicapped children may reflect motor limitations rather than conceptual deficiencies. The degree of impairment is also critical. Thalidomide individuals and congenital amputees possess at least one functional limb or segment that could potentially be employed in the formation of motor schemes. These children will circumvent the expected impairments by compensating creatively for the handicaps (Eagle, 1985). Even in extreme conditions of physical impairment, a child may still have control of at least one means of interaction with the environment (Sinclair, 1971). For example, eye movements or perhaps motor activities involved in chewing could be sufficient for motor schemes to develop.

Severely quadriplegic children are more impaired than congenital amputees and thalidomide children. Thus, in addition to impairment of both arms and legs, the trunk, eye movements, and mouths are often spastic, rigid, or exceptionally hypotonic. But congenitally physically impaired infants often have more diffuse brain damage, extending to nonmotor areas. In each case, it is difficult to identify the unique contribution of organic as opposed to experiential factors in any observed cognitive delays (Eagle, 1985). Even when organic contributions can be ruled out, other sorts of deprivation, such as social deprivations, are often associated with physical handicaps.

But most importantly, physically handicapped individuals may still experience large amounts of tactile-kinesthetic information from eye, mouth, and head movements and the feelings arising from other bodily functions. These bodily experiences may be sufficient for the coordination of many action schemes that underlie cognitive growth. Moreover, recent research shows that normally occurring sensory experience has a major role in species-specific instinctive behaviors that have traditionally been thought to be an outcome of heredity (Gottlieb, 2002). In this view, the nervous system does not develop fully or normally without the benefit of normally occurring sensory experience. Young infants and children may not necessarily need to have all their limbs, or be able to move their bodies in normal ways, for them still to benefit enormously from simple and complex action patterns as they develop fundamental concepts. Thus, even disabled children will have sufficient bodily experiences to form a wide variety of image schemas, including CONTAINMENT, BALANCE, SOURCE-PATH-GOAL, LINKAGE, and so on.

Multimodal Perception

Many studies in developmental psychology show that young children find abstract similarities between different sensory experiences. Infants seem able to connect visual information with tactile information. For example, 6-month-old infants were given one of two pacifiers to suck that had different textures (Meltzoff & Borton, 1979). The surface of one pacifier was smooth, whereas the other one had a ribbed surface. At first, the infants sucked on the their pacifiers without seeing the objects. In a second part of the experiment, the infants were shown large pictures of both pacifiers. As expected, the majority of the infants preferred looking at the pacifier that they had just been sucking. This preference for congruence suggests that even 1-month-old infants have some understanding of cross-modal equivalence.

Babies can also make cross-modal connections between auditory and visual information. For instance, 4-month-old infants viewed simultaneous films of two rhythmic events; a woman playing "peek-a-boo," and a baton hitting a wooden block (Spelke, 1976). While they were viewing the films, an audiotape, centered between the two screens, was played that was appropriate to one of the films. The infants preferred to look at the visual events that matched the auditory source. This too is evidence for some understanding of cross-modal equivalence.

Infants as young as 2 to 5 months old are capable of perceiving coherent unitary multimodal events, such as the relationship between a person's face and voice, on the basis of temporal synchrony and shared rhythm between the movements of the mouth and the timing of the speech (Dodd, 1979; Lewkowicz, 1996), as well as between the shapes of the lips and the corresponding vocal sounds (Kuhl & Meltzoff, 1982). By age 5–7 months, infants can match their own body motions, experienced proprioceptively, with a visual display of the motion, on the basis of shared temporal and spatial information (Bahrick & Watson, 1985; Bahrick, 1995; Rochet, 1995; Schumaker, 1986). Thus, when a 5-month-old observes a live video display of her own legs moving, alongside one of an infant's legs, she can distinguish the two and prefers to watch the novel display of the other infant.

Detection of intermodal relations is not just a case of association of two experiences that happen to occur simultaneously. For example, 3-month-old infants were familiarized with different visible and audible filmed events (Bahrick, 1988). One film depicted a hand shaking a clear plastic bottle containing one very large marble. The other film depicted a hand shaking a similar bottle containing a number of very small marbles. Four conditions varied in their pairings of film and sound tracks as to whether the appropriate track (one or many marbles) was paired with a film or whether a track was synchronous with the film or not. Only one group of infants was acquainted with films paired with the appropriate, synchronized sound tracks. After familiarization, an internal preference test was given to each group of infants with two films presented side by side while a single central track played. The data showed that learning did occur with greater familiarization, resulting in a preference for matching the film specified by its appropriate sound track. But, most importantly, learning was confined to just one group of infants, namely, those most familiar with the appropriate synchronized pairing of sight and sound. Equal opportunity to associate with an inappropriate sound track did not lead to a preference for that combination on the preference test. These findings show that very young children exhibit an ability to acquire abstract relations between events in different sensory modalities.

A different line of research on how children find abstract similarities between different sensory experiences comes from work on synesthesia. In one early study, infants were challenged to construct a similarity relationship between two events that shared no physical features or history of co-occurrence (e.g., a pulsing tone and paired slides of a dotted line and a solid line). Nine- to 12-month-old infants looked longer at the dotted line than at the solid line in the presence of a pulsing tone, suggesting that a metaphorical match was construed (Wagner et al., 1981). Similarly, they looked more at an arrow pointing upward when listening to an ascending tone and at a downward arrow when listening to a descending tone. The infants were thus able to recognize an abstract dimension that underlay two physically and temporally dissimilar events (e.g., discontinuity in the pulsing tone and discontinuity in the dotted line). Another study demonstrated that four-year-olds already perceive and conceive of similarities between pitch and brightness (e.g., low pitch equals dim; high pitch equals bright) and between loudness and brightness (e.g., soft equals dim; loud equals bright). These findings are especially important because they parallel the idea that adults project image-schemas from one domain onto another, for example, conceptualizing quantity in terms of verticality (e.g., MORE IS UP and LESS IS DOWN).

Finally, more recent research examined whether infants can construe an abstract unity between a facial expression of emotion (e.g., joy) and an auditory event (e.g., an ascending tone), events that also share no physical features or history of co-occurrence (Phillips et al., 1990). The 7-month-old infants in this study did not categorize different facial expressions of joy and anger. But the infants did look significantly longer at joy, surprise, and sadness when these facial expressions were matched with ascending, pulsing, and descending and continuous tones, respectively. Because the auditory and visual events in this experimental task were substantially different, infants had to act upon the events within a short period of time to bring meaning (i.e., determine equivalences) to the disparity. Thus, infants had to determine the equivalence between facial expressions and auditory events. This is a striking demonstration of how infants metaphorically match disparate events to construe some meaning in facial expressions of emotion.

There are three basic principles of intermodal perception (Bahrick, 2000). First, global, abstract intermodal relations are detected earlier than are more specific nested relations. For example, global relations involve shared synchrony, as when the sight and sound of a hammer hitting the ground are synchronized. Nested relations are more specific and reveal details about an events, such as that a specific object makes a specific sound when hitting the ground, whereas a compound object (e.g., a tray of cutlery) makes a complex set of sounds.

The second principle claims that amodal relations are perceived earlier than arbitrary relations. Thus, a person's voice is always synchronized with his or her mouth movements in such a way that the synchrony provides amodal information. But the precise sound of the voice is arbitrary and cannot be specified in advance. Moreover, it is not possible to predict the specific sound that a red object will make when dropped onto the floor.

The third principle holds that the detection of amodal relations facilitates perceptual learning about arbitrary relations. For instance, when an infant perceives the synchrony between his or her mother's face and voice, he or she learns to associate the unique sounds of the voice with that person. If the two modalities are not synchronized, then the association of face and voice will not be learned. This principle guides the young infant through a maze of sights, sounds, and other natural mental combinations and provides a way of organizing perceptual experience that leads infants to more mature knowledge of adults.

The experimental work on multimodal perception is quite relevant to an embodied perspective on cognitive development. This work clearly demonstrates that young children are capable of making cross-modal, or cross-sensory, connections, which enable them to understand important aspects of objects and events in the world. Yet these cross-modal connections also form the bases of image schemas that underlie many concrete and abstract concepts.

Imitation

Imitation is an embodied cognitive activity. Piaget suggested that infants lack the skill to imitate adult actions, such as tongue protrusion and mouth opening, before the age of 8 or 9 months. But infants as young as 42 minutes after birth have crude imitative abilities, such as when they initiate moving tongue protrusions, mouth openings, and lip movements of an adult

(Meltzoff, 1990; Gallagher & Meltzoff, 1996). This ability to match visual with proprioceptive actions may be assumed to represent a "supramodal representational system" or an embryonic body schema (Meltzoff, 1990).

Piaget argued that deferred imitation is not exhibited under 18 months when infants are unable to form mental representations apart from immediate environmental stimuli. Yet 6-month-olds exhibit deferred imitation, or the ability to imitate an action seen 24 hours earlier, such as an adult's facial expression (Collie & Hayne, 1999; Meltzoff & Moore, 1994). At 9 months of age, infants can copy adults' actions on objects (Meltzoff, 1990) and can reproduce event sequences after a delay (Carver & Bauer, 1999). Later on, by 14 months, infants can model a range of adult, as well as peer, behaviors toward different objects (Hanna & Meltzoff, 1993; Meltzoff, 1990). Meltzoff (1995) demonstrated that 18-month-olds will go beyond imitation per se and will perform the intended (i.e., initiated but not completed) actions of a model following a brief retention interval. These studies clearly show that deferred imitation is not a final achievement of the sensorimotor period but emerges early on and becomes more sophisticated by the end of toddlerhood.

Three hypotheses have been proposed to explain infants' surprising imitative abilities (Meltzoff & Moore, 2000). First, imitation may be based on reinforcement from the parents. But parents are unaware of having some of the behaviors imitated in the first four weeks of life. Parental reinforcement, therefore, seems implausible as the source of early infant imitation.

Second, imitation may be based on an innate releasing mechanism (Anifeld, 1996). According to this idea, lip protrusion and sequential finger movement are fixed-action patterns that get released when infants see corresponding adult gestures. However, the variety of infants' gestures suggests that their imitative abilities are not due to a small set of fixed-action patterns.

A final possibility is that imitation is based on the infant's capacity to represent visually and proprioceptively perceived information on a form common to both modalities. Under this view, the infant compares sensory information from her own bodily movements to a "supramodal" representation of the visually perceived gesture and construct a match between them. Meltzoff and Moore (1992, 1997) contend that true imitation is made possible by active intermodal mapping (AIM) mechanisms that enable infants to make cross-modal equivalence between body transformations that are seen or heard and those that are felt on the basis of their own tactile-kinesthetic action to generate the matching response. This idea is consistent with the possibility that children's early sensorimotor actions provide part of the basis for abstract representational systems used in successful imitation.

Yet the psychological primitive underlying infants' imitation may not necessarily be due to either a body schema, or some developing representational system. Instead, imitation may reflect primal animation of the tactile-kinesthetic body (Sheets-Johnstone, 1999). Whether infants are copying pure body movements of others, or how others interact with objects, their imitation reflects a dynamically attuned body and an organizing kinesthetic liveliness. What the infant sees is a replication of the dynamics of its own felt movement. Under this view, imitation is just one facet of learning to move oneself. In some cases, perhaps, reproducing an event may be evoked not through memory, but via the mere presence of an object and the actions that it may typically elicit or afford. This possibility emphasizes how sensorimotor activity is integral to infants' understanding of objects, even when an infant has not previously performed these actions on a specific object. Of course, this idea is limited to conventional motor patterns and cannot explain babies' developing abilities to recreate novel sequences or actions (see Mandler, 2004).

Another instance of imitation is evident in older infants' analogical reenactment of previously seen events. Piaget argued that sensorimotor behavior becomes representational via a process of interiorization. Overt behavior serves as the model for understanding real-world events via a process of analogy, specifically "motor analogies." Piaget observed that his own children imitated certain spatial relations that they had seen in the physical world using their own bodies. For instance, Piaget's children imitated the opening and closing of a matchbox by opening and closing their hands and mouths. Piaget suggested that this behavior showed that the infants are trying to understand the mechanism of the matchbox through a motor analogy, reproducing a kinesthetic image of opening and closing. Mental imagery was then argued to develop out of kinesthetic imitations as a result of progressive interiorization.

In fact, various studies demonstrate that infants as young as 10 months can make spatial relational mappings, which can be readily transferred to new objects by infants of 13 months (Bauer, 1996; Chen, Sanchez, & Campbell, 1997). In Chen et al. (1997), infants were presented with a doll that was out of their reach. The doll was also behind a box and had a string attached to it that was lying on a visible cloth. Infants could bring the doll within reach by performing a series of actions, such as removing the box and pulling the cloth so that they could pull the string attached to the toy. Once infants could successfully perform this action and pull the doll toward themselves, they were presented with two different scenarios, each using identical tools (cloths, boxes, and strings). However, these new problems differed in that the cloths, boxes, and strings were all different from those encountered before. Moreover, in this new problem, two strings and two cloths were presented, although only one pair could reach the toy.

Children 10 and 13 months old were tested in this experiment. Some of the older infants worked out the solution to reaching the toy on their own, whereas others modeled their parents' solution before successfully solving the problem. Once the first problem was solved, the 13-month-old infants transferred an analogous solution to the second and third problem. But the 10-month-olds focused on one salient perceptual cue before they could analogously move the first solution onto the second and third problems. These data generally support Piaget's contention that analogical transfer, based on sensorimotor schemes, is a critical part of how infants learn to represent and reenact real-world events (see Gibbs, 1994 for a further discussion of the relevant developmental evidence here).

Developing a Theory of Others' Minds

One of the hallmarks of child development is the acquisition of a "theory of mind." Evidence of the child's developing theory of mind comes from several sources, most notably false-belief experiments. In these studies, a participant is asked about the thoughts and actions of another person or character who lacks certain information that the participant knows. A participant knows, for instance, that a candy box contains pencils. Someone else enters the room and the participant is asked, "What will the other person say is in the candy box?" Four-year-olds typically respond correctly that the other person will think there are candies in the box. But 3-year-olds are unable to see that the other person may falsely believe that there are candies in the box and respond that the other person will say that there are actually pencils in the box.

Several theories have been proposed to account for this developmental milestone. The "theory theory" claims that children's theory of mind is generated as an innately specified domain-specific mechanism, or a theory of mind module, particularly designed for reading others' minds (Baron-Cohen, 1995; Leslie, 1991; Tooby & Cosmides, 1995). At first, the child develops a first-order belief that allows him or her to distinguish her own beliefs from someone else's. Later, around the age of 3 or 4, the child acquires an ability to notice another person's thoughts about a third person's thoughts (a second-order belief attribution).

In contrast to theory theory, simulation theory argues that a person understands something of another individual's mind by pretending to be in that person's shoes. More specifically, an observer tries to make his or her own mind emulate the thought processes that the other person is experiencing given the present situation. By recreating the other person's presumed thought processes, the observer will come to understand that person's point of view.

There is a large literature devoted to the debate between the "theory theory" and "simulation" views. Both positions maintain that the child's developing theory of mind comes about as the child develops a theoretical stance involving the possible existence of mental states in others. A common assumption underlying both theories is the "mentalistic assumption"

(Gallagher, 2001), which states that "to know another person is to know that person's mind, and their means to know their beliefs, desires, or intentional states" (Gallagher, 2001: 91). People use their "theory" to explain and predict the behavior of others.

The false-belief paradigm, however, fails to account for many aspects of primary intersubjectivity available to children around the age of 4 that may be critical in children's abilities to read others' minds (Bloom & German, 2001). Something clearly happens around age 4 and the false-belief task may tap into some parts of this specialized cognitive ability. But explaining and predicting, as required by the false-belief task, are indeed specialized activities, and do not reflect much about how children, or others, normally interact with one another, and to some extent, read each other's minds. Experimental participants must adopt third-person perspective to solve these problems, whereas second-person intentions are the typical ways we interact with one another. Moreover, false-belief tasks require metarepresentational processes that are conscious, as opposed to the primary unconscious way people engage with and read others.

In general, the empirical demonstrations that a child acquires a theory of mind at some age so he or she can consciously explain or predict what someone else, whom her or she is not interacting with, knows is not proof that the child's primary understanding of others is rooted solely in a theory of mind capabilities.

There is a third possible theory to consider. This alternative suggests that children's theory of mind is not primarily based on developing a theory of the other, or constructing an internal simulation. Instead, understanding another person is a form of embodied practice (Gallagher, 2001). Even prior to developing an ability to read other's minds, young children engage in embodied practices that are sensorimotor, perceptual, emotional, and nonconceptual. These practices "constitute our primary access for understanding others, and continue to do so even after we attain a theory of mind abilities" (p. 85).

Infants and young children may acquire a "theory of mind" without necessarily developing a mentalistic theory of the other. Even before the acquisition of a putative theory-of-mind module, infants examine the bodies and expressive movements of others to recognize people's intentions or to find the meaning of some object. As early as 9–14 months, infants look to the eyes of others to help interpret the meaning of an ambiguous event (Phillips, Baron-Cohen, & Rutter, 1992). Thus, a child can understand that another person is looking at a door and may have some intention vis-à-vis that door from the person's expressive body movements. Infants 5–7 months old can detect relationships between visual and auditory information specifying emotional expressions (Walker, 1982). This perception of emotion is especially noted from the movement of others, rather than from an infant having a theory or simulation of an emotional event. As mentioned earlier, 5-month-olds recognize the emotional nature of human movement, as demonstrated in their preferential attentiveness to human shapes in point-light displays of actions (Bertenthal et al., 1994). The emotional states of others are not something that infants must infer, but something that is directly perceived in the movement and experience of other's behaviors (Allison & Puce, & McCarthy, 2000). This also explains why 11-month-olds can recognize the intentional boundaries in some continuous scenes (Baldwin & Baird, 2001), and why 18-month-olds can understand what other persons intend to do, and may even, under some situations, complete actions that another person had not completed (Meltzoff, 1995). None of these abilities demand that the child must infer the mental states of others.

Gallagher argues that even before a child develops a theory of mind, he or she already has understandings of others, and this experience includes "(a) an understanding of what it means to be an experiencing subject, (b) an understanding of what it means that certain kinds of entities (but not others) in the environment are indeed such subjects, and (c) an understanding that in some way these entities are similar to and in other ways different from oneself" (Gallagher, 2001: 86). Meltzoff and Brooks (2001) speculate, along these lines, that infants' construal of human acts as intentional and goal-directed arises from a "like me" analogy that acts as the starting point for social cognition.

Most generally, this alternative claims that primary intersubjectivity is not just a precursor to children's developing theory of mind. Instead, primary intersubjectivity comprises a set of embodied practices that are primary, not just in the developmental sense, but in the sense that anyone can explain or predict what other people believe, desire, or intend in the practice of their own minds (Gallagher, 2001).

Finally, the child's acquisition of a theory of mind also involves entering a community of minds, where people with different minds communicate for common purposes and understandings (Nelson et al., 2003). Thus, the burden of constructing a model of minds does not rest on the child's individual cognitive processes, but rather "is a gift from the larger community that incorporates these constructs into its language and its talk about concerns of people within the community" (Nelson et al., 2003: 43). This view is consistent with an experientialist view of cognitive development in which the sources of what children know are seen as rooted both in the conditions of experience in the special social and cultural world, and in the phenomenology of experiencing on the part of the child. The results of two studies of 3- and 4-year-old children engaging in different theory-of-mind tasks and discussing their responses suggests that changes in the understanding of their own and other's mental states reflect their participation in communities in which social interactions are directed toward specific pragmatic purposes.

Mental Imagery

Embodied action may be critical to children's developing imagery abilities. Studies show that the ability of children (ages 5–8) to form dynamic mental images of objects is greatly facilitated if they first engage in overt manipulation of the objects (Wolff & Levin, 1972). Interestingly, this was true even when the children had no visual access to their movements or to the objects being manipulated. Other studies show that handling objects is critical to children's success in mental rotation tasks, at least up until the ages of 9 and 10 (Zabalia, 2002). Both sets of findings support Piaget's idea on the role of overt and covert activity in the creation of mental imagery.

The importance of embodied movement in imagery is also shown in a different study in which children either watched someone build four simple block buildings, looked at the completed buildings, pretended to build the building along with the experimenter, or constructed the buildings themselves while looking at pictures of them (Corriss & Kose, 1998). Afterwards, the buildings were removed and the children were asked to reconstruct the configurations. Children were more accurate when they either imagined or actually constructed the buildings, rather than looking at the finished products or watching the construction. These results show that if children in some way act physically, either by mimicking the building process or by performing the construction, they have a much clearer mental image of the building. Imagining actions of oneself is more effective than imagining the actions of another person. The results support the theory that imagination is an action-based process.

Conclusion

Developmental psychologists continue to debate the role that sensorimotor activity plays in cognitive development. Although there is a large body of evidence suggesting specific ways that different embodied experiences underlie various aspects of cognitive growth, too much of the developmental work ignores the child's own tactile-kinesthetic experiences in bootstrapping cognition. Let me present one final example of this problem.

Children's understanding of the concept of balance has been extensively studied by developmental psychologists, especially in the context of children's physical reasoning skills. Most generally, this work demonstrates that as children get older, they are to take account of more variables in dealing with different balancing tasks. For example, the study of how children learn to balance objects is primarily seen as a matter of learning how to combine information about different physical variables. Of course, both children and adults can engage in different balancing activities, better than they can explain how they do it. The tasks used to assess children's understandings of the balance concept involve showing a child some pictures of a seal trying to balance a ball on its nose and asking the child to select the one in which the seal was balancing the ball correctly (Pine & Messer, 2003). A different task required children to actually place a set of six blocks on each side of a fulcrum so that all the blocks would balance. In one study, 5- and 6-year-old children engaged in these and other balancing tasks over the course of 5 days. Not surprisingly, the children improved over this time, but they still experienced difficulties in explaining correct balancing behavior, suggesting that they did not have adequate conscious access to representations about balancing.

I have no doubt about the accuracy of these findings. But it is remarkable that the study of children's developing ideas about balance did not acknowledge the child's own tactile-kinesthetic experiences of balancing across sensory modalities and full-bodied sensations and movements. Balance is not an abstract idea or principle that we learn as a rule, but is something that is a constant part of our embodied experiences as living organisms. The image schema for BALANCE arises from these varying embodied activities, and, as argued in earlier chapters, is a critical part of many abstract concepts. My plea for developmental psychologists is to find clever ways of assessing how concepts such as balance, or balancing, may be grounded in embodiment, and not to assume that solving physical reasoning problems somehow develops as a pure cognitive competence apart from sensory, embodied experience.

My argument in favor of an embodied perspective on cognitive development is not entirely consistent with Piaget's claim, because he underestimated young children's cognitive abilities, and assumed, incorrectly, that higher-level forms of cognition are abstracted away from sensorimotor action. As I suggested in previous chapters, many of our embodied experiences are incorporated into our conceptual and linguistic representations. Moreover, our phenomenological bodily experiences continue to reaffirm and ground cognitive symbols.

8

Emotion and Consciousness

The stream of consciousness reveals many insights into who we are, how we think, and what we feel. Consider the case of Charlie Kaufman, a character in the film *Adaptation*, played by Nicholas Cage. Kaufman is a screenwriter who has been hired to adapt a book published by Susan Orleans on people who are fanatical about orchids. Unfortunately, Kaufman struggles with this assignment and worries about an upcoming meeting with his agent. As he paces in his living room one morning, trying to come up with ideas for the adaptation, Kaufman thinks to himself (in voice over):

> I'm old. I'm fat. I'm bald. (reaches for notebook, catches sight of bare feet) My toenails have turned strange. I am old. I am – (flipping through notebook, paces) I have nothing. She'll think I'm an idiot. Why couldn't I stay on that diet? She'll pretend not to be disappointed, but I'll see that look, that look – (passes mirror, glances quickly at reflection, looks away) God, I'm repulsive. (another glance) But as repulsive as I think? My Body Dysmorphic Disorder confuses everything. I mean, I know people call me Fatty behind my back. Or Fatso. Or facetiously Slim. But I also realize this is my perverted form of self-aggrandizement, that no one talks about me at all. What possible interest is an old, bald, fat man to anyone?

Many people, like despondent Charles Kaufman, struggle with the ebb and flow of their emotional states, and emotions often dominate the stage of consciousness. Each of us may not have the same negative self-image that Kaufman has, but all people typically experience running narratives in the mind's theater about themselves, other people, and the world around them. Our inner voices typically produce bits and pieces of thoughts rather than fully formed sentences. This narrative is tightly linked to the self, because we feel that the voice is the "I" talking. The language-like quality of the stream of consciousness suggests to many that consciousness is quite divorced from the body, again reaffirming Descartes' famous observation, "I think, therefore I am." But the highly private, idiosyncratic nature of consciousness has mostly discouraged scientific psychologists, and others, from studying these aspects of the mind.

Fortunately, the situation in cognitive science has now changed. Both emotions and consciousness are now recognized as ideal phenomena through which to study the relationship between mind and body. One important conclusion that is slowly emerging from this work is that both emotions and consciousness partly arise from, and are expressed in, embodied action. This chapter describes the importance of embodiment in emotion and consciousness.

Emotion

The Language of Emotions

The way we speak about emotion provides a significant clue to understanding emotional experience. A poignant example of how people experience their emotions in terms of embodied movements, which have both texture and depth, is seen in the following conversation between a man and his psychotherapist where the two participants negotiate the meaning and personal implications of several metaphors (Ferrara, 1994: 139–41). Howard is a client in his thirties who is talking with Judy, his therapist, in their third session. One month earlier, Howard had been fired from his job as an orderly in a hospital because of suspicion over some missing drugs. Howard maintained that he did not steal the drugs and was eventually reinstated.

JUDY: "When you have a problem, what do you do with it?"

HOWARD: "I usually let it be a problem. I don't usually do anything much or I... I was thinking about that the other day."

JUDY: "Does the problem go away if you don't do anything about it?"

HOWARD: "No, it gets worse... or it just complicates things as you go further down the road."

JUDY: "Can you look at your own life, kind of on a continuum? Look down the road of that line and see what that's gonna do... in your life?"

HOWARD: "Look on down the road."

JUDY: "Yeah, kinda visualize what un... your own life will be like if you don't deal with some of it... your problems... Can you see how it might complicate... your life?"

HOWARD: "It will just continue the way it is."

JUDY: "Kind of like a snowball... effect."

HOWARD: "No no not a snowball. Just kinda floating, floating down the river."

JUDY: "Floating down the river."

HOWARD: "That's what I'm doing now. That's what I was afraid I was gonna go back into all this. I said something the first time I talked to you about."

JUDY: "Yeah."
HOWARD: "Floating and being afraid of going back into floating. That's just you know, floating, drifting ..."
JUDY: "So you're adrift right now?"
HOWARD: "Yeah. And feel dead and I feel like I'm – I drink to feel a little bit deader. No, that's not true."
JUDY: "Feel depressed ... or numb?"
HOWARD: "Yeah."
JUDY: "Numb, you feel?"
HOWARD: "Yeah. Yeah."
JUDY: "What's it like to be floating down the river? Tell me more."
HOWARD: "It's comfortable. It's safe ... Everything just keeps on an even keel, you know."
JUDY: "Mmmhmm."
HOWARD: "You're just kinda floating ..."
JUDY: "Kind of in a canoe? ... going down the river, or"
HOWARD: "No, more like a great ole big barge ... on a great old big river."
JUDY: "Barge, very stable, kinda."
HOWARD: "Yeah, plenty of room to spread out and ... sit in the sun. Yeah, and you don't have to worry about falling off the edge."
JUDY: "Mmhmm."
HOWARD: "And sun, you know, it's kinda hazy. It's not really clear sun. It's kinda hazy."
Judy; "Mmhmm."
HOWARD: "Kinda half asleep, that what's it's like ..."
JUDY: "What happens when you kind of come to the ... falls, the falls that are down there, about two miles down the river?"
HOWARD: "Get the hell off the river."
JUDY: "That's certainly one way to handle it. Get out."
HOWARD: "I feel a lot of discomfort. That's what happened just last month. I hit those falls last month." (noise)
JUDY: "I don't know why it did that. So that's what happened ... um this ... last time there was kind of um ... an external situation that sort of forced you out of your boat."
HOWARD: "It was uncomfortable but I was, I was pretty, I was enjoying it too. And I didn't want to go back to just floating. It was uncomfortable and I was out, I don't know, I been floating a long time."
JUDY: "Mmhmm ... Well, you've found that it works for you ... in a sense."
HOWARD: "What works for me?"
JUDY: "Floating."
HOWARD: "Because I'm ... stay ... comfortable and"
JUDY: "In a sense, but it may ... now be inappropriate. It may not be working as well ... as it did in the past."

HOWARD: "Mnnn. Yeah, I'd like to have a little excitement now and then"
JUDY: "Some rapids"
HOWARD: "Yeah (laughs) Something I can keep in control of maybe and not drown. But . . . yeah, I think I am bored."

This conversation is notable because of the way embodied metaphors structure the discourse. For instance, the client, Howard, introduces the metaphorical idea of his future life as being "down the road." The therapist picks up on this idea and asks Howard to elaborate on the metaphor in her questions abut visualizing the road ahead and whether he feels adrift at present. Howard provides more detail when he rejects the therapist's question about life being like a "snowball effect" (i.e., a forceful felt movement of being swept away uncontrollably). Instead, his experience feels like "Just kinda floating, floating, down the river." Client and therapist further extend their metaphorical characterization of how Howard feels about his life by talk of keeping "on an even keel," experiencing "some rapids," and not having "to worry about falling off the edge." The metaphorical meanings here seem quite appropriate, and perhaps highly desirable, in this therapeutic context. Howard and Judy's conversation illustrates the value of felt movement in talking about one's emotional experiences.

When undergoing a strong emotional experience, we feel as if we are in the grasp of an emotion, as if we are being swept away by its hold and force. Many cognitive linguistic studies on the metaphorical nature of emotion talk illustrate the importance of movement in people's emotional experiences (Harker & Wierzbicka, 2001; Kovecses, 2000a, 2000b; Yu, 1999). For instance, Kovecses (2000a, 2000b) provides numerous examples of how emotions are understood as forces that appear to change people's embodied positionings. Consider some of these conceptual metaphors, and relevant linguistic examples, that are specific instantiations of the generic-level EMOTION IS FORCE metaphor:

EMOTION IS AN OPPONENT
"He was seized by emotion."
"He was struggling with his emotions."
"I was gripped by emotion."
"She was overcome by emotion."

EMOTION IS A WILD ANIMAL
"His emotions ran away with him."
"She kept her emotions in check."
"He couldn't hold back his feelings."

EMOTION IS A SOCIAL FORCE
"He was driven by fear."
"His whole life was governed by passion."
"He was ruled by anger."

EMOTION IS A NATURAL FORCE
"I was swept off my feet."
"I was overwhelmed by her love."

EMOTION IS A MENTAL FORCE
"Our emotions often fool us."
"His emotions deceived him."
"She was misled by her emotions."

EMOTION IS INSANITY
"She was beside herself with emotion."

EMOTION IS PHYSICAL AGITATION
"The speech stirred everyone's feelings."
"I am all shook up."
"He was slightly ruffled by what he heard."
"The children were disturbed by what they saw."

EMOTION IS A PHYSICAL FORCE
"When I found out, it hit me hard."
"That was a terrible blow."
"She knocked me off my feet."
"They gravitated toward each other immediately."
"I was magnetically drawn to her."
"I am attracted to her."
"That repels me."

These different conceptual metaphors together illustrate the most pervasive folk theory of the emotion process in English (Kovecses, 2000b): (1) cause of emotion – force tendency of the cause of emotion – (2) self has emotion – force tendency of emotion – (3) self's force tendency – emotion's force tendency – (4) resultant effect. This schema reflects our basic understanding of emotions as different physical/embodied forces interacting with one other.

Emotions as Felt Movements

The linguistic evidence suggests that embodiment is central to understanding emotional experience. Most cognitive theories admit that an important body component in the emotion process is the readiness to take action (Lazarus, 1991; Oatley, 1992). This readiness to act is a corporeal felt urge to do something – approach someone, strike something or someone, touch something, run away from something or someone, and so on. Emotion is not identical to simple action such kicking, embracing, running, and so on, but reflects a change in postural attitude, or an affective sense of such action (Sheets-Johnstone, 1999).

The fundamental relation between embodied action and emotion is captured by the idea that to "be moved" refers to feeling as if one is in a different position in regard to one's situation. The word "emotion" is derived from the Latin "e" (out) and "movere" (to move). The emphasis on movement in emotion is a recurrent theme in the psychological literature. For example, Adler (1931: 42) defined emotions as "psychological movement forms, limited in time," whereas Arnold and Gasson (1954: 294) suggested "that an emotion or an affect can be considered as the felt tendency toward an object judged suitable, or away from an object judged unsuitable, reinforced by specific bodily changes according to the type of emotion." Having an emotion may clearly involve some sense of bodily movement.

One early study surveyed people about their sense of movement when they were thinking of different emotion terms (Manaster, Cleland, & Brooks, 1978). Participants rated their felt movement (i.e., either toward others or away from others) for 140 emotion terms. The results showed that there were a group of 20 emotion words that tended to move people toward others (e.g., love, jolly, affectionate, sexy, confident, sentimental), and another group of 20 emotion words that moved people away from others (e.g., hate, humiliated, sulky, bitter, guilty, aggravated). Other studies show a strong association between affect and spatial positioning, such that people are faster to classify positive words as "good" when they are presented toward the top of a computer screen, and negative words as "bad" when they are in the lower portion of the screen (Meier & Robinson, 2004). These results are consistent with our metaphorical ideas that GOOD IS UP and BAD IS DOWN (Lakoff & Johnson, 1980, 1999). Findings such as these support the idea that the primary feeling of having an emotional experience is that of being moved. Each emotion reflects different, sometimes subtle, bodily movements. We may at times experience some emotion as a state of passively being moved rather than as moving ourselves.

Emotional experience involves our perceptible source of meaningful change in a situation and in ourselves under some circumstance. Emotions arise as we become displaced and dislocated to another position in adaptive response to some situation. One way of characterizing the felt dimension of emotional experience is in terms of "affective space," or the space we move through as we experience distinct emotions (Cataldi, 1996). This idea of affective space is nicely illustrated by considering how we hesitate in advancing when worried, gently blossom when in love, distinctly loiter about when sad or depressed, or suddenly burst forward when feeling outraged.

People experience their emotions as movements toward something in themselves. When people feel joy, they have repositioned themselves as being "on top of the world," or when they feel emotionally troubled, then they experience a burden on "one's shoulders," where there is a downward turn of the body as the head drops and the person slouches. Feeling superior to another makes us feel as if we are "looking down" on that person, or that he or she is "beneath us." Feeling admiration for another makes us "look up" to that person.

Different emotions imply varying levels of removedness from others. When I feel overwhelmed, the world seems too close, suffocating me. Being in love suggests a closeness or proximity to our loved one, whereas hatred repositions us away from others. When I feel lonely, I experience my body as separated from others. Feeling fear drives us away from others, and is accompanied, like all emotions, by a complex set of action tendencies.

Consider the following phenomenological account of the kinesthetics involved in fear (Sheets-Johnstone, 1999: 269): "An intense and unceasing whole-body tension drives the body forward. It is quite unlike the tension one feels in a jogging run, for instance, or in a run to greet someone. There is a hardness to the whole body that congeals it into a singular tight mass; the driving speed of the movement condenses airborne and impact mounts into a singular continuum of motion. The head-on movement is at times erratic; there are sudden changes of direction. With these changes, the legs move suddenly apart, momentarily widening the base of support and bending at the knee, so that the whole body is lowered. The movement is each time abrupt. It breaks the otherwise unrelenting and propulsive speed of movement. The body may suddenly swerve, dodge, twist, duck, or crouch, and the head may swivel about before the forward plunging run with its acutely concentrated and unbroken energies continues."

As this passage reveals, affective space has a sensuous feel to it, a texture that makes it neither purely mental, or reducible to the physiological body. In fact, the cognitive component of emotion may be based on these felt, tactile dimensions of emotional feeling (Cataldi, 1996). This is precisely why we speak of having been "touched" when we have been emotionally affected by something, as when a situation is felt as "touching." It would be surprising if emotion and touch did not overlap given that we talk of "feeling" in connection with the body.

For instance, we sense "butterflies in our stomach" when feeling anxious (such as when first falling in love). This feeling cannot be objectively defined as a spastic stomach apart form some situation that elicits this response. After all, we may feel a spastic stomach without experiencing any particular emotion, such as when something we ate upsets our stomachs. This is why when feeling apprehensive we experience butterflies fluttering in our stomach, rather than, more simply, having a spastic stomach. The embodied feeling here is kinesthetically similar to butterflies fluttering because we sense our apprehension as an intermingling of things we can touch on the "outside" (e.g., butterflies fluttering) with the feeling "inside" our stomach. Thus, emotions are not simply or completely "mental sensations" but rely on tactile, felt feelings from the outside that become part of our inner emotional experiences.

Moving through affective space has a textured, palpitably felt dimension, just in the way that we can feel different textures of substances we touch with our skin. Physical substances we touch have a depth to them, and this is precisely why our emotions are also experienced at different levels of depth. The language people use to talk about the nuances of their emotions, once again, reveals important aspects of the textured, in-depth feel of different emotions. Consider some of the felt textures associated with different emotions (Cataldi, 1996). For example, when feeling very frightened, we feel our bodies to be frozen solid, almost "petrified"; we are radiant with love or bask in pride, or drown in sorrow, or effervescently bubble over in happiness, or blissfully walk on air in joy, or wallow in self-pity, or cautiously trend on pins and needles when feeling apprehensive. We feel steamy when lustful; we feel dry, stifled, and stale when bored. Yet being serene feels smooth, whereas gratitude has a plush, or lavish feel. When we are simply worn out, we may feel affectively stuck in some situations, as when we are in a pinch or a jam.

Most generally, each emotion is distinguishable by skin-deep textures that are felt when we move through affective space. Furthermore, the greater the emotional extreme, the more depth we feel in our textured experiences. An emotional state need not be revealed in immediate overt actions, but it certainly implies the high probability of actions that will soon be directed outward from an individual into the world (Freeman, 1999). Such states are easily recognized and explained as intentional in many situations, but in others they seem to boil up spontaneously and illogically within an individual in defiance of intent.

In cases when we do not move our bodies, we feel our emotions as if something within us has moved (De Rivera, 1977). An emotion may have distinctive kinetic forms that are dynamically congruent with it, but these forms are not identical with the emotion. We may distinguish between an emotion, in terms of its affective feel and any postural attitudes it exhibits, and the actual kinesthetic form that manifests the emotion. People may corporeally experience an emotion, even though the actual body movement does not occur. Thus, people may inhibit the movement associated with an emotion if necessary. We may learn to mentally simulate our actions – moving quickly, flailing our arms around, getting red in the face, and so on – without engaging in these actions. In this way, emotions are kinesthetic or potentially kinesthetic, and what is kinetic may be affective or potentially affective (Sheets-Johnstone, 1999).

Basic Emotions and Facial Expressions

Most cognitive scientists ignore the importance of full-bodied movement in empirical studies of emotions. However, over the past 30 years, one kind of bodily action, facial expressions, has been extensively studied. One widely held belief is that specific facial expressions indicate, and define, universal "basic emotions" (Ekman, 1992, 1994). This view holds the following assumptions (adopted from Fernandez-Dols, Carrera, & Casado, 2002):

(a) There are a small number (seven plus or minus two) of basic emotions.
(b) Each basic emotion is genetically determined, universal, and discrete.
(c) Each basic emotion is a coherent pattern of facial behavior, physiology, and instrumental action.
(d) Any state lacking its own distinct facial expression is not a basic emotion. There is consensus about the existence of six basic emotions: happiness, surprise, fear, anger, disgust, and sadness.
(e) All emotions other than the basic ones are subcategories or mixtures of the basic emotions.
(f) Expressions of emotion are spontaneous. Voluntary facial expressions can simulate spontaneous ones.
(g) Different cultures establish different display rules. Display rules inhibit, exaggerate, or mask spontaneous expression.
(h) The expressions of basic emotions are easily recognized by all human beings.
(i) The ability to recognize an expression of basic emotion is innate rather than culturally determined.
(j) The true criteria for the existence of a basic emotion are to be found in people's facial movements. Verbal reports of emotion can be bypassed.
(k) The meaning of a facial expression of basic emotion is invariant across changes in the context in which it is produced.

These specific assumptions are supported by empirical studies in which participants are shown a small set of pictures of prototypical facial expressions and asked to assign each one to a category of basic emotion (e.g., happiness, sadness, anger, fear, disgust, and surprise). The results show that people in many different cultures regularly associate specific facial expressions with particular emotions (Ekman, 1985).

However, there are several methodological problems with these studies that raise questions about their interpretation (Fernandez-Dols et al., 2002; Russell, 1995). First, the experimenters in these studied did not usually speak the participants' languages in the cross-cultural studies. Many of the terms used to specify basic emotions may have had a different meaning for the native speakers than for the experimenters. Second, most of the studies used forced-choice response formats that may have compelled participants to pair specific faces with particular emotion terms in a way they would not do in ordinary life. Thus, the "recognition" of emotion in these facial experiments is not necessarily representative of universal entities known by an individual, but is rather an attribution in which people link some emotions to some facial patterns using lay explanations that lack any necessary or sufficient relationship to the actual experience of emotion and its behavioral consequences. For example, people may frown when they threaten someone, and most people are angry before they threaten someone. An ideal description would say that people frown when they are angry. A realistic description of the situation would say that the person is angry and afterward frowns when threatening another person. Empirical studies show, in fact, that people will associate facial expressions with a person's actual statement to someone about his or her emotion (e.g., "You harmed my son!"), but not to statements reflecting a person's thoughts (e.g., "So, he harmed my son!") (Fernandez-Dols et al., 2002). This suggests that facial expressions may reflect something that happens after the emotional experience, but not necessarily simultaneous with it.

The idea that facial expressions are natural, automatic expressions of inner emotional experiences is also at odds with empirical work showing that adults' spontaneous facial expressions during intense emotional episodes are surprisingly rare (Ferndanez-Dols & Ruiz-Belda, 1997). Lack of facial expression can, in particular contexts, be as informative as intense facial displays (Carrera-Levillain & Fernandez-Dols, 1994). One analysis of paintings in the Prado suggests that smiles are displayed by vulgar, drunk, or crazy models or by children. Smiling was not linked, as it is today, with beauty. A fixed, open smile was a sign of simpleness, not of happiness (Fernandez-Dols et al., 2002).

Furthermore, a significant body of work suggests that many emotional facial expressions are strategic, or intentionally produced (Gibbs, 1999a). For instance, one study observed the facial displays of bowlers (Kraut & Johnston, 1979). Observers were positioned both behind the waiting pit and in the back of the pin-setting machine at the end of the lane. This allowed observers to chart the bowlers' behavior as they rolled the ball, watched the ball roll, and as they pivoted to face the members of the bowling party. Bowlers rarely smiled when facing the pins, but did smile frequently when they pivoted to face their friends in the waiting pit. The outcome of the roll, which one might expect to affect the bowler's emotion, bore little relationship to the production of smiles.

A different study analyzed the facial displays of Olympic gold medal winners during the award ceremonies (Fernandez-Dols & Ruiz-Belda, 1995). The athletes only smiled when interacting with others and rarely did so alone. Even though the athletes were judged by observers to be very happy, the fact that they only smiled when looking at or talking to others suggests the importance of psychological beliefs and desires (e.g., intentions to communicate information about oneself to others) in regulating emotional behavior.

One behavior that is widely considered a readout of inner emotional states is that of motor mimicry. We cringe when we hear of another's fear, and grit our teeth when confronted with someone's anger. But we now know that motor mimicry is communicative. For instance, one empirical demonstration of the intrinsically intentional function of facial displays showed that the timing of a wince of empathetic pain depended on the availability of the display to its intended audience (Bavelas et al., 1986). In one study, an experimenter staged an event where he dropped a color TV monitor onto his apparently already injured finger in full view of the experimental participant. When the experimenter directly faced the participant, the participant frequently displayed a sympathetic wince, but when the experimenter turned away right after dropping the TV, any initial wincing by the participant quickly ceased. Again, many aspects of our nonverbal displays are specifically directed to an audience and timed to be recognized by the intended recipient.

Finally, other research showed that observers could easily identify the type of odor (good, bad, or neutral) from the emotional facial expressions of the raters only when the raters knew that they were being observed, not when they thought they were making their ratings alone (Gilbert, Fridlund, & Sabini, 1987). Similarly, people emit few spontaneous facial expressions when eating sweet and salty sandwiches by themselves, but emit many facial expressions when eating these sandwiches with other people (Brighton et al., 1977).

These findings contradict the traditional view that facial expressions are by nature nonverbal readouts of pure, or genuine, emotions rather than social, communicative displays. A person's overt emotional behavior is not a genuine "spillover" from inner vicarious experiences, but has a distinctly communicative function. Even when we talk to ourselves and deploy facial displays in the course of these acts, we are being communicative. Thus when we are alone we often treat ourselves as interactants (Fridlund, 1994).

An emotional expression need not be fully conscious for it to be understood as an intentional act. Research shows that people have the tendency to automatically mimic and synchronize movements, facial expressions, postures, and emotional vocalizations with those displayed by others – a phenomenon called "emotional contagion" (Hatfield, Cacioppo, & Rapsom, 1992). Emotional contagious behaviors still express actions, as people intend to emotionally converge with those around them. We can, of course, consciously display, for example, pretend smiles in situations where we do not feel especially happy. These emotional displays often have a different bodily appearance than do behaviors that are less self-conscious (Ekman, 1994). Yet many of the socially determined, intentionally based emotional expressions observed in the above-mentioned studies (e.g., the smiles of Olympic athletes when receiving their medals) are quite genuine and have none of the characteristics usually associated with pretend emotional displays. It is a mistake, then, to assume that only involuntary, nonaction emotional displays are "genuine." Expressing oneself emotionally can be intentional and genuine at the same time.

Emotions and Bodily Changes

Psychologists have long debated the relationship between emotional experience and bodily changes, beyond those conveyed by the face. William James, one hundred years ago, suggested that the feelings of emotion are associated with the bodily changes that accompany or follow the perception of some exciting fact (James, 1882). He noted, "The various permutations and combinations of which these organic activities as susceptible makes it abstractly possible that no shades of emotion, however slight, should be without a bodily reverberances as unique, when taken in its totality, as is to emotional mood itself" (James, 1898: 1066).

Neurophysiologists have focused their attention on the anatomical structures that underlie emotion. Papez (1937), for example, proposed that there exists an entire circuit comprising the interconnections between the hypothalamus, anterior thalamus, cingulate gyrus, and hippocampus. Limbic structures, such as the amygdala, have been shown to play a crucial role in emotions (Aggleton & Mishkin, 1986; Damasio, 1994; LeDoux, 1998).

But psychophysiologists have followed James in exploring the extent to which emotions are differentiated by autonomic nervous system activity. Much of this research has centered on the "specificity-debate," or whether various emotions can be distinguished by unique patterns of somatovisceral arousal (Cacioppo et al., 1993; Ekman & Davidson, 1994; Panksepp, 1998). Some psychophysiologists attempt to demonstrate specificity by comparing two or more emotions on the basis of such measures as skin temperature, heart rate, respiration, finger temperature, skin conductance, facial temperature, and blood pressure (Ax, 1953; Ekman, Levenson, & Friesen, 1983; Levenson et al., 1992). For example, heart rate and temperature go up when people feel angry, but go down when they feel sad.

Yet other psychophysiologists argue that bodily awareness is insufficient to distinguish between different emotional experiences (Mandler, 1984; Schachter & Singer, 1962). Bodily awareness in emotion experience is merely awareness of general arousal, and emotion experience is based crucially on cognitive attributions of the cause of bodily arousal. An emotion is arousal plus a cognitive label for it in terms of anger, sadness, joy, and so on. In some cases, people misattribute arousal to some source that is not responsible for what they are consciously feeling.

Some empirical research has explored people's felt bodily sensations when experiencing different emotions. One study asked a group of psychology students to imagine a scene in which they might experience a specific emotion and to write down the characteristics that define that specific emotional experience (Parkinson, 1995). Two-thirds of participants' emotional definitions referred to some bodily symptoms. Many emotions corresponded to very specific changes in the body. Anger, for instance, was closely associated with tension, rising temperature, and feeling hurt, whereas fear was related to feeling nausea, cold sweat, and increased heart rates. Specific body symptoms were less related to happiness and sadness. Consequently, bodily changes may not accompany all emotional experiences to the same degree.

A different study asked participants to remember different emotional experiences and mark a schematic diagram of the areas of the front and back of the human body that were involved in what they felt (Nieuwenhuyse, Offenberg, & Frijda, 1987). People generally responded that certain emotions were deeply associated with localized internal body symptoms. For example, fear is localized in the abdomen and anal areas. Some emotions seem to spread over the entire body, such as when we feel a certain glow from being in love. It is difficult to understand the causal relationship between body symptoms and emotion in this study, however, because it did not distinguish between bodily symptoms, consequences of emotions for future human actions, and experiences compatible with our responses to emotion.

Another project attempted to demonstrate that body movements and postures are specific for certain emotions to some degree (i.e., that body movements and postures reflect not only the quantity of an emotion, but also its quality) (Walbott, 1998). A sample of 224 videotapes, in which actors and actresses portrayed the emotions of joy, happiness, sadness, despair, fear, terror, cold anger, hot anger, disgust, contempt, shame, pride, guilt, and boredom was analyzed for their body movements and postures. The results showed that 66% of the movement and posture categories distinguished significantly between emotions or subclasses of emotion studied. For instance, an erect body posture is very rare when one experiences the emotion of shame, sadness, or boredom. During these emotional states actors much more often chose a collapsed body posture. Lifting the shoulders, on the other hand, is typical for elated joy and hot anger, but rather infrequent for all other emotions. Moving the shoulders forward is frequent for disgust, as well as for despair and fear, compared to other emotions. For different types of head movements and head postures significant differences also arose between emotions. Orientation of the head directly toward the camera is least frequent during boredom experiences. On the other hand, moving the head downward is most typical of disgust. Moving the head backward, that is, raising the chin, can be observed rather frequently during boredom, but also during pride and elated joy, compared to the other emotions.

The most significant variation among emotions is seen in different types of hand and arm postures and movements. Lateralized hand/arm movements are most frequent during hot anger, cold anger, and interest, that is, rather active emotions. Arms stretched out to the front indicate the same three emotions and in addition, elated joy in comparison to the other emotions. Arms stretched sideways are especially typical for terror, but less often used for all other emotions. Crossing arms in front of the body is rather frequent during pride experiences, as well as during disgust. Opening and closing of the hands is again typical of some active emotions, such as hot anger and elated joy, but also of despair and fear. Overall, a discriminant analysis showed that it is possible to correctly classify different emotions, far above chance level, based on the analysis of movement patterns alone. This implies that distinctive patterns of movement and postural behavior may be associated with at least some emotions.

The results of all these studies are consistent with the idea that people believe different emotions to be associated with different localized bodily symptoms. Whether these beliefs about links between the body and emotional experiences reflect actual physiological responses to emotion is less clear. Visceroception research shows, in fact, that people are very poor perceivers of their physiological changes (Pennybaker, 1982; Rime, Philippot, & Cisamolo, 1990). Many scholars argue that the process of symptom perception is at least partly determined by individuals' personal and cultural expectations about their physiological states. If a culture has a folk psychological stereotype that people are "hot" with anger, or "cold" with fear, they will then retrospectively report feeling hot with anger regardless of whether they actually felt hot when they were angry (Phillippot & Rime, 1997). Thus, the reporting of the bodily sensations associated with emotions may be a theory-driven process, reflecting various kinds of social schemata.

One way to understand the relation of physiology to emotional experience is to examine individuals with physical handicaps. Does decreased bodily sensation reduce the intensity of emotions? One study interviewed 25 adult men, with no psychiatric problems, who had suffered spinal injuries and lost all sensation below the site of the injury (Hohmann, 1966). The patients were questioned about their sexual feelings, fear, grief, sentimentality, and overall emotionality. Most of the men reported decreases in sexual feeling since their injury. Those with injuries at the neck level reported large decreases. One man said that before injury his sexual feelings were "a hot, tense feeling all over my body," but since the accident "it doesn't do anything for me" (p. 148). One man, whose injury was at the high chest level, talked about fear. One day he was fishing on a lake when a storm came up and a log punctured his boat. He said "I knew I was sinking, and I was afraid all right, but somehow I didn't have that feeling of trapped panic that I know I would have had before" (p. 150).

Along with decreases in sexual feelings, fear, and anger, most participants reported an increase in feelings that might be called sentimentality, feeling tearful and choked up on occasions such as partings. But some of these results may be due to participants getting older and changing their cognitive appraisals of events that lead to different emotions and emotional intensity. For example, one participant said about anger "Now I don't get a feeling of physical animation . . . Sometimes I get angry when I see some injustice. I yell and cuss and raise hell because if you don't do it sometimes I've learned that people will take advantage of you, but it just doesn't have the heat in it. It's a mental kind of anger" (p. 151).

This study seems to support James's claim that emotion begins in bodily sensation. But other research presents a different conclusion. For example, one study interviewed 37 subjects who had suffered spinal injuries during the previous 1 to 8 years (mean of 4.5 years) (Bermond et al., 1991). Participants were asked about the intensities of their physiological disturbances in relation to the subjective intensities of emotional experiences. Specifically, participants were asked to remember two experiences of fear, one from before their injuries and one from afterward, and describe what caused them to feel this way. Overall, participants reported more significant experiences of fear following the injury than before, even though purely physiological disturbances in the postinjury emotion had diminished.

Participants also rated their fear, anger, grief, sentimentality, and joyfulness on scales indicating increases and decreases since their injury. Neither in the whole group, nor in the 14 individuals with the greatest sensory loss (i.e., those with neck injuries), was there any general decrease in rated emotional intensity. Most participants reported little change on most scales, though some reported some increases in intensity since their injury. These findings are difficult to reconcile with James's predictions.

One problem with the research on physical handicaps and emotions is that people in Western cultures are often aware of bodily sensations that are part of an emotion without being aware of them as an emotion. One study found that 18% of all consultations with general medical practitioners were found to be cases of anxiety or depression in which the persons complained of bodily symptoms but were not aware of specific affective or cognitive symptoms and had poor recognition of their emotional states (Bridges & Goldberg, 1992).

A different way to think about the role of the body in emotional experience is to see if particular body movements may induce specific emotions. One proposal suggests that some facial expressions have emotional effects by constricting flow through blood vessels in the face (Zajonc, Murphy, & Inglehart, 1989). These facial constrictions affect blood flow through parts of the brain, which then produce temperature changes that are affectively experienced as positive or negative. To test this idea, native German speakers were asked to read a number of stories aloud. Some of these stories were filled with words requiring them to make movements with their mouths and lips that were just like the facial expressions of disgust, whereas the other stories had few such words. Participants liked the stories inducing the disgust expression less than they did other stories, even though the two kinds of stories were virtually identical in content.

Participants in another study were asked simply to hold a pen in the mouth, thus making the muscle movements characteristic of a smile without the participants realizing it (Strack, Martin, & Stepper, 1988). As they did this, participants judged whether different cartoons were humorous. These participants thought the cartoons were funnier than did a control group who made the same judgments without holding a pencil in their mouths.

Participants in a related study were asked to judge the personality of a fictitious person who was described in very neutral terms (Berkowitz & Troccoli, 1990). Half of the subjects heard the descriptions while holding a pen between their teeth without using their lips. Holding a pen like this forces the face into an expression similar to that of smiling. The remaining participants heard the same descriptions while biting down on a towel, which provokes an expression s similar to frowning. Participants who were smiling rated the fictitious person in far more positive terms than did participants who were frowning. This finding suggests that when the body is placed into a situation that is highly correlated with an emotion (e.g., smiling or frowning face), this constrains other cognitive (that is, embodied) processing. A different experiment induced people to draw their eyebrows together in a way that mimicked a sad face (Larsen, Kasimatis, & Frey, 1992). These peoples' judgments of pictures were sadder than a control group, although they did not know that their eyebrow pose had implied sadness.

All of the above studies suggest that making certain facial expressions prompts people to experience slightly different affective states. But facial feedback may not be a necessary component for emotional experience. Studies show that stroke patients who had lost the ability to make facial expressions had no loss in emotional experience (Ross & Mesulam, 1979), and patients with Moebius syndrome with congenital loss of facial movement have no apparent deficit in emotional experience (Cole, 1997). This clinical data implies that feedback from facial expressions is not an essential component of emotional experience.

Do particular body movements, other than facial expressions, initiate specific emotions? Participants in one study adopted three different postures without being told what these body poses represented (Duclos et al., 1989). In one posture, characteristic of fear, the participants kept their heads facing forward as they leaned their upper bodies backward while twisting them slightly and dipping one shoulder, similarly to how they would react when a sudden danger had unexpectedly appeared. Another posture, generally associated with sadness, required people to fold their hands in their laps, drop their heads forward, and let their bodies sag. The third posture was an anger pose. Participants placed their feet flat on the floor, clenched their hands tightly, and leaned their bodies forward. After each pose was held for a brief period, the participants rated their feelings at that time. Participants reported the strongest feelings for the mood that was characteristically associated with each posture. Thus, emotion-related body movements, as well as facial expressions, appear to initiate at least some kinds of emotional experiences, even if only at a low level of intensity.

Of course, emotion-related muscular movements can affect our thoughts as well as our feelings. People make different attributions when sad than when angry. Sadness heightens the chance that people will attribute their life circumstances to situational forces, whereas when feeling angry, people are more apt to regard some person as specifically responsible for what happens to them. Moreover, differences in causal attributions can be produced by getting people to adopt either a sad or an angry pose in their faces and bodies (Keltner, Ellsworth, & Edwards, 1993).

One case study provides some support for the idea that merely participating in the action tendency associated with some emotion may easily cause one to feel that emotion (Damasio, 2003). A 65-year-old woman with Parkinson's disease had recently undergone a treatment of having tiny electrodes implanted bilaterally in the brain stem. These electrodes emit a low-intensity, high-frequency electrical current that alters the functioning of the motor nucleus. Most patients experience remarkable recovery after the surgery and are quickly able to walk normally and precisely move their hands. But determining where the electrodes should be implanted in order not to create unwanted side effects can be tricky. This patient, for example, experienced an unexpected event when the electric current passed through one of the contact sites on her left side. She immediately slumped, cast her eyes down and to the right, leaned to the right, and appeared very sad. Soon the woman started crying, and then sobbing, and she started describing how sad she felt, and that she had no energy left to continue living. The surgeon in charge of the treatment realized the problem and abandoned the procedure. Just a few seconds later, the patient's behavior returned to normal and she seemed completely perplexed about what had just happened.

This case illustrates how activation of the brain stem nucleus that controls specific motor actions, realized as an ensemble of movements of the facial muscles, movements of the mouth, pharynx, larynx, and diaphragm, all necessary for crying, will facilitate one's feeling quite sad. Even though no event had occurred to induce sadness, nor was the patient prone to experiencing such sadness beforehand, emotion-related thought (feeling sad) could affect the emotion-action sequence that had begun.

A different kind of research focuses on bodily cues to reading other people's emotions. Some studies suggest that adults use six specific body cues to infer people's different emotional states (Boone & Cunningham, 1998): (1) frequency of upward arm movements, (2) the duration of time the actor's arms are kept close to the body, (3) the amount of muscle tension,

(4) the duration of time the actor leans forward, (5) the number of directional changes in an actor's face and torso, and (6) the number of tempo changes an actor makes in a particular sequence of movements. Experiments indicate that the six cues help observers discriminate different emotions when watching actors move without speaking. For instance, anger was distinguished by a greater number of directional changes in the face and torso and a greater number of tempo changes. Observers distinguished happiness from sadness and fear by a greater number of upward arm movements and by the increase in time in which the arms are positioned away from the torso, such as when an actor throws his hands above his head and kept his arms outstretched. Actors were seen as sad when they kept their heads down with a slumped body posture (i.e., less muscle tension). Fear was detected when an actor's body was rigid and his head was kept up and alert.

Other empirical research investigated people's recognition of emotion from gait (Montpare, Goldstein, & Clausen, 1987). Participants viewed videotaped displays of walkers and judged which of four emotions (happiness, sadness, anger, and pride) the walkers were expressing. Walkers read brief scenarios describing emotional situations and were instructed to imagine themselves in the situation and to walk accordingly. Participants performed better than chance levels in identifying sadness, anger, happiness and pride from the walkers' gait. People were less proficient at identifying pride compared to sadness or anger. A further analysis of the walkers who conveyed the most consistent emotions to observers revealed that angry gaits were most heavy-footed,and sad gaits had the lowest amount of arm swinging. Angry and proud gaits had the longest stride lengths. Happy gaits were faster-paced than the other gaits. Consistent with these findings, other work demonstrates that people can recognize happy dances when all they can see are points of light placed at the dancers' main joints (Brownlow et al., 1997). Not surprisingly, depressed people tend to gesture less and hold their heads down more than nondepressed people (Segrin, 1998). These data support the idea that emotional information is revealed in gait.

The different empirical studies looking at the relation of particular body movements and emotional experiences, including reading of other people's emotions, tend to individually analyze the influence of one factor (facial movements, body postures, perception of gait) in defining specific emotions. It is sometimes hard, in this case, to determine whether scholars necessarily wish to claim that the independent variable studied necessarily serves as the sole causal reason for different emotional experiences. However, some psychologists openly advocate a complex view of the body's role in emotional experience. For example, Berkowitz (2000) claims that emotional experience arises from the integration of bodily sensations with other associated mental representations, including previously acquired conceptions of how one customarily feels in a certain class of situations. Suppose that Joe is faced with a bully who has just insulted him. Joe's body reacts quickly. His heart beats faster, his face becomes hot, his mouth clamps shut, his brows draw together, and his fists clench. Joe also may recall other times when he has been insulted and the feelings that he had experienced on these occasions, as well as the stories he had read, seen, and heard about anger-provoking occurrences. Joe's mind actively integrates all of these inputs, guided to some degree by his conception of what anger is like, with the result that Joe feels/thinks "I am angry."

This integrated view of emotions suggests that certain beliefs about both the body and emotional expressions are partly constitutive of subjectively felt emotions. Under this perspective, naive theories about emotions should play an important role in people's reports about their affective states. In fact, a variety of research indicates that there is at least some cultural variation in bodily and mental emotion experience. Linguistic studies show that speakers from different cultures differ in regard to how much attention is paid to the body in emotion talk. For example, Russian participants discursively construct emotions as an action process expressed in a number of external behaviors, whereas American participants present emotions as internal states (Pavlenko, 2002; Wierzbicka, 1999).

Empirical studies reveal other cultural differences in emotional experience. For example, emotions are located and experienced in the body much more frequently by Chinese and Taiwanese than by North Americans (Kleinman, 1982). Anger in Chinese individuals is frequently located and experienced in the chest and heart, depression is often experienced in terms of something pressing into the chest, or down on the head, and grief may be experienced in terms of a kind of back pain. Chinese, in contrast to North Americans, very rarely describe emotion experiences in terms of "intrapsychic feelings," such as personal thoughts. Rather, they comment on emotion experience only to a caused situation and to its somatic and intrapersonal effect and not personal cognition. Thus, an individual's or a culture's tacit folk model of self and of emotion will influence the form of emotional experiences.

But despite this cultural variation, there remains a large degree of similarity across cultures in their association of body experience and emotion. One large study of people in 37 countries in five continents examined people's embodied states (based on 10 questions) for seven emotional states (Scherer and Wallbott, 1994). Although some statistical differences appeared across cultures, the overall amount of variance explained was much larger for the effects of emotion than for the effects of culture.

A related study asked American, German, Polish, and Russian students to report in which parts of the body they felt anger, envy, fear, and jealousy (Hupka et al., 1996). Extending the number of body questions to 31, the researchers actually showed significant effects of culture for 8 out of these 31 variables in the case of anger, for 6 of them in the case of envy, for 9 of them for the case of fear, and for 6 of them for the case of jealousy. Thus, there

TABLE 8.1.

Emotion	Evaluation	Action	World-Focused
Joy	Enhanced	Buoyant, light, easy to move, able	Open, inviting, nonresistant, supportive
Sadness	Diminished	Heavy, unable, weak	Empty, closed, burdening, lacking in attractiveness
Anger	Impeded, compressed, pushed back	Ready to push out	Impeding, compressing, requiring force to remove blocking agent
Fear	About to be overwhelmed, pierced, destroyed	Self-protecting	Overwhelming, piercing, disintegrative
Shame	Stained	Shrinking, self-occluding	The impinging gaze of others
Pride	Augmented	Increasing the exposed self	The welcoming gaze of others

appear to be some differences of people's bodily expressions of emotions across cultures. However, once again, cross-cultural similarity seemed to predominate. In fact, other studies showed that between 6% and 8% of the bodily sensation variance is accounted for by cultural differences (Philippot & Rime, 1997). These analyses showed that some emotions, including the social emotions (joy, guilt, shame, and disgust), yield more cultural variations than others (anger, fear, sadness, and surprise). Similarly, certain bodily sensations, such as temperature and respiratory changes or muscular sensations, are marked by more cultural variations than others. The relation between culture and body expressions of emotion is clearly complex.

Finally, one recent theory proposed that any emotion state is a combination of evaluative descriptions (ED), based on cognitive appraisals, and an action attribute (AA) (Lambie & Marcel, 2002). A single ED is not inevitably associated with any one AA. A single specific emotion episode (e.g., sadness) may vary over time or in the degree to which the experience is of the ED or AA. This is seen especially in coping with emotions where the different coping strategies involve focusing on either evaluating aspects (e.g., negative thoughts), or bodily responses (e.g., one's breathing). There is also no one-to-one determinate relation between a particular ED and a particular AA; each emotional state is defined by a combination of the two. This theory also acknowledges how emotions can be both self-focused (bodily physicality) and world-focused (hodological space). Presented in Table 8.1 are examples of several typical emotions, their characteristic EDs and AAs, and their world-focused space (adapted from Lambie & Marcel, 2002: 238).

In conclusion, the essence of any emotion is not completely captured by the way it is articulated in the body. For instance, if I am in some situation that makes me feel frustrated to the point of extreme agitation, I may feel as if I am about to blow up, I may loudly voice some sounds or words, I may begin to clench my fists and shake them deliberately, as if fighting an imaginary opponent, or I may consciously swear something must be done and even take action to reposition myself given the situation. All these felt expressions of gestures, thoughts, and behavior combined may make me feel as if I am right there "in touch" with the essence of anger. But the essence of anger is never completely captured by the particular bodily displays I produce. In some instances, I may express anger through complete silence and a blue face. I may, on other occasions, when angry, display a reddened face with tensed eyebrows and pursed lips but speak with a calm voice. These observations lend credence to the idea that affective processes are "emotional gestalts" that emerge from a complex of "interacting environmental, bodily, and cognitive variables" (Thagard & Nerb, 2002: 275). Let me explore this idea in more detail below.

A Dynamical View of Emotional Expression

Chapter 3 presented a dynamical model of intentional actions that is relevant to exploring emotional expressions (Gibbs & Van Orden, 2003). Imagine that you walk down the street, come across someone you know, and smile. Why did you do this? Was your smile intentional or an automatic response to seeing someone you knew? As shown above, there is much research to demonstrate that people may strategically express emotions in the sense of intending to communicate specific messages. But are other emotional expressions, such as having sweaty palms when nervous, also intentional? This folk-level analysis does not adequately capture intentionality or the psychological dynamics of emotional expression. A dynamic systems perspective on emotional expressions, as self-organized critical states, may yield a unified view of emotional expressions as a natural consequence. Dynamic systems have a capacity for self-control whereby they reduce a set of potential actions (e.g., the large set of potential ways to greet a friend) to that which is actually expressed, such as a particular smiling demeanor. Self-organization reduces the degrees of freedom for action until a human face becomes a context-appropriate "special device," a smiling device, frowning device, or whatever will suit the singular set of circumstances in which the action is situated. This capacity is creative and exquisitely context-sensitive, in the sense that it produces a singular action tailored to a particular context.

Under the dynamical view, emotional expressions are on a par with intentional contents. The intention one feels to purposefully smile, or raise one's hand to wave hello, or enact some other greeting, all result from a person's capacity for self-organization. Intentions attendant on self-organization entail a potential to purposefully smile, for example, even before the desire to smile reaches awareness (Ellis, 2002; Shaw, 2001). Intentional actions, such as purposefully smiling, start with the idea that self-organized dynamical structures are globally stable even though they may compose local sources of disorder. Thus a complex system can be driven toward local instabilities in the interaction of external circumstances and the system's own internal dynamic processes.

For example, feeling happy when seeing a friend can precipitate local instability, not only neurologically, but also in abstract relations at cognitive and emotional "levels." By forming an intention, say to smile, when seeing a friend, a cognitive phase-change may find a locally more stable trajectory (i.e., a better match between the "friend bearing" situation and the possibilities for friendly discourse). The new intention restructures ("prunes") the vast set of behavioral possibilities, excluding all but a potential set of friendly actions. These intentional limits on the potential set avoid the need to consider and evaluate every logical and physical possibility for action (Shaw & Turvey, 1999). Thus, the emergent intention to let a friend know of your happiness to see him or her prunes the set of possibilities down to the act of smiling, excluding other possibilities such as writing the person a note, shaking his or her hand, whispering to him or her, and so forth.

A dynamical view also accommodates other aspects of emotional expression. For instance, people sometimes experience an emotion without displaying any outward bodily reaction. People may also minimize, or inhibit, an emotional behavior in some situations, or even substitute one expression for another (e.g., smiling when feeling angry). These noncorrespondences may be expected to occur if emotional expressions are recruited for display in the interaction of intentions and circumstances (rather than causal chains). This approach may also explain how people can produce certain facial expressions that are codeable as being emotional when it is unlikely that emotion is being experienced. This may be explained by incorporating nonemotional facial expressions within the framework of self-organization.

For example, a face can produce a continuum of muscle actions that may potentially combine in an infinite number of configurations. Nevertheless, only a limited subset of these configurations actually occur. The face assumes only a circumscribed set of patterned states due to constraints imposed by lower-level synergistic relationships among muscle actions (i.e., coordinative structures of motor control). There are limits (embodied constraints) on the ways muscles can come together in combination. Such coordinative structures might emerge in several different ways besides apparent evolutionary sources. Another source might be the experience of an emotion itself (e.g., surprise). However, the same facial action ensemble might also appear if only some of its components were produced in an instrumental action.

For example, brow raising is a facial action that may occur alone or in combination with other facial expressions. One developmental study with 5- and 7-month-old infants showed that raised brow movements significantly co-occurred with heads-up and/or eyes-up movements (Michel, Camras, & Sullivan, 1992). Raised eyebrows occurred more often when a raised head and/or gaze was required to look at things. This suggests that raised eyebrows are part of a coordinative motor structure involving actions of the head, eyes, and brows. The operation of this coordinative structure may determine whether infants produce a variant of expressing interest involving raised eyebrows when they are displaying this emotion. Again, raised eyebrows may sometimes be produced when head and/or gaze is lifted but the emotion of interest is not present. Other studies show that infants produce surprised expressions in situations in which their brows are raised, as when an infant opens its mouth to orally explore an object (Camras, Lambrecht, & Michel, 1996).

Most generally, these results suggest that coordinative structures, emergent in one context, can be recruited in other contexts for a variety of purposes. This recruitment would take place over lower-level synergistic relationships among facial muscle actions. As a consequence, the emotion-relevant facial configuration might sometimes be produced when no emotion was being experienced. Unique and exclusive ties may not be found between emotions and their corresponding facial expressions, or other bodily actions; no singular causal chain can be traced through the body. A key consequence of these ideas is the elimination of the conventional distinction between intentional and automatic emotional expression. It simply disappears once we view emotional expressions as emergent dynamical structures.

Knowing How We Feel: The Interaction of Emotion and Consciousness

Most of us have some sense of how we usually feel at any given moment. Yet as described earlier, people often misunderstand what they are feeling, and on some occasions we struggle to define how we feel. Philosopher Naitka Newton (2000) asks "how can I know how I feel?" and attempts to answer this question in the context of a dynamical approach to emotion and consciousness. A typical response to this question focuses on our ability to observe our own mental states, including those related to various thoughts and desires, which are critical to our having some understanding of our own minds. But Newton suggests, alternatively, that knowing how we feel is best characterized as a self-organized process. Consider the following situation (Newton, 2000: 102):

> I want to keep writing this paper. I also want to stop and take a nap. Both images are attractive, in that there are no vivid obstacles accompanying the imagery. But I cannot image doing both at the same time. If I imagine taking a nap now, then

that imagery activates pleasurable images of drifting off to sleep, but also other imagery of resuming the writing later with great difficulty. If I imagine continuing to write, that imagery activates anticipatory imagery of increasing discomfort, but also other imagery of being able to sleep later without worrying about the paper. The latter imagery wins the competition, at least on this occasion.

Newton suggests that her decision about how she feels can be described in dynamical terms about self-organization processes that operate at two levels: the self-organizing system as a whole (serving internal homeostasis while seeking interaction with the environment to satisfy organismic goals such as nourishment and reproduction), and consciousness. Consciousness is also a self-organizing activity (see below) and is directed toward intentional action. But knowing what one consciously feels is not a matter of observing the contents of mind, or introspecting about our present experience. Instead, we know our minds by enacting mental states.

For instance, Newton knows what she feels in the case of her paper writing by noting, "I feel a reluctance to go on working, but it makes me anxious to think of taking a nap before I am finished, so I basically feel as if I want to go on until the paper is done" (Newton 2000: 103). She is therefore specifically conceptualizing her feelings, not by observing them, but rather by "imaginatively perform[ing] alternative actions in an effort to identify the emotion they best satisfy" (Newton 2000: 103). In this way, the feeling she had arose from enacting relevant activities in imagination. Knowing how one emotionally feels about some situation depends upon these kinds of imaginative, and in some cases real-world, embodied action. Enactment facilitates competition between various subsystems of the self-organizing whole, with the result that they can become better organized and directed toward the pursuit of a single goal. As we will now see, conscious states of mind are emotionally driven responses of a goal-oriented body in dynamic interaction with the environment.

Consciousness

The topic of consciousness is at the heart of the mind-body problem. Do conscious thoughts exist in a realm separate from the body and bodily experience? Or might consciousness be intimately tied to embodied activity, not only within the brain, but also in the full body in action? Of course, the traditional dualist position asserts that consciousness must have some nonmaterial existence. Many contemporary scholars believe, however, that consciousness must have some neural correlates (Crick & Koch, 1996; Metzinger, 2000; and see Jackendoff, 1987 and Prinz, 2001 for a related claim that there is an intermediate level of internal representation between sensory processing and higher-level thought). In fact, there is a huge effort in recent research to characterize the neural correlates of consciousness employing neuroimaging techniques.

But as Chalmers (1996: 384) correctly argues, "The facts about consciousness do not just fall out of facts about the structure and firing of neural processes." There remains an explanatory gap between these processes and the experiential level – the so-called "hard problem" of consciousness. Even if there are important correlations between neural systems and conscious experience, it is not clear that this evidence proves the existence of a content match between the two (Noe & Thompson, 2004). For instance, as Noe and Thompson (2004: 11–12) note in regard to the evidence of certain cell firings during perception of a vertical line, the perceptual experience "of a vertical line is never just a matter of the registration of the presence of a vertical line in this way. The perceptual experience as of a vertical line will represent the line as against a background, and as occupying a certain position in egocentric space, that is, as occupying a certain spatial relation to you, the embodied perceiver." Thus, the receptive field content and the content of the perceptual experience are two different kinds of content. In line with my discussion in Chapter 3 of the problems of reducing bodily experience to neural firings in the somatosensory cortex, there is no way to determine the receptive-field content of neurons apart from consideration of the sensorimotor content of the entire animal in action (Varela et al., 1991). My argument, following this perspective, is that understanding how consciousness arises from animate motion, and more specifically the dynamical interactions of brains, bodies in motion, and the environment, is the best way to close this explanatory gap and ultimately solve the "hard problem." Let me discuss this idea more fully.

Defining Consciousness and Its Functions

The essence of consciousness is experience: those things that are before your mind right now, such as different perceptions, bodily sensations, thoughts, feelings, images, and so on. As described at the beginning of this chapter, the elements of mental experience appear to float in a continuous narrative stream that endures as long as we are awake or alive. Most consciousness scholars today do not believe that this stream represents all there is to consciousness, or even that there is a single, definite stream of consciousness. "(i)nstead, there are multiple channels in which specialized circuits try, as parallel pandemoniums, to do their various things, creating multiple drafts as they go . . . some get promoted to further functional roles by the activity of a Virtual Machine in the brain" (Dennett, 1992: 253–4). Thus, defining consciousness in terms of the stream of consciousness alone underestimates the complexity of mental experience, even if this stream reveals much about the process and content of consciousness. Nevertheless, conscious ideas and images are always owned in a highly physical and body-based way (Donald, 2001; James, 1892). We own our conscious thoughts in the same way that we feel ownership of our bodies. Conscious experiences are not ethereal, but quite often have a raw feel to them that is testimony to their embodied nature. Cognitive scientists do not yet completely understand the physical nature of this embodied ownership, yet the sense of consciousness as something that is part of us, and our bodies, is quite real.

The psychologist George Miller once wrote that "Consciousness is a word worn smooth by many tongues" to note that consciousness is used to refer to many aspects of mental experience, ranging from simple awareness to complex reflexive experiences of self-consciousness. At the very least, though, consciousness has several unique features, compared to other events such as sleep/coma, habituated events, unconscious problem-solving, involuntary actions (Baars, 1988):

1. Conscious experience involves generally broadcast information. Thus, this information is available to all effectors and action schemas.
2. Conscious events are internally consistent. This distinguishes consciousness from dreams, even when the content of dreams are generally broadcast.
3. Conscious events are informative (i.e., they place a demand for adaptation on other parts of the system).
4. Conscious events require access by the self-system.
5. Conscious events may require perceptual/imaginal events of some duration.

One popular position holds that consciousness primarily functions as a spotlight, directed to a point in the theater of the mind by attention (Baars, 1988). Consciousness integrates multiple sensory inputs and disseminates them to a wide audience of different modules within the nervous system. In this way, conscious operations confer a number of evolutionary advantages (Mandler, 1975). For example:

1. Consciousness enables the covert testing of possible ways of interacting with the immediate environment. This consideration of complex input-output contingencies eliminates the need for overt testing of actions that may have harmful consequences.
2. Consciousness makes it possible to reformulate long-range plans, involving the retrieval of information for long-term memory, modification of that information, remembering new plans, and so forth.
3. Consciousness provides a troubleshooting function for systems that normally operate unconsciously, but only become conscious when they fail. For example, if one is driving a car and the brakes suddenly fail, awareness is immediately redirected to the task in hand, enabling repair work to get under way.

These functions enable people to react reflectively rather than automatically and provide for more adaptive transactions between the organism and the environment. Most generally, consciousness is directly tied to action, both when these actions are physically performed and when they are just mentally entertained. Yet consciousness does not exist along a single dimension. At the very least, three types of consciousness may be distinguished (Shannon, 1997). The most basic form is sensual being, or corporeal consciousness (Sheets-Johnstone, 1998). Sensual experience differentiates the living or animate from the inanimate or dead. Inanimate objects do not respond to the environment in the dynamic moment-by-moment way that living organisms do. The second form of consciousness is mental awareness, which ordinarily provides something about the contents, but not processes, of cognition. Finally, reflection is perhaps the highest form of consciousness, where creatures not only are aware of their present embodied situations, but can reflect on themselves in terms of both past and prospective actions.

Consciousness and Enactment

Conscious experience is fundamentally grounded in perceptually guided activity in the environment. As we move about the world, various information becomes available to our perceptual systems (i.e., affordance) that specifies points of view sequentially occupying different spatial locations. The things that we are most conscious of are those that offer opportunities for action. The affordances that arise from our bodily interactions with objects produce in us a fleeting, and usually inhibited, inner movement that brings them into consciousness. This perceptual grounding, together with our subjective experience of our bodies supports the experience of consciousness. The serial and unitary nature of conscious experience is a fundamental consequence of the embodied and situational character of the mind (Carlson, 1997; Damasio, 1994). This view of conscious experience differs from Dennett's (1992) claim that the serial character of consciousness is due to culturally transmitted memes (or ideas).

The idea that consciousness depends upon movement has a long, albeit sporadic, history in psychology. Washburn (1916) argued that consciousness is tied to "tentative movements" that are diminished versions of real action. He speculated that the cortex, not the muscles, was the locus of these tentative movements for consciousness. Bodily action and attitude were crucial to the ways of meaning in Tichener's (1909) view. Thus, the meaning a person gives to a situation depends on the bodily sensations experienced in that context.

Several contemporary cognitive scientists argue that consciousness is clearly associated with basic sensory and motor processes (Ellis, 2002; Newton, 1996, 2000). Several neuroscientists have argued that thought arises from the activation of sensorimotor images (Damasio, 1994;

Edelman, 1992) that capture memories of how someone has in the past moved or felt his or her body in certain ways. The philosopher Newton (1996, 2000) proposed that our conscious experience of embodied images grounds our concept of intentionality. This directedness upon an object, the hallmark of intuitive mental states, concerns the experienced directedness of a physical action toward a goal. As Newton states "Our apparent introspective awareness of the intentionality of mental states is our conscious experience of the sensorimotor imagery that constitutes these states" (Newton, 2000: 105). People experience consciousness when sensorimotor imagery in working memory, consisting of sensory and motor associations distributed across the cortex, is combined with ongoing sensory and somatosensory input. This image provides something of what it would be like to prefer a certain action (Newton, 2000).

Movement is related to consciousness, because consciousness is rooted in animate motion. Some psychologists emphasize that the major function of consciousness is enactment (Shannon, 1997). Enactment is a mental activity in which people simulate concrete, embodied action in the real world without overtly performing this action (e.g., imagining a conversation, mentally rotating an object to imagine it from a different viewpoint). Shannon (1997) provides an example of enactment where he was thinking about a forthcoming trip to reside at the Cite Universitate in Paris. The conscious contents of Shannon's thoughts were an imagined conversation with S, a friend who had previously stayed at the same university. The conversation emerged as a sequence of ideas in Shannon's mind:

1. They gave me a room at the Cite Universitate.
2. Do you know whether they give you sheets there?
3. Oh, I can ask S if they give you sheets at the Universitate.

This mundane sequence is nonetheless remarkable. Shannon specifically enacted in his mind a conversation in which he posed to S a question, yet only afterward did he decide to perform the desired action in the real world. Enacting the conversation in the mind was necessary for the decision to actually ask S the question. In this manner, enactment is not simply a thought sequence we entertain but action actually performed. Enactment is not pure mental computation, but is fundamentally constituted by action. Consciousness enables people to find natural, efficient ways of performing actions in the world. Different thought experiments (Gedankenexperimentum) are wonderful examples of enactment in which people mentally create entities and explore hypothetical states of action through active manipulation of these entities. Recognizing the tight relationship between kinesthetic action and cognition (i.e., the decisions we make) demonstrates that there is not a mysterious gap between cognitive abilities and consciousness (Shannon, 1997). In fact, the ability to control our consciously held thoughts may make use of the same cerebro-cerebellar dynamics employed in the control of organism-environmental interactions (Ito, 1993). Neuroimaging studies show, consistent with this idea, that delusions of control often seen in schizophrenia may be related to problems in the functioning of the cerebro-cerebellar loops that enable people to recognize that our thoughts originate with us (Frith, Blakemore, & Wolport, 2000).

The varied detailed bodily feelings that arise from movements provide the fundamental grounding for consciousness (Sheets-Johnstone, 1999). Consciousness is not a neural state that acts in the preparation of action, but fundamentally emerges from action. The basic kinesthetic abilities by which any creature distinguishes parts of itself as an animate form constitute a "corporeal consciousness." A creature's corporeal consciousness is primarily focused on the movement of its own body. As creatures move, they break from their resting positions and initiate movement by responding appropriately to the surrounding environmental context. There is an inherent kinesthetic specificity of animate form that provides for a wide range of movement possibilities – a series of "I cans," which constitute a creator's sense of agency. Creatures differ sensually in their own proprioceptive actions in the present movement as they begin crawling, undulating, flying, elongating, contracting, and so on.

Under this view, consciousness is not solely limited to human experience; it is not solely a natural product, but a visceral, complex biological faculty. "Consciousness is thus not in matter, it is a dimension of living form, in particular, a dimension of living form that moves" (Sheets-Johnstone, 1999: 60). A primitive form of intentionality exists in any animal that exists in worlds of sensorimotor representation used in the pursuit of goals (Newton, 1996).

Conscious thoughts differ depending on whether the focused content is the self or the world. Consider the situation of pressing your forefinger on the horizontal edge of a table. Simply through a shift in attention, you can experience either (a) the sensation on the inner end of your finger, of indentation and pressure, which has a shape and orientation, or (b) the perception of the edge of an external object, which has shape, texture, orientation, mass, and location. The single informational state due to reception in your finger in mechanical contact with another object can lend itself to awareness of either of the above, or both. Attention to the world yields haptic perceptual experience (the table edge); attention to one's body yields tactile sensation (felt pressure on the finger). In attention, either the external world or body becomes figure.

Some interesting differences exist between these two attentional patterns. First, bodily sensations move with one's own movement, whereas externally perceived object features do not. Second, they are known uniquely through proprioception awareness. Third, they have hedonic qualities of a kind different from externally perceived objects or features. These differences in spatial reference frames, spatial properties, epistemic properties, and hedonic properties emphasize that even though one's body is experienced as located in the world, the two are not homogeneous parts of the same experiential world. This is why the following syllogism is invalid: There is a pain in my hand, my hand is on the table, therefore the pain is on the table.

These distinctions also suggest interesting differences between the ownership of the experiential content. The contents of bodily sensation are experienced as owned in a way in which the contents of haptic perception (a surface, edge, object) are not. Tactile pressure, pain, itch, is "mine" or "yours" and "I am hot or in pain." The haptic perception of the table edge is mine or yours, but the perceived table edge is not. Such a distinction in experiences could only obtain if one's body and its states are experienced as one's (physical) self. In general, any sensation and experienced state of action readiness are part of the experienced states of the body that is me (Gallagher & Marcel, 1999).

Altered States of Consciousness

Altered, or nonordinary, states of consciousness have not been widely studied or discussed within the cognitive sciences. But one remarkable phenomenological investigation of the various effects of Ayahuasca on conscious experience reveals several insights into the embodied nature of some aspects of conscious experience. Shannon (2002) examined in great detail the reports of dozens of Ayahuasca users, including his own, particularly in the context of indigenous Amazonian cultures. Ayahuasca is a brew made from several plants that is used in religious rites and tribal ceremonies, and most recently by various syncretic religious groups that bring together Christian and Amerindian traditions. Ayahuasca inebriation includes feelings of overall heightened sensitivity, enhanced meaningfulness, faster mentation, and more energy, along with more specific effects such as visual imagery, enhanced metaphoricity (i.e., seeing-as), more synesthesia, and greater fluidity (i.e., openness to new ways of seeing). Ayahuasca drinkers often report that the divide between the self and nonself is significantly diminished and that they sometimes experience a marvelous sense of transcendence beyond the normal human condition.

Shannon's (2002) analysis of Ayahuasca experience revealed that there are two types of nonordinary conscious experience (Consciousness 4 and 5), which are extensions beyond three ordinary types of consciousness (Consciousness 1, 2, and 3) (Shannon, 1997). Consciousness 1 consists of the undifferentiated quality of sensual being, relating to the fact that sentient agents are in touch with the external, real world. Consciousness 2 is a differentiated, well-defined state that encompasses all thought sequences, mental images, dreams, and daydreams. Consciousness 3 is self-consciousness or a second-order ability to reflect upon the mind's own productions. All of these types of consciousness are interrelated and compose a coherent, unified system. In normal, waking life, we continually float between these three types of conscious experiences.

There are two additional types of consciousness that characterize nonordinary states of consciousness under the influence of Ayahuasca. Consciousness 4, like Consciousness 1, consists of direct sensual experience from contact with the real world. However, in Consciousness 4, undifferentiated mentation appears to be independent, externally given, rather than a product of one's own mind. Consciousness 5 refers to what is sometimes called "super" or "cosmic" consciousness, in which one's experience transcends human agency.

The two types of nonordinary consciousness are described as being similar to skilled bodily performance, specifically in the paradox of being immersed in bodily activity, while still being able to focus on aspects of the present environment. Ayahuasca experience is likened, for example, to one's playing one's own mind in the way that a master musician plays a musical instrument. A master pianist can immerse himself or herself into the act of playing the piano and seem to be at one with the instrument. Yet he or she can also maintain some distance from this activity to critically reflect on his or her performance. Thus, there is a constant, dynamic flow between the feeling of total immersion and of critical reflection. In a similar way, the master "ayahuasquero" exhibits the contradictory skill of being grounded in the world and being able to soar high above without constraint. Grounding is achieved through straight body posture while sitting, stable breathing, having a relaxed psychological attitude, and contemplation with distraction. This enables drinkers to "immerse themselves in the otherly realms of Ayahuasca" (Shannon, 2002: 352). But drinkers can immediately shift their attention to real-world events, ranging from assisting others undergoing a difficult Ayahuasca experience to chasing a dog from the place where the Ayahuasca session is occurring.

A different analogy for characterizing nonordinary consciousness is that of dancing. Dancers often find themselves in states of consciousness that are quite similar to those labeled as "altered," such as "flow" states (Csikszentmihalyi, 1990). As the dancer is fully engaged in movement, he or she feels immersed in a separate reality of sorts, thus separating himself or herself from the domain of life existing outside the dancer at that moment. When dancing with others, as in pas de deux, dancers sometimes feel their personal identities being transformed so they become one with their partners. But skilled dancers still can be aware of what is going on, both with themselves and in the immediate environment. Shannon claims that this example perfectly illustrates important aspects of Ayahuasca inebriation.

Hallucination experience is not simply perceptual, because it also pertains to action. When Ayahuasca drinkers experience perceptual visions, they often stop being mere spectators and assume roles as actors. A person may step into the scene of his vision, but remain still and simply observe. Yet he can also move about the scene, sometimes interacting with other beings and objects in the scene as if in reality, and sometimes moving about with no interaction with others. On occasion, this embodied immersion is accompanied by feelings of metamorphosis, as if one had transformed into another person or creature. Some enactments are especially meaningful to people because they involve personal performances that they would not ordinarily accomplish in real life. Consider the following brief example (Shannon, 2002: 158): "I was climbing a very high mountain. I have never done any mountaineering in my life and the feat was quite difficult for me. I almost got to the top but could not carry on any further. Then a fairy came, gave me a push and I reached the summit. It was a most gratifying experience."

The importance of enactment in aspects of nonordinary consciousness is not limited to internal thoughts, because Ayahuasca drinkers often enact aspects of their visions, or engage in activities such as singing, dancing, or playing instruments, often in remarkable ways that give overt evidence of this special state of mind.

Consciousness and Self-Organization

Many cognitive scientists believe that the first step toward constructing a scientific theory of consciousness is to discover the neural correlates of consciousness. As noted above, this strategy ignores the "hard problem" of explaining the gap between neural structures and experiential content. But even understanding the neural basis of consciousness is best done at the level of dynamical brain signatures (large-scale dynamical patterns of activity over multiple frequency bands) rather than the structural level of specific circuits or classes of neurons. This dynamical approach to understanding consciousness gives little reason to search for matches in the content between internal mental representations and conscious experience. The processes crucial for consciousness cut across brain-body-world divisions, as part of an individual's embodied capabilities, rather than being limited to neural events in the head (Thompson & Varela, 2001).

The relationship between neural dynamics and conscious situated agents can be described in terms of the participation of neural processes in the "cycle of operation" that constitutes the agent's life (Thompson & Varela, 2001). Three kinds of cycles can be distinguished (Thompson & Varela, 2001).

Cycles of organismic regulation of the entire body. The main basis for this regulation is the autonomic nervous system, in which sensors and effectors to and from the body link neural processes to build homeodynamic processes of the internal organs and viscera. Emotional states – reflecting the links between the autonomic nervous systems and the limbic system via the hypothalamus – are part and parcel of homeodynamic regulation. In this way, organism regulation has a pervasive affective dimension that manifests in the range of affective behavior and feeling that makes up sentience – the feeling of being alive (often referred to as primal or core consciousness).

Cycles of sensorimotor coupling with the environment provide the organism with a sense of how it moves based on what it senses. The substrate of these cycles is the sensorimotor pathways of the body, which are mediated in the brain by multiple neocortical regions and subcortical structures. Transient neural assemblies mediate the coordination of sensory and motor surfaces and sensorimotor coupling with the environment constrains and modulates this neural dynamic.

Finally, cycles of intersubjective interaction provide for the recognition of intentional meaning in verbal and nonverbal actions. Neural structures, such as the amygdala, the ventromedial frontal cortices, and the right somatosensory related cortices, are known to be important in social cognition based on our reading of other people's bodies. Intersubjectivity involves distinct forms of sensorimotor coupling, such as seen in mirror neurons. These neurons display the same pattern of activity both when the animal accomplishes certain goal-directed hand movements and when the agent observes another person performing the same action. Thus, the recognition of intentional meaning of actions in others apparently depends on patterns of neural activity in premotor areas that are similar to those internally generated to produce the same type of action.

Most generally, these three levels of cycles suggest how consciousness depends on the manner in which brain dynamics are embedded in the somatic and environmental context of the animal's life. The coupled dynamics of brain, body, and environment exhibit self-organization and emergent processes at multiple levels and that emergence involves both upward causation and downward causation. Upward causation occurs when neural activity influence cognitive operations and phenomenological experience. Downward causation occurs at multiple levels in these systems, including that of conscious cognitive acts in relation to local neural activity.

Although conscious cognitive acts may be emergent phenomena, they can still have causal effects on local neuronal activity. This suggests that one can observe a moment of consciousness and its substrate large-scale neural assemblies at the level of local properties of neuronal activity. One case study supports this claim (Varela, 2002). When an epileptic patient was engaged in different particular cognitive tasks (i.e., visual and auditory discrimination tasks), this activity influenced specific effects in the local activity given by an epileptic discharge. Thus, deterministic temporal patterns within the apparently random fluctuation of human epileptic activity can be modulated during cognitive tasks. An analysis of the periodic orbit in this person's brain activity showed that the act of perception contributes in a specific manner to "pushing" the epileptic activities toward unstable periodic orbits, a clear case of downward causation. In this way, conscious experience, as a unified global pattern of brain activity, may have a downward causative effect on local neural activity.

At first glance, the idea of downward causation seems at odds with the classic, but still controversial finding that conscious will (i.e., a person deciding to act) may not be the ultimate cause of simple hand movements (Libet, 1985). But Libet's studies only refer to simple one-way causation from conscious will to simple body action. The point of Varela's work is to offer a dynamical model of consciousness that does not see consciousness as merely localized brain activity. Instead, consciousness is best understood as a whole-organism activity in which the person is situated or coupled with the world in terms of dynamical interactions of brain, body, and world. A different study, in fact, showed synchronic patterns of brain activity correlating with ongoing experiences (i.e., a person's sense of preparation and quality of perception) in trained participants' performance on a depth-perception task (Lutz, Lachaux, Martinerie, & et al., 2002). But the relation between presenting the visual object and the ongoing brain activity is dependent upon what happens before and after an individual experimental trial. Thus, understanding the dynamics of a single moment of consciousness is not merely a matter of momentary brain–subjective experience correlations, because any conscious experience is characterized in terms of both the ongoing activity preceding stimulation and the activity following it. This work, more generally, aims to show how first-person data can, and must, be used to interpret neural data when constructing theories of mind and body. This perspective is clearly in an early stage of theoretical development (see Varela & Shear, 1999). Yet the dynamical theory offers the prospect of closing the explanatory gap between minds and bodies.

One implication of the dynamical perspective on consciousness is that consciousness may extend beyond the confines of an individual's head, and may be temporally extended beyond any single moment in time (see Donald, 2001; Wilson, 2004 for similar claims). Each of us may be aware of our immediate experience within a few seconds of time. But most moments of awareness are temporally extended, and include longer time-scales of minutes, hours, and days, when we consciously think about learning a complex skill, creating a narrative, following the directions on a map, or some other complex set of instructions (Wilson, 2004). These different instances of awareness make use of environmental and cultural tools that help off-load cognition into the real world. As is the case in many cases of reasoning (see Chapter 5), it may be difficult to distinguish purely internal aspects of consciousness from those that extend through the body and out into the physical/cultural world. Similarly to seemingly singular acts of perception, such as observing a mug in front of us (see Chapter 3), many moments of conscious awareness are structured around the sensorimotor contingencies of what we may, can, or will do with the objects that are the immediate focus of attention. Even feelings of bodily pain also are not just perceived as passive sensations, but are directed outward toward how a bodily part, such as an injured knee, would feel engaging in various physical actions. These different experiences reflect the "as-if" quality of consciousness, which encompasses both what we experienced in the past and what we could experience in the future. Consciousness, then, is not simply tied to a very short moment in time, such as a few seconds in our phenomenal "stream of consciousness," and instead expands across longer past, present, and future time-scales that are fundamentally tied to complex interactions of brains, bodies, and world.

Conclusion

Emotions and consciousness are both directly tied to human action. We feel different emotions as movement through affective space that defines who we are at any moment in time. Different emotions have varying effects on the body, even if it may be impossible to strictly define individual emotions in terms of specific bodily sensations. But emotional expressions can be characterized, and even predicted, by specific dynamical patterns of interaction between brain, body, and world. This dynamical perspective on emotional expression dissolves the traditional divide between behaviors that are automatically generated and those that are intentionally produced. Both kinds of expressions arise as emergent products of self-organizing processes that constrain the degrees to which various emotions are felt, expressed, and acted on. As such, emotions cut across brain, body, and world, and are thus neither purely mental nor purely physiological phenomena.

Conscious experiences are also not purely mental, but exist as kinds of actions, even when these actions are not manifested by full-bodied behavior. These actions are not abstract and colorless, because people usually experience distinct bodily sensations when they engage in conscious reflection. Of course, consciousness occurs at different levels of experience, yet each level is constituted by its own sensations of felt movement, either in terms of the body's direct interaction with the world or when we imagine ourselves engaging in past or future actions. A dynamical systems framework is most capable of describing how consciousness emerges from interactions of brain, body, and world rather than being a specific result of brain-state activations, or just some immaterial substance with no tie to human bodies.

Emotions and consciousness are tightly linked in enabling us to consider appropriate courses of action for immediate and long-term goals. Cognitive science has traditionally voiced skepticism of first-person investigations of human experience. But it is clear that the study of both emotions and consciousness demands further understanding of how first-person experiences of how we feel and are conscious correspond to third-person properties of brains and bodies that are beyond our phenomenological awareness. This is the task of phenomenological cognitive science, which aims to close the traditional explanatory gaps in the study of emotions and consciousness, and which aims to give embodied action its rightful place in the scientific study of the mind.

9

Conclusion

Bodily experiences matter greatly in mental life. No longer is cognition divorced from considerations of the body and our phenomenological experiences of our bodies, because mind and body are deeply intertwined. The previous chapters describe the mass of empirical evidence in favor of an embodied view of thought and language. This work is representative of a second wave in the history of cognitive science that dramatically differs from the traditional view of mind as purely symbolic, computational, and disembodied. Although there are alternative ways of explaining aspects of some of this evidence, the collective weight of this work is very impressive in suggesting a unified view of mind and body.

Most discussions of embodiment in cognitive science focus exclusively on particular topics, such as the two visual systems (Chapter 3) or embodied grounding for metaphor (Chapters 4 and 6) debates. Scholars then draw general conclusions about the possibility of embodied cognition from consideration of these specific research areas. One motivation for this book was to provide a fuller picture of embodiment that cuts across the many areas of cognitive science research, including perception/action, concepts, mental imagery, memory, language, development, consciousness, and so on. I have aimed to more completely represent various disciplinary and subdisciplinary approaches to embodied cognition than is typically done in discussions of the mind-body problem. This broad sweep of the empirical literature makes it difficult to offer a single, explicit model that best characterizes the precise ways in which bodily experience shapes each aspect of perception, cognition, and language. But the work presented in this book surely demonstrates in myriad ways that embodied activity is central to mental life.

A key part of my search for the embodied mind is the embodiment premise (repeated here from Chapter 1). This states:

People's subjective, felt experiences of their bodies in action provide part of the fundamental grounding for language and thought. Cognition is what occurs when the body engages the physical, cultural world and must be studied in terms of the dynamical interactions between people and the environment. Human language and thought emerge from recurring patterns of embodied activity that constrain ongoing intelligent behavior. We must not assume cognition to be purely internal, symbolic, computational, and disembodied, but seek out the gross and detailed ways that language and thought are inextricably shaped by embodied action.

This premise reflects a methodological imperative for cognitive science. Accordingly, cognitive scientists must not assume that any aspect of perception, cognition, or language arises from disembodied processes unless an explicit search has failed to find mind-body connections. Too much of the debate about embodiment in cognitive science is done in the abstract, where scholars take principled positions about the autonomy of perception, cognition, action, or language and then only pursue research fitting with these ideals. Embodied cognition is often dismissed, or seen as irrelevant to the true goals of cognitive science, without appropriate efforts to seek out the "gross and detailed ways" in which mind and body are linked. Experimental psychologists, in particular, have historically aimed to reduce bodily effects on human performance in laboratory studies, precisely because of the prevailing belief that embodied action has little to do with the essence of cognition or language.

Yet the work described in this book clearly offers a dramatically different view of the many possibilities for how embodied action and experiences of the body are related to a wide variety of human cognitive performance. Of course, this does not imply that all searches for the embodied foundations of perception, cognition, or language will necessarily find mind-body correspondences. Nothing in what I have argued in this book necessarily indicates that the mind is completely, irreducibly embodied. But there is surely enough empirical evidence to suggest that a careful search for mind-body connections will often find such links. For this reason, cognitive scientists embracing disembodied views of mind and language should take on the challenge of doing the right scientific thing by looking for embodiment in cognition before espousing any theoretical position that denies the body its rightful place in understanding the human mind.

Cognitive science includes ideas and research from scholars in several related disciplines, including psychology, linguistics, philosophy, computer science (artificial intelligence), neuroscience, and anthropology. Scholars from many other academic disciplines, such as biology, education, literature, and the arts, also contribute to the ongoing discourse about the origins and functions of the human mind that is, in my view, part of the wider web of cognitive science. Despite the continued acknowledgment from almost all cognitive scientists of the need for interdisciplinary research and perspectives in formulating comprehensive theories of the human mind, there remains a strong tendency for scholars to privilege methods and data from their own respective academic fields. For instance, cognitive psychologists often dismiss ideas from linguistics and philosophy, precisely because these disciplines do not engage in scientific work using hypothetico-deductive methods, such as those employed in the natural sciences. At the same time, there is a strong reductionist pull within cognitive science to explain matters about cognition in terms of specific brain states and patterns of neural activation.

Conducting rigorous scientific studies on human cognition is surely important, and the data from brain-imaging studies, for example, provide important constraints on the embodied mind, as evident in my discussion of this work in the previous chapters. But I reject claims that cognitive linguistics and phenomenological evidence have little bearing on cognitive science theories because they are not based on behavioral or neuropsychological studies. The systematic study of language, including examining possible language-mind and language-mind-body correspondences, is vital to understanding abstract thought and the grounding of symbols in embodied experience. Cognitive scientists who dismiss cognitive linguistic work are missing critically important empirical, even if not experimental, evidence on the embodied mind and language. There are various questions about the reliability of the methods employed by cognitive linguists (Gibbs, 1996), but systematic exploration of linguistic structure and behavior should clearly be part of the methodological tools in cognitive science's bag of tricks for understanding the embodied mind. At the very least, cognitive scientists must, once more, be able to explain why it is that people talk in the embodied ways they do, without appeal to embodied experience, before they can reject cognitive linguistic and cognitive psychological claims about the fundamentally embodied character of language and thought.

The tendency to privilege one's own working methods in debates about the mind-body problem is surely quite natural. But there is a major downside to this normal scientific bias. By insisting that data from phenomenological reports, behavioral measures, or functional neuroimaging, to take three examples, are the best ways to discover principles of cognition, or even the embodied mind, cognitive scientists of whatever stripe too narrowly define the causal locus of what is "cognitive." Part of the problem here is that cognitive scientists too often assume that there are single causes underlying complex human behaviors. In most cases, these singular causes are highly localized functional or anatomical mechanisms that are far removed from the whole organism acting in complex environments. For example, in cognitive psychology and neuropsychology, observed performance in laboratory tasks (e.g., the overall variability in response times, error rates, recognition rates) is divided into component effects using linear statistical models (e.g., analysis of variance), and these component effects are assumed to originate in causal components of mind. Thus, behavior is understood to be the sum of strictly separable pieces, plus some noise. Furthermore, the presence of an effect is equated with the presence of a mental structure/representation and the absence of an effect is equated with the absence of a mental structure/representation.

This "effects = structures" logic is deeply flawed, especially in its implicit assumption that behavioral tasks can be unpacked to reveal individual components of mind that are the single causes for behavior. One place where this effects = structure fallacy has had unfortunate consequences in cognitive science is in the use of double-dissociation logic in behavioral and neuropsychological studies (Plaut, 1995; Shallice, 1988; Van Orden, Pennington, & Stone, 2001). Under the standard logic, a double dissociation between performances on materials from two different experimenter-defined categories is assumed to rely on separate modules specialized for processing the different categories of materials. Consider some typical findings from this paradigm. A double dissociation between living things and artifacts in picture naming and property verification has been used to argue for separate modules for different semantic categories (Warrington & McCarthy, 1987). A double dissociation in reading abstract versus concrete nouns has been used to argue for separate modules for abstract and concrete nouns (Warrington, 1981). Moreover, a double dissociation in production of past tenses of exception words versus regular words has been used to argue for separate brain mechanisms for words and rules (Pinker, 1991; Pinker & Ulmann, 2002). Various parallel-distributed/connectionist processing models have offered alternative accounts for these data in terms of a single, integrated interactive mechanism instead of separate modules (Farah & McClelland, 1991; Plaut, 1995). But more generally, the observed patterns of dissociation demonstrating autonomous or independent representations (single causes) simply reaffirm the inevitable consequent of assuming that there were autonomous representations in the first place (Van Orden, Jansen op de Haar, & Bosman, 1997; Van Orden et al., 2001).

The effort to explain human performance in terms of singular causes is also evident in contemporary brain-imaging studies, which also adhere to the "effects = structure" fallacy. Thus, dissociations in performance on some experimental task are correlated with varying patterns of neural activity. Researchers then conclude from such studies that the neural basis for some cognitive behavior is rooted in particular brain sites or patterns of neural activation. Some scholars even contend that this type of neuropsychological evidence is the real location and causal basis for the embodied mind.

As noted earlier, these types of arguments about the neural basis for thought and language are far from my own vision of the embodied mind. I clearly do not ignore research findings from neuropsychology, as evident in my frequent mention of this work in the previous chapters. But there is something deeply problematic in how cognitive scientists typically interpret neuropsychological findings, especially in their aim to identify specific brain sites as the singular causal locations for different types of human performance. First, showing that a particular brain area is "lit up" under certain conditions says nothing about what the rest of the brain is doing, and indeed contributing to human performance. Second, the brain does not work in isolation, but is part of an organic whole that includes the nervous system and kinesthetic sensations of the body in action. Asserting that specific brain sites are the causal loci of particular kinds of cognitive performance completely misses the full-bodied nature of cognition. Embodiment shapes cognitive performance not only as a distal, or ultimate cause, but also as a proximate cause, in the sense that bodily experience continually influences ongoing cognition over the course of an individual's lifetime. Finally, painting a picture of human cognition as performance-brain state correspondences creates a distorted image of mind as completely defined by what is on the inside of the skull/body. Yet the traditional separation of mind and environment misses the important ways in which minds are shaped by, and extended into, the physical/cultural world through bodily action.

The strong tendency in cognitive science to posit autonomous, disembodied representations is also clearly seen in theories on the modularity of mind. For example, Fodor (1983) argued that the mind is made up of genetically specified, independently functioning modules, such as those responsible for vision, motor actions, and language. Information from the environment passes first through a system of sensory transducers that transform the data into formats each special-purpose module can process. Each module then outputs data in a common format for central, domain-general processing. These modules are assumed to be hardwired (not assembled from more primitive processes), of fixed neural architecture (specified genetically), domain-specific, fast, and informationally encapsulated (i.e., insensitive to the operation of other modules or central cognitive goals).

In recent years, various cognitive scientists have revised Fodor's original idea to suggest that many aspects of higher-order cognition may also be modular. For example, evolutionary psychologists argue that instead of a uniform learning procedure, single long-term memory, and a small set of inference engines, the mind is really a grab bag of quite specialized knowledge-and-action stories, developed in a piecemeal fashion (over evolutionary time) to serve specific, adaptively important ends (Sperber, 2001; Cosmides & Tooby, 1997). Thus, there are specific modules for thinking about spatial relations, tool use, comprehension, social understanding, and so on. Unlike earlier proposals on modularity, these newer theories even assume that there are modules working within other modules, such as the comprehension module being embedded within the specialized theory-of-mind module (Sperber, 2000). Modularity theory embraces the traditional view of the mind as being composed of autonomous components, even if it holds the additional belief that these components are domain-specific and evolutionarily determined. Although there may be specific modules for different kinds of bodily action, modularity theory downplays the role of embodied experience in the development, and continued operation, of cognitive processes.

I am enthusiastic about any effort to think about human cognition in terms of devices that solve adaptive problems for full-bodied organisms in complex environments. Indeed, there may be a variety of specialized, genetically determined devices that underlie different kinds of human performance. But modularity theorists appear blind to the importance of lived, embodied experience in cognition in their desire to reduce cognitive processes to specialized modules. Many behaviors may appear to be modular and domain-specific. But these effects may be better understood as functional outcomes of an individual's self-organizing abilities rather than as evidence of underlying, causal mechanisms. As noted earlier, part of the problem here rests with the guiding assumption that complex human behaviors may be caused by autonomous components of mind. Among modularity scholars, there is no effort given to seeing what is common across modules, or even to describing how these modules interact to produce adaptive behavior.

For example, consider two different human behaviors, two people talking with one another, and two people walking across a room and through a narrow doorway. What do these different events have in common? Most cognitive scientists would answer that these are very different human activities, and indeed, these behaviors would probably be studied by very different types of scholars. But both events require a kind of coordination that is rooted in physical action. Even the two people talking are engaged in a kind of embodied coordination that is established through their body positions and speech actions. Just as the two people walking through a narrow doorway must tacitly negotiate who enters the doorway first, the two speakers must also cooperate in such a way as to meet their individual and joint goals. Both events then rely on embodied coordination for their successful completion, and as such have something in common that is rooted in embodied experience. In this way, modularity theorists who posit a vast number of independent modules of mind completely miss what is common across different modules, some of which may involve embodied action. Of course, it is not surprising that modularity scholars miss embodied regularities in cognitive performance, because they never look for mind-body correspondences in their empirical and theoretical endeavors. This neglect is a major problem for contemporary cognitive science.

I hasten to add here that embracing an embodied view of cognition does not at all imply that there must be domain-general mechanisms underlying human cognitive behavior. After all, there may be different specialized, domain-specific mechanisms that drive adaptive behavior. But these mechanisms may be variously embodied to some degree (i.e., shaped by embodied action both ontogenetically and phylogenetically) and may also be part of specific patterns of interaction of brain, body, and world rather than functional, independent components of the mind/brain.

Dynamic systems theories offer alternative ways of thinking about cognitive performance that properly acknowledge embodied experience and do not assume that cognition should be reduced to single, autonomous components of mind. As described earlier, this alternative view invokes a reciprocal form of causality in which every part of a system is always present in each behavior of that system. Each of the parts continuously affects, along a different time scale, the overall behavior of the system to the point that its independent contribution cannot be sorted out from the behavior of the whole. Most important, the performance of cognitive systems emerges from coordinated activity among interdependent sensorimotor ensembles. These strongly nonlinear, qualitative transformations show the impossibility of reducing cognitive performance to singularly causal neural assembles, or even singularly causal component oscillations. This self-organizing gestalt allows fluid continuity between action and perception, and organism and environment. Not surprisingly, this approach to cognition not only explains many empirical findings without appealing to specific underlying representations, but more importantly, places proper attention to the fully embodied whole organism in the scientific study of mental life.

It is somewhat unclear whether this theoretical approach may be able to explain all aspects of adaptive human performance. Nonetheless, the previous chapters make it evident that the dynamical systems approach is amenable to describing the diversity of human experiences ranging from low-level aspects of perception/action up to emotion and consciousness. Dynamical systems theory most certainly best captures my argument that embodied cognition arises from, and is sustained through, ongoing interactions between brains, bodies, and world.

My argument in favor of a dynamical systems approach to cognition may seem at odds with my claims, in various places, that embodied action underlies part of people's conceptual representations. Dynamical systems theorists generally aim to describe human performance as a self-organized process without any need for explicit, internal mental representations as the causal basis for adaptive behavior. Advocates of embodied representations suggest that many conceptual symbols include significant information about the motoric actions involved when people perceive and think about concrete objects and abstract ideas. There is much debate in cognitive science over whether explicit "representations" are needed in cognitive theories of the human mind. Many of these discussions are quite interesting (e.g., Clark, 1997, 1998; Doffner, 1999; Markman & Deitrich, 2000; Prinz & Barsalou, 2001; van Gelder, 1998) and echo some of the same arguments that occurred 50 years ago at the birth of the cognitive revolution, when behaviorism was cast aside in the study of human thought processes. Defenders of "representations" conclude that dynamical systems may characterize reactive cognitive agents, but that some form of internal representations is needed to account for higher-order aspects of cognition.

An embodied approach to the study of cognition does not, in my view, demand that researchers either embrace or abandon representationalism in theories of mind. I am clearly impressed with the power of dynamical systems theory to account for a wide variety of perceptual and cognitive phenomena, including purely mental acts involving intentions, beliefs, and desires. Yet I remain open to the possibility that some aspects of cognition may require internal mental representations, at least some of which should be deeply shaped by embodied experience. But I also reject the automatic reflex to posit representations as the driving causal force for human performance, as is done far too often in cognitive science. Adopting a dynamical perspective properly acknowledges the body's role in cognitive behavior as brain, body, world interactions. Under this perspective, there is less temptation to simply reduce cognitive performance to singular, autonomous, and disembodied components of mind. My hope is that cognitive science will continue the research trends described in this book and further explore the lived body by properly acknowledging how embodied experiences shape and guide cognitive performance in real-world contexts.

References

Abbott, V., Black, J., & Smith, E. (1985). The representation of scripts in memory. *Journal of Memory and Language, 24*, 179–99.
Adler, A. (1931). *What life should mean to you*. Oxford: Little, Brown.
Adolph, K. (1997). Learning in the development of infant locomotion. *Monographs of the Society for Research in Child Development, 62*.
Adolph, K. (2000). Specificity of learning: Why infants fall over a vertiable cliff. *Psychological Science, 11*, 290–5.
Adolphs, R., Damasio, H., Tranel, D., Cooper, G., & Damasio, A. (2000). A role for somatosensory cortices in the visual recognition of emotion as revealed by three-dimensional lesion mapping. *Journal of Neuroscience, 20*, 2683–90.
Aggleton, J., & Mishkin, M. (1986). The amygdala: Sensory gateway to the emotions. In R. Plutchik & H. Kellerman (Eds.), *Emotion: Theory, research, and experience* (pp. 281–9). Orlando, FL: Academic Press.
Aglioti, S., Goodale, M., & DeSouza, J. (1995). Size-contrast illusions deceive the eye but not the hand. *Current Biology, 5*, 679–85.
Agre, P., & Chapman, D. (1987). Pengi: An implementation of a theory of activity. Proceedings of *AAAI-87*. Menlo Park: AAAI.
Ahsen, A. (1995). Self-report questionnaires: New directions for imagery research. *Journal of Mental Imagery, 19*, 107–22.
Akshoomoff, N., Courchesne, E., & Townsend, J. (1997). Attention coordination and anticipatory control. *International Review of Neurobiology, 411*, 575–98.
Alibali, M., & DiRusso, A. (1999). The function of gesture in learning to count: More than keeping track. *Cognitive Development, 14*, 37–56.
Alibali, M., Kita, S., & Young, A. (2000). Gesture and the process of speech production: We think, therefore we gesture. *Language and Cognitive Processes, 15*, 593–613.
Allison, T., Puce, R., & McCarthy, G. (2000). Social perception for visual cases of the STS region. *Trends in Cognitive Science, 4*, 267–78.
Andrews, E. (1995). Seeing is believing: Visual categories in the Russian lexicon. In E. Contini-Morava & B. Goldberg (Eds.), *Meaning as explanation* (pp. 363–77). Berlin: Mouton de Gruyter.

Anifeld, M. (1996). Only tongue protrusion modeling is matched by neonates. *Developmental Review, 16*, 149–61.

Arditi, A., Holtzman, J., & Kosslyn, S. (1988). Mental imagery and seeing experiences in congenital blindness. *Neuropsychologia, 26*, 1–12.

Arnold, M. (1946). On the mechanism of suggestion and hypnosis. *Journal of Abnormal and Social Psychology, 41*, 107–28.

Arnold, M., & Gasson, S. (1954). Feelings and emotions as dynamic factors in personality integration. In M. Arnold & S. Gasson (Eds.), *The human person* (pp. 294–313). New York: Ronald.

Asci, F. (2003). The effect of physical fitness training on trait anxiety and physical self-concept of female university students. *Psychology of Sports and Exercise, 4*, 255–64.

Attneave, F., & Olson, R. (1967). Discriminability of stimuli varying in physical and retinal orientation. *Journal of Experimental Psychology, 74*, 149–57.

Ax, A. (1953). The physiological differentiation between fear and anger in humans. *Psychosomatic Medicine, 15*, 433–42.

Ayer, A. (1936). *Language, truth, and logic*. London: Gollancz.

Ayers, T., & Jonides, J. (1979). Differing suffix effects for the same physical suffix. *Journal of Experimental Psychology: Human Learning & Memory, 5*, 315–21.

Baars, B. (1988). *A cognitive theory of consciousness*. New York: Cambridge University Press.

Babcock, M., & Freyd, J. (1988). Perception of dynamic information in static handwritten forms. *American Journal of Psychology, 101*, 111–30.

Bach-y-Rita (1996). Sustitucion sensorielle et qualia. In J. Proust (Ed.), *Perception et intermodalite* (pp. 81–100). Paris: Presses Universitaires de France.

Baddeley, A. (1986). *Working memory*. Oxford, England: Clarendon Press.

Baddeley, A., & Hitch, G. (1974). Working memory. In G. Bower (Ed.), *The psychology of learning and memory: Vol. 8* (pp. 47–89). New York: Academic Press.

Baddeley, A., & Lieberman, K. (1980). Spatial working memory. In R. Nickerson (Ed.), *Attention and performance VIII* (pp. 521–39). Hillsdale, NJ: Erlbaum.

Bahrick, L. (1988). Intermodal learning in infancy: Learning on the basis of two kinds of invariant relational in audible and visible events. *Child Development, 59*, 197–209.

Bahrick, L. (1995). Intermodal origins of self-perception. In P. Rochat (Ed.), *The self in infancy* (pp. 349–73). Amsterdam: North-Holland.

Bahrick, L. (2000). Increasing specificity in development of intermodal perception. In D. Muir & A. Slater (Eds.), *Infant development: The essential readings* (pp. 119–37). Malden, MA: Blackwell.

Bahrick, L., & Watson, S. (1985). Detection of intermodal proprioceptive-visual contingency as a potential basis for self-perception in infancy. *Developmental Psychology, 21*, 963–73.

Bai, D., & Bertenthal, B. (1992). Locomotor structure and the development of spatial search skills. *Child Development, 63*, 215–26.

Bailey, D. (1998). Getting a grip: A computational model of the acquisition of verb semantics for hand actions. Unpublished Ph.D. dissertation, International Computer Science Institute, University of California, Berkeley.

Baillargeon, R. (1986). Representing the existence and location of hidden objects: Object permanence in 6- and 8-month-old infants. *Cognition, 23*, 21–41.

Baillargeon, R. (1987a). Object permanence in 3.5 and 4.5 month-old infants. *Developmental Psychology, 23*, 655–64.
Baillargeon, R. (1987b). Young infants' responding about the physical and spatial properties of a hidden object. *Cognitive Development, 2*, 179–200.
Baillargeon, R. (1993). The object concept revisited: New direction in the investigation of infant's physical knowledge. In C. Granud (Ed.), *Visual perception and cognition in infancy* (pp. 265–313). Hillsdale, NJ: Erlbaum.
Baillargeon, R. (1994). Object permanence in young infants: Further evidence. *Child Development, 62*, 1227–46.
Baillargeon, R. (1995). Physical reasoning in infancy. In M. Gazzaniga (Ed.), *Physical reasoning in infancy* (pp. 187–204). Cambridge, MA: MIT Press.
Baillargeon, R. (2000). How do infants learn about the physical world. In D. Muir & A. Slater (Eds.), *Infant development: The essential readings* (pp. 195–212). Malden, MA: Blackwell.
Baillargeon, R. (2004). Infants' physical reasoning. *Current Directions in Psychological Science, 13*, 89–94.
Baillargeon, R., & DeVos, J. (1991). Object permanence in young infants: Further evidence. *Child Development, 114*, 1227–41.
Baillargeon, R., DeVos, J., & Graber, M. (1989). Location memory in 8-month-old infants in a non-search AB task: Further evidence. *Cognitive Development, 4*, 345–67.
Baillargeon, R., & Graber, M. (1988). Evidence of location memory in 8-month-old infants in a non-search AB task. *Developmental Psychology, 24*, 502–11.
Baillargeon, R., Needham, A., DeVos, J. (1992). The development of young infants' intuitions about support. *Early Development and Parenting, 1*, 69–78.
Baillargeon, R., Spelke, E., & Wasserman, S. (1985). Object permanence in five-month-old infants. *Cognition, 20*, 191–208.
Baker, L. (2000). *Bodies and persons*. New York: Cambridge University Press.
Baldwin, D., & Baird, J. (2001). Discerning intentions in dynamic human action. *Trends in Cognitive Sciences, 5*, 171–8.
Ballard, D., Hayhoe, M., Pook, P., & Rao, R. (1997). Deictic codes and the embodiment of cognition. *Behavorial and Brain Sciences, 20*, 723–67.
Bargh, J., Chen, M., & Burrows, L. (1996). Automaticity of social behavior: Direct effects of trait construct and stereotype activation on action. *Journal of Personality and Social Psychology, 71*, 230–44.
Baron-Cohen, S. (1995). *Mindblindness*. Cambridge, MA: MIT Press.
Barsalou, L. (1983). Ad hoc categories. *Memory & Cognition, 11*, 211–27.
Barsalou, L. (1985). Ideals, central tendency, and frequency of instantiation as determinants of graded structure in categories. *Journal of Experimental Psychology: Learning, Memory, & Cognition, 11*, 629–54.
Barsalou, L. (1987). The instability of graded structure in concepts. In U. Neisser (Ed.), *Concepts and conceptual development: Ecological and intellectual factors in categorization* (pp. 101–40). New York: Cambridge University Press.
Barsalou, L. (1989). Intra-concept similarity and its implications for inter-concept similarity. In S. Vosniadou & A. Ortony (Eds.), *Similarity and analogical reasoning* (pp. 76–121). New York: Cambridge University Press.
Barsalou, L. (1991). Deriving categories to achieve goals. In G. H. Bower (Ed.), *The psychology of learning and motivation: Advances in research and theory, Vol. 27* (pp. 1–64). New York: Academic Press.

Barsalou, L. (1995). Flexibility, structure, and linguistic vagary in concepts: Manifestations of a compositional system of perceptual symbols. In A. Collins, S. Gathercole, M. Conway, & P. Morris (Eds.), *Theories of memory*. Hillsdale, NJ: Erlbaum.

Barsalou, L. (1999a). Perceptual symbol systems. *Behavioral and Brain Sciences, 22,* 577–660.

Barsalou, L. (1999b). Language comprehension: Archival memory or preparation for situated action. *Discourse Processes, 28,* 61–80.

Barsalou, L. (2002). Being there conceptually: Simulating categories in preparation for situated action. In N. Stein & P. Bauer (Eds.), *Representation, memory, and development: Essays in honor of Jean Mandler* (pp. 1–15). Mahwah, NJ: Erlbaum.

Barsalou, L. (2003). Situated simulation in the human conceptual system. *Language & Cognitive Processes, 18,* 513–562.

Barsalou, L., & Medin, D. (1986). Concepts: Fixed definitions or dynamic context-dependent representations? *Cahiers de Psychologie Cognitive, 6,* 187–202.

Bassili, J. (1978). Facial motion in the perception of faces and emotional expression. *Journal of Experimental Psychology: Human Perception and Performance, 4,* 373–9.

Basso, K. (1990). *Western Apache language and culture: Essays in linguistic anthropology*. Tucson: University of Arizona Press.

Bateson, G. (1972). *Steps to an ecology of mind*. Chicago: University of Chicago Press.

Bauer, P. (1996). What do infants recall of their lives? Memory for specific events by one- to two-year-olds. *American Psychologist, 51,* 29–41.

Bauer, P. (1997). Development of memory in early childhood. In N. Cowan (Ed.), *The development of memory in childhood* (pp. 83–111). Hove, England: Psychology Press.

Bavac-Cikoja, D., & Turvey, M. (1995). Does perceived size depend on perceived distance? An argument for extended haptic perception. *Perception and Psychophysics, 57,* 216–24.

Bavelas, J., Black, A., Lemery, C., & Mullet, J. (1986). "I show how you feel": Motor mimicry as a communicative act. *Journal of Personality and Social Psychology, 50,* 322–9.

Beach, K. (1988). The role of external mnemonic system in acquiring an occupation. In M. Gruneberg & P. Morris (Eds.), *Practical aspects of memory* (pp. 342–6). Oxford: Wiley.

Beardsworth, T., & Buckner, T. (1981). The ability to recognize oneself from a video recording of one's movement without seeing one's body. *Bulletin of the Psychonomic Society, 18,* 19–22.

Becker, A., & Ward, T. (1991). Children's use of shape in extending novel labels to animate objects: Identity versus postural change. *Cognitive Development, 6,* 3–16.

Beer, F. (2001). *The meanings of war & peace*. College Station: Texas A & M Press.

Beer, R. (1997). The dynamics of adaptive behavior. *Robotics and Autonomous Systems, 20,* 257–89.

Beer, R. (2003). The dynamics of active categorical perception in an evolved model agent. *Adaptive Behavior, 11,* 209–43.

Beitel, D., Gibbs, R., & Sanders, P. (2001). The embodied approach to the polysemy of the spatial preposition "on." In H. Cuyckens (Ed.), *Polsemy in cognitive linguistics* (pp. 241–60). Amsterdam: Benjamins.

Bergan, B., & Chang, N. (in press). Simulation-based language understanding in embodied construction grammar. In J.-O. Ostman & M. Fried (Eds.), *Construction grammar(s): Cognitive and cross-linguistic dimensions*. Amsterdam: Benjamins.

Berko, J., Burke, L., Craven, J., & Sarlo, N. (1992). The importance of motor activity in sensorimotor development: A perspective for children with physical handicaps. *Human Development, 35*, 226–40.

Berkowitz, L. (2000). *Causes and consequences of feelings*. New York: Cambridge University Press.

Berkowitz, L., & Troccoli, B. (1990). Feelings, direction of attention, and expressed evaluations of others. *Cognition and Emotion, 4*, 305–25.

Bermond, B., Nieuwenhuyse, B., Fasolti, S., & Schuerman, J. (1991). Spinal cord lesions, peripheral feedback, and intensities of emotional feelings. *Cognition and Emotion, 5*, 201–20.

Bermudez, J., Marcel, A., & Eilan, N. (Eds.) (1995). *The body and the self*. Cambridge, MA: MIT Press.

Bertenthal, B. (1993). Infants' perception of biomechanical motions: Intrinsic and knowledge-based constraints. In C. Granrud (Ed.), *Visual perception and cognition in infancy* (pp. 175–214). Hillsdale, NJ: Erlbaum.

Bertenthal, B., & Campos, J. (1987). New directions in the study of early experience. *Child Development, 58*, 560–7.

Bertenthal, B., Campos, J., & Barrett, K. (1984). Self-produced locomotion: An organizer of emotional, cognitive, and social development in infancy. In R. Ende & R. Harmon (Eds.), *Continuties and discontinuities in development* (pp. 174–210). New York: Plenum.

Bertenthal, B., Campos, J., & Kermoian, R. (1994). An epigenetic perspective on the development of self-produced locomotion and its consequences. *Current Directions in Psychological Science, 3*, 140–5.

Bertenthal, B., & Pinto, J. (1993). Complementary processes in the perception and production of human movements. In L. Smith and E. Thelen (Eds.), *A dynamic systems approach to development: Applications* (pp. 209–39). Cambridge, MA: MIT Press.

Berthier, N., DeBlois, S., Poirer, C., Novack, M., & Clifton, R. (2000). Where's the ball? Two- and three-year olds reasons about unseen events. *Developmental Psychology, 36*, 394–401.

Berthoz, A. (2000). *The brain's sense of movement*. Cambridge, MA: Harvard University Press.

Bigelow, A. (1992). Locomotion and search behavior in blind infants. *Infant Behavior and Development, 15*, 179–89.

Blakemore, S-J., Wolpert, D., & Firth, C. (2000). Why can't you tickle yourself? *NeuroReport, 11*, R11–R16.

Bloch, H. (1990). Structure and function of early sensorymotor coordinations. In H. Bloch & B. Bertenthal (Eds.), *Sensorymotor organization and development in infancy and early childhood* (pp. 163–78). New York: Kluwer Academic.

Bloom, L. (1993). *Language development from two to three*. New York: Cambridge University Press.

Bloom, P., & German, T. (2001). Two reasons to abandon the false belief task as a test of theory of mind. *Cognition, 77*, B25–B31.

Bogartz, R., & Shinsky, J. (1998). On the perception of partially-occluded objects in 6-month-olds. *Cognitive Development, 13*, 141–63.

Boone, T., & Cunningham, J. (1998). Children's decoding of emotion in expressive body movements: The development of cue attunement. *Developmental Psychology, 34*, 1007–14.

Boroditsky, L. (2000). Metaphoric structuring: Understanding time through spatial metaphors. *Cognition, 75*, 1–28.

Boroditsky, L. (2001). Does language shape thought? English and Mandarin speakers' conception of time. *Cognitive Psychology, 43*, 1–22.

Boroditsky, L., & Ramscar, M. (2002). The roles of body and mind in abstract thought. *Psychological Science, 13*, 185–9.

Boschker, M., Bakker, F., & Michaels, C. (2002). Effect of mental imagery in realizing affordances. *Quarterly Journal of Experimental Psychology, 55A*, 775–92.

Botvinick, J., & Cohen, J. (1998). Rubber hands 'feel' touch that eyes see. *Nature, 391*, 756.

Bourdieu, P. (1977). *Outline of a theory of practice*. New York: Cambridge University Press.

Bower, G., Black, J., & Turner, T. (1979). Scripts in memory for texts. *Cognitive Psychology, 11*, 177–220.

Brandt, S., & Stark, L. (1997). Spontaneous eye movements during visual imagery reflects the contents of the visual scene. *Journal of Cognitive Neuroscience, 9*, 27–38.

Brass, M., Bekkering, H., Wohlschlager, A., & Prinz, W. (2000). Compatibility 6 between observed and executed finger movements: Comparing symbolic, spatial, and imitative cues. *Brain & Cognition, 44*, 124–43.

Brecht, M., Singer, W., & Engel, A. (1998). Correlation analysis of corticotectal interactions in the cat visual system. *Journal of Neurophysiology, 79*, 2394–2407.

Bridgeman, B. (1983). Mechanisms of space constancy. In A. Hein & M. Jeannerod (Eds.), *Spatially-oriented behavior* (pp. 263–79). New York: Springer.

Bridgeman, B. (2000). Interaction between vision for perception and vision for behavior. In Y. Rossetti & A. Revonsuo (Eds.), *Interaction between dissociated implicit and explicit processing* (pp. 17–40). Amsterdam: Benjamins.

Bridgeman, B., Kirch, M., & Sperling, A. (1981). Segregation of cognitive and motor-oriented systems of visual position perception. *Perception & Psychophysics, 29*, 336–42.

Bridgeman, B., Lewis, S., Heit, G., & Nagle, M. (1979). Relations between cognitive and motor-oriented systems of visual position perception. *Journal of Experimental Psychology: Human Perception and Performance, 5*, 692–700.

Bridgeman, B., Peery, S., & Anand, S. (1997). Interaction of cognitive and sensorimotor maps of visual space. *Perception & Psychophysics, 59*, 456–69.

Bridges, K., & Goldberg, D. (1992). Somatization in primary health care: Prevalence and determinants. In B. Cooper & R. Eastwood (Eds.), *Primary health care and psychiatric epidemiology* (pp. 341–50). London: Routledge.

Brighton, V., Segal, A., Werther, P., & Steiner, J. (1977). Facial expression and hedonic response to taste stimuli. *Journal of Dental Research, 56*, B161.

Brooks, L. (1968). Spatial and verbal components of the act of recall. *Canadian Journal of Psychology, 22*, 349–68.

Brooks, R. (1991). Intelligence without representations. *Artificial Intelligence, 47*, 139–59.

Brooks, R. (2002). *Flesh and machine: How robots will change us*. New York: Pantheon.
Browder, J., & Gallagher, J. (1948). Dorsal cordotomy for painful phantom limb. *Annals of Surgery, 128*, 456–69.
Browman, C., & Goldstein, L. (1992). Articulatory phonology: An overview. *Phonetica, 49*, 155–80.
Browman, C., & Goldstein, L. (1995). Dynamics and articulatory phonology. In R. Port & T. van Gelder (Eds.), *Mind as motion: Explorations in the dynamics of cognition* (pp. 175–94). Cambridge, MA: MIT Press.
Brown, J., Collins, A., & Duguid, P. (1989). Situated cognition and the culture of learning. *Educational Researcher, 18*, 32–42.
Brownlow, S., Dixon, A., Egbert, C., & Radcliffe, R. (1997). Perception of movement and dancer characteristics for point-light displays of dance. *Psychological Record, 47*, 411–21.
Brugger, P., Regard, M., & Shiffrar, M. (2000). Hand movement observation in a person born without hands: Is body schema innate? Meeting of the Swiss Neurological Society, London, England, Sept. 2000.
Brugman, C., & Lakoff, G. (1988). Cognitive typology and lexical networks. In S. Small, G. Gorrell, & M. Tanenhaus (Eds.), *Lexical ambiguity resolution* (pp. 477–508). Palo Alto, CA: Morgan Kaufman.
Brugman, C., & McCaulay, M. (1986). Interacting semantic systems: Mixtec expressions of location. *Berkeley Linguistic Society, 12*, 315–27.
Bruner, J., Goodnow, J., & Austin, G. (1956). *A study of thinking*. New York: Wiley.
Bruno, N. (2001). When does action resist visual illusions? *Trends in Cognitive Science, 5*, 379–82.
Bryant, D., & Wright, G. (1999). How body asymmetries determine accessibility in spatial function. *Quarterly Journal of Experimental Psychology, 52A*, 487–508.
Bullitt-Jones, M. (1999). *Hunger: A memoir of desire*. New York: Knopf.
Burgess, C. (2000). Theory and operational definitions in computational memory models. *Journal of Memory and Language, 43*, 482–8.
Burgess, C., & Lund, K. (2000). The dynamics of meaning in memory. In E. Dietrich & A. Markman (Eds.), *Cognitive dynamics* (pp. 117–56). Mahwah, NJ: Erlbaum.
Burton, G. (1992). Nonvisual judgments of the crossability of path gap. *Journal of Experimental Psychology: Human Perception and Performance, 18*, 698–713.
Butcher, C., & Goldin-Meadow, S. (2000). Gesture and the transition from one- to two-word speech: When hand and mouth come together. In D. McNeil (Ed.), *Language and gesture: Window into thought and action* (pp. 167–91). New York: Cambridge University Press.
Butler, S., Berthier, N., & Clifton, R. (2002). Two-year-olds' search strategies and visual tracking in a hidden displacement task. *Developmental Psychology, 38*, 581–90.
Butterworth, B., & Beattie, G. (1978). Gesture and silence as indicators of planning in speech. In R. Campbell & P. Smith (Eds.), *Recent advances in the psychology of language* (pp. 347–60). New York: Plenum.
Butterworth, B., & Hadar, U. (1989). Gesture, speech, and computational stages: A reply to McNeil. *Psychological Review, 96*, 168–74.
Butterworth, G. (1993). Dynamic approaches to infant perception and action: Old and new theories about the origins of knowledge. In L. Smith & E. Thelen (Eds.),

A dynamic systems approach to development: Applications (pp. 171–87). Cambridge, MA: MIT Press.

Cacioppo, J., Klein, D., Bernston, G., & Hatsfield, E. (1993). The psychophysiology of emotion. In M. Lewis & J. Haviland (Eds.), *Handbook of emotions* (pp. 119–42). New York: Guilford Press.

Camras, L., Lambrecht, L., & Michel, G. (1996). Infant "surprise" expressions as coordinative motor structures. *Journal of Nonverbal Behavior, 20*, 183–95.

Carlson, R. (1997). *Experienced cognition*. Mahwah, NJ: Erlbaum.

Carpenter, P., & Eisenberg, P. (1978). Mental rotation and the frame of reference in blind and sighted individuals. *Perception & Psychophysics, 23*, 117–24.

Carpenter, W. (1874). *Principles of mental physiology, with their applications to the training and discipline of the mind and the study of its morbid conditions*. New York: Appelton.

Carreiras, M., Carriedo, N., Alonso, M., & Fernandez, A. (1997). The role of verb tense and verb aspect in the foregrounding of information during reading. *Memory & Cognition, 25*, 438–46.

Carrera-Levillain, P., & Fernandez-Dols, J-M. (1994). Neutral faces in context: Their emotional meaning and their function. *Journal of Nonverbal Behavior, 18*, 281–289.

Carroll-Phelen, B., & Hampson, P. (1996). Multiple components of the perception of musical sequences: A cognitive neuroscience analysis and some implications for auditory imagery. *Music Perception, 13*, 517–61.

Carver, L., & Bauer, P. (1999). When the event is more than the sum of its parts: 9-month-olds' long-term ordered recall. *Memory, 7*, 147–74.

Cary, M., & Carlson, R. (1999). External support and the development of problem-solving routines. *Journal of Experimental Psychology: Learning, Memory, and Cognition, 25*, 1053–70.

Case, R. (1992). *The mind's staircase*. Hillsdale, NJ: Erlbaum.

Cassell, J., Bickmore, T., Campbell, L., Vihjammsson, H., & Yan, H. (2001). More than just a pretty face: Conversational protocols and the affordances of embodiment. *Knowledge-Based Systems, 14*, 55–64.

Castiello, U. (1996). Grasping a fruit: Selection for action. *Journal of Experimental Psychology: Human Perception & Performance, 23*, 582–603.

Cataldi, S. (1996). *Emotion, depth, and flesh*. Albany: State University of New York Press.

Chalmers, D. (1996). *The conscious mind*. New York: Oxford University Press.

Chambers, D., & Reisberg, D. (1992). What an image depicts depends on what an image means. *Cognitive Psychology, 24*, 145–74.

Chen, Z., Sanchez, R., & Campbell, T. (1997). From beyond to within their grasp: Analogical problem solving in 10- and 13-month-olds. *Developmental Psychology, 33*, 790–801.

Churchland, P. (1984). *Matter and consciousness*. Cambridge, MA: MIT Press.

Churchland, P. (1985). Reduction, qualia, and the direct introspection of brain states. *Journal of Philosophy, 82*, 8–28.

Churchland, P., Ramachandran, V., & Sejinowski, T. (1994). A critique of pure vision. In C. Koch & J. Davis (Eds.), *Large-scale neuronal theories of the brain* (pp. 23–60). Cambridge, MA: MIT Press.

Cienki, A. (1998). Straight: An image schema and its metaphorical extensions. *Cognitive Linguistics, 9*, 107–49.

Clancey, W. (1997). *Situated cognition: On human knowledge and computer representations*. New York: Cambridge University Press.

Clark, A. (1996). *Being there: Putting brain, body, and world together*. Cambridge, MA: MIT Press.

Clark, A. (1997). The dynamic challenge. *Cognitive Science, 21*, 461–81.

Clark, A. (2003). *Natural-born cyborgs: Minds, technologies, and the future of human intelligence*. New York: Oxford University Press.

Clark, H. (1996). *Using language*. New York: Cambridge University Press.

Clarke, E. (2001). Meaning and the specification of motion in music. *Musicae Scientiae, 5*, 213–34.

Clarke, S., & French, R. (1978). Can congenital amputees achieve academically? *American Corrective Therapy Journal, 32*, 7–11.

Clearfield, M. (2000). The role of locomotor experience in the development of navigational memory. Unpublished Ph.D. dissertation.

Clement, C. (1987). Applying general principles to novel problems as a function of learning history: Abstraction from examples vs. studying general statements. *Dissertation Abstracts International, 48*, 585.

Coccia, M., Bartolini, M., Luzzi, S., Provinciali, L., & Ralph, M. (2004). Semantic memory is an amodal, dynamic system: Evidence from the interaction of naming and object use in semantic dementia. *Cognitive Neuropsychology, 21*, 515–27.

Cohen, L., & Oakes, L. (1993). How infants perceive a simple causal event. *Developmental Psychology, 29*, 421–433.

Colcombe, S., & Wyer, R. (2001). The role of prototypes in the mental representation of temporally related events. *Cognitive Psychology, 44*, 67–105.

Cole, J. (1995). *Pride and the daily marathon*. Cambridge, MA: MIT Press.

Cole, J. (1997). On "being faceless": Selfhood and facial embodiment. *Journal of Consciousness, 4*, 467–84.

Cole, M., Hood, L., & McDermott, R. (1997). Concepts of ecological validity: Their differing implications for comparative cognition. In M. Cole & Y. Engestroem (Eds.), *Mind, culture, and activity* (pp. 48–58). New York: Cambridge University Press.

Collie, R., & Hayne, H. (1999). Deferred imitation by 6- and 9-month-old infants: More evidence for declarative memory. *Developmental Psychobiology, 35*, 83–90.

Cooper, L., & Shepard, R. (1982). *Mental imagery and their transformations*. Cambridge: MIT Press.

Connell, J. (1989). A colony architecture for an artificial machine. AI Tech Report 1152, MIT AI Labs, August.

Corballis, M. (1994). Neuropsychology of perceptual functions. In D. Zaidel (Ed.), *Neuropsychology handbook of perception and cognition* (2nd ed.) (pp. 83–104). San Diego, CA: Academic Press.

Corriss, D., & Kose, G. (1998). Action and imagination in the formation of images. *Perceptual and Motor Skills, 87*, 979–83.

Cosmides, L., & Tooby, J. (1997). Dissecting the computational architecture of social inference mechanisms. Characterizing human psychological adaptations. Ciba Foundation symposium, No. 208 (pp. 132–61). New York: Wiley.

Craighero, L. (1996). Grasping a fruit: Selection for action. *Journal of Experimental Psychology: Human Perception and Performance, 22*, 582–603.

Craighero, L., Fadiga, L., Rizzolatti, G., & Umilta, C. (1999). Action for perception: A motor-visual attentional effect. *Journal of Experimental Psychology: Human Perception and Performance, 25*, 1673–92.

Creem, S., & Proffitt, D. (1998). Two memories for geographical slant: Separation and interdependence of action and awareness. *Psychonomic Bulletin and Review, 5*, 22–36.

Crick, F., & Koch, C. (1996). Why neuroscience may be able to explain consciousness. *Scientific American, 273*, 84–85.

Crott, W., & Cruse, A. (2004). *Cognitive Linguistics*. New York: Cambridge University Press.

Csikszentmihalyi, M. (1990). *Flow: The psychology of optimal experience*. New York: Perennial.

Csordas, T. (Ed.) (1994). *Embodiment and experience*. New York: Cambridge University Press.

Cutting, J., Proffitt, D., & Kozlowski, L. (1978). A biomechanical invariant for gait perception. *Journal of Experimental Psychology: Human Perception and Performance, 4*, 357–72.

Damasio, A. (1989). Time-locked multiregional retroactivation: A system-level proposal for the neural substrate of recall and recognition. *Cognition, 33*, 25–62.

Damasio, A. (1994). *Descartes' error: Emotion, reason, and the human brain*. New York: G.P. Putnam & Sons.

Damasio, A. (1999). *The feeling of what happens: Body and emotion in the making of consciousness*. New York: Harcourt Brace & Co.

Damasio, A. (2003). *Looking for Spinoza: Joy, sorrow, and the feeling brain*. New York: Harcourt.

Damasio, A., & Damasio, H. (1994). Cortical systems for retrieval of concrete knowledge: The convergence zone framework. In C. Koch & J. Davis (Eds.), *Large-scale neuronal theories of the brain* (pp. 61–74). Cambridge, MA: MIT Press.

Decety, J., & Grezes, J. (1999). Neural mechanisms subserving the perception of human action. *Trends in Cognitive Science, 3*, 172–78.

Decety, J., Grezess, J., Costes, N., Perani, D., Jeannerod, M., Procyk, E., Grassi, F., & Fazio, F. (1997). Brain activity during observation of actions: Influence of action content and subject's strategy. *Brain, 120*, 1763–77.

Decety, J., Jeannerod, M., & Problanc, C. (1989). The timing of mentally represented actions. *Behavioral Brain Research, 34*, 35–42.

Decety, J., Perani, D., Jeannerod, M., Bettinardi, V., Tadary, B., Woods, R., Mazziotta, J., & Fazio, F. (1994). Mapping motor representations with PET. *Nature, 371*, 600–2.

DeLoache, J., Uttal, D., & Rosengren, K. (2004). Scale errors offer evidence for a perception-action dissociation early in life. *Science, 304*, 1027–9.

Dennett, D. (1992). *Consciousness explained*. Boston: Little Brown.

De Rivera, J. (1977). *A structural theory of the emotions*. New York: International Universities Press.

Descartes, R. (1984). *The philosophical writings of Descartes: vol. 2*. New York: Cambridge University Press.

Dewey, J. (1896). The reflex arc concept in psychology. *Psychological Review, 3*, 357–70.

Dewey, J. (1934). *Art as experience*. New York: Minton, Balch.

Dewey, J. (1938). *Logic: The theory of inquiry*. New York: Henry Holt.

Diamond, A. (1991). Neuro-psychological insights into the meaning of object concept development. In S. Carey and R. Gelman (Eds.), *The epigenesis of mind: Essays on biology & cognition* (pp. 67–110). Hillsdale, NJ: Erlbaum.

Dijksterhuis, A., & van Knippenberg, A. (1998). The relation between perception and behavior, or how to win a game of Trivial Pursuit. *Journal of Personality and Social Psychology, 74*, 865–77.

Dijksterhuis, A., Bargh, J., & Miedema, J. (2001). Of mice and mackerels: Attention and automatic social behavior. In H. Bless & J. Forgas (Eds.), *Subjective experience in social cognition and behavior* (pp. 37–51). Philadelphia: Psychology Press.

DiPelligrino, G., Fadiga, L., Fogassi, L., Gallese, V., & Rizzolatti, G. (1992). Understanding motor events. *Experimental Brain Research, 91*, 176–80.

diSessa, A. (1993). Toward an epistemology of physics. *Cognition & Instruction, 10*, 105–225.

Dodd, B. (1979). Lipreading in infancy: Attention to speech in and out of synchrony. *Cognitive Psychology, 11*, 478–84.

Doffner, G. (1999). The connectionist route to embodiment and dynamicism. In A. Riegler, M. Peschl, & A. von Stein (Eds.), *Understanding representation in the cognitive sciences: Does representational need reality?* (pp. 23–32). New York: Kluwer.

Donald, M. (2001). *A mind so rare: The evolution of human consciousness*. New York: Norton.

Dorman, M., Studdert-Kennedy, M., & Raphael, L. (1977). Stop-consonant recognition: Release bursts and formant transitions as functionally equivalent, context-dependent cues. *Perception & Psychophysics, 22*, 109–22.

Douglas, M. (1970). *Natural symbols*. New York: Pantheon.

Downing, L. (2000). *Negation, text worlds, and discourse: The pragmatics of fiction*. Mahwah, NJ: Erlbaum.

Duclos, S., Laird, J., Schneider, E., Sexter, M., Stern, L., & Van Lighten, O. (1989). Emotion-specific effects of facial expressions and postures on emotional experience. *Journal of Personality and Social Psychology, 57*, 100–8.

Eagle, R. (1985). Deprivation of early sensorimotor experience and cognition in the severely involved cerebral palsy child. *Journal of Autism, and Developmental Disorders, 15*, 269–83.

Edelman, G. (1992). *Bright air, brilliant fire: On the matter of the mind*. New York: Basic Books.

Eimer, M. (1995). Stimulus-response compatibility and automatic response activation: Evidence from psychophysiological studies. *Journal of Experimental Psychology: Human Perception and Performance, 21*, 335–59.

Ekman, P. (1985). Telling lies: clues to deceit in the marketplace, politics, and marriage. New York: Norton.

Ekman, P. (1992). Are there basic emotions? *Psychological Review, 99*, 550–3.

Ekman, P. (1994). Strong evidence for universals in facial expressions: A reply to Russell's mistaken critique. *Psychological Bulletin, 115*, 268–87.

Ekman, P., & Davidson, R. (Eds.) (1994). *The nature of emotions*. New York: Oxford University Press.

Ekman, P., Levenson, R., & Friesen, W. (1983). Autonomic nervous system activity distinguishing among emotions. *Science, 221*, 1208–10.

Ellis, N., & Hennelly, R. (1980). A bilingual word-length effect: Implications for intelligence testing and the relative ease of mental calculation in Welsh and English. *British Journal of Psychology, 71*, 43–52.

Ellis, R. (1995). *Questioning consciousness.* Amsterdam: Benjamins.
Ellis, R. (2002). Efferent brain processes and the enactive approach to consciousness. *Journal of Consciousness Studies, 7*, 40–52.
Ellis, R., & Tucker, M. (2000). Micro-affordances: The potentiation of components of action by seen objects. *British Journal of Psychology, 91*, 457–71.
Emmorey, K. (2002). *Language, cognition, and the brain: Insights from sign language research.* Mahwah, NJ: Erlbaum.
Emmorey, K., Kosslyn, S., & Bellugi, U. (1993). Visual imagery and visual-spatial language: Enhanced imagery abilities in deaf and hearing ASL signers. *Cognition, 46*, 139–81.
Engelkamp, J. (1998). *Memory for actions.* Hove, England: Psychology Press.
Engelkamp, J., & Zimmer, H. (1984). Motor programme information as a separable unit. *Psychological Research, 46*, 283–297.
Epstein, W. (1973). The process of 'taking-into-account' in visual perception. *Perception, 2*, 267–85.
Farah, M., Hammond, K., Levine, D., & Calvanio, R. (1988). Visual and spatial mental imagery: Dissociable systems of representation. *Cognitive Psychology, 20*, 439–62.
Farah, M., & McClelland, J. (1991). A computational model of semantic memory impairment: Modality specificity and emergent category-specificity. *Journal of Experimental Psychology: General, 120*, 339–57.
Farnell, B. (1995). *Do you see what I mean? Plains Indian sign talk and the embodiment of action.* Austin: University of Texas Press.
Feldman, J., & Narayanan, S. (2004). Embodiment in a neural theory of language. *Brain & Language, 89*, 385–92.
Fernandez-Dols, J-M., & Carrera, P. (1994). Neutral faces in context: Their emotional meaning and their function. *Journal of Nonverbal Behavior, 11*, 287–99.
Fernandez-Dols, J-M., Carrera, P., Casado, C. (2002). The meaning of expression: Views from art and other sources. In L. Anolli, R. Ciceri, & G. Riva (Eds.), *Say not to say: New perspectives on miscommunication* (pp. 117–34). Amsterdam: IOS Press.
Fernandez-Dols, J-M., & Ruiz-Belda, M. (1995). Are smiles signs of happiness? Gold medal winners at the Olympic games. *Journal of Personality and Social Psychology, 69*, 1113–19.
Ferrara, K. (1994). *Therapeutic ways with words.* New York: Oxford.
Fery, J.-C. (2003). Differentiating visual and kinesthetic imagery in mental practice *Canadian Journal of Experimental Psychology, 57*, xx–xx.
Fillmore, C. (1982). Frame semantics. In Linguistic Society of Korea (Ed.), *Linguistics in the morning calm* (pp. 111–38). Hansin, Seoul.
Finke, R. (1989). *Principles of mental imagery.* Cambridge: MIT Press.
Finke, R., & Freyd, J. (1985). Transformations of visual memory induced by implied motions of pattern elements. *Journal of Experimental Psychology: Learning, Memory, and Cognition, 11*, 780–94.
Finke, R., Freyd, J., & Shyi, G. (1986). Implied velocity and acceleration induce transformations of visual memory. *Journal of Experimental Psychology: General, 115*, 175–88.
Fisher, S. (1990). The evolution of psychological concepts about the body. In T. Cash & T. Pruzinsky (Eds.), *Body images: Development, deviance, and change* (pp. 3–20). New York: Guilford.

Fitzpatrick, P., Carello, C., Schmidt, R., & Corey, D. (1994). Haptic and visual perception of an affordance for upright posture. *Ecological Psychology, 6*, 265–88.

Flanagan, O. (2002). *The problem of the soul: Two visions of mind and how to reconcile them*. New York: Basic Books.

Flanagan, R., & Beltzer, M. (2000). Independence of perceptual and sensorimotor prediction in the size-weight illusion. *Nature Neuroscience, 3*, 737–41.

Flanagan, R., King, S., Wolpert, D., & Johansson, R. (2001). Sensorimotor prediction and memory in object manipulation. *Canadian Journal of Experimental Psychology, 55*, 87–95.

Fletcher, C., van den Broek, P., & Arthur, E. (1996). A model of narrative comprehension and recall. In B. Britton & A. Graesser (Eds.), *Models of understanding text* (pp. 142–64). Mahwah, NJ: Erlbaum.

Fletcher, R. (1994). Levels of representation in memory for discourse. In M. Gernsbacher (Ed.), *Handbook of psycholinguistics* (pp. 589–608). San Diego: Academic Press.

Flores d'Arcais, G., & Schreuder, R. (1982). Semantic activation during object naming. *Psychological Research, 49*, 153–9.

Fodor, J. (1983). *The modularity of mind*. Cambridge, MA: MIT Press.

Fogel, A., & Hannan, T. (1985). Manual actions of nine- to fifteen-week-old human infants during face-to-face interactions with their mothers. *Child Development, 56*, 1271–9.

Foster, D. (1983). Visual discrimination, categorical identification, and categorical rating in brief displays of curved lines: Implications for discrete encoding processes. *Journal of Experimental Psychology: Human Perception and Performance, 9*, 785–806.

Foster, J., & Strack, F. (1996). Influence of overt head movement on memory for valenced words: A case of conceptual-motor compatibility. *Journal of Personality and Social Psychology, 71*, 421–30.

Fowler, C. (1986). An event approach to the study of speech perception from a direct-realist perspective. *Journal of Phonetics, 14*, 3–28.

Fowler, C. (1987). Perceivers as realists, talkers too: Commentary on papers by Strange, Diehl et al., and Rakerd and Verbrugge. *Journal of Memory & Language, 26*, 574–87.

Fowler, C. (1994). Auditory "objects" – The role of motor activity in auditory perception and speech perception. In K. Pribram (Ed.), *Origins: Brain and self-organization* (pp. 593–603). Hillsdale, NJ: Erlbaum.

Fowler, C., & Rosenblum, D. (1991). The perception of phonetic gestures. In I. Mattingly & M. Studdert-Kennedy (Eds.), *Modularity and the motor theory of speech perception* (pp. 33–59). Hillsdale, NJ: Erlbaum.

Franz, V., Gegenfurtner, K., Buelthoff, H., & Fahle, M. (2000). Grasping visual illusions: No evidence for a dissociation between perception and action. *Psychological Science, 11*, 20–5.

Freeman, N., Lloyd, S., & Sinha, C. (1980). Infant search tasks reveal early concepts of containment and canonical usage of objects. *Cognition, 8*, 243–62.

Freeman, W. (1991). The physiology of perception. *Scientific American, 264*, 78–87.

Freeman, W. (2001). *How brains make up their minds*. New York: Columbia University Press.

Freyd, J. (1987). Dynamic mental representation. *Psychological Review, 94,* 429–38.
Freyd, J., & Finke, R. (1984). Representational momentum. *Journal of Experimental Psychology: Learning, Memory, and Cognition, 10,* 126–32.
Freyd, J., & Finke, R. (1985). A velocity effect for representational momentum. *Bulletin of the Psychonomic Society, 23,* 443–6.
Freyd, J., & Johnson, J. (1987). Probing the time course of representational momentum. *Journal of Experimental Psychology: Learning, Memory, and Cognition, 10,* 126–32.
Freyd, J., & Jones, K. (1994). Representational momentum for a spiral path. *Journal of Experimental Psychology: Learning, Memory, and Cognition, 20,* 968–76.
Freyd, J., Kelly, M., & DeKay, M. (1990). Representational momentum in memory for pitch. *Journal of Experimental Psychology: Learning, Memory, and Cognition, 16,* 1107–17.
Freyd, J., & Pantzer, T. (1995). Static patterns moving in the mind. In S. Smith, T. Ward, & R. Finke (Eds.), *The creative cognition approach* (pp. 181–204). Cambridge: MIT Press.
Freyd, J., Pantzer, T., & Cheng, J. (1988). Representing statics as forces in equilibrium. *Journal of Experimental Psychology: General, 117,* 395–407.
Friberg, A., & Sundberg, J. (1994). Does music performance allude to locomotion? A model of final ritardandi derived from measurements of stopping runners. *Journal of the Acoustical Society of America, 105,* 1469–84.
Friberg, A., & Sundberg, J. (1999). Does music performance allude to locomotion? A model of final ritardandi derived from measurements of stopping runners. *Journal of the Acoustical Society of America, 105,* 1469–84.
Friberg, A., Sundberg, J., & Fryden, L. (2000). Music for motion: Sound level envelopes of tones expressing human locomotion. *Journal of New Music Rsearch, 24,* 199–210.
Fridlund, A. (1994). *Human facial expression.* San Diego: Academic Press.
Friedman, R., & Foerster, J. (2000). The effect of approach and avoidance motor actions on the elements of creative insight. *Journal of Personality and Social Psychology, 79,* 477–92.
Frith, C., Blakemore, S., & Wolport, D. (2000). Explaining the symptoms of schizophrenia: Abnormalities in the awareness of action. *Brain Research Reviews, 31,* 357–63.
Gainotti, G., Silveri, M., Daniele, A., & Giustolisi, L. (1995). Neuroimagining correlates of category-specific semantic disorders: A critical survey. *Memory, 3,* 247–64.
Gallagher, S. (1995). Body schema and intentionality. In J. L. Bermudez & A. Marcel (Eds.), *The body and self* (pp. 225–44). Cambridge, MA: MIT Press.
Gallagher, S. (2001). The practice of mind: Theory, simulation, or primary interaction? *Journal of Consciousness Studies, 8,* 83–103.
Gallagher, S., & Marcel, A. (1999). The self in contextualized action. *Journal of Consciousness Studies, 6,* 212–28.
Gallagher, S., & Meltzoff, A. (1996). The emerging sense of self and others: Merleau-Ponty and recent developmental studies. *Philosophical Psychology, 9,* 211–33.
Gallese, V. (2000). The inner sense of action: Agency and motor representations *Journal of Consciousness Studies, 7,* 23–40.
Gallese, V., Ferari, P., & Umilta, M. (2002). The mirror matching system: A shared manifold for intersubjectivity. *Behaviorial and Brain Sciences, 25,* 35–6.

Gallese, V., & Goldman, A. (1998). Mirron neurons and the simulation theory of mind reading. *Trends in Cognitive Science, 2*, 439–50.
Gardner, H. (1983). *Frames of mind: The theories of multiple intelligences*. New York: Basic Books.
Gardner, H. (1985). *The mind's new science: A history of the cognitive revolution*. New York: Basic Books.
Gardner, R., Martinez, R., & Sandoval, Y. (1987). Obesity and body image: An evaluation of sensory and non-sensory components. *Psychological Medicine, 17*, 927–32.
Garrod, S., & Sanford, A. (1985). On the real-time character of interpretation during reading. *Language and Cognitive Processes, 1*, 43–61.
Garry, M., & Polaschik, D. (2000). Imagination and memory. *Current Directions in Psychological Science, 9*, 6–10.
Geeraerts, D. (1993). Vagueness's puzzles, polysemy's vagueness. *Cognitive Linguistics, 4*, 223–72.
Geeraerts, D. (1997). *Diachronic prototype semantics: A contribution to historical lexicography*. Oxford: Clarendon.
Geertz, C. (1979). *Meaning and order in Morocan society*. New York: Cambridge University Press.
Gelman, R. (1991). Epigenetic foundations of knowledge structures: Initial and transcendent construction. In S. Carey and R. Gelman (Eds.), *Epigenesis of mind: Essays in biology and cognition* (pp. 293–322). Hillsdale, NJ: Erlbaum.
Gelman, R., Durgin, F., & Kaufman, L. (1995). Distinguishing between animates and inanimates: Not by motion alone. In D. Sperber & D. Premack (Eds.), *Causal cognition* (pp. 150–84). New York: Oxford University Press.
Gentner, D., Imai, M., & Boroditsky, L. (2002). As time goes by: Understanding time as spatial metaphor. *Language and Cognitive Processes, 17*, 537–65.
Georgopoulos, A., Lurito, J., Petrides, M., Schwartz, A., & Massey, J. (1989). Mental rotation of the neuronal population vector. *Science, 243*, 234–36.
Gergely, G., Nadasdy, Z. Csiba, G., & Biro, S. (1995). Taking the intentional stance at 12 months of age. *Cognition, 56*, 165–93.
Gergely, G., & Watson, J. (1999). Early socio-emotional development: Contingency perception and the social-biofeedback model. In P. Rochat (Ed.), *Early social cognition: Understanding others in the first months of life* (pp. 101–36). Mahwah, NJ: Erlbaum.
Gergen, K. (1991). *The saturated self*. New York: Basic Books.
Gerlach, C., Law, I., & Paulson, O. (2002). When action turns into words: Activation of motor-based knowledge during categorization of manipulable objects. *Journal of Cognitive Neuroscience, 14*, 1230–9.
Geurts, K. (2002). *Culture and the senses: Bodily ways of knowing in an African community*. Berkeley: University of California Press.
Gibbs, R. (1994). *The poetics of mind: Figurative thought, language, and understanding*. New York: Cambridge University Press.
Gibbs, R. (1996). Why many concepts are metaphorical. *Cognition, 61*, 309–19.
Gibbs, R. (1999a). *Intentions in the experience of meaning*. New York: Cambridge University Press.
Gibbs, R. (1999b). Moving metaphor out of the head and into the cultural world. In R. Gibbs & G. Steen (Eds.), *Metaphor in cognitive linguistics* (pp. 145–66). Amsterdam: Benjamins.

Gibbs, R., Beitel, D., Harrington, M., & Sanders, P. (1994). Taking a stand on the meanings of "stand": Bodily experience as motivation for polysemy. *Journal of Semantics, 11*, 231–51.

Gibbs, R., & Berg, E. (2002). Mental imagery and embodied activity. *Journal of Mental Imagery, 26*, 1–30.

Gibbs, R., & Franks, H. (2002). Embodied metaphor in women's narratives about their experiences with cancer. *Health Communication, 14*, 139–65.

Gibbs, R., Lima, P., & Francuzo, E. (2004). Metaphor in thought and language is grounded in embodied experience. *Journal of Pragmatics, 36*, 1189–210.

Gibbs, R., & Matlock, T. (2000). Psycholinguistics and mental representations. *Cognitive Linguistics, 10*, 263–9.

Gibbs, R., & O'Brien, J. (1990). Idioms and mental imagery: The metaphorical motivation for idiomatic meaning. *Cognition, 36*, 35–68.

Gibbs, R., Strom, L., & Spivey-Knowlton, M. (1997). Conceptual metaphor in mental imagery for proverbs. *Journal of Mental Imagery, 21*, 83–110.

Gibbs, R., & Tenney, Y. (1980). The concept of scripts in understanding stories. *Journal of Psycholinguistic Research, 9*, 275–84.

Gibbs, R., & Van Orden, G. (2003). Are emotional expressions intentional? A self-organizational approach. *Consciousness & Emotion, 4*, 1–16.

Gibson, E. (1988). Exploratory behavior in the development of perceiving, acting, and the acquiring of knowledge. *Annual Review of Psychology, 39*, 1–41.

Gibson, J. (1962). Observations on active touch. *Psychological Review, 69*, 477–90.

Gibson, J. (1966). *The senses considered as perceptual systems*. Boston.

Gibson, J. (1968). What gives rise to the perception of motion? *Psychological Review, 57*, 335–46.

Gibson, J. (1979). *The ecological approach to visual perception*. Boston: Houghton Mifflin.

Gilbert, A., Fridlund, A., & Sabini, J. (1987). Hedonic and social determinants of facial displays to odors. *Chemical Senses, 12*, 355–63.

Glenberg, A. (1997). What is memory for? *Behavioral and Brain Sciences, 20*, 1–55.

Glenberg, A. (1999). Why mental models need to be embodied. In G. Rickert & C. Habel (Eds.), *Mental models in discourse processing* (pp. 77–90). Amsterdam: Elsevier.

Glenberg, A., & Robertson, D. (2000). Symbol grounding and meaning: A comparison of high-dimensional and embodied theories of meaning. *Journal of Memory and Language, 43*, 379–401.

Glenberg, A., Meyer, M., & Lindem, K. (1987). Mental models contribute to foregrounding during text comprehension. *Journal of Memory and Language, 26*, 69–83.

Glenberg, A., Schroeder, J., & Robertson, D. (1998). Averting the gaze disengages the environment and facilitates remembering. *Memory & Cognition, 26*, 651–8.

Glucksberg, S. (2001). *Understanding figurative language*. New York: Oxford University Press.

Glucksberg, S. (2002). Emotion language: A new synthesis? *Contemporary Psychology, 47*, 764–6.

Glucksberg, S., Brown, M., & McGlone, M. (1993). Conceptual metaphors are not automatically accessed during idiom comprehension. *Memory & Cognition, 21*, 711–19.

Glucksberg, S., & Keysar, B. (1990). Understanding metaphorical comparisons: Beyond similarity. *Psychological Review, 97*, 3–18.

Goff, L., & Roediger, H. (1998). Imagination inflation for action events: Repeated imaginings leads to illusory recollection. *Memory & Cognition, 26*, 20–33.

Goffman, E. (1959). *The presentation of self in everyday life*. New York: Doubleday.

Goffman, E. (1976). Response cries. *Language, 54*, 787–815.

Goldap, C. (1992). Morphology and semantics of Yucatec space relators. *Zeitschrift fur Phonetik, Sprachwissenschaft und Kommunikationsforschung, 45*, 612–25.

Goldberg, A. (1995). *Constructions*. Chicago: University of Chicago Press.

Goldfield, E. (1993). Dynamic systems in development: Action systems. In L. Smith & E. Thelen (Eds.), *A dynamic systems approach to development: Applications* (pp. 51–70). Cambridge, MA: MIT Press.

Goldie, P. (2000). Explaining expressions of emotion. *Mind, 109*, 25–38.

Goldinger, S. (1995). Echoes of echoes? An episodic theory of lexical access. *Psychological Review, 105*, 251–79.

Goldman, A. (1970). *A theory of action*. Englewood Cliffs, NJ: Prentice-Hall.

Goodale, M., & Humphrey, G. (1998). The objects of action and perception. *Cognition, 67*, 181–207.

Goodale, M., & Murphy, K. (2000). Space and the brain: Different neural substrates for allocentric and egocentric forms of reference. In T. Metzinger (ed.), *Neural correlates of consciousness* (pp. 189–202). Cambridge, MA: MIT Press.

Goodwin, C. (1981). *Conversational organization: Interaction between speakers and hearers*. New York: Academic Press.

Goossens, L., Pauwels, B., Rudzka-Ostyn, M., Simon-Venderberger, J., & Varpays, J. 1995. *By word of mouth: Metaphor, metonymy, and linguistic action in a cognitive perspective*. Amsterdam: Benjamins.

Gorfein, D. (Ed.) (2001). *On the consequences of meaning selection: Principles of resolving lexical ambiguity*. Washington, DC: APA Books.

Gottlieb, F. (2002). On the epigenetic evolution of species-specific perception: The developmental manifold concepts. *Cognitive Development, 17*, 1287–310.

Gouin-Decarie, T. (1969). A study of the mental and emotional development of the thalidomide child. In B. Foss (Ed.). *Determinants of infant behavior* (pp. 167–187). London: Methuen.

Grady, J. (1997). Theories are buildings revisited. *Cognitive Linguistics, 8*, 267–90.

Grady, J. (1999). A typology of motivation for conceptual metaphor: Correlation vs. resemblance. In R. Gibbs & G. Steen (Eds.), *Metaphor in cognitive linguistics* (pp. 79–100). Amsterdam: Benjamins.

Graesser, A., Singer, M., & Trabasso, T. (1994). Constructing inferences during narrative text comprehension. *Psychological Review, 101*, 371–95.

Graesser, A., Woll, S., Kowalski, D., & Smith, D. (1980). Memory for typical and atypical actions in scripted activities. *Journal of Experimental Psychology: Human Learning and Memory, 6*, 503–15.

Grafton, S., Fadiga, L., Arbib, M., & Rizzolatti, G. (1997). Premotor cortex activation during observation and naming of familiar tools. *Neuroimage, 6*, 231–6.

Granott, N., & Paziale, J. (Eds.) (2002). *Microdevelopment: Transition processes in development and learning*. New York: Cambridge University Press.

Green, D. (2001). Understanding microworlds. *Quarterly Journal of Experimental Psychology, 54A*, 879–911.

Greenberg, J. (1978). *Universals of human language: Vol. 3*. Stanford, CA: Stanford University Press.

Greene, R., & Samuel, A. (1986). Recency and suffix effects in serial recall of musical stimuli. *Journal of Experimental Psychology: Learning, Memory and Cognition, 12*, 517–24.

Gregory, R., & Wallace, J. (1963). *Recovery from early blindness: A case study*. Monograph No. 2. Experimental Psychology Society.

Grezes, J., & Decety, J. (2001). Functional anatomy of execution, mental simulation, observation, and verb generation of actions: A meta-analysis. *Human Brain Mapping, 12*, 1–19.

Grush, R. (2004). The emulation theory of representation: Motor control, imagery, and perception. *Behavioral and Brain Science, 27*, 377–396.

Hadamard, J. (1945). *The psychology of invention in the mathematical field*. Princeton, NJ: Princeton University Press.

Hadar, U. (1989). Two types of gesture and their role in speech production. *Journal of Language and Social Psychology, 8*, 221–8.

Hadar, U., Wenkert-Olenik, D., Krauss, R., & Soroker, N. (1998). Gesture and the processing of speech: Neuropsychological evidence. *Brain & Language, 62*, 107–126.

Haith, M. (1997). The development of future thinking as essential for the emergence of skill in planning. In S. Friedman & Scholnick (Eds.), *The developmental psychology of planning: Why, how, and when do we plan?* (pp. 25–42). Mahwah, NJ Erlbaum.

Halff, H., Ortony, A., & Anderson, R. (1976). A context-sensitive representation of word meaning. *Menory & Cognition, 4*, 378–84.

Hall, C., Bernoties, L., & Schmidt, D. (1995). Interference effects of mental imagery on a motor task. *British Journal of Psychology, 86*, 181–90.

Hamilton, E., & Cairns, H. (1961). *Plato: The collected dialogues*. Princeton, NJ: Princeton University Press.

Hanna, E., & Meltzoff, A. (1993). Peer imitation by toddlers in laboratory and daycare contexts: Implications for social learning and memory. *Developmental Psychology, 29*, 701–17.

Hanrahan, C., Tetreau, B., & Sarrazin, C. (1995). Use of imagery while performing dance movement. *International Journal of Sport Psychology, 26*, 413–30.

Hardy, L., & Callow, N. (1999). Efficacy of external and internal visual imagery perspectives for the enhancement of performances on tasks in which form is important. *Journal of Sport and Exercise Psychology, 21*, 95–112.

Harker, J., & Wierzbicka, A. (Eds.) (2001). *Emotion in crosslinguistic perspective*. New York: Mouton de Gruyter.

Harman, K., Humphrey, G., & Goodale, M. (1999). Active manual control of object views facilitate object recognition. *Current Biology, 9*, 1315–18.

Harnad, S. (1990). The symbol grounding problem. *Physica D, 42*, 335–46.

Hatano, G., & Osawa, K. (1983). Digit memory of grand experts in abacus-derived mental calculation. *Cognition, 5*, 47–53.

Hatfield, E., Cacioppo, J., & Rapsom, R. (1992). Primitive emotional contagion. In M. Clark (Ed.), *Review of personality and social psychology: Vol. 14. Emotion and social behavior* (pp. 151–77). Newbury Park, CA: Sage.

Hatsopoulos, N., & Warren, W. (1991). Resonance tuning in rhythmic arm movements. *Journal of Motor Behavior, 28*, 3–14.

Healey, A. (1982). Short-term memory for order information. In G. Bower (Ed.), *The psychology of learning and motivation: Vol. 16* (pp. 191–238). New York: Academic Press.

Hecht, H., Vogt, S., & Prinz, W. (2001). Motor learning enhances perceptual judgment: A case for action-perception transfer. *Psychological Research, 65*, 3–14.

Heidegger, M. (1962). *Being and time*. New York: Harper & Row.

Heine, B. (1989). Adpositions in African languages. *Linguistique Africaine, 2*, 77–127.

Heine, B. (1997). *Cognitive foundations of grammar*. New York: Oxford University Press.

Heine, B., Ulrike, C., & Hunnemeyer, F. (1991). *Grammaticalization: A conceptual framework*. Chicago: University of Chicago Press.

Heller, J. (1961). *Catch-22*. New York: Knopf.

Hemingway, E. (1960). *The collected poems of Ernest Hemingway*. San Francisco: Pirated Edition.

Henderson, W., & Smyth, G. (1948). Phantom limbs. *Journal of Neurology, Neurosurgery, Psychiatry, 11*, 88–117.

Heptulla-Chatterjee, S., Freyd, J., & Shiffrar, M. (1996). Configural processing in the perception of apparent biological motion. *Journal of Experimental Psychology: Human Perception and Performance, 22*, 916–29.

Hermer, L., & Spelke, E. (1994). A geometric process for spatial reorientation in young children. *Nature, 370*, 57–9.

Hertenstein, M. (2002). Touch: Its communicative function in infancy. *Human Development, 45*, 70–94.

Hewes, G. (1983). The invention of phonemically-based language. In E. de Grolier (Ed.), *Glossogenetics: The origins and evolution of language* (pp. 143–62). Paris: Harwood Publishers.

Heywood, C., & Kentridge, R. (2000). Affective blindsight? *Trends in Cognitive Sciences, 4*, 125–6.

Hohmann, G. (1966). Some effects of spinal cord lesions on experienced emotional feelings. *Psychophysiology, 3*, 143–56.

Hommel, B. (1995). Stimulus-response compatibility and the Simon effect: Toward an empirical clarification. *Journal of Experimental Psychology: Human Perception and Performance, 21*, 764–75.

Hommel, B. (1996). S-R compatibility effects without response uncertainty. *Quarterly Journal of Experimental Psychology, 49A*, 546–71.

Hommel, B., Musseler, J., Aschersleben, G., & Prinz, W. (2001). The theory of event coding (TEC): A framework for perception and action planning. *Behavorial and Brain Sciences, 24*, 849–937.

Hornstein, S., & Mulligan, N. (2001). Memory of action events: The role of objects in memory of self- and other-performed tasks. *American Journal of Psychology, 114*, 199–217.

Howes, D. (2003). *Sensual relations: Engaging the senses in culture and social theory*. Ann Arbor: University of Michigan Press.

Hubbard, T. (1990). Cognitive representation of linear motion: Possible direction and gravity effects in judged displacement. *Memory & Cognition, 18*, 299–309.

Hubbard, T. (1995). Cognitive representations of motion: Evidence for friction and gravity analogues. *Journal of Experimental Psychology: Learning, Memory, and Cognition, 21*, 241–54.

Hubbard, T. (1996). Representational momentum, centripetal force, and curvilinear impetus. *Journal of Experimental Psychology: Learning, Memory, and Cognition, 22*, 1049–62.

Hubbard, T. (1999). How consequences of physical properties influence mental representation: The environmental invariants hypothesis. In P. Killeen & W. Uttal (Eds.), *Fechner Day 99: The end of 20th-century psychophysics, Proceedings of the 15th annual meeting of the International Society for Psychophysics* (pp. 274–9). Tempe, AZ: International Society for Psychophysics.

Hubbard, T., & Bharacha, J. (1988). Judged displaced in apparent vertical and horizontal motion. *Perception & Psychophysics, 44*, 211–21.

Humphrey, N. (1974). Vision in a monkey without striate cortex: A case study. *Perception, 3*, 241–55.

Hupka, R., Zaleski, Z., Otto, J., Reidl, L., Tarabrina, N. (1996). Anger, envy, fear, and jealousy as felt in the body: A five-nation study. *Cross-Cultural Research, 30*, 243–64.

Husserl, E. (1977). *Phenomenological psychology*. The Hague: Martinus Nijhoff.

Husserl, E. (1980). *Ideas pertaining to a pure phenomenology and to a phenomenological philosophy*. Boston: Kluwer Academic.

Hutchins, E. (1995). *Cognition in the wild*. Cambridge: MIT Press.

Hutchinson, W., Davis, K., Lozano, A, Tasker, R., & Dostrovsky, J. (1999). Pain-related neurons in the human cingulated cortex. *Nature Neuroscience, 2*, 403–5.

Iacoboni, M., Woods, R., & Mazziotta, J. (1998). Brain-behavior relationships: Evidence from practice effects or spatial stimulus-response compatibility. *Journal of Neurophysiology, 76*, 321–31.

Intos-Peterson, M., & Roskos-Ewoldsen, B. (1987). Sensory-perceptual qualities of images. *Journal of Experimental Psychology: Learning, Memory, & Cognition, 15*, 188–99.

Ito, M. (1993). Movement and thought: Identical control mechanisms by the cerebellum. *Trends in Neuroscience, 16*, 448–50.

Ito, M. (1999). Imagined movement and response programming. *Journal of Mental Imagery, 23*, 71–84.

Iverson, J., & Thelen, E. (1999). Hand, mouth, and brain: The dynamic emergence of speech and gesture. *Journal of Consciousness Studies*, 11–12, 19–40.

Ivry, R., & Fiez, J. (2000). Cerebellum contributions to cognition and imagery. In M. Gazzaniga (Ed.), *The new cognitive neuroscience* (pp. 999–1011). New York: Plenum.

Jackendoff, R. (1987). *Consciousness and the computational mind*. Cambridge, MA: MIT Press.

Jackendoff, R., & Aaron, D. (1991). Review of G. Lakoff & M. Turner, More than cool reason: A filed guide to poetic metaphor. *Language, 67*, 320–38.

Jackson, F. (1982). Epiphenomenal qualia. *Philosophical Quarterly, 32*, 127–36.

Jackson, F. (1986). What Mary didn't know. *Journal of Philosophy, 83*, 291–5.

Jackson, J. (1994). Chronic pain and the tension between the body as subject and object. In T. Csordas (Ed.), *Embodiment and experience* (pp. 201–28). New York: Cambridge University Press.

Jacobson, E. (1932). Electrophysiology of mental activities. *American Journal of Psychology, 44*, 677–94.

James, K., Humphrey, K., & Goodale, M. (2001). Manipulating and recognizing virtual objects: Where the action is. *Canadian Journal of Experimental Psychology, 55*, 111–20.

James, W. (1890). *The principles of psychology*. New York: MacMillan.

James, W. (1892). *Psychology: Briefer course*. Cambridge, MA: Harvard University Press.

James, W. (1895). The knowing of things together. *Psychological Review, 2,* 105–24.

Jarvella, R., & Collas, J. (1974). Memory for the intentions of sentences. *Memory & Cognition, 2,* 185–8.

Jeannerod, M. (1994). The representing brain: Neural correlates of motor intention and imagery. *Behaviorial and Brain Sciences, 17,* 187–245.

Jeannerod, M. (1995). Mental imagery in the motor cortex. *Neuropsychologica, 33,* 1419–32.

Jeannerod, M. (1999). To act or not to act: Perspectives in the representation of action. *Quarterly Journal of Experimental Psychology: Human Experimental Psychology, 52,* 1–29.

Johansson, G. (1973). Visual perception of biological motion and a model for its analysis. *Perception and Psychophysics, 14,* 201–11.

Johnson, M. (1987). *The body in the mind*. Chicago: University of Chicago Press.

Johnson, M. (1991). Knowing through the body. *Philosophical Psychology, 4,* 3–20.

Johnson, M. (1993). Conceptual metaphor and embodied structures of meaning. *Philosophical Psychology, 6,* 413–22.

Johnson, S. (2000). Thinking ahead: The case for motor imagery in prospective judgments of prehension. *Cognition, 74,* 33–70.

Juarrero, A. (1999). *Dynamics in action: Intentional behavior as a complex system*. Cambridge, MA: MIT Press.

Jusczyk, P. (1995). Infants' detection of the sound patterns of words in fluent speech. *Cognitive Psychology, 29,* 1–23.

Kaczmarek, K., & Bach-y-Rita, P. (1995). Tactile displays. In W. Barfield & Furness, T. (Eds.), *Virtual environments and advanced interface design* (pp. 349–414). New York: Oxford University Press.

Kaiser, M., & Proffitt, D. (1987). Observers' sensitivity to dynamic anomalies in collision. *Perception and Psychophysics, 42,* 275–80.

Kalnins, I., & Bruner, J. (1973). The coordination of visual observation and instrumental behavior in early infancy. *Perception, 2,* 307–14.

Kandel, S., Orliaguet, J.-P., & Viviani, P. (2000). Perceptual anticipation in handwriting: The role of implicit motor competence. *Perception & Psychophysics, 62,* 706–16.

Kant, I., (1787/1927). Immanuel Kant's Critique of pure reason : in commemoration of the centenary of its first publication. New York: MacMillan.

Karmiloff-Smith, A. (1992). *Beyond modularity: A developmental perspective on cognitive science*. Cambridge, MA: MIT Press.

Kaschak, M., & Glenberg, A. (2000). Constructing meaning: The role of affordances and grammatical constructions in sentence comprehension. *Journal of Memory and Language, 43,* 508–29.

Kay, P., & Fillmore, C. (1999). Grammatical constructions and linguistic generalizations: The "what's X doing Y?" construction. *Language, 75,* 1–33.

Keefe, D., & McDaniel, M. (1993). The time course and durability of predictive inferences. *Journal of Memory and Language, 32,* 446–63.

Keen, R. (2003). Representation of objects and events: Why do infants look so smart and toddlers look so dumb? *Current Directions in Psychological Science, 12,* 79–83.

Kelly, M., & Freyd, J. (1987). Explorations of representational momentum. *Cognitive Psychology, 19*, 369–401.

Kelso, J. (1995). *Dynamic patterns: The self-organization of brain and behavior.* Cambridge, MA: MIT Press.

Keltner, D., Ellsworth, P., & Edwards, K. (1993). Beyond simple pessimism: Effects of sadness and anger on social perception. *Journal of Personality and Social Psychology, 64*, 740–52.

Kennedy, J., Gabia, P., & Nicholls, A. (1991). Tactile pictures. In M. Heller & W. Schift (Eds.), *The psychology of touch* (pp. 263–99). Hillsdale, NJ: Erlbaum.

Kermoian, R., & Campos, J. (1988). Locomotor experience: A facilitator of spatial cognitive development. *Child Development, 59*, 908–17.

Kerr, N. (1983). The role of vision in "visual imagery" experiments: Evidence from the congenitally blind. *Journal of Experimental Psychology: General, 112*, 265–77.

Kimura, D. (1973). The asymmetry of the human brain. *Scientific American, 228*, 70–8.

Kintsch, W. (1988). The role of knowledge in discourse comprehension: A construction-integration model. *Psychological Review, 95*, 163–82.

Kintsch, W. (1998). *Comprehension: A paradigm for cognition.* New York: Cambridge University Press.

Kirsh, D. (1995). The intelligent use of space. *Artificial Intelligence, 73*, 31–68.

Kirsh, D., & Maglio, P. (1994). On distinguishing epistemic from pragmatic action. *Cognitive Science, 18*, 513–49.

Klatt, D. (1989). Review of selected models of speech perception. In W. Marseln-Wilson (Ed.), *Lexical representations and processes* (pp. 169–226). Cambridge, MA: MIT Press.

Klatzky, R. (1994). On the relation between motor imagery and visual imagery. *Behavioral and Brain Sciences, 17*, 212–13.

Klatzky, R., Lederman, S., & Metzger, V. (1985). Identifying objects by touch: An expert system. *Perception and Psychophysics, 37*, 299–307.

Klatzky, R., Loomis, J., Lederman, S., & Wake, H. (1993). Haptic identification of objects and their depictions. *Perception & Psychophysics, 54*, 170–78.

Klatzky, R., Pellegrino, J., McCloskey, B., & Doherty, S. (1989). Can you squeeze a tomato?: The role of motor representations in semantic sensibility judgments. *Journal of Memory and Language, 28*, 56–77.

Kleinman, A. (1982). Neurasthenia and depression: A study of somatization and culture in China. *Culture, Medicine, and Psychiatry, 6*, 117–89.

Knoblich, G., & Flach, R. (2001). Predicting the effects of action: Interaction of perception and action. *Psychological Science, 12*, 467–72.

Knoblich, G., Seigerschmidt, E., Flach, R., & Prinz, W. (2002). Authorship effects in the production of handwriting strokes: Evidence for action simulation during action perception. *Quarterly Journal of Experimental Psychology, 55*A, 1027–46.

Knuf, L., Aschersleben, G., & Prinz, W. (2001). An analysis of ideomotor action. *Journal of Experimental Psychology: General, 130*, 779–98.

Kohler, E., Keysers, C., Umilta, M., Fogassi, L., Gallese, V., & Rizzolatti, G. (2002). Hearing sounds, understanding actions: Action representation in mirror neurons. *Science, 297*, 846–48.

Koivisto-Alanko, P. (1998). Mechanisms of semantic change in nouns of cognition: A general model. In J. Coleman & C. Kay (Eds.), *Lexicology, semantics and lexicography* (pp. 35–54). Amsterdam: Benjamins.

Koleck, M., Bruchon-Schweitzer, M., Cousson-Gelie, F., Gillard, J., & Quintard, B. (2002). The body-image questionnaire: An extension. *Perceptual and Motor Skills, 94*, 189–96.

Kolstad, V. (1991). *Understanding of containment in 5.5 month-old infants*. Poster presented at the meeting of the Society for Research in Child Development, Seattle: Washington.

Kopp, C., & Shaperman, J. (1973). Cognitive development in the absence of object manipulation during infancy. *Developmental Psychology, 9*, 430.

Koslowski, L., & Cutting, J. (1977). Recognizing the sex of a walker from a dynamic point-light display. *Perception & Psychophysics, 21*, 575–80.

Kosslyn, S. (1987). Seeing and imagining in the cerebral hemisphere: A computational approach. *Psychological Review, 94*, 148–75.

Kosslyn, S. (1994). Image and brain: The resolution of the imagery debate. Cambridge, MA: MIT Press.

Kosslyn, S., Cave, M., Provost, D., & von Gierke, S. (1988). Sequential processes in image generation. *Cognitive Psychology, 20*, 319–43.

Kosslyn, S., DiGirolamo, G., & Thompson, W. (1998). Mental rotation of object versus hands: Neural mechanisms revealed by positron emission tomography. *Psychophysiology, 35*, 151–61.

Kosslyn, S., Thompson, W., Wraga, M., & Alpert, N. (2001). Imagining rotation by endogenous versus exogenuous forces: Distinct neural mechanisms. *Neuroreport, 12*, 2519–25.

Kotchoubey, B. (2001). About ham and eggs – perception and action, ecology, and neuroscience: A reply to Michaels (2000). *Ecological Psychology, 13*, 123–33.

Kourtzi, Z., & Kanwisher, N. (2000). Activation in human MT/MST by static images with implied motion. *Journal of Cognitive Neuroscience, 12*, 48–55.

Kourtzi, Z., & Shiffrar, M. (1997). One-shot view invariance in a moving world. *Psychological Science, 8*, 461–6.

Kourtzi, Z., & Shiffrar, M. (1999). Dynamic representations of human body movement. *Perception, 28*, 49–62.

Kovecses, Z. (2000a). *Metaphor and emotion: Language, culture and body in human feeling*. New York: Cambridge University Press.

Kovecses, Z. (2000b). Force and emotion. In L. Albertazzi (Ed.), *Meaning and cognition* (pp. 145–68). Amsterdam: Benjamins.

Krauss, R. (1998). Why do we gesture when we speak? *Current Direction in Psychological Science, 7*, 54–60.

Krauss, R., & Hadar, U. (1999). The role of speech-related arm/hand gestures in word retrieval. In L. Messing & R. Campbell (Eds.), *Gesture, speech, and sign* (pp. 93–116). New York: Oxford University Press.

Kraut, R., Fussell, S., & Siegel, J. (2003). Visual information as a conversational resource in collaborative physical tasks. *Human-Computer Interaction, 18*, 13–49.

Kraut, R., & Johnston, R. (1979). Social and emotional messages of smiling: An ethological approach. *Journal of Personality and Social Psychology, 37*, 1539–1553.

Krist, H., Fieberg, E., & Wilkening, F. (1993). Intuitive physics in action and judgment: The development of knowledge about projectile motion. *Journal of Experimental Psychology: Learning, Memory, & Cognition, 19*, 952–966.

Kugler, P., & Turvey, M. (1987). *Information, natural law, and the self-assembly of rhythmic movement*. Hillsdale, NJ: Erlbaum.

Kuhl, P., & Miller, J. (1975). Speech perception by the chinchilla: Voiced-voiceless distinction in alveolar plosive consonants. *Science, 190*, 69–72.

Kuhl, P., & Meltzoff, A. (1987). The bimodal perception of speech in infancy. *Science, 218*, 1138–41.

Kuzouka, H., Oyama, S., Yamazaki, K., Suzuki, K., & Mitsuishi, M. (2000). GestureMan: A mobile robot that embodies a remote instructor's actions. *Proceedings of the CSCW 2000* (pp. 155–62). New York: ACM.

Lachs, K., & Pisoni, D. (2004). Specification of cross-modal source information in isolated kinematic displays of speech. *Journal of the Acoustical Society of America, 116*, 507–18.

Laeng, B., & Teodorescu, D-S. (2002). Eye scanpaths during visual imagery reenacts those of perception of the same visual scene. *Cognitive Science, 26*, 207–31.

Lakoff, G. (1987). *Women, fire, and dangerous things: What our categories reveal about the mind*. Chicago: University of Chicago Press.

Lakoff, G. (1990). The invariance hypothesis: Is abstract reasoning based on image-schemas? *Cognitive Linguistics, 1*, 39–74.

Lakoff, G. (1993). The contemporary theory of metaphor. In A. Ortony (Ed.), *Metaphor and thought* (pp. 202–251). New York: Cambridge University Press.

Lakoff, G., & Johnson, M. (1980). *Metaphors we live by*. Chicago: University of Chicago Press.

Lakoff, G., & Johnson, M. (1999). *Philosophy in the flesh*. New York: Cambridge University Press.

Lakoff, G., & Nunez, R. (2000). *Where mathematics comes from: How the embodied mind brings mathematics into being*. New York: Basic Books.

Lambek, M., & Strathern, A. (Eds.) (1998). *Bodies and persons: Comparative perspectives from Africa and Melanesia*. New York: Cambridge University Press.

Lambie, J., & Marcel, A. (2002). Consciousness and the varieties of emotion experience: A theoretical framework. *Psychological Review, 109*, 219–59.

Landau, J., Libkuman, T., & Wildman, J. (2002). Mental simulation inflates performance estimates for physical abilities. *Memory & Cognition, 30*, 372–9.

Lang, P. (1995). The emotion probe: Structure of motivation and attention. *American Psychologist, 50*, 372–85.

Langacker, R. (1991). *Image, word, and symbol*. Berlin: de Gruyter.

Larsen, R., Kasimatis, M., & Frey, K. (1992). Facilitating the furrowed brow: An unobtrusive test of the facial feedback hypothesis applied to unpleasant affect. *Cognition and Emotion, 6*, 321–38.

Lazarus, R. (1991). *Emotion and adaptation*. New York: Oxford University Press.

Leander, K. (2002). Silencing in classroom interaction: Drawing and relating social space. *Discourse Processes, 34*, 193–235.

Leder, D. (1990). *The absent body*. Chicago: University of Chicago Press.

Lederman, S., & Klatzky, R. (1990). Haptic exploration and object representation. In M. Goodale (Ed.), *Vision and action: The control of grasping* (pp. 98–109). Norwood, NJ: Ablex.

Lederman, S., & Klatzky, R. (2003). Feelng surfaces and objects remotely. In R. Nelson (Ed.), *The somatosensory system: Deciphering the brain's own body image* (pp. 103–20). New York: C Press.

LeDoux, J. (1998). *The emotional brain*. London: Weidenfeld & Nicolson.

Leslie, A. (1982). The perception of causality in infants. *Perception, 11*, 173–86.

Leslie, A. (1988). The necessity of illusion: Perception and thought in infancy. In L. Weiskrantz (Ed.), *Thought without language* (pp. 185–210). Oxford: Clarendon.

Leslie, A. (1994). ToMM, ToBY, and agency: Core architecture and domain specificity. In L. Hirschfeld & S. Gelman (Eds.), *Mapping the mind* (pp. 119–48). New York: Cambridge University Press.

Leslie, A., & Keeble, S. (1987). Do six-month-old infants perceive causality? *Cognition, 25*, 265–85.

Levenson, R., Ekman, P., Heider, K., & Friesen, W. (1992). Emotion and autonomic nervous system activity in the Minangkabau of West Sumatra. *Journal of Personality & Social Psychology, 62*, 972–88.

Levin, D., & Simons, D. (1997). Failure to detect changes to attended objects in motion pictures. *Psychonomic Bulletin & Review, 4*, 501–506.

Levins, J., & Lewontin, R. (1985). *The dialectical biologist*. Cambridge, MA: Harvard University Press.

Levinson, S. (1994). Vision, shape, and linguistic description: Tzeltal body-part terminology and object description. *Linguistics, 32*, 791–855.

Lew, A., & Butterworth, G. (1997). The development of hand-mouth coordination in 2- to 5-month-old infants: Similarities with reaching and grasping. *Infant Behavior and Development, 20*, 59–69.

Lewkowicz, D. (1996). Perception of auditory -visual temporal synchrony in human infants. *Journal of Experimental Psychology: Human Perception and Performance, 22*, 1094–106.

Leyton, M. (1992). *Symmetry, causality, mind*. Cambridge, MA: MIT Press.

Li, L., & Warren, W. (2002). Retinal flow is sufficient for steering during observation. *Psychological Science, 13*, 485–97.

Libby, L. (2003). Imagining perspective and source monitoring in imagination inflation. *Memory & Cognition, 31*, 1072–81.

Liberman, A. (1970). The grammars of speech and language. *Cognitive Psychology, 1*, 301–23.

Liberman, A. (1991). Speech: A special code. In A. Liberman (Ed.), *Learning, development and conceptual change* (pp. 121–145). Cambridge, MA: MIT Press.

Liberman, A., Cooper, F., Shankweiler, D., & Studdert-Kennedy, M. (1967). Perception of the speech code. *Psychological Review, 74*, 431–61.

Liberman, A., & Mattingly, I. (1985). The motor theory of speech perception revisited. *Cognition, 21*, 1–36.

Liberman, A., & Mattingly, I. (1989). A specialization for speech perception. *Science, 243*, 489–94.

Liberman, A., & Whalen, D. (2000). On the relation of speech to language. *Trends in Cognitive Science, 4*, 187–96.

Libet, B. (1985). Unconscious cerebral initiative and the role of conscious will in voluntary action. *Behavioral and Brain Sciences, 8*, 529–66.

Liljedahl, P. (2001). Embodied experience of velocity and acceleration: A narrative. *Journal of Mathematical Behavior, 20*, 439–45.

Lloyd, S., Sinha, C., & Freeman, N. (1981). Spatial references systems and the canonicality effect in infant search. *Journal of Experimental Child Psychology, 32*, 1–10.

Logie, R. (1995). *Visuo-spatial working memory*. Hillsdale, NJ: Erlbaum.

Logie, R., & Marchetti, C. (1991). Visuo-spatial working memory: Visual, spatial, or central executive? In R. Logie & M. Denis (Eds.), *Mental images in human cognition* (pp. 105–15). Oxford: North-Holland.

Logie, R., & Pearson, D. (1997). The inner eye and the inner scribe of visuo-spatial working memory: Evidence for developmental fractionation. *European Journal of Cognitive Psychology, 9*, 241–57.

Loring, D., Meador, K., Allison, J., & Wright, J. (2000). Relationship between motion and linguistic activation using fMRI. *Neurology, 54*, 981–3.

Low, S. (1994). Embodied metaphors: Nerves as lived experience. In T. Csordas (Ed.), *Embodiment and experience* (pp. 139–62). New York: Cambridge University Press.

Luff, P., Heath, C., Kuzuoka, Hi., Hindmarsh, J., Yamazaki, K., & Oyama, S. (2003). Fractured ecologies: Creating environments for collaboration. *Human-Computer Interaction, 18*, 51–84.

Maalej, Z. (2004). Figurative language in anger expressions in Tunisian Arabic: An extended view of embodiment. *Metaphor and Symbol, 19*, 51–75.

Mack, A., & Rock, I. (1998). *Inattentional blindness*. Cambridge, MA: MIT Press.

MacNeilage, P. (1975). Preliminaries to the study of single motor unit activity in speech musculature. *Journal of Phonetics, 1*, 55–71.

MacWhinney, B. (1998). The emergence of language from embodiment. In B. MacWhinney (Ed.), *The emergence of language* (pp. 213–56). Mahwah, NJ: Erlbaum.

Manaster, G., Cleland, C., & Brooks, J. (1978). Emotions as movement in relation to others. *Journal of Individual Psychology, 34*, 244–53.

Mandler, G. (1975). *Mind and emotion*. New York: Wiley.

Mandler, G. (1984). *Mind and body: Psychology of emotion and stress*. New York: Norton.

Mandler, J. (1992). How to build a baby – 2. *Psychological Review, 99*, 587–604.

Mandler, J. (1998). Babies think before they speak. *Human Development, 41*, 116–26.

Mandler, J. (2004). *The foundations of mind: Origins of conceptual thoughts*. New York: Oxford University Press.

Mandler, J., Bauer, P., & McDonough, L. (1991). Separating the sheep from the goats: Differentiating global categories. *Cognitive Psychology, 23*, 263–98.

Manusov, V., & Rodriguez, M. (1989). Intentionally based nonverbal messages: A perceiver's perspective. *Journal of Nonverbal Behavior, 13*, 15–24.

Markman, A., & Deitrich, E. (2000). In defense of representation. *Cognitive Psychology, 40*, 135–71.

Marks, D. (1999). Consciousness, mental imagery, and action. *British Journal of Psychology, 90*, 567–85.

Marmor, G., & Zaback, L. (1976). Mental rotation by the blind: Does mental rotation depend on visual imagery? *Journal of Experimental Psychology: Human Perception and Performance, 2*, 515–21.

Marrone, R. (1990). *Body of knowledge: An introduction to body/mind psychology*. Albany, NY: SUNY Press.

Marschark, M. (1994). Gesture and sign. *Applied Psycholinguistics, 15*, 209–36.

Martin, A., Ungerleider, L., & Haxby, J. (2000). Category specificity and the brain: The sensory-motor model of semantic representation of objects. In M. Gazzaniga (Ed.), *The new cognitive neurosciences* (2nd edition) (pp. 1023–36). Cambridge, MA: MIT Press.

Martin, A., Wiggs, C., Ungerleider, L., & Haxby, J. (1996). Neural correlates of category-specific knowledge. *Nature, 379*, 649–52.

Martin, E. (1994). *Flexible bodies: Tracking immunity in American culture from the days of polio to the age of AIDS*. Boston: Beacon.

Massaro, D. (1987). *Speech perception by ear and by eye: A paradigm for psychological inquiry*. Hillsdale, NJ: Erlbaum.

Matisoff, J. (1978). *Variational semantics in Tibeto-Burman: The organic approach to linguistic comparison*. Occasional paper of the Wolfenden Society. Philadelphia: Institute for the Study of Human Issues.

Matlock, T. (2004). Fictive motion as cognitive simulation. *Memory & Cognition, 32*, 1389–1400.

Maturana, H. (1980). Biology of cognition. In H. Maturana & F. Varela (Eds.), *Autopoiesis and cognition: The realization of the living* (pp. 5–58). Boston: Reidel.

Maturana, H. (1983). What it is to see? *Archivos de Biologica y Medicina Experimentales, 16*, 255–69.

Mayberry, R., & Jacques, J. (2000). Gesture production during stuttered speech: Insights into the nature of gesture-speech integration. In D. McNeil (Ed.), *Language and gestures* (pp. 199–214). New York: Cambridge University Press.

McCloskey, M., & Kohl, D. (1983). Naive physics: The curvilinear impetus principle and its role in interactions with moving objects. *Journal of Experimental Psychology: Learning, Memory, & Cognition, 9*, 146–56.

McDonnell, P. (1988). Developmental responses to limb deficiencies and limb replacement. *Canadian Journal of Psychology, 42*, 120–43.

McGlone, M., & Harding, J. (1998). Back (or forward) to the future: The role of perspective in temporal language comprehension. *Journal of Experimental Psychology: Learning, Memory, and Cognition, 24*, 1211–23.

McGurk, H., & MacDonald, J. (1976). Hearing lips and seeing voices. *Nature, 264*, 746–8.

McNeil, D. (1992). *Hand and gesture: What gestures reveal about thought*. Chicago: University of Chicago Press.

Medin, D., Lynch, E., Coley, J., & Atran, S. (1997). Categorization and reasoning among tree experts: Do all roads lead to Rome? *Cognitive Psychology, 32*, 49–96.

Meier, B., & Robinson, M. (2004). Why the sunny side is up: Associations between affect and vertical position. *Psychological Science, 15*, 243–7.

Meltzoff, A. (1990). Foundations for developing a concept of self: The role of imitation in relating self to other and the value of social mirroring, social modeling, and self practice in infancy. In D. Cicchetti & M. Beeghly (Eds.), *The self in transition* (pp. 139–64). Chicago: University of Chicago Press.

Meltzoff, A. (1995). Understanding the intentions of others: Re-enactment of intended acts by 18-month-old children. *Developmental Psychology, 31*, 838–50.

Meltzoff, A., & Borton, R. (1979). Intermodal matching by human noenates. *Nature, 282*, 403–4.

Meltzoff, A., & Brooks, R. (2001). "Like me" as building block for understanding other minds: Bodily acts, attention, and intention. In B. Malle, L. Moses, & D. Baldwin (Eds.), *Intentions and intentionality: Foundations of social cognition* (pp. 171–91). Cambridge, MA: MIT Press.

Meltzoff, A., & Moore, M. (1992). Early imitation within a functional framework: The importance of person identity, movement, and development. *Infant Behavior and Development, 15*, 479–505.

Meltzoff, A., & Moore, M. (1994). Imitation, memory, and the representation of persons. *Infant Behavior and Development, 17*, 83–99.

Meltzoff, A., & Moore, M. (1997). Explaining facial imitation: A theoretical model. *Early Development and Parenting, 6*, 179–92.

Meltzoff, A., & Moore, M. (2000). (a) Imitation of facial and manual gestures by human neonates (b) Resolving the debate about early imitation. In D. Muir & A. Slater (Eds.), *Infant development: The essential readings. Essential readings in development psychology* (pp. 167–81). Malden, MA: Blackwell.

Meltzoff, A., & Moore, M. (2001). Imitation of facial and manual gestures by human neonates: Resolving the debate about early imitation. In D. Muir & A. Slater (Ed.), *Infant development: The essential readings* (pp. 167–81). Malden, MA: Blackwell.

Merleau-Ponty, M. (1962). *Phenomenology of perception*. London: Routledge & Kegan Paul.

Merzenich, M., Kaas, J., Wall, J., Nelson, R., Sur, M., & Felleman, D. (1983). Topographic reorganization of somatosensory cortical Area 3B and 1 in adult monkeys following restricted deafferentation. *Neuroscience, 8*, 33–56.

Metzinger, T. (Ed.) (2000). *Neural correlation of consciousness.* Cambridge, MA: MIT Press.

Michel, G., Camras, L., & Sullivan, J. (1992). Infant interest expressions as coordinative motor structures. *Infant Behavior and Development, 15*, 347–58.

Michotte, A. (1963). *The perception of causality*. New York: Basic Books.

Miller, J., & Stigler, J. (1991). Meanings of skill: Effect of abacus expertise in number representation. *Cognition & Instruction, 8*, 29–67.

Milner, D., & Dyde, R. (2003). Why do some perceptual illusions affect visually guided action, when others don't? *Trends in Cognitive Sciences, 7*, 10–11.

Milner, D., & Goodale, M. (1995). *The visual brain in action*. New York: Oxford University Press.

Mitchell, R., & Gallaher, M. (2001). Embodying music: Matching music and dance as movement. *Music Perception, 19*, 65–85.

Möller, R. (1999). Perception through anticipation: A behavior-based approach to visual perception. In A. Riegler, M., Peschl, & A. von Stein (Eds.), *Understanding representation in the cognitive sciences* (pp. 169–76). New York: Kluwer Academic.

Montessori, M. (1914). *Dr. Montessori's own handbook*. London: Heineman.

Montpare, J., Goldstein, S., & Clausen, A. (1987). The identification of emotions from gait information. *Journal of Nonverbal Behavior, 1*, 33–42.

Morrow, D., Bower, G., & Greenspan, S. (1989). Updating situation models during narrative comprehension. *Journal of Verbal Learning and Verbal Behavior, 28*, 292–312.

Mulligan, N., & Hornstein, S. (2003). Memory for actions: Self-performed tasks and the reenactment effect. *Memory & Cognition, 31*, 412–21.

Munakata, Y., McClelland, J., Johnson, M., & Siegler, R. (1997). Rethinking infant knowledge: Toward an adaptive process account of success and failure on object permanence. *Psychological Review, 104*, 686–713.

Murphy, G. (1996). On metaphoric representations. *Cognition, 60*, 173–204.

Murphy, G. (2002). *The big book of concepts*. Cambridge, MA: MIT Press.

Murphy, S. (1990). Models of imagery in sports: A review. *Journal of Mental Imagery, 89*, 216–23.

Murray, C. (2001). The experience of body boundaries by Siamese twins. *New Ideas in Psychology, 19*, 117–30.

Murray, I., & Trevarthen, C. (1986). The infant's role in mother-infant communication. *Journal of Child Language, 13*, 15–29.

Murray, J., Klin, C., & Myers, J. (1993). Forward inference in narrative text. *Journal of Memory and Language, 32*, 464–73.

Nairne, J., & Walters, V. (1983). Silent mouthing produces modality and suffix-like effects. *Journal of Verbal Learning and Verbal Behavior, 22*, 475–483.

Nakamura, R., & Mishkin, M. (1980). Chronic blindness following non-visual cortical lesions. *Brain Research, 188*, 572–7.

Narayanan, S. (1997). Moving right along: A computational model of metaphoric reasoning about events. Unpublished Ph.D. dissertation, International Computer Science Institute, University of California, Berkeley.

Needham, A. (2001). Object recognition and object segregation in 4.5 month-old infants. *Journal of Experimental Child Psychology, 78*, 3–24.

Needham, A., & Baillargeon, R. (1993). Intuitions about support in 4.5-month-olds. *Cognition, 47*, 121–48.

Needham, A., Barrett, T., & Peterman, K. (2002). A pick-me-up for infants' exploratory skills: Early simulated experiences reaching for objects using 'sticky mittens' enhances young infants' object exploration skills. *Infant Behavior & Development, 25*, 279–95.

Neisser, U. (1993). The self perceived. In U. Neisser (Ed.), *The perceived self: Ecological and interpersonal sources of self-knowledge* (pp. 3–21). New York: Cambridge University Press.

Nelson, K., Skwerer, D., Goldman, S., Henseler, S., Presler, N., & Walkenfeld, F. (2003). Entering a community of minds: An experientialist approach to a theory of mind. *Human Development, 46*, 24–46.

Neruda, P. (1972). *The captain's verses.* Evanston, IL: Northwestern University Press.

Neumann, C. (2001). Is metaphor universal? Cross-linguistic evidence from German and Japanese. *Metaphor and Symbol, 16*, 123–42.

Newcombe, N. (2002). The nativist-empiricist controversy in the context of recent research in spatial and quantitative development. *Psychological Science, 13*, 395–401.

Newton, N. (1996). *Foundations of understanding.* Amsterdam: Benjamins.

Newton, N. (2000). Conscious emotion in a dynamic system: How I can know how I feel. In R. Ellis & N. Newton (Eds.), *Caldrons of consciousness* (pp. 91–108). Amsterdam: Benjamins.

Nicolelis, M., & Fanselow, E. (2002). Thalamocortical optimization of tactile processing according to behavioral state. *Nature Neuroscience, 5*, 517–523.

Nielsen, T. (1963). Volition: A new experimental approach. *Scandanavian Journal of Psychology, 4*, 225–30.

Nieuwenhuyse, B., Offenberg, L., & Frijda, N. (1987). Subjective emotion and reported body experience. *Motivation and Emotion, 11*, 169–82.

Noe, A. (2004). *Action in perception.* Cambridge, MA: MIT Press.

Noe, A., & O'Reagan, K. (2002). On the brain-basis of visual consciousness: A sensorimotor account. In A. Noe & E. Thompson (Eds.), *Vision and mind* (pp. 567–98). Cambridge, MA: MIT Press.

Noe, A., & Thompson, E. (2004). Are there neural correlates of consciousness? *Journal of Consciousness Studies, 11*, 3–28.

Nolfi, S., & Floreano, D. (2000). *Evolutionary robotics: The biology, intelligence, and technology of self-organizing machines*. Cambridge, MA: MIT Press.

Nyberg, L., Habib, R., McIntosh, A., & Tulving, E. (2000). Reactivation of encoding-related brain activity during memory retrieval. *Proceedings of the National Academy of Sciences, 97*, 11,120–4.

Nygaard, L., Sommers, M., Mitchell, S., & Pisoni, D. (1994). Speech perception as talker-contingent process. *Psychological Science, 5*, 42–6.

Oatley, K. (1992). *The best laid schemes: The psychology of emotion*. New York: Cambridge University Press.

O'Brien, E., & Albrecht, J. (1992). Comprehension strategies in the development of a mental model. *Journal of Experimental Psychology: Learning, Memory, & Cognition, 18*, 777–84.

Ochs, E., Jacoby, S., & Gonzales, P. (1994). Interpretive journeys: How physicists talk and travel through graphic space. *Configurations, 2*, 157–72.

Odling-Smee, F. (1988). Niche-constructing phenotypes. In H. Plotkin (Ed.), *The role of behavior in evolution* (pp. 73–132). Cambridge, MA: MIT Press.

Ojemann, G. (1994). Cortical stimulation and recording in language. In A. Kertesz (Ed.). *Localization and Neuroimaging in Neuropsychology* (pp. 35–55). San Diego, CA: Academic Press.

Ojemann, G., & Mateer, C. (1979). Human language cortex: Localization of memory, syntax, and sequential motor-phoneme identification systems. *Science, 205*, 1401–3.

Olson, E. (2003). Personal identity. In S. Stich & T. Warfield (Eds.), *The Blackwell guide to philosophy of mind* (pp. 352–68). New York: Blackwell.

O'Regan, K. (1992). Solving the "real" mysteries of visual perception: The world as an outside memory. *Canadian Journal of Psychology, 46*, 461–88.

O'Regan, K., & Noe, A. (2001). A sensorimotor account of vision and visual consciousness. *Behavioral and Brain Sciences, 24*, 939–1031.

O'Regan, K., Resnick, R., & Clark, J. (1997). Picture changes during blinks: Not seeing where you look and seeing where you don't look. *Investigative Ophthalmology and Visual Science, 38*, S707.

Oudejams, R., Michaels, C., Bakker, F., & Dolne, M. (1996). The relevance of action in perceiving affordances: Perception of the catchableness of fly balls. *Journal of Experimental Psychology: Human Perception and Performance, 22*, 879–91.

Paillard, J. (1987). Cognitive versus sensorimotor encoding of spatial information. In P. Ellen & C. Thinus-Blanc (Eds.), *Cognitive processes and spatial orientation in animals and man* (pp. 35–54). Dordrecht, Netherlands: Martinus Nijhoff.

Paivio, A. (1986). *Mental representations: A dual-coding approach*. Oxford: Oxford University Press.

Pandya, V. (1993). *Above the forest: A study of Andamanese ethnoemology, cosmology, and the power of ritual*. New York: Oxford University Press.

Panksepp, J. (1998). *Affective neuroscience*. New York: Oxford University Press.

Papez, J. (1937). A proposed mechanism of emotion. *Archives of Neurology and Psychiatry, 38*, 725–43.

Parkinson, B. (1995). *Ideas and realities of emotion*. London: Routledge.

Parsons, L. (1987a.) Imagined spatial transformations of one's body. *Journal of Experimental Psychology: General, 116*, 172–91.

Parsons, L. (1987b). Imagined spatial transformations of one's hands and feet. *Cognitive Psychology, 19*, 178–241.

Parsons, L. (1994). Temporal and kinematic properties of motor behavior reflected in mentally simulated action. *Journal of Experimental Psychology: Human Perception and Performance, 20*, 709–30.

Parsons, L., & Fox, P. (1998). The neural basis of implicit movements used in recognising hand shape. *Cognitive Neuropsychology, 15*, 583–615.

Parsons, L., Fox, P., Downs, J., Glass, T., Hirsch, T., Martin, C., Jerabek, P., & Lancaster, J. (1995). Use of implicit motor imagery for visual shape discrimination as revealed by PET. *Nature, 375*, 54–58.

Pavlenko, A. (2002). Emotions and the body in Russian and English. *Pragmatics & Cognition, 10*, 207–41.

Pazzani, M. (1997). Influence of prior knowledge on concept acquisition: Experimental and computational results. *Journal of Experimental Psychology: Learning, Memory, and Cognition, 17*, 416–32.

Pecher, D., Zeelenberg, R., & Barsalou, L. (2003). Verifying different modality properties for concepts produces switching costs. *Psychological Science, 14*, 119–24.

Pecher, D., Zeelenberg, R., & Raaijmakers, J. (1998). Does pizza prime coin? Perceptual processing in lexical decision and pronunciation. *Journal of Memory and Language, 38*, 407–18.

Pennybaker, J. (1982). *The psychology of physical symptoms*. New York: Springer-Verlag.

Philippot, P., Rime, B. (1997). The perception of bodily sensations during emotion: A cross-cultural perspective. *Polish Psychological Bulletin, 28*, 175–88.

Phillips, R., Wagner, S., Fell, C., & Lynch, M. (1990). Do infants recognize emotion in facial expressions? Categorical and metaphorical evidence. *Infant Behavior and Development, 13*, 71–84.

Phillips, W., Baron-Cohen, S., & Rutter, M. (1992). The role of eye contact in goal detection: Evidence from normal infants and children with autism or mental handicaps. *Development & Psychopathology, 4*, 375–83.

Piaget, J. (1952). *The origins of intelligence in childhood*. New York: International Universities Press.

Piaget, J. (1954). *The construction of reality in the child*. New York: Basic Books.

Piaget, J. (1975). *The equilibrium of cognitive structures*. Paris: Presses Universitairse de France.

Piaget, J., & Inhelder, B. (1969). *The psychology of the child*. London: Routledge & Kegan Paul.

Pine, K., & Messer, D. (2003). The development of representations as children learn about balancing. *British Journal of Developmental Psychology, 21*, 285–301.

Pinker, S., & Ullman, M. (2002). The past and future of past tense. *Trends in Cognitive Sciences, 6*, 456–63.

Plaut, D. (1995). Double-dissociation without modularity: Evidence from connectionist neuropsychology. *Journal of Clinical and Experimental Neuropsychology, 17*, 291–321.

Pollio, H., Henley, T., & Thompson, C. (1997). *The phenomenology of everyday life*. New York: Cambridge University Press.

Port, R., & van Gelder, T (Eds.) (1995). *Mind as motion: Explorations in the dynamics of cognition*. Cambridge, MA: MIT Press.

Premack, D. (1990). The infant's theory of self-propelled objects. *Cognition, 36*, 1–16.

Presson, C., & Montello, D. (1994). Updating of rotational and translational body movements: Coordinate structures of perceptual spaces. *Perception, 23*, 1447–55.

Preston, S., & de Waal, F. (2002). Empathy: Its ultimate and proximate bases. *Behavioral and Brain Sciences, 25*, 1–25.

Pribram, K. (1991). *Brain and perception: Holonomy and studies in figural processing*. Hillsdale, NJ: Erlbaum.

Prinz, W. (1997). Perception and action planning. *European Journal of Cognitive Psychology, 9*, 129.

Prinz, J. (2002). *Furnishing the mind: Concepts and their perceptual basis*. Cambridge, MA: MIT Press.

Prinz, J., & Barsalou, L. (2000). Steering a course for embodied representations. In E. Deitrich & A, Markman (Eds.), *Cognitive dynamics: Conceptual and representational changes in humans and machines* (pp. 51–78). Mahwah, NJ: Erlbaum.

Proffitt, D., Creem, S., & Zosh, W. (2001). Seeing mountains in mole hills: Geographical-slant perception. *Psychological Science, 12*, 418–23.

Pulvermueller, F. (1999). Words in the brain's language. *Behavorial and Brain Sciences, 22*, 253–336.

Putnam, H. (1975). *Mind, language, and reality: Philosophical papers, Vol. 2*. New York: Cambridge University Press.

Quinn, J. (1994). Toward a clarification of spatial processing. *Quarterly Journal of Experimental Psychology*, 47A, 465–80.

Quinn, N. (1991). The cultural basis of metaphor. In J. Fernandez (Ed.), *Beyond metaphor: The theory of tropes in anthropology* (pp. 56–93). Stanford, CA: Stanford University Press.

Radcliff-Brown, A. (1964). *The Andaman islanders*. New York: Free Press.

Ramachandran, V., & Blakeslee, S. (1998). *Phantoms in the brain*. London: Fourth Estate.

Ramachandran, V., & Hirstein, W. (1997). Three laws of qualia: What neurology tells us about the biological functions of consciousness. *Journal of Consciousness Studies, 4*, 429–57.

Redding, G., & Wallace, B. (1997). *Adaptive spatial alignment*. Mahwah, NJ: Erlbaum.

Reed, C., & Farah, M. (1995). The psychological reality of the body schema: A test with normal participants. *Journal of Experimental Psychology: Human Perception and Performance, 21*, 334–43.

Regier, T. (1996). *The human semantic potential*. Chicago: University of Chicago Press.

Reisberg, D., Rappaport, I., & O'Shaughnessy, M. (1984). Limits of working memory: The digit span. *Journal of Experimental Psychology: Learning, Memory and Cognition, 10*, 203–21.

Reiser, J., Doxey, P., McCarrell, N., & Brooks, P. (1982). Wayfinding and toddlers' use of information from an aerial view of a maze. *Developmental Psychology, 18*, 714–20.

Reiser, J., Lockman, J., & Pick, H. (1980). The role of visual experience in knowledge of spatial layout. *Perception and Psychophysics, 28*, 185–90.

Reiser, J., & Rider, E. (1991). Young children's spatial orientation with respect to multiple targets when walking without vision. *Developmental Psychology, 27*, 97–107.

Remez, R., Fellowes, J., & Rubin, P. (1997). Talker identification based on phonetic information. *Journal of Experimental Psychology: Human Perception & Performance, 23*, 651–661.

Repp, B. (1998). Musical motion in perception and performance. In D. Rosenbaum & C. Collyer (Eds.), *Timing of behavior: Neural, psychological, and computational perspectives* (pp. 125–41). Cambridge, MA: MIT Press.

Resnick, A., O'Regan, K., & Clark, J. (1997). To see or not to see: The need for attention to perceive changes in scenes. *Psychological Science, 8*, 368–73.

Richardson, D., & Spivey, M. (2000). Representation, space, and Hollywood Squares: Looking at things that aren't there anymore. *Cognition, 76*, 269–75.

Richardson, D., Spivey, M., Barsalou, L., & McRae, K. (2003). Spatial representations activated during real-time comprehension of verbs. *Cognitive Science, 27*, 767–80.

Rieser, J., & Rider, E. (1991). Young children's spatial orientation with respect to multiple targets while walking without vision. *Developmental Psychology, 27*, 97–107.

Rime, B., Philippot, P., & Cisamolo, D. (1990). Social schemata of peripheral changes in emotion. *Journal of Personality and Social Psychology, 59*, 38–49.

Rizzolatti, G. (1994). Nonconscious motor images. *Behavioral and Brain Sciences, 17*, 220.

Rizzolatti, G., & Arbib, M. (1998). Language within our grasp. *Trends in Neuroscience, 21*, 188–194.

Rizzolatti, G., Fogassi, L., & Gallese, V. (1997). Parietal cortex: From sight to action. *Current Opinion in Neurobiology, 7*, 562–67.

Rizzolatti, G., Riggio, L., & Sheliga, B. (1994). Space and selective attention. In C. Umilta & M. Moscovitch (Eds.), *Attention and performance 15: Conscious and nonconscious information processing* (pp. 232–65). Cambridge, MA: MIT Press.

Rochat, P. (1989). Object manipulation and exploration in 2- to 5-month-old infants. *Developmental Psychology, 28*, 871–84.

Rochat, P. (2001). *The infant's world*. Cambridge, MA: Harvard University Press.

Rosch, E. (1975). Cognitive reference points. *Cognitive Psychology, 7*, 532–57.

Rosch, E. (1999). Reclaiming concepts. *Journal of Consciousness Studies, 6*, 61–77.

Rosch, E., & Mervis, C. (1975). Family resemblances: Studies in the internal structure of categories. *Cognitive Psychology, 7*, 573–605.

Rosch, E., Mervis, C., Gray, W., Johnson, M., & Boyes-Braem, P. (1976). Basic objects in natural categories. *Cognitive Psychology, 8*, 382–439.

Roseblad, B., & von Hofsten, C. (1994). Repetitive goal-directed arm movements in children with development coordination: Role of visual information. *Adapted Physical Activity, 11*, 190–202.

Rosenbaum, D. (1991). *Human motor control*. New York: Academic Press.

Rosler, F., Heil, M., & Hennighausen, E. (1995). Distinct cortical activation patterns during long-term memory retrieval of verbal, spatial, and color information. *Journal of Cognitive Neuroscience, 7*, 51–65.

Ross, B. (1990). Reminding-based category learning. *Cognitive Psychology, 22*, 460–92.

Ross, B. (1999). Postclassification category use: The effects of learning to use categories after learning to classify. *Journal of Experimental Psychology: Learning, Memory, and Cognition, 25*, 743–57.

Ross, B., Perkins, S., & Tenpenny, P. (1990). Reminding-based category learning. *Cognitive Psychology, 22*, 460–92.

Ross, E., & Mesulam, M-M. (1979). Damaged language functions of the right-hemisphere for prosody and emotional feeling. *Archives of Neurology, 36*, 144–8.

Rossi, S., Tecchio, F., Pasqualetti, P., Ulivelli, M., Pizzella, V., Romani, G., Passero, S., Battistini, N., & Rossini, P. (2002). Somatosensory processing during movement observation in humans. *Clincal Neurophysiology, 113*, 16–24.

Rotenberg, K., & Sullivan, C. (2003). Children's use of gaze and limb movement cues to infer deception. *Journal of Genetic Psychology, 164*, 175–87.

Roth, E., & Shoben, E. (1983). The effect of context on the structure of categories. *Cognitive Psychology, 15*, 346–78.

Rothman, G. (1987). Understanding order of movement in youngsters with cerebral palsy. *Perceptual and Motor Skills, 65*, 391–7.

Rovee-Collier, C., & Hayne, H. (2000). Memory in infancy and early childhood. In E. Tulving & F. Craik (Eds.), *The Oxford handbook of memory* (pp. 267–82). New York: Oxford University Press.

Rumelhart, D. (1980). Schemata: The building blocks of cognition. In R. Spiro, B. Bruce, & W. Brewer (Eds.), *Theoretical issues in reading comprehension* (pp. 33–58). Hillsdale, NJ: Erlbaum.

Rumelhart, D., & McClelland, J. (1986). (Eds.), *Parallel distributed processing: Volume 1 – Foundations*. Cambridge, MA: MIT Press.

Runson, S., & Frykolm, G. (1981). Visual perception of lifted weights. *Journal of Experimental Psychology: Human Perception and Performance, 7*, 733–40.

Russell, J. (1995). Facial expressions of emotion: What lies beyond minimal universality? *Psychological Bulletin, 118*, 379–91.

Salway, A., & Logie, R. (1995). Visuospatial working memory, movement control, and executive demands. *British Journal of Psychology, 86*, 253–69.

Sartre, J.-P. (1956). *Being and nothingness*. New York: Philosophical Library.

Schachter, S., & Singer, J. (1962). Cognitive, social, and physiological determinants of emotional state. *Psychological Review, 69*, 379–99.

Schank, R. (1982). *Dynamic memory*. New York: Cambridge University Press.

Schank, R., & Abelson, R. (1976). *Scripts, plans, goals, and understanding*. Hillsdale, NJ: Erlbaum.

Scheper-Hughs, N., & Lock, M. (1987). The mindful body: A prolegomenon to future work in medical anthropology. *Medical Anthropology Quarterly, 1*, 6–41.

Scherer, K., & Wallbott, H. (1994). Evidence for universality and cultural variation of differential emotion response patterning. *Journal of Personality and Social Psychology, 66*, 310–28.

Schladt, M. (1997). *Kognitive Strukturen von Korerteilvokabularien in kenianischen Sprachen*. Cologne: Institut fur Afrikanistik, University of Cologne.

Schreuder, R., Flores D'Arcais, G., & Glazenborg, G. (1984). Effects of perceptual and conceptual similarity in semantic priming. *Psychological Research, 45*, 339–354.

Schwartz, D. (1999). Physical imagery: Kinematic versus dynamical models. *Cognitive Psychology, 38*, 433–64.

Schwartz, D., & Black, T. (1996). Analog imagery in mental model reasoning: Depictive models. *Cognitive Psychology, 30*, 154–219.

Schwartz, D., & Black, T. (1999). Inferences through imagined actions: Knowing by simulated doing. *Journal of Experimental Psychology: Learning, Memory, and Cognition, 25*, 116–36.

Schwartz, D., & Holton, D. (2000). Tool use and the effect of action on the imagination. *Journal of Experimental Psychology, Learning, Memory, and Cognition, 26*, 1655–65.

Scott, C., Harris, R., & Rothe, A. (2001). Embodied cognition through improvisation improves memory for dramatic monologue. *Discourse Processes, 31*, 293–305.
Scruton, R. (1997). *The aesthetics of music*. Oxford: Clarendon Press.
Segal, S., & Fusella, S. (1970). Influences of imaged pictures and sounds on detection of visual and auditory signals. *Journal of Experimental Psychology, 83*, 458–64.
Segrin, C. (1998). Interpersonal communication patterns associated with depression and loneliness. In P. Anderson & L. Guerrero (Eds.), *Handbook of communication and emotion* (pp. 215–42). San Diego: Academic Press.
Seifert, C., Robertson, S., & Black, J. (1985). Types of inferences generated during reading. *Journal of Memory and Language, 24*, 405–22.
Shallice, T. (1988). *From neuropsychology to mental structure*. New York: Cambridge University Press.
Shannon, B. (1997). What is the functions of consciousness? *Journal of Consciousness Studies, 5*, 295–308.
Shannon, B. (2002). *The antipodes of the mind: Charting the phenomenology of the Ayahuasca experience*. New York: Oxford University Press.
Sharkey, N., & Sharkey, A. (1987). What is the point of integration? The loci of knowledge-based facilitation in sentence processing. *Journal of Memory and Language, 26*, 255–76.
Sharkey, N., & Ziemke, T. (1998). A consideration of the biological and psychological foundations of autonomous robotics. *Connection Science, 10*, 361–91.
Shaw, R. (2001). Processes, acts, and experiences: Three stances on the problem of intentionality. *Ecological Psychology, 13*, 636–51.
Shaw, R., & Turvey, M. (1999). Ecological foundations of cognition II: Degrees of freedom and conserved quantities in animal-environment systems. In R. Nunez & W. Freeman (Eds.), *Reclaiming cognition* (pp. 111–23). Bowling Green, OH: Imprint Academic.
Shebilske, W. (1977). Visuomotor coordination in visual direction and position constancies. In W. Epstein (Ed.), *Stability and constancy in visual perception: Mechanisms and processes* (pp. 89–112). New York: Wiley.
Sheets-Johnstone, M. (1998). Consciousness: A natural history. *Journal of Consciousness Studies, 5*, 260–94.
Sheets-Johnstone, M. (1999). *The primacy of movement*. Amsterdam: Benjamins.
Shepard, R. (1984). Ecological constraints on internal representations: Resonant kinematics of perceiving, imagining, thinking, and dreaming. *Psychological Review, 91*, 417–47.
Shepard, R., & Metzler, J. (1971). Mental rotation of three-dimensional objects. *Science, 171*, 701–3.
Sherrington, C. (1906). *The integrative action of the nervous system*. New York: C. Scribner's Sons.
Shiffrar, M., & Pinto, J. (2002). The visual analysis of bodily motion. In W. Prinz and B. Hommel (Eds.), *Common mechanisms in perception and action* (pp. 381–400). New York: Oxford University Press.
Shirouzu, H., Miyake, N., & Masukawa, H. (2002). Cognitively active externalization for situated reflection. *Cognitive Science, 26*, 469–501.
Shontz, F. (1969). *Perceptual and cognitive aspects of bodily experience*. New York: Academic Press.
Shore, B. (1996). *Culture in mind*. New York: Oxford University Press.

Shore, P., & Repp, B. (1995). Musical motion and performance: Theoretical and empirical perspectives. In J. Link (Ed.), *The practice of performance* (pp. 55–83). New York: Cambridge University Press.

Shweder, R. (1991). *Thinking through cultures: Explorations in cultural psychology.* Cambridge, MA: Harvard University Press.

Simon, J. (1969). Reactions toward the source of stimulation. *Journal of Experimental Psychology, 81,* 174–6.

Simon, J., & Ruddell, A. (1967). Auditory S-R compatibility: The effect of irrelevant cue on information processing. *Journal of Applied Psychology, 51,* 433–5.

Simons, D., & Chabris, C. (1999). Gorillas in our midst: Sustained inattentional blindness for dynamic events. *Perception, 28,* 1059–74.

Sinclair, H. (1971). Sensorimotor activity patterns as a condition for the acquisition of syntax. In R. Huxley & E. Ingram (Eds.), *Language acquisition: Models and methods* (pp. 121–45). Oxford: Academic Press.

Sitskoorn, M., & Smitsman, A. (1991). *Infants' visual perception of relative size in and containment and support events.* Paper presented at the Biennial Meeting of the International Society for the Study of Behavioral Development, Minneapolis.

Sitskoorn, M., & Smitsman, A. (1995). Infants' perception of dynamic relations between objects: Passing through or support? *Developmental Psychology, 31,* 437–47.

Slamecka, N., & Graf, P. (1978). The generation effect: Delineation of a phenomenon. *Journal of Experimental Psychology: Human Learning and Memory, 4,* 592–604.

Smeets, J., & Brenner, E. (1995). Perception and action are based on the same visual information. *Journal of Experimental Psychology: Human Perception and Performance, 21,* 19–31.

Smets, G., Strappers, P., & Overbeeke, L., & van der Mast, C. (1995). Designing in virtual reality: Perception-action coupling and affordances. In K. Carr & R. England (Eds.), *Simulated and virtual realities: Elements of perception* (pp. 189–208). Philadelphia: Taylor & Francis.

Smith, C. (1981). *A search for structure: Selected essays on science, art, and history.* Cambridge, MA: MIT Press.

Smith, L., Thelen, E., Titzer, R., & McLin, D. (1999). Knowing in the context of acting: The task dynamics of the A-not-B error. *Psychological Review, 106,* 235–60.

Smyth, M., & Waller, A. (1998). Movement imagery in rock climbing: Patterns of interference from visual, spatial and kinesthetic secondary tasks. *Applied Cognitive Psychology, 12,* 145–57.

Solomon, K. (1997). The spontaneous use of perceptual representations during conceptual processing. Doctoral dissertation. University of Chicago.

Solomon, K., & Barsalou, L. (2001). Representing properties locally. *Cognitive Psychology, 43,* 129–69.

Spelke, E. (1976). Infants' intermodal perception of events. *Cognitive Psychology, 8,* 626–36.

Spelke, E. (1988). When perceiving ends and thinking begins: The apprehension of objects in infancy. In Albert Yonas (Ed.), *Perceptual development in infancy* (pp. 197–234). Hillsdale, NJ: Erlbaum.

Spelke, E. (1990). Origins of visual knowledge. In D. Osherson & S. Kosslyn (Eds.), *Visual cognition and action: An invitation to cognitive science* (pp. 92–127). Cambridge, MA: MIT Press.

Spelke, E. (1991). Physical knowledge in infancy: Reflections on Piaget's theory. In S. Carey & R. Gelman (Eds.), *The epigenesis of mind: Essays on biology and cognition* (pp. 133–64). Hillsdale, NJ: Erlbaum.

Spelke, E. (1994). Initial knowledge: Six suggestions. *Cognition, 50*, 431–45.

Spelke, E. (1998). Nativism, empiricism, and the origins of knowledge. *Infant Behavior & Development, 21*, 181–200.

Spelke, E., Breinlinger, K., Macomber, S., & Jacobson, K. (1992). Origins of knowledge. *Psychological Review, 99*, 605–32.

Spelke, E., & Newport, E. (1998). Nativism, empiricism, and the development of knowledge. In R. Lerner (Ed.), *Handbook of child psychology: Vol. 1. Theoretical models of human development* (5th Edition) (pp. 275–340). New York: Wiley.

Spelke, E., Philip, A., & Woodward, A. (1995). Infants' knowledge of object motion and human action. In D. Sperber & D. Premack (Eds.), *Causal cognition* (pp. 44–78). New York: Oxford University Press.

Spence, J., Smith, L., & Thelen, E. (2001). Tests of a dynamic systems account of the A-not-B error: The influence of prior experience in the spatial memory abilities of two-year-olds. *Child Development, 72*, 1327–46.

Sperber, D. (2001). In defense of massive modularity. In E. Dupoux (Ed.), *Language, brain, and cognitive development: Essays in honor of Jacques Mehler* (pp. 47–57). Cambridge, MA: MIT Press.

Sperry, R. (1939). Action current study in movement coordination. *Journal of General Psychology, 20*, 295–313.

Spivey, M., & Geng, J. (2001). Oculomotor mechanism activated by imagery and memory: Eye movements to absent objects. *Psychology Research, 65*, 235–241.

Stampe, D. (1976). Cardinal numeral systems. *Chicago Linguistic Society, 12*, 594–609.

Stanfield, R., & Zwaan, R. (2001). The effect of implied orientation derived from verbal context on picture recognition. *Psychological Science, 12*, 153–6.

Steels, L. (1994). Cooperation between distributed agents through self-organization. In Y. Demazeau & J.-P. Muller (Eds.), *Decentralized AI* (pp. 175–96). Amsterdam: North-Holland.

Steri, A., Spelke, E., & Rameix, E. (1993). Modality-specific and amodal aspects of object perception in infancy: The case of active touch. *Cognition, 47*, 251–79.

Stern, D. (1985). *The interpersonal world of the infant*. Cambridge, MA: Harvard University Press.

Stevens, J., Fonlupt, P., Shiffrar, M., & Decety, J. (2000). New aspects of motion perception: Selective neural encoding for apparent human movement. *Neuroreport, 11*, 109–15.

Stevens, K., & Blumstein, S. (1981). The search for invariant acoustic correlates of phonetic features. In P. Eimas & J. Miller (Eds.), *Perspectives on the study of speech* (pp. 1–38). Hillsdale, NJ: Erlbaum.

Stewart, J. (1983). Perception of animacy. Dissertation Abstracts International, *43*, 2376–7.

Stiefehagen, R., Yang, J., & Waibel, A. (2002). Modeling focus of attention for meeting index based on multiple cues. *IEEE Transactions on Neural Networks, 13*, 928–38.

Stigler, J. (1984). Mental abacus: The effect of abacus training on Chinese children's mental calculation. *Cognitive Psychology, 16*, 145–76.

Stigler, J., Lee, S., & Stevenson, H. (1986). Digit memory in Chinese and English: Evidence for a temporally limited store. *Cognition, 23*, 1–20.

Stoerig, P., & Cowey, A. (1992). Wavelength discrimination in blindsight. *Brain, 115*, 425–44.

Stoffregen, T., Gordan, K., Sheng, Y.-Y., & Flynn, S. (1997). Perceiving affordance for another person's actions. *Journal of Experimental Psychology: Human Perception and Performance, 25*, 120–36.

Stoller, P. (1989). *The taste of ethnographic things: The senses in anthropology*. Philadelphia: University of Pennsylvania Press.

Stolz, T. (1994). *Sprachdynamik*. Bochum: Brockmeyer.

Strack, F., Martin, L., & Stepper, S. (1998). Inhibiting and facilitating conditions of the human smile: A nonobtrusive test of the facial feedback hypothesis. *Journal of Personality and Social Psychology, 54*, 768–77.

Strauss, C., & Quinn, N. (1997). *A cognitive theory of meaning*. New York: Cambridge University Press.

Strathern, A. (1996). *Body thoughts*. Ann Arbor: University of Michigan Press.

Studdert-Kennedy, M. (1981). The emergence of phonetic structure. *Cognition, 10*, 301–306.

Studdert-Kennedy, M. (1983). The phoneme as perceptuomotor stimulus. In A. Allport & D. MacKay (Eds.), *Language perception and production: Relationships between listening, speaking, reading, and writing* (pp. 67–84). San Diego: Academic Press.

Suchman, L. (1987). *Plans and situated action: The problem of human-machine communication*. New York: Cambridge University Press.

Sudnow, D. (1978). *Ways of the hand: The organization of improvised conduct*. Cambridge, MA: Harvard University Press.

Suprenant, A., Pitt, M., & Crowder, R. (1993). Auditory recency in immediate memory. *Quarterly Journal of Experimental Psychology, 46A*, 193–223.

Sweetser, E. (1986). Polysemy vs. abstraction: Mutually exclusive or complementary. In D. Feder, M. Niepokuj, V. Nikforidou, & M. Van Clay (Eds.), *Papers from the Twelfth Meeting of the Berkeley Linguistics Society* (pp. 528–38). Berkeley, CA: Berkeley Linguistic Society.

Sweetser, E. (1990). *From etymology to pragmatics: The mind-body metaphor in semantic structure and semantic change*. New York: Cambridge University Press.

Talmy, L. (1988). Force dynamics in language and cognition. *Cognitive Science, 12*, 49–100.

Talmy, L. (1996). Fictive motion in language and cognition. In P. Bloom & M. Peterson (Eds.), *Language and space* (pp. 211–276). Cambridge, MA: MIT Press.

Talmy, L. (2000). *Toward a cognitive semantics*. Cambridge, MA: MIT Press.

Tanaka, S., & Inui, T. (2002). Cortical movement for action imitation of hand/arm positions versus finger configurations: An fMRI study. *NeuroReport, 13*, 1599–1602.

Taub, S. (2001). *Language from the body*. New York: Cambridge University Press.

Thagard, P., & Nerb, J. (2002). Emotional gestalts: Appraisal, change, and the dynamics of affect. *Personality and Social Psychology Review, 6*, 274–82.

Thelen, E. (2000). Grounded in the world: Developmental origins of the embodied mind. *Infancy, 1*, 3–28.

Thelen, E., & Smith, L. (1994). *Dynamic systems approach to development: Applications*. Cambridge, MA: MIT Press.

Thelen, E., Schoener, G., Scheier, C., & Smith, L. (2001). The dynamics of embodiment: A field theory of infant perservative reaching. *Behavorial and Brain Science, 24*, 1–86.

Thomas, A., Bulevich, J., & Loftus, E. (2003). Exploring the role of repetitive and sensory exploration in the imagination inflation effect. *Memory & Cognition, 31*, 630–40.

Thomas, N. (1999). Are theories of imagery theories of imagination? An active perception approach to conscious mental content. *Cognitive Science, 23*, 207–45.

Thompson, E., & Varela, F. (2001). Radical embodiment: Neural dynamics and consciousness. *Trends in Cognitive Science, 5*, 418–25.

Thompson, E., Palacios, A., & Varela, F. (2002). Ways of coloring: Comparative vision as a case study. In A. Noe & E. Thompson (Eds.), *Vision and mind* (pp. 351–418). Cambridge, MA: MIT Press.

Tilley, C. (1994). *A phenomenology of landscape*. Oxford: Oxford University Press.

Tipper, S. (1985). The negative priming effect: Inhibiting priming by ignored objects. *Quarterly Journal of Experimental Psychology, 37A*, 571–91.

Titchner, E. (1909). *Lectures on the experimental psychology of the thought processes*. New York: Macmillan.

Todd, N. (1999). Motion in music: A neurobiological perspective. *Music Perception, 17*, 115–126.

Tooby, J., & Cosmides, L. (1995). Mapping the evolved functional organization of mind and brain. In M. Gazzaniga (Ed.), *The cognitive neurosciences* (pp. 1185–95). Cambridge, MA: MIT Press.

Tranel, D., Damasio, H., & Damasio, A. (1997). A neural basis for the retrieval of conceptual knowledge. *Neuropsychologia, 35*, 1319–27.

Traugott, E., & Dasher, R. (2002). *Regularity in semantic change*. New York: Cambridge University Press.

Trevarthen, C. (1977). *The interpersonal world of the infant*. New York: Basic Books.

Tucker, M., & Ellis, R. (1998). On the relations between seen objects and components of potential actions. *Journal of Experimental Psychology: Human Perception and Performance, 24*, 830–46.

Turing, A. (1950). Computing machinery and intelligence. *Mind, 59*, 433–63.

Turvey, M., Solomon, H., & Burton, G. (1989). An ecological analysis of knowing by wielding. *Journal of the Experimental Analysis of Behavior, 52*, 387–407.

Ungerleider, L., & Miskin, M. (1982). Two cortical visual systems. In D. Ingle, M. Goodale, &. Mansfield (Eds.), *Analysis of visual behavior* (pp. 549–86). Cambridge, MA: MIT Press.

Valenti, S., & Costall, A. (1997). Visual perception of lifted weight from kinematic and static (photographic) displays. *Journal of Experimental Psychology: Human Perception and Performance, 23*, 181–98.

Vallee-Tourangeau, F., Anthony, S., & Austin, N. (1998). Strategies for generating multiple instances of common and ad hoc categories. *Memory, 6*, 555–92.

Van der Heijden, A., Mussler, J., & Bridgeman, B. (1999). On the perception of position. In G. Aschersleben, T. Bachmann, & J. Musseler (Eds.), *Cognitive contributions to the perception of spatial and temporal events* (pp. 19–37). Amsterdam: Elsevier.

van der Meer, A., van der Weel, R., & Lee, D. (1995). The functional significance of arm movements in neonates. *Science, 267*, 693–5.

van Geert, P. (1991). A dynamic systems model of cognitive and language growth. *Psychological Review, 98,* 3–53.

van Gelder, T. (1998). The dynamical hypothesis in cognitive science. *Behavorial and Brain Sciences, 21,* 615–65.

van Leeuwen, L., Smitsman, A., & van Leeuwen, C. (1994). Affordances, perceptual complexity, and the development of tool use. *Journal of Experimental Psychology: Human Perception and Performance, 20,* 174–91.

Van Orden, G., Jansen op de Haar, M., & Bosman, A. (1997). Complex dynamic systems also predict dissociations, but they do not reduce to autonomous components. *Cognitive Neuropsychology, 14,* 131–65.

Van Orden, G., Pennington, B., & Stone, G. (2001). What do double dissociations prove? *Cognitive Science, 25,* 111–72.

van Rooij, D., Bongers, R., & Haselager, W. (2002). A non-representational approach to imagined action. *Cognitive Science, 26,* 345–75.

Varela, F. (2002). Upward and downward causation in the brain: Case studies in the emergence and efficacy of consciousness. In Y. Yasue & M. Jibu (Eds.), *No matter, never mind: Proceedings of toward a science of consciousness* (pp. 95–117). Amsterdam: Benjamins.

Varela, F., & Shear, J. (Eds.) (1999). *The view from within.* Imprint Academics: Kluwer.

Varela, F., Thompson, E., & Rosch, E. (1991). *The embodied mind.* Cambridge, MA: MIT Press.

Vishton, P., Rea, J., Cutting, J., & Nunez, L. (1999). Comparing effects of the horizontal-vertical illusion on grip scaling and judgment: Relative versus absolute, not perception versus action. *Journal of Experimental Psychology: Human Perception and Performance, 25,* 1659–72.

Viviani, P. (2002). Motor competence in the perception of dynamic events: A tutorial. In W. Prinz & B. Hommel (Eds.), *Common mechanisms in perception and action* (pp. 406–42). New York: Oxford University Press.

Viviani, P., Baud-Bovy, G., & Redolfi, M. (1997). Perceiving and tracking kinesthetic stimuli: Further evidence of motor-perception interactions. *Journal of Experimental Psychology: Human Perception and Performance, 23,* 1232–52.

Viviani, P., & Stucchi, N. (1992a). Biological movements look uniform: Evidence of motor-perceptual interactions. *Journal of Experimental Psychology: Human Perception & Performance, 18,* 603–23.

Viviani, P., & Stucchi, N. (1992b). Motor-perceptual interactions. In G. Stelmach & J. Requin (Eds.), *Tutorials in motor behavior II* (pp. 229–48). Amsterdam: North-Holland.

Vogt, S. (1995). On the relations between perceiving, imagining and performing in the learning of cyclical movement sequences. *British Journal of Psychology, 86,* 191–216.

Wagman, J., & Carello, C. (2001). Affordances and inertial constraints in tool use. *Ecological Psychology, 13,* 173–95.

Wagner, S., Winner, E., Cicchetti, D., & Gardner, H. (1981). Metaphorical mappings in human infants. *Child Development, 52,* 728–31.

Walker, A. (1982). Intermodal perception of expressive behavior by human infants. *Journal of Experimental Child Psychology, 33,* 514–35.

Wallbott, H. (1998). Bodily expression of emotion. *European Journal of Social Psychology, 28,* 879–96.

Wang, S.-H., Baillargeon, R., & Brueckner, L. (2004). Young infants' reasoning about hidden objects: Evidence from violation-of-expectation tasks with test trials only. *Cognition, 93*, 167–98.
Warren, W. (1984). Perceiving affordances: Visual guidance of stair climbing. *Journal of Experimental Psychology: Human Perception and Performance, 10*, 683–703.
Warrington, E., & McCarthy, R. (1987). Categories of knowledge: Further fractionations and an attempted integration. *Brain, 110*, 1273–96.
Warrington, E., & Shallice, T. (1984). Category-specific semantic impairment. *Brain, 107*, 829–54.
Washburn, M. (1916). *Movement and mental imagery*. Boston: Houghton Mifflin.
Wegner, D. (2002). *The illusion of conscious will*. Cambridge, MA: Harvard University Press.
Wegner, D., & Wheatley, T. (1999). Apparent mental causation: Sources of the experience of will. *American Psychologist, 54*, 480–492.
Weiskrantz, L. (1980). Varieties of residual experience. *Quarterly Journal of Experimental Psychology, 32*, 365–86.
Weiskrantz, L., Warrington, E., Sanders, M., & Marshall, J. (1974). Visual capacity in the hemianopic field following restricted occipital ablation. *Brain, 97*, 709–29.
Welch, R. (1978). *Perceptual modification: Adapting to altered sensory environments*. New York: Academic Press.
Werner, A. (1904). Note on the terms used for "right hand" and "lefthand" in the Bantu languages. *Journal of the African Society, 13*, 112–16.
Wexler, M., Kosslyn, S., & Berthoz, A. (1998). Motor processes in mental rotation. *Cognition, 68*, 77–94.
Wheeler, M., Peterson, S., & Buckner, R. (2000). Memory's echo: Vivid remembering reactivates sensory-specific cortex. *Proceedings of the National Academy of Sciences, 97*, 11,125–9.
White, P. (1999). Toward a causal realist account of causal understanding. *American Journal of Psychology, 112*, 605–42.
Wierzbicka, A. (1999). *Emotions across languages and cultures: Diversity and universals*. New York: Cambridge University Press.
Wilcox, P. (2001). *Metaphor in American sign language*. Washington, DC: Gallaudet University Press.
Wilson, M. (2001). The case for sensorimotor coding in working memory. *Psychonomic Bulletin and Review, 8*, 49–57.
Wilson, M. (2002). Six views of embodied cognition. *Psychonomic Bulletin and Review, 9*, 625–36.
Wilson, M., & Emmorey, K. (1997). A visuospatial phonological loop in working memory: Evidence from American Sign Language. *Memory & Cognition, 25*, 313–20.
Wilson, M., Iverson, A., & Emmorey, K. (2000). Further investigation of the phonological similarity effect for sign language: Two effects of spatial similarity. Manuscript submitted for publication.
Wilson, N., & Gibbs, R. (2005). Real and imagined body movement primes metaphor comprehension. Manuscript submitted for publication.
Wilson, R. (2004). *Boundaries of the mind: The individual in the fragile sciences – cognition*. New York: Cambridge University Press.

Wilson, T. (2002). *Strangers to ourselves: Discovering the adaptive unconscious.* Cambridge, MA: Harvard University Press.

Winkler, C. (1994). Rape trauma: Contexts of meaning. in T. Csordas (Ed.), *Embodiment and experience* (pp. 248–68). New York: Cambridge University Press.

Wohlschlager, S., & Wohlschlager, A. (1998). Mental and manual rotation. *Journal of Experimental Psychology: Human Perception and Performance, 24,* 397–412.

Wolff, P. (1999). Space perception and intended action. In G. Aschersleben, T. Bachmann & J. Musseler (Eds.), *Cognitive contributions to the perception of spatial and temporal events* (pp. 43–630. Amsterdam: Elsevier.

Wolff, P., & Levin, J. (1972). The role of overt activity in children's imagery production. *Child Development, 43,* 537–47.

Woodward, A. (1999). Infants' abilities to distinguish between purposeful and non-purposeful behaviors. *Infant Behavior and Development, 22,* 145–60.

Wright, T. (2001). Karen in motion: The role of physical enactment in developing an understanding of distance, time, and speed. *Mathematical Behavior, 20,* 145–62.

Wu, L., & Barsalou, L. (2001). Grounding concepts in perceptual simulations: I. Evidence from property generation. Manuscript submitted for publication.

Xu, F., & Carey, S. (1996). Infants' metaphysics: The case of numerical identity. *Cognitive Psychology, 30,* 111–53.

Yarbus, A. (1965). Role of eye movements in the visual process. Oxford: Nauka.

Yu, N. (1999). *The contemporary theory of metaphor: Perspectives from Chinese.* Amsterdam: Benajmins.

Yu, N. (2003). Chinese metaphors of thinking. *Cognitive Linguistics, 14,* 141–66.

Zabalia, M. (2002). Action and mental imagery in children. *Anne Psychologique, 102,* 409–22.

Zajonc, R., Murphy, S., Inglehart, M. (1989). Feeling and facial efference: Implication of the vascular theory of emotion. *Psychological Review, 96,* 395–416.

Ziemke, T. (1999). Rethinking grounding. In A. Riegler, M. Peschl, & A. von Stein (Eds.), *Understanding representation in the cognitive sciences* (pp. 177–90). New York: Kluwer Academic.

Zimler, J., & Keenan, J. (1983). Imagery in the congenitally blind: How visual are visual images? *Journal of Experimental Psychology: Learning, Memory, and Cognition, 9,* 269–82.

Zubin, D., & Choi, S. (1984). Orientation and gestalt: Conceptual organizing principles in the lexicalization of space. In D. Testen, V. Misha, & J. Drogo (Eds.), *Papers from the parasession of lexical semantics* (pp. 333–45). Chicago: Chicago Linguistics Society.

Zwaan, R. (1996). Processing narrative time shifts. *Journal of Experimental Psychology: Learning, Memory, & Cognition, 22,* 1196–1207.

Zwaan, R., Magliano, J., & Graesser, A. (1995). Dimensions of situated model construction in narrative comprehension. *Journal of Experimental Psychology: Learning, Memory, & Cognition, 21,* 386–97.

Zwaan, R., Stanfield, R., & Yaley, R. (2002). Language comprehenders mentally represent the shapes of objects. *Psychological Science, 13,* 168–71.

Index

CPSIA information can be obtained at www.ICGtesting.com
Printed in the USA
BVOW040126060112

279932BV00003B/36/P

9 780521 811743